Contemporary Disney Animation

To my father

Contemporary Disney Animation

Genre, Gender and Hollywood

Eve Benhamou

EDINBURGH
University Press

Edinburgh University Press is one of the leading university presses in the UK. We publish academic books and journals in our selected subject areas across the humanities and social sciences, combining cutting-edge scholarship with high editorial and production values to produce academic works of lasting importance. For more information visit our website: edinburghuniversitypress.com

© Eve Benhamou, 2023, 2024

Edinburgh University Press Ltd
The Tun – Holyrood Road
12 (2f) Jackson's Entry
Edinburgh EH8 8PJ

First published in hardback by Edinburgh University Press 2023

Typeset in 11/13 Adobe Garamond Pro by
IDSUK (DataConnection) Ltd

A CIP record for this book is available from the British Library

ISBN 978 1 4744 7612 6 (hardback)
ISBN 978 1 4744 7613 3 (paperback)
ISBN 978 1 4744 7614 0 (webready PDF)
ISBN 978 1 4744 7615 7 (epub)

The right of Eve Benhamou to be identified as author of this work has been asserted in accordance with the Copyright, Designs and Patents Act 1988 and the Copyright and Related Rights Regulations 2003 (SI No. 2498).

Contents

List of Figures   vii
Acknowledgements   ix

Introduction   1
1   Animating a Formula: Disney, Genre and Hollywood Animation   22

Part 1 Disney and Romance

2   Reanimating Fantasies of Fairy-tale Romance: Disney Nostalgia and *The Princess and the Frog*   51
3   The DreamWorks Formula and the Post-feminist Disney Couple: *Tangled*'s Romantic Parodies   77
4   Brave New Tale? Reframing Love and Romance in *Frozen*   100

Part 2 Disney and Action Adventure

5   Animating the Digital Action-adventure Spectacle   125
6   Disruption/Containment: Gender, Marvel and Disney's Superheroes   150
7   Animal Action Buddies: Disney's Anthropomorphic Reimaginings in *Zootopia*   180
8   Reflections of/on Contemporary Disney Animation: *Ralph Breaks the Internet*   206

Filmography   221
References   226
Index   242

Figures

1.1	Shrek tears the page of the formulaic fairy-tale book. From *Shrek*	35
1.2	Robert's incredulity challenges Disney's formulaic fairy-tale musical. From *Enchanted*	44
1.3	Robert embraces sentimental fairy-tale romance, embodied by Giselle. From *Enchanted*	44
2.1	Eudora reads *The Frog Prince* to young Tiana and Charlotte. From *The Princess and the Frog*	58
2.2	Tiana and Naveen's fairy-tale wedding is infused with post-feminist nostalgia. From *The Princess and the Frog*	63
2.3	Tiana and Naveen's unexpected second 'kiss'. From *The Princess and the Frog*	72
3.1	Flynn questions the integrity of the diegetic musical. From *Tangled*	82
3.2	Rapunzel's excitement at visiting the theme-park inspired kingdom. From *Tangled*	85
3.3	'I See the Light' celebrates Disney's formulaic display of coupledom. From *Tangled*	93
4.1	The reunited sisters are central to *Frozen*'s happy ending. From *Frozen*	111
4.2	*Frozen* prioritises 'sensitive and sweet' homme-com hero Kristoff. From *Frozen*	116
4.3	Elsa reclaims the camp performance of Disney's witches. From *Frozen*	120
5.1	Hiro's 'pre-production' work for Baymax. From *Big Hero 6*	138
5.2	Ralph represented as a plasticine-like deranged monster. From *Wreck-It Ralph*	140

5.3	Sea adventure initially represents a fantasy for Moana. From *Moana*	146
6.1	Superheroes' spectacular muscular physique as a ridiculous fantasy. From *Big Hero 6*	158
6.2	Baymax as a hybrid superhero. From *Big Hero 6*	161
6.3	'Mini-Maui' re-enacts Maui's spectacular feats. From *Moana*	164
6.4	Elsa's powers reveal the 'plasmatic' freedom of animation. From *Frozen*	171
7.1	Judy is framed as a minuscule, defenceless creature. From *Zootopia*	187
7.2	Judy's over-the-top performance of the attacked prey. From *Zootopia*	196
7.3	Zootopia as an enchanting Disney theme park. From *Zootopia*	198
8.1	The princesses repurpose their fairy-tale icons into weapons. From *Ralph Breaks the Internet: Wreck-It Ralph 2*	210
8.2	Vanellope demystifies the formulaic Disney musical. From *Ralph Breaks the Internet: Wreck-It Ralph 2*	212
8.3	Shank, Vanellope and Ralph form a 'buddy' triangle. From *Ralph Breaks the Internet: Wreck-It Ralph 2*	217

Acknowledgements

My first thanks go to Gillian Leslie, her colleagues at Edinburgh University Press, as well as Eliza Wright, for making this a smoother publication experience than I could have wished for.

This book began as a doctoral thesis at the University of Bristol. I pass on my immense gratitude to my supervisors for their dedicated guidance, patience, and enthusiasm for my project. Kristian Moen's illuminating advice and constant encouragement have been invaluable. Sarah Street has always provided insightful feedback and assistance. My sincere appreciation goes to the University of Bristol for its financial support. Thanks must also go to my examiners, Pete Falconer and Susan Smith: the book is richer for their ideas and constructive criticism.

I am particularly grateful to my fellow PhD students at Bristol for their thought-provoking observations on my research and infectious passion for cinema. The long film discussions over cake or ice cream were fully appreciated. Special thanks go to Miguel Gaggiotti, Dominic Lash, Hoi Lun Law, Steven Roberts, Polly Rose and Sarah Watts. The denizens of the Arts & Humanities graduate school also provided joyful and animated support. Special praise goes to Jawaher Alghamdi, Rhiannon Easterbrook, Bethany Pleydell and Dana Ramona.

Many thanks to my former colleagues at Swansea University for providing encouragement and opportunities to share my research as the book developed, and to Joanna Rydzewska for her mentorship.

The British Association of Film, Television and Screen Studies (BAFTSS) has represented an important support network for me to develop as a researcher. I am very grateful to members who shared advice and expertise throughout this time, including Christopher Holliday, Catherine Lester, Chris Pallant and Sam Summers, and to anyone who listened to my papers. Thanks in particular to Malcolm Cook, who provided crucial input and invaluable insight at key stages of the project.

I am forever indebted to my mother for her unwavering confidence in me and in my work, and for fostering my love of film through an extensive home video library and regular trips to the cinema. Extra doses of gratitude to Aurélie, Marie-Céline, Marielle, Séverine, Sophie and Victoria.

Last but not least, thanks to Juliet, the family pug, the best real-life Disney animal sidekick one could ask for.

Introduction

> Oh, come on! Princesses and cartoon characters?! Barf! (Vanellope in the official trailer for *Ralph Breaks the Internet: Wreck-It Ralph 2*, Phil Johnston and Rich Moore, 2018)[1]

The official trailer for *Ralph Breaks the Internet*, the sequel to *Wreck-It Ralph* (Rich Moore, 2012), showcases a strikingly self-reflexive, tongue-in-cheek, and slightly altered sequence from the computer-animated film. While video-game 'bad guy' Ralph (John C. Reilly) and his young kart-racing friend Vanellope (Sarah Silverman) travel through the Internet's immersive worlds, the intrepid little girl is directed to 'Oh My Disney', the company's fan-targeted promotional website. Passing through the gates of the Magic Kingdom and catching sight of iconic characters, from Snow White and Rapunzel to *Winnie the Pooh*'s Eeyore, Vanellope is frustrated and annoyed: she had been promised adventure and excitement, not what she assumes to be the boringly predictable and childish home of 'princesses and cartoon characters'. As a flying robotic figure rushes over her and offscreen, she realises her mistake. A computer-generated camera pan reveals an unexpectedly expansive space where a multitude of props and characters – the Death Star, Iron Man, the Luxo Lamp, Dumbo – float over and move through sections labelled 'Star Wars', 'Marvel', 'Pixar', which surround the central 'Disney Animation' area. Looking forward to venturing into these various worlds, Vanellope excitedly exclaims, 'Cool!' Like the computer-generated camera pan, this book unveils and explores the multifaceted interactions between the studio's contemporary animated output, Disney's live-action properties, and wider generic trends within mainstream animation and Hollywood cinema.

Throughout its history, the Disney studio has asserted and maintained its leadership over mainstream American animation through a delicate balance, continuously reinventing its output while preserving what has been perceived and promoted as a distinctive aesthetic, narrative style and overall brand. In the late 1990s and early 2000s, Disney faced important challenges, including internal corporate tensions and the novel competition from computer-animation studios, notably Pixar and DreamWorks, along with growing academic and popular criticisms regarding predictable plots and retrograde gender portrayals. This has led to a phase of significant revision and expansion of the studio's animated blueprint since the late 2000s, paralleled by the company's unprecedented corporate growth under new leadership, and resulting in box office records and new-found critical acclaim. It is precisely this singular phase of the studio's recent history, from 2008 to 2018, that *Contemporary Disney Animation: Genre, Gender and Hollywood* investigates. From production and marketing to critical reception, this decade has been described as both the return and renewal of Disney animation (Haswell 2019: 92). This phenomenon was epitomised by the success of *Frozen* (Chris Buck and Jennifer Lee, 2013), which was the first Disney animated feature to both be awarded the Oscar for Best Animated Film in 2014 and gross more than $1 billion worldwide – remaining the highest grossing animated film of all time until 2019.[2] *Frozen* also crystallises some of the studio's major generic influences and distinct reworkings since the late 2000s: a self-aware, post-feminist fairy tale reappropriating romantic-comedy and Marvel superhero tropes. Such a claim reflects the wider aims of the book. Rather than approaching animated features such as *Frozen* as belonging to a cohesive, strictly delimited canon identified with the studio's brand – 'Disney films' – or through potentially reductive labels such as 'children's movies', this book illuminates the ways they interact with a much wider generic milieu, both within and beyond Disney.

Providing an in-depth study of contemporary Disney animation from the perspective of genre combined with a focus on gender, the book considers theatrically released animated features as its corpus of focal texts, including close textual analyses of *Bolt* (Byron Howard and Chris Williams, 2008), *The Princess and the Frog* (Ron Clements and John Musker, 2009), *Tangled* (Nathan Greno and Byron Howard, 2010), *Wreck-It Ralph*, *Frozen*, *Big Hero 6* (Don Hall and Chris Williams, 2014), *Zootopia* (Byron Howard and Rich Moore, 2016), *Moana* (Ron Clements and John Musker, 2016) and *Ralph Breaks the Internet*.[3] I focus on the 2008–18 decade for several reasons. With the animated films released during this period, Disney strove to re-envision its canon and reinvigorate components of its identity by engaging both with its past animated output and with a notably expanding range of properties. As will be examined throughout the book, the films explicitly and consistently reference, reappropriate and revise the studio's animated intertext, from self-aware lines of dialogue to a more subtle restaging of musical and romantic motifs; from parodic to more nostalgic approaches towards specific aesthetic tropes and constructions of gender. In parallel, these animated films interact with and are impacted by a wider set of generic tropes, beyond Disney's animated canon. The company's substantial acquisitions – from animation studios to live-action properties – constitute an overwhelmingly vast cinematic universe, as illustrated in the trailer for *Ralph Breaks the Internet*, opening new frameworks through which to understand Disney animation. While the Disney company had notably grown with the addition of businesses, film and entertainment companies since the 1980s, the scope and pace of this expansion significantly increased in the late 2000s (Wasko 2020: 36). Investigating this specific decade also contrasts with most scholarship on Disney, which tends to consider the globality of the studio's output from the 1930s onwards (Davis 2006, 2013; Pallant 2013; Mollet 2020; Wasko 2020), and wider studies of contemporary mainstream animation, which examine Disney's 2000s and 2010s output in relation to other animation studios (Holliday 2018a; Brown 2021). Building on these works, this book provides a focused and distinctive panorama of contemporary Disney animation.

The timeframe of the book starts in 2008 with the release of *Bolt*, the film that signalled the 'start of Disney's regeneration' following the company's acquisition of Pixar (Haswell 2019: 97). The input of Pixar co-founders Ed Catmull and John Lasseter, who became respectively President and Chief Creative Officer of Disney Animation in 2006, was pivotal to *Bolt* and all subsequent features, emphasising the influence of Pixar's computer-animated aesthetic and generic tropes over Disney. Also released in 2008 was *Iron Man* (Jon Favreau), the first instalment in the highly successful Marvel Cinematic Universe, which imposed the superhero film as the major genre of the decade. Disney's acquisition of Marvel in 2009 notably impacted the historic animation studio. For the first time, a well-known company with extremely lucrative properties beyond animated films (comics, live-action films, television series), a well-established fan base and a distinct generic identity was incorporated within Disney – Marvel characters appeared in Disney stores and theme parks alongside Disney Princesses. Amy Davis observes that Marvel along with Lucasfilm, which Disney acquired in 2012, tend to be examined in terms of 'economics, corporatization, and fan controversies . . . "satellite" brands' which, although linked to Disney, are ultimately considered separately (2019: 6). Focusing on film texts and generic tropes, I unpack the multiple interactions within Disney's expanded cinematic universe, considering most specifically Pixar and Marvel in relation to Disney animation. The timeframe of the book ends in 2018 with *Ralph Breaks the Internet*, which functions as a highly self-reflexive retrospective of the studio's expansion and generic reimaginings since 2008. The year 2018 also corresponds to the appointment of Jennifer Lee as new Chief Creative Officer, marking the end of a distinct phase in Disney animation history.[4]

In what follows, the Introduction contextualises and maps the specific approach of the book. First, I locate animated films, and Disney more specifically, within genre studies, and show how a generic framework can open up new perspectives on contemporary mainstream animation and challenge the compartmentalisation of animation and live action in film studies. I subsequently explore how combining genre with gender, a key component of both contemporary genre studies and analyses of Disney, and the concept of post-feminism can help us investigate the complexity of the studio's current output, and its multifaceted relationship with Hollywood generic trends.

Mainstream American Animation and Genre

Disney animated films are often marginalised, sometimes excluded from scholarship on genre: looking at studies of the musical, which represents one of the most significant generic influences throughout the studio's canon, particularly highlights their consistent sidelining. Rick Altman's major work *The American Film Musical* (1989) points to the various obstacles that limit or prevent the presence of Disney's output in such scholarship. Altman's approach to genre analysis considers both the 'building blocks' of musicals – recurring traits such as 'attitudes, characters, shots, locations, sets' – and the 'structures into which they are arranged' (1984: 10). This dual approach uncovers convergences with other genres, and the ways individual films can 'innovate by combining the syntax of one genre with the semantics of another' (Altman 1984: 12). This allows us, for example, to illuminate the relationship, or family resemblances, between 'non-musical' screwball comedies and 1930s Fred Astaire–Ginger Rogers musicals – syntactically similar despite their semantic differences (Altman 1989: 168). Yet, Altman's study of the musical still ultimately prioritises narrative structure, as the 'love plot' is selected as the central tenet of the genre (Moine 2008: 60). Many Disney animated features, such as *Dumbo* (Ben Sharpsteen, 1941) and *Peter Pan* (Clyde Geronimi and Wilfred Jackson, 1953), do not fit this syntactic blueprint: these are not studied as 'musicals' since they do not focus on romance. More surprisingly, those that syntactically fit Altman's categorisation through the importance of their love plot, such as *Cinderella* (Clyde Geronimi and Wilfred Jackson, 1950) and *Sleeping Beauty* (Clyde Geronimi, 1959), are only briefly mentioned (1989: 104), and do not even feature in a section dedicated to 'fairy tale' musicals. More recent studies illustrate further this marginalisation. Barry Langford's chapter on musicals includes a short paragraph on the late 1980s/early 1990s wave of Disney animated musicals: despite their critical and commercial success, they are overlooked as an anomaly considering the 'irreversible decline' of the genre in that period (2005: 99). In *The Oxford Handbook of the American Musical*, the discussion of animated musicals is limited to one chapter (Smith 2011).

These examples suggest that the syntactic and semantic specificities of Disney's animated musicals, such as the presence of magic, anthropomorphic animals and imaginary worlds, seem to clash too heavily with live-action musicals, representing obstacles to their consideration.

This marginalisation goes beyond the musical, and affects animated films beyond Disney. These are largely absent from canonical works, such as Steve Neale's *Genre and Hollywood* (2000), as well as more contemporary edited collections, such as Lincoln Geraghty and Mark Jancovich's *The Shifting Definitions of Genre: Essays on Labeling Films, Television Shows and Media* (2008), Barry Grant's *Film Genre Reader IV* (2012), or Mary Harrod and Katarzyna Paszkiewicz's *Women Do Genre in Film and Television* (2018). The fact that animation is 'cordoned off' in most discussions of American genres mirrors to some extent its historical marginalisation as a production practice and sporadic presence at the box office (Goldmark and Keil 2011: 5). However, in the past thirty years, animated films have secured a prominent place within Hollywood's landscape. The increasing pace of Disney releases since the late 1980s, the growing number of animation studios and divisions, and the industry-wide adoption of computer animation in the 2000s have opened up the market (Brown 2012: 205). The multiplication of highly successful franchises such as Pixar's *Toy Story* (1995, 1999, 2010, 2019), DreamWorks' *Shrek* (2001, 2004, 2007, 2010) and Disney's *Frozen* (2013, 2019), along with the creation of the 'Best Animated Feature' category at the Oscars in 2001, highlights the box-office weight and critical recognition animation has gained. Why would genre studies disregard some of the most popular and significant releases from contemporary Hollywood?

Such disregard points to implied hierarchies between genres: Hollywood animation is most often associated with genre labels that have become pejorative terms, the children's film and family film being prime examples.[5] It is primarily in generic studies of children's and family films that animation features prominently.[6] Their assumed audience demographic tends to be prioritised over their semantics or syntactic structure. Mark Jancovich explains that 'definitions of genre are seldom free from evaluative prescriptions' (2001: 34). From this perspective, the children's film/family film crystallises what Altman describes as a 'bad object' (1999: 113). The 'juvenile qualifier ("children's") is often used pejoratively' (Hermansson and Zepernik 2019: 9) with 'patronising' undertones, suggesting 'excessive sentiment' (Brown 2012: 9–10). The fact that mainstream children's films/family films are often 'blockbusters' opens them to further denigration due to their 'commercialism' (ibid.: 10). A number of scholars have highlighted the simplistic association of animation with children's films, considerably constraining its generic scope.[7] Such derogatory labels provide further contextualisation for the marginalisation of animated films within genre studies.

Disney has not only reinforced the reductive association of Hollywood animation with children's/family films but has come to crystallise the epitome of a generic 'bad object'. Between the 1930s and 1950s, Disney imposed itself as the most important American feature-animation studio; in the 1950s–60s, when the influence of the Hays Code started to wane, it consolidated its status as the major purveyor of 'family entertainment' and 'safe' content, unlike live-action Hollywood films, which increasingly depicted onscreen sex and violence (Davis 2019: 2–3). Since then, it has transformed into a global purveyor of entertainment with a vast range of related merchandise and theme parks, and a multimedia conglomerate playing a central role in American culture. This positioning has helped reinforce the association between animation and children's/family film, and the preconceptions regarding the medium. For example, Susan Napier relies on Disney to illustrate the lack of depth of most American animated texts (2005: 9). Critics and academics similarly often read and evaluate Disney's animated output as formulaic, involving 'predictability of content, fixed narrational norms, regulatory conventions, and repeating regimes of representation' (Holliday 2019: 118). For its detractors, the Disney formula is shorthand for sentimentalism and conservative portrayals of gender and authority (Zipes 2011: 88), as will be discussed in Chapter 1. Connoting commercialism, family content and formulaic storylines, Disney animated features combine most preconceptions surrounding mainstream animation, which further explains their marginalisation within genre studies.

Considering Disney's long history of cel animation, namely the studio's primary production process up until the mid-2000s, reveals a potentially deeper reason for the isolated status of its output within genre studies, beyond evaluative prescriptions, semantics and syntactic differences: its visual and ontological clash with live action. Many animation scholars, such as Paul Wells, argue that the 'difference' of medium between live action and animation justifies studying animated films in isolation from their live-action counterparts: the former's 'very aesthetic and illusionism . . . potentially prompts alternative ways of seeing and understanding what is being represented' (2009: 5). Suzanne Buchan argues that animation poses indeed 'an aesthetic puzzle not fully solved by live-action based film studies approaches and methodologies' (2013: 8). Relying on distinct critical frameworks, these animation scholars argue for a departure from conventional generic analysis when examining animated films. Buchan regards animation as a 'cinematic form that can have more to do with sculpture, algorithms or painting than with the genres of narrative live-action cinema' (ibid.: 2). Such 'intrinsic difference as a form' leads Wells to argue that animation 'may support and relate to established definitions of genre but will ultimately be defined by its own generic terms and conditions' (2002a: 44). This differentiating approach is particularly fruitful when looking at experimental animation or specific processes such as silhouette, cut-out, plasticine or puppet animation: animated films which ostentatiously contrast with the aesthetic conventions of live-action cinema.

Yet, as will be discussed in Chapter 1, Disney animation has always maintained a balance between imitating and departing from such conventions: the studio's contemporary computer-animated output is particularly illuminating in that regard. Within Hollywood, computer animation 'has become the core ingredient of contemporary moving-image production', from the feature-length output of Pixar and DreamWorks to the computer-animated environments and characters of Marvel's live-action blockbusters (Pallant 2015: 3). Such predominance highlights a degree of aesthetic porousness between live action and animation. Compositing, namely the use of computer-animation techniques to alter or enhance live-action images, particularly encourages this 'collapse of boundary' (Husbands and Ruddell 2019: 7). Both *How to Train Your Dragon* (Dean DeBlois and Chris Sanders, 2010) and *The Hobbit: The Desolation of Smaug* (Peter Jackson, 2013), for example, comparably strive for believability, disguising the digital constructedness of their backgrounds and cinematography. Aesthetics represents 'an immense area' in which animation and live-action media may overlap (Furniss 2014: 5). This converging aspect represents one of the entry points of Disney animated films into live-action dominated genre studies.

Christopher Holliday's recent work on computer animation qualifies these convergences: computer-animated films are studied as forming a separate generic framework in themselves, 'connected through their own internal structures and attributes, rather than simply governed by the rule-based familiarity of live-action genres' (2018a: 32–3). Such an approach reveals some illuminating semantic and syntactic connections between computer-animated films, such as the recurring themes of object transformation and obsolescence, and the prominence of the journey narrative (ibid.: 41, 220). However, it perpetuates to some extent Wells's and Buchan's isolationist approach: a specific animation technique becomes the primary criterion of genre analysis. Regarding Disney, this approach fruitfully challenges the predominance of the 'formula' as 'structuring principle' of study (Holliday 2019: 115), showing how the studio's recent films are 'visibly informed, shaped and moulded by their contact with computer-animated films that circulate beyond the Disney canon' (ibid.: 121). However, this also dilutes to some extent the studio's distinctiveness in the animation market.

Disney contemporary animated features are not only in dialogue with other computer-animated films, but they also interact with Disney's rich intertext and paratext, including the company's affiliated output, and with the studio's own generic and aesthetic history. Unlike Pixar or DreamWorks, Disney stands out in the Hollywood landscape through its large canon of cel animation and ever-expanding portfolio of live-action studios and features. This permeates the production and reception of Disney's contemporary computer-animated films. The release of cel-animated fairy tale *The Princess and the Frog* in 2009, labelled 'anomalous' for the 'Digital Disney period' by Holliday (2019: 131), testifies to such enduring influence; it notably follows from live-action *Enchanted* (Kevin Lima, 2007) and frames subsequent computer-animated *Tangled* and *Frozen*. These complex interactions point to the specificity of Disney's relationship to genres, beyond the computer-animated film context.

Expanding Holliday's approach, it is useful to identify a wider set of connecting criteria and overarching modes. Deborah Thomas refers to 'certain broad categories', namely the 'melodramatic, the comedic and the romantic', which 'cut across the generic field' (2000: 9). Thomas examines the 'alternative structures' of their narrative, and the corresponding distinct moods conveyed within their diegetic worlds and experienced by the audience (ibid.: 13–14). Some authors have fruitfully applied broader generic categories – or modes – to animated films, in an attempt to challenge isolationist approaches characterising both animation and genre studies, and the theoretical divides between animation and live action. Interrogating the historical 'affinity' of short animation for comedy, Daniel Goldmark and Charlie Keil explore the 'fluid and ongoing' interchange between animated humour and live-action comedy, considering cartoons to be a 'hybrid form . . . that borrowed brazenly from recognized comic conventions but expanded on them' (2011: 3, 5, 7). Similarly, Holliday and Alexander Sergeant interrogate the 'obviousness' of the connection between animation and fantasy, 'highlighting the complex set of relationships that can exist' between the two (2018: 2).

Comedy and fantasy are modes that have historically been associated with animation, yet looking at paratexts for contemporary Disney animated features, namely the surrounding discourses of publicity, promotion and reception which play a crucial role in creating generic expectations, reveals more unexpected correspondences and influences. *Zootopia* has been compared with *L.A. Confidential* (Curtis Hanson, 1997) and *48 Hrs.* (Walter Hill, 1982), suggesting parallels with the crime film and cop buddy film (Travers 2016; Collin 2016b), while *Frozen*'s heroine, Princess Anna, has been described as a 'contemporary rom-com heroine' (Merry 2013). Such singular comparisons parallel the various generic influences and frameworks explicitly acknowledged by the filmmakers themselves, as discussed throughout the book. These paratextual clues challenge generic understandings of Disney, and represent an insightful starting point from which to reassess the studio's contemporary animation.

Therefore, from the perspective of genre studies, mainstream animation as exemplified by Disney and live action need to be studied alongside each other. The discrepancy between the position of animated films within contemporary Hollywood and within academia must be challenged. Theoretical approaches to genre and animation need to overcome the marginalisation of the animated medium to reveal the multiplicity of generic influences, reappropriations and confluences at work between mainstream animated and live-action films, challenging their perceived status as 'bad objects'. This does not mean, however, that the specificities of animation as a form should entirely be discarded. I share Wells's postulate on the potential of animation in offering a commentary upon genre as understood within live-action cinema through the distinctive credentials of animated forms (2002a: 48). These include, for example, the self-reflexive impulses of animation, the importance of visual and thematic metamorphosis, the aesthetics of caricature and slapstick, and characterisation through anthropomorphism. Taking these particularities into account does not necessarily involve using a different generic language, or separating animation from live-action study, as the works of Goldmark and Keil, and Holliday and Sergeant reveal. Janet Staiger points out that 'the critical function of using categories is to see things perhaps not otherwise visible' (2008: 86). Relying on the same generic tools while acknowledging animation specificities helps expand and challenge the understanding of genre within live-action dominated genre studies, and unpack the multiple generic reworkings at the core of contemporary mainstream animated films.

REFRAMING CONTEMPORARY DISNEY ANIMATION

Contemporary Disney Animation: Genre, Gender and Hollywood offers a fresh approach to Disney's contemporary animated films, building on and informing animation scholarship and genre studies, and mapping out productive intersections between the two. Applying genre studies to animation sheds new light on our current understanding of film genres. It opens new areas of cinema to generic analysis, foregrounding the key role of mainstream animated features in re-envisioning well-established live-action genres. Applying genre studies to animation also opens new perspectives on the analysis of mainstream animated features, revealing the multiplicity of generic influences at work within these films. Such a focus challenges not only isolationist approaches but also reductive labels associated with mainstream animated films. This framework allows us to reconsider Disney contemporary animated features, repositioning these films at the centre of the current Hollywood landscape. These animated films interact with live-action genres in ways that are specific both to their animation medium and to the studio's distinct aesthetic style, and its intertextual and paratextual universe.

Regarding genre, I adopt a semantic/syntactic approach to contemporary Disney animation, with a particular emphasis on hybridity. Several authors consider the latter to be a 'hallmark' of genres (Berry-Flint 2004: 39), analysed as 'inherently processual' (Langford 2005: 278), 'interfertile' (Altman 1998: 24) and frequently overlapping (Neale 2000: 3). Such a focus on hybridity is key to reassessing specific film texts, genres and filmmakers.[8] I follow from Neale, who calls for a more 'flexible approach to Hollywood's output', considering 'hybrids and combinations' beyond 'a handful of canonical films' (2000: 254). This approach is particularly fruitful in relation to animated features: within genre studies, they are indeed non-canonical, at the margins of works focusing on well-established live-action genres. The primary focus of the book will be on the film texts, supported by a discussion of associated paratexts. A film may be 'classified differently in different institutional contexts', whether that be within the process of production, marketing or critical reception (Geraghty and Jancovich 2008: 4). This expanded approach to genre reveals some generic tensions, unexpected combinations and creative hybridisations within Disney's animated film texts.

A complementary approach to generic hybridity is the use of broader categories: I rely on two modes, namely romance and action adventure, as primary lenses in order to unpack Disney's reappropriation and re-envisioning of genres. I have selected these two specific modes for several reasons. First, there are parallels between the two, as underlined by Yvonne Tasker: each mode 'emerges from and participates in any number of allied genres and sub-genres ... theories of genre hybridity and multiplicity are central to [their] understanding' (2015: 20). Conceptualising action as a 'mode' points simultaneously to a way of telling and visualising a story, and to specific kinds of stories told through very diverse features (ibid.: 21). Romance is 'necessarily ... intertwined' with a variety of narratives: the presence of mutual desire 'as a central concern' is also pervasive throughout many films and genres (Thomas 2000: 9–10). Considering the scope of these two modes, they represent productive frameworks which encompass the wide range of genres influencing and reappropriated by contemporary Disney animation, from screwball and chick flick to superhero film and buddy movie.

Second, as I will show throughout the book, these two modes correspond to two major facets of Disney's contemporary generic identity. Romance is essential to the studio's constructed formula and its canon of fairy-tale musicals, the tropes of which are strikingly revived, revisited and reworked throughout Disney's latest cycle of animated fairy tales (2009–13). Action adventure is ubiquitous throughout Disney's extended cinematic universe, from Pixar to Marvel, and Hollywood cinema: the studio's contemporary animated films consistently engage with tropes associated with these other properties and wider trends. The tensions and convergences between the two modes translate the studio's double impulse throughout its 2008–18 output: preserving and reinventing Disney's iconic formula, while expanding its generic identity.

Third, I focus on romance and action adventure in order both to propose new generic frameworks for Disney and mainstream animation – beyond the children's/family film, comedy or fantasy – and to highlight the significant presence of these modes beyond live-action contexts. The book investigates how Disney animated films reappropriate various genres of romance and action adventure, often in humorous and challenging ways, and how these genres are re-envisioned by Disney animation, revealing distinctive interactions and variations. These generic reappropriations resonate not only with contemporary discourses surrounding film genres and animation aesthetics but also with gender portrayals.

Genre, Gender and Post-feminism

Constructions of gender represent a recurring focus within Disney studies, and are central to the studio's contemporary revision of its own recurring set of tropes. Most notably, the character of the Disney Princess crystallises Disney's complex relationship with its own past canon and formula, and the way it engages with Hollywood's generic trends. Combining genre as an analytical framework with a focus on gender fruitfully expands and enriches – often isolationist – discourses on both contemporary Disney and the studio's gender portrayals. This perspective reveals the multifaceted ways in which Disney has revised and renewed its contemporary animated output. Genre is essential to understanding how contemporary Disney aesthetics, narrative conventions and associated paratexts interact with a wide variety of contemporary filmic tropes, while renegotiating the studio's animated legacy. I argue that an intersectional, post-feminist framework, and more specifically the idea of a 'post-feminist spectrum', further illuminates such a delicate, sometimes uneasy balance within the context of Disney's gender portrayals, challenging binary readings of a key aspect of Disney studies.

Throughout genre studies, Heidi Wilkins observes that 'genre and gender are frequently . . . inextricably linked' (2016: 1). Beyond the recurring and persisting combination of specific genders with particular genres both onscreen and throughout popular and critical discourses – as illustrated by the 'orientation' of the romantic comedy towards and 'consumption by female audiences' (San Filippo 2021: 6) – gender plays a pivotal role in generic mutations and hybridisations. Tasker observes that the semantics and syntactic structure of a predominantly male genre are significantly altered and problematised when women become central protagonists. Using early 1990s action cinema as a case study, Tasker points out that 'the increased inclusion of women in action roles has both contributed to and been part of the ways in which the genre has evolved' (1998: 68). Therefore, cinematic gender (re)constructions depend on and impact film genres. More contemporary works have further analysed the intrinsic connection between gender and genre, as illustrated by studies of the romantic comedy (Alberti 2013; Kaklamanidou 2014), the action film (Brown 2015) and the superhero film (Kent 2021). Christine Gledhill argues that such an approach opens new perspectives for the analysis of gender in film: 'genre offers a "constellation" of cultural, aesthetic, and ideological materials, containing . . . a more inclusive range of possibilities than allowed by ideologically driven "readings"' (2012: 4).

The latter readings have dominated studies of Disney's portrayals of gender: critics' and academics' recurring aim has been to unveil their conservative and/or progressive aspects, often leaning towards one end of the spectrum. Authors writing on early Disney fairy tales such as *Snow White and the Seven Dwarfs* (David Hand, 1937), *Cinderella* and *Sleeping Beauty* emphasise their reductively retrograde – even 'sexist' (Zipes 1995: 36) – construction of femininity. Subsequent fairy tales including *The Little Mermaid* (Ron Clements and John Musker, 1989), *Beauty and the Beast* (Gary Trousdale and Kirk Wise, 1991) and *Aladdin* (Ron Clements and John Musker, 1992) have been perceived as perpetuating such portrayals behind a more progressive façade. For example, Susan Hines and Brenda Ayres underline the ultimately superficial feminist impulse of the films, focusing on their heteronormative closure and the design of the princesses (2003: 7), while Janet Wasko highlights the lack of interaction between women and more particularly the absence of mothers (2020: 142).

In parallel, other authors have striven to rehabilitate these portrayals. A striking example is Douglas Brode's discussion of Disney's early fairy tales as 'protofeminist' fables featuring 'strong women' such as fairy godmothers (2005: 173, 191) – a reading that is arguably not as convincing when applied to the heroines. Rebecca-Anne Do Rozario's more nuanced account reconsiders the late 1980s/early 1990s princess as a disruptive agent within the patriarchal narrative structure of the fairy tales – a role formerly performed by the female villain (2004: 57). Beyond such well-known fairy-tale heroines, Amy Davis underlines the presence of more independent female protagonists in films such as *The Rescuers* (John Lounsbery and Wolfgang Reitherman, 1977) and *The Black Cauldron* (Ted Berman and Richard Rich, 1985). What particularly characterises such approaches is the emphasis on the evolution of Disney's constructions of femininity: what Davis describes as a gradual move away from the 'passive' female characters of the past to more 'active' heroines (2006: 224).

Disney's contemporary gender portrayals have mostly been approached from a similar perspective, as exemplified by popular and critical accounts of *Frozen*. Michael Macaluso observes that, 'whereas Disney has usually been criticised for reinforcing traditional ... gender norms ... *Frozen* is being celebrated for its feminist qualities of sisterhood' (2016: 73). By contrast, other authors argue that this film merely perpetuates Disney's past gender representations beyond their surface of 'seemingly triumphant liberation' (Streiff and Dundes 2017: 8), as epitomised by Jack Zipes's observation that the 'film manages to create an aura of originality and modernity while actually repeating the same story and embracing the same ideology that Walt Disney fostered in the 1930s' (2016: 9).

Such approaches regarding Disney's constructions of gender pose two main issues. First, they tend to replicate the isolationist standpoint of some animation scholars. These gender portrayals are considered from a very limited generic perspective – the fairy tale, princess films – or within a generic vacuum: Disney's animated canon represents the primary context of study. Analysing *Frozen*'s Elsa solely in the light of Snow White or *The Little Mermaid*'s Ariel is necessarily limiting; wider influences beyond Disney tend to be missed. For example, Clare Bradford argues that contemporary Disney heroines' 'ostensibly more modern' trajectory to romance 'incorporates episodes of conflict between partners, eventually resolved when the couple acknowledges their love for each other' (2012: 181). This analysis fails to acknowledge the significant influence of genres of romance on the syntactic structure of these films and on Disney's wider revision of the studio's constructions of femininity. It is precisely through these 'episodes of conflict', in typical romantic-comedy fashion, that the heroines demonstrate their wit and are gradually positioned on the same footing as their male counterparts. Therefore, the study of gender is intrinsically linked to the study of genre, providing a wider context to the 'ostensibly more modern' film narratives and their gender portrayals. Relying on generic frameworks not conventionally associated with animated films, such as action genres, reframes and reveals new ways to approach gender in *Wreck-It Ralph*, *Frozen* and *Moana*. Foregrounding the multilayered generic influences at work within these films emphasises the correspondingly multifaceted aspects of Disney's contemporary gender constructions. Authors who have started to include genre in their analysis of Disney's portrayals of femininity, focusing most notably on interactions between fairy tale and musical (Do Rozario 2004; Bunch 2017), bring 'contradictions and complexities to the surface' (Bunch 2017: 90).

Such an emphasis on contradictions and complexities differs from the tendency in both academic and critical accounts to rely on binary categorisations, which represents a second recurring issue throughout studies of Disney. 'Distinct disagreements' emerge throughout these accounts (Wasko 2020: 143). The studio's gender constructions are characterised as either positive or negative, regressive or progressive, traditionalist or feminist, and most often in academic works, apparently subversive yet actually stereotypical: these approaches fail to grasp the complexity of the studio's contemporary constructions of femininity and masculinity. Writing on popular representations of girlhood, Sarah Projansky insists that attention needs to be focused on the 'inextricable combination of disruption and containment' at the core of contemporary portrayals of female characters (2007: 69) – beyond reductive dichotomies.

Post-feminism represents a particularly useful framework, in combination with genre studies, which 'transcends binary divisions' (Genz 2009: 52). Initially used to characterise a particular moment in late twentieth-century feminist history in the West, 'simultaneously marked by backlash politics and by the pleasures and possibilities of "new" femininities' (Gillis and Hollows 2009: 8), it is still relevant in the context of Disney's latest output. Rosalind Gill argues that, in a contemporary cultural moment 'seemingly characterised by a multiplicity of (new and old) feminisms which co-exist with revitalized forms of anti-feminism and popular misogyny', it remains 'a relatively stable patterned yet contradictory sensibility' (2016: 612, 621). The latter corresponds to a set of discourses circulated through mass media and popular culture which 'simultaneously' acknowledges the 'importance of gender equality while perpetuating profoundly hierarchical gender cultures' (Tasker 2020: 672). I follow from academics such as Angela McRobbie, Diane Negra, Yvonne Tasker and Stéphanie Genz who highlight the ambiguities, even paradoxes of such discourses, which fuse 'empowerment rhetoric with traditionalist identity paradigms' (Negra and Tasker 2007: 18), indicating 'both a dependence on and an independence from feminism' (Genz 2009: 50).

Such 'double entanglement' (McRobbie 2009: 6) helps contextualise and unpack Disney's contemporary gender constructions, and the tensions between semantics, syntactic structure and paratext. Disney's pioneering role, longevity and synergistic presence is unique within mainstream animation. Every contemporary Disney animated feature, introduced with the iconic fairy-tale castle logo, is intrinsically linked to the studio's past canon, intertextually evoking and drawing on earlier animated characters, while inviting connections with more recent images of femininity and masculinity circulated throughout and beyond Disney's wider cinematic universe. This multifaceted, often contradictory gendered dialogue is best approached through the framework of post-feminism. Applying Gill's remarks to Disney animation, critical uses of post-feminism

> neither fall into a celebratory trap of seeing all instances of mediated feminism as indications that [the studio's films] have somehow 'become feminist,' but nor do they fail to see how entangled feminist ideas can be with pre-feminist, anti-feminist, and backlash ones. (Gill 2016: 622)

Therefore, post-feminism allows us to reassess Disney's contemporary constructions of gender, beyond binary categorisations.

Much critical work on post-feminism has opened up the term to 'intersectional interrogation' (Gill 2017: 612). Jess Butler observes that, while post-feminist discourse 'can and does make space for women of colour within its boundaries, it strictly regulates and polices the forms their participation may take' (2013: 50). Gill observes similar mechanisms in relation to the growing visibility of lesbian and bisexual women in mainstream media: they 'do not exist somehow outside a post-feminist sensibility' (2017: 614). In other words, 'rather than simply an exclusion of racial and sexual others, post-feminism primarily represents an affirmation of a white heterosexual subject' (Butler 2013: 49). Such intersectional interrogation highlights further the ambiguities and paradoxes underlying post-feminist discourses on gender, and represents an important prerequisite in order to address Disney's contemporary constructions of femininity. Since the 1990s, increased attention has been focused on Disney's portrayal of race (Wasko 2020: 150), and more specifically on the depiction of non-white heroines (Ma 2003; Naidu Parekh 2003; Staninger 2003; Lacroix 2004). *The Princess and the Frog*'s introduction of an African American princess in the overwhelmingly white animated space of Disney's fairy tales accentuated such critical and academic debates. An intersectional approach combined with a post-feminist framework and a generic lens illuminate the disruptive potential of such a portrayal, while examining the specific boundaries framing this unique figure within Disney's animated canon. Still in the fairy-tale context, such an approach can also unpack the singular subversion performed by *Frozen*'s Elsa, a heroine whose depiction does not fit into Disney's explicitly heteronormative constructions of romance. Several authors have adopted a queer reading to locate and examine representations which subtly challenge norms of gender and sexuality throughout Disney's animated films (Griffin 1999; Sweeney 2013; Letts 2016). Such representations tend to correspond to supporting characters or villains; by contrast, the centrality of Elsa's character, as well as the scope of her popularity, are arguably unprecedented. While a detailed analysis of Elsa's potential queerness, which may involve a comprehensive account of the critical reception and fan readings of this character, is beyond the scope of this book, I rely on this critical lens in order to specifically explore the extent to which her portrayal destabilises Disney's most codified genre of gender, namely fairy-tale femininity.

Considering gender as a pivotal tool of genre, the book examines Disney's constructions of gender as central to the studio's re-envisioning of both its own canon and wider generic trends. As a complementary framework, post-feminism illuminates the contradictions and paradoxes of these portrayals. While such a focus on femininity/masculinity may seem to reproduce rigid binaries, it is important to acknowledge that these categories are central not only to Disney's marketing and merchandising strategies but also to wider contemporary portrayals of gender. Post-feminist discourse 'looks backward and forward simultaneously' (Tasker 2020: 672), nostalgically yet knowingly reviving 'essentialized' conceptions of gender (Negra 2009: 123). As will be discussed throughout the book, such essentialised constructions of femininity and masculinity still underpin, to varying degrees, Disney's contemporary constructions of gender.

Some scholars, however, have pointed out the potential limits of post-feminism. Authors such as Benjamin Brabon and Stéphanie Genz have observed the 'value judgement' conferred by some feminist critics on texts perceived as post-feminist, sceptically viewed as the 'abatement' and 'depoliticization of the feminist movement' (2009: 18–19). From this perspective, the typically post-feminist entanglement of feminist and anti-feminist ideas inevitably leads to the dilution or, in Shelley Cobb and Diane Negra's words, the 'scrambling of feminist precepts' (2017: 764). Another binary subsequently arises, echoing the regressive versus progressive dichotomy: gender portrayals are perceived as either wholly and truly feminist or 'post-feminist'. Imelda Whelehan considers the latter to be 'boring and frustrating to analyse because [their] message requires little unpacking and lies prominently on the surface' (2010: 159). Such an understanding not only creates a new hierarchy among contemporary film texts but also considerably limits the complexity of post-feminism as a critical tool. Describing a text as reflecting post-feminist discourses would necessarily imply that it relies on a superficial empowerment rhetoric, and that its traditionalist impulse inevitably determines its construction of femininity, for example. This approach to post-feminism applied to Disney's output would lead to a new critical impasse, suggesting that the inescapable weight of the studio's past gender portrayals uniformly impacts contemporary Disney films and consistently constrains their subversive potential.

I propose to combine the idea of a 'post-feminist spectrum' with the framework of genre studies to maintain a more nuanced and precise approach. Disney's contemporary output borrows from and reworks numerous generic tropes: the latest fairy-tale cycle, building on an iconic, conventional Disney genre, could be placed towards the traditionalist end of the spectrum; action-adventure gender constructions would be found at the other, more empowering end. Such positioning is far from stable, considering the particularly hybrid nature of individual films such as *Frozen*: specific sequences and characters foreground different degrees of disruption/containment. Therefore, Disney's post-feminist combination of feminist and anti-feminist ideas is not fixed: these animated films represent what Brabon and Genz term 'a site of struggle over the meanings of feminism' (2009: 25). A focus on genre combined with an intersectional lens particularly illuminates their fluid movement across the post-feminist spectrum, and avoids a restrictive application of the term 'post-feminism'. Disney's contemporary animated films are neither retrograde nor progressive, but rather varyingly combine generic images drawing on the studio's own past canon, the wider cinematic universe, as well as other computer-animated features and contemporary live-action genres. They disrupt and preserve aspects of the studio's formulaic gender portrayals in multiple and heterogeneous ways.

DISNEY, ROMANCE AND ACTION ADVENTURE

The overarching concerns of this book are: how do the studio's contemporary animated features interact with Disney's past canon, the studio's wider cinematic universe, and popular Hollywood trends? How do these animated films combine and rework a wide range of generic tropes while challenging and re-envisioning canonical genres, revisiting and expanding the studio's formula in the process?

The first chapter provides a brief history of Disney animation through the perspective of the Disney formula. I start by examining the studio's output and unpacking the idea of the Disney formula as constructed between the late 1930s and 1990s, before analysing how it was challenged specifically by Pixar's and DreamWorks' early computer-animated features in terms of aesthetic, tone and style. The chapter subsequently focuses on Disney's 2000s generic experiments and reappropriations as responses to the studio's competitors, using *Lilo & Stitch* (Dean DeBlois and Chris Sanders, 2002), *Chicken Little* (Mark Dindal, 2005) and *Enchanted* as main case studies, and providing context to Disney's wider generic approaches from 2008 onwards.

Part 1 (Chapters 2, 3 and 4) examines *The Princess and the Frog*, *Tangled* and *Frozen* through the lens of romance. With this cycle of fairy-tale adaptations released between 2009 and 2013, Disney returned to what has been perceived as the iconic genre of the studio. Fairy tales in which romance plays an essential part, such as *Snow White and the Seven Dwarfs*, *Cinderella* and

Beauty and the Beast have represented major successes. Their popularity has been preserved through merchandising, theme-park attractions, sequels and remakes, but also significantly challenged through the irreverent competition of DreamWorks' *Shrek* franchise. With *The Princess and the Frog*, *Tangled* and *Frozen*, Disney has both nostalgically revived and shrewdly revisited semantics, syntactic structures and gender portrayals characterising earlier fairy tales, engaging with multiple genres of romance. The animation studio has explicitly looked inwards, throughout its past canon, in order to renew and reinvent its iconic generic formula.

In Chapter 2, I examine how *The Princess and the Frog* and its paratexts revive the studio's formulaic fairy-tale romance, building on several layers of nostalgia intrinsic to the Disney brand while engaging with the neo-traditional romantic comedy. *The Princess and the Frog*'s parallel interactions with the screwball comedy, and reliance on playful self-reflexivity generically revise and complicate aspects of Disney's formulaic fairy-tale romance, particularly in relation to the portrayal of the studio's first black princess. I rely on the complementary generic lens of the 'memory film' (Cook 2005: 4) to unpack the idealised vision of the American past arising from Disney's nostalgic fantasy fairy-tale world.

Chapter 3 approaches *Tangled* as an explicitly parodic reappropriation of Disney's fairy-tale formula, borrowing both from DreamWorks' *Shrek* and post-feminist 'genres of gender' from the contemporary romantic comedy (Alberti 2013: 3). The chapter explores Disney's imitation of DreamWorks' specific type of tonal and generic parody, particularly notable in the first half of the film, and epitomised through the textual and paratextual portrayal of Flynn Rider. I examine the tensions between these parodic impulses and the persistence of Disney's idealised and sentimental romance. Flynn's initially conflictual relationship with Rapunzel and the very duality of his characterisation – both Flynn and Eugene – crystallise these tensions, also reflected in the gendered portrayal of the two leads, which both subverts and reclaims the tropes of the Disney Prince, Princess and couple.

Chapter 4 examines how *Frozen* engages with Disney's wider animated fairy-tale intertext, considering Pixar's *Brave* (Mark Andrews and Brenda Chapman, 2012), and interacts with several strands of the romantic mode – chick flick, 'homme-com' (Jeffers McDonald 2009: 152), screwball. Through such interactions, the film explicitly questions the primacy and plausibility of fairy-tale romance and its underpinning, 'true love', notably revising the studio's formula in the process. The film relies on narrative and character doubling – sister and love plots, Anna and Elsa, Hans and Kristoff – representing the culmination of Disney's shift to a different generic regime of verisimilitude, from fairy tale to romantic comedy. Through the portrayal of

Elsa, *Frozen* also introduces alternative generic trajectories beyond heteronormative romance.

The second part of the book (Chapters 5, 6 and 7) examines Disney's wider contemporary output through the lens of action adventure. With the release of *Bolt*, *Wreck-It Ralph*, *Big Hero 6*, *Zootopia* and *Moana*, Disney has ventured into a generic mode perceived as more unexpected for the studio, which has yet been ubiquitous within Hollywood cinema and mainstream animation. Action-adventure genres represent particularly interesting entry points to explore how Disney has renegotiated its generic identity since the company's acquisition of Pixar and Marvel, looking outwards to renew its output while distinctly challenging and re-envisioning popular tropes. Genres of romance and action adventure have also converged: to borrow Celestino Deleyto's terms, they have 'come into contact', vied for dominance and 'transformed' (2009: 14). My discussion of *Frozen* in both parts, and of *Ralph Breaks the Internet* in Chapter 8, unpacks these generic hybridisations. It is worth noting that, considering the timeframe of the book, *Frozen*'s multifaceted generic identity and the spectacular scope of its related properties – four short films (2015, 2017, 2019, 2020), a theatrically released sequel (2019) and a mini-series (2021) at the time of writing – I solely focus on the original 2013 film text, although some occasional references will be made to these intertexts throughout the following chapters.[9]

In Chapter 5, I analyse the studio's multifaceted reworking of the digital action spectacle. *Bolt*, *Wreck-It Ralph*, *Big Hero 6* and *Moana* not only playfully transpose the dazzling aesthetics and thrills of live-action action-adventure films to computer animation, as pioneered and influenced by Pixar, but also self-reflexively reveal and challenge the *mise en scène* behind such impressive displays. Reframing the action spectacle as musical performances, these films reinvent and expand the convergences between the two genres. I particularly examine *Moana* as an example of the 'action musical', pointing to Disney's distinct re-envisioning of action adventure, which relies on its aesthetic and generic history.

Chapter 6 focuses on Disney's reworking of gender as constructed in one of the most popular contemporary action-adventure genres, the Marvel superhero film. The latter frames the exertion of characters' extraordinary abilities as a potentially dangerous performance which oscillates between disruption and containment, before being ultimately mastered. I examine how *Wreck-It Ralph*, *Frozen*, *Big Hero 6* and *Moana* highlight, mock, challenge and re-envision the gendered nature of such a performance through the prism of Disney animation. Studying these films from the generic lens of the superhero films opens up new perspectives on both this action-adventure genre and Disney's contemporary canon, and most particularly the studio's portrayals of post-feminist femininity.

Chapter 7 unpacks *Zootopia*'s anthropomorphising of action-adventure cinema. The film translates tropes from the live-action cop buddy film to animation through a distinct anthropomorphic lens, questioning and reworking the gendered imbalance of the genre in the process. Through its reframing of the post-feminist action heroine and her narrative trajectory, the film also gently mocks Disney's own formulaic tropes. However, the film deals more ambiguously with other representational configurations, especially regarding race. This chapter examines how *Zootopia* both addresses issues of bias and micro-aggressions more strikingly than other contemporary Disney animated features and reproduces to some extent problematic configurations.

As a concluding chapter, Chapter 8 relies on *Ralph Breaks the Internet* to map the book's main discoveries regarding Disney's re-envisioning of its contemporary animation, illuminating distinct generic combinations and wider shifts that have marked a particular phase of the studio's history. With characters travelling from the digital action world of 'Slaughter Race' to the familiar kingdom of 'Oh My Disney', this animated sequel represents the culmination and fusion of Disney's parallel impulses between 2008 and 2018: self-reflexive revision and generic expansion. Via genres of romance and action adventure, *Ralph Breaks the Internet* playfully deconstructs the studio's fairy-tale tropes, extends the scope of the musical and re-envisions its action framework, reflecting the gradual prominence of this mode throughout Disney's output. This concluding chapter also reflects on the fruitfulness of genre analysis as applied to Disney films, foregrounding the multiple enlightening intersections between live-action cinema and animation.

Focusing on specific contemporary case studies, and placing them within the wider contexts of Disney's cinematic universe, as well as Hollywood cinema, the book offers a fresh approach to both genre studies and studies on Disney.

Notes

1. The official trailer for *Ralph Breaks the Internet* was released in June 2018.
2. *Frozen* remained the highest grossing animated film of all time ($1.3 billion gross worldwide) until 2019, when it was replaced by Disney's *The Lion King* remake (Jon Favreau, 2019; $1.6 billion gross). See Brown 2021: 15.
3. *Zootopia*'s release title in the United Kingdom is *Zootropolis*. In this book, I will refer to the original American title.
4. The eviction of John Lasseter followed accusations of sexual misconduct towards employees. See Maddaus 2017; Marotta 2018.
5. It should be noted that such assumptions in critical and popular accounts tend to be specific to mainstream American animation. Anglophone scholars of Japanese animation, for example, have consistently highlighted the 'breadth and variety of anime's interactions with genre' (Denison 2015: 14). Susan

Napier describes anime as 'everything that Western audiences are accustomed to seeing in live-action films – romance, comedy, tragedy, adventure, even psychological probing' (2005: 6–7).

6. See for example Brown 2012; Howe and Yarbrough 2014; Beeler and Beeler 2015.
7. See Wells 1998: 175; Furniss 2014: 225; Denis 2020: 10.
8. Christine Gledhill, for example, acknowledges 'genre mixing' as central to women media makers' 're-writing' of tropes critically constructed as masculine or feminine (2018: xii–xiii). Noel Brown's study of the family film explores examples as varied as *Star Wars* (George Lucas, 1977) and *Mrs Doubtfire* (Chris Columbus, 1993), illuminating their shared 'specific ideological overtones, emotive aspects and commercial intent' (2012: 12). Celestino Deleyto examines the 'fundamental' influence of the romantic comedy on 'the social and sexual dynamics' of a wide range of films, from *Rear Window* (Alfred Hitchcock, 1954) to *Before Sunset* (Richard Linklater, 2004), that are not traditionally included in studies of this genre (2009: 51).
9. Shorts include theatrically released *Frozen Fever* (Chris Buck and Jennifer Lee, 2015) and *Olaf's Frozen Adventure* (Stevie Wermers-Skelton and Kevin Deters, 2017). *Myth: A Frozen Tale* (Jeff Gipson, 2019), *Once Upon a Snowman* (Dan Abraham and Trent Correy, 2020) and the mini-series *Olaf Presents* (Hyrum Osmond, 2021) were released on Disney's streaming platform Disney+. The sequel to *Frozen* is *Frozen II* (Chris Buck and Jennifer Lee, 2019).

CHAPTER 1

Animating a Formula: Disney, Genre and Hollywood Animation

> You want reality? Here you go, chief. The show's too predictable. The girl's in danger, the dog saves her from the creepy English guy, we get it. There's always a happy ending, and our focus groups tell us 18-to-35-year-olds are unhappy. They're not happy with happy . . . if you lose so much as half a rating point, so help me I will fire everyone in this room, starting with you!
> (Mindy Parker in *Bolt*, Byron Howard and Chris Williams, 2008)

Early in *Bolt*, a network representative (Mindy) challenges the presumptuous television director of the action series 'Bolt', in which the canine hero (also named Bolt) unknowingly stars. Despite the apparent success and appeal of the series, suggested by its impressive budget, dazzling special effects, endearing animal protagonist and associated merchandise, the formulaic aspect of each episode is starting to bore audiences. Mindy's brief, unequivocal statement is her answer to the patronising and overconfident director, who is convinced that his approach is the most effective. Yet, he is forced to adapt both by revising the structure of the following episodes and even by borrowing from other genres to maintain the show's popularity: the film notably concludes with an episode relying on science-fiction tropes.

This sequence not only plays a pivotal role within *Bolt*'s narrative, leading to Bolt's separation from his beloved owner Penny and his journey to find her, but also reflects the wider struggles that Disney had faced in the mid-1990s and 2000s. While Disney had always dominated and defined mainstream feature animation, a series of critical and commercial failures, paralleled by the rise of new and highly successful studios, seriously disrupted this monopoly. While Pixar reinvented the aesthetic of mainstream animation by consolidating and popularising a particular style of computer animation, DreamWorks promoted a distinctive tone, humour and generic approach which exerted a 'considerable influence' on 2000s animation (Summers 2020: 2). The output of these major studios was produced, marketed and received as different from, one often opposed to the idea of the Disney formula, especially its perceived predictability, sentimentality and cheerfulness, as referred to in *Bolt*. The emergence of newer animation studios, including Blue Sky, Illumination and Sony, further challenged Disney's monopoly. The argument between the director and Mindy also hints at internal tensions characterising this period of Disney's history. In 1994, Disney's then CEO, Michael Eisner, fired head of Walt Disney Studios Jeffrey Katzenberg, who subsequently established DreamWorks SKG with Steven Spielberg and David Geffen (Price 2009: 168–9). In 2005, Eisner's failure to renew a partnership agreement with Pixar – Disney was co-producing and distributing Pixar films until then – led to his removal as CEO: he was replaced by Robert Iger in 2006, which led to tremendous changes throughout Disney's hierarchy.

This chapter investigates this transitional phase, at times tumultuous and experimental, of Disney's history, from the mid-1990s to the late 2000s. It examines how profound industrial changes, both within Disney and in the wider mainstream animation landscape, impacted the studio's animated output, and most specifically its generic identity and associated formula. Analysing this period provides key context to subsequently address the focus of the book, namely the animated films released from 2008 onwards. The mid-1990s and 2000s exemplify Disney's continuous efforts to reinvent itself, yet are unique in the company's history: the studio was being increasingly sidelined within the unprecedently saturated market of mainstream animation. The arrival of Pixar and DreamWorks notably altered Disney: during this period, the studio adopted different approaches towards its own canon, ultimately leading to the double impulse analysed in the rest of the book: self-reflexive parody and nostalgic celebration, generic revision and expansion.

The first part of the chapter focuses on the construction and consolidation of the idea of the Disney formula, providing a brief history of Disney animation until the mid-1990s in the process. I argue that the formula can be approached as the combination of a distinct, seemingly cohesive animation aesthetic characterised by believability and sentimentalism, and a discursive emphasis on specific genres, notably the musical and the fairy tale, all supported by a growingly imposing synergistic machine. The second part explores the extent to which major emerging competitors Pixar and Dream-Works challenged such a formula visually, tonally and generically. I examine specifically these two studios for several reasons: in addition to their considerable influence, enormous commercial success and critical acclaim in the 2000s, they stand out through their inextricable link to Disney, from their corporate history to the positioning of their animated output. A close analysis of the wider animation landscape of this era, including the films from Blue Sky and Illumination, would be beyond the scope of this book.[1] The third part focuses on Disney's responses to these challenges throughout its early 2000s animated output and associated paratexts, investigating generic experiments and imitations. Relying on detailed analyses of *Lilo & Stitch* (Dean

DeBlois and Chris Sanders, 2002), *Chicken Little* (Mark Dindal, 2005) and *Enchanted* (Kevin Lima, 2007), I examine how the studio's formula seemingly disappeared, resurfacing to be mocked before being explicitly reclaimed following corporate changes. These films, and notably the animation/live-action hybrid *Enchanted*, are pivotal to understanding Disney's specific post-Pixar and post-DreamWorks approach towards its own canon and wider Hollywood live-action genres.

Disney's Rule over Mainstream Animation: Constructing and Consolidating a Formula

Throughout its history, Disney's predominant position within and considerable influence on mainstream animation has encouraged a 'view of homogeneity in the field and an understanding in the public imagination that "animation" is Disney' (Wells 2002b: 49). Undeniably, as a studio, Disney has played a pivotal role within the evolution and perception of animation. One characteristic that has been consistently observed is an emphasis on sentimentalism, permeating aesthetics, narratives and style. Looking at short and later feature-length animation in the 1930s and 1940s, this is conveyed through charming and comic anthropomorphic characters, and the representation of an ideal, interdependent relationship between human beings and the natural world, as epitomised in *Snow White and the Seven Dwarfs* (David Hand, 1937) (Whitley 2012: 2, 8–9). David Whitley observes that such characteristics have often been 'construed in a negative mode within academic criticism' and perceived as 'conservatively sentimental': 'a pandering to popular taste that mitigates against developing the art of animation in more probing, thoughtful or challenging forms' (ibid.: 2). Yet, this apparent emphasis on sentimentality was often counterbalanced by more challenging impulses. Steven Watts argues that these animated films were inspired by both 'nineteenth-century sentimental realism and modernist art, . . . innovative elements and tradition' (1997: 102). Watts coined the term 'sentimental modernism' to define Disney's combination of 'naturalism and fantasy', 'nonlinear, irrational, quasi-abstract modernist explorations' with tropes from the Victorian past such as 'exaggerated sentimentality, clearly defined moralism, and disarming cuteness' (ibid.: 104–5). This combination can be observed most strikingly in the various musical sequences of *Fantasia* (Ben Sharpsteen et al., 1940). In the 1930s and 1940s, Disney animated films recurrently included free-flowing, sometimes nightmarish sequences which explore characters' distorted perspective and consciousness, before returning to more naturalistic and reassuringly peaceful states. The 'Pink Elephants on Parade' in *Dumbo* (Ben Sharpsteen, 1941) or Snow

White's terrifying flight through the forest illustrate the surreal potential of Disney's version of anthropomorphism, beyond its associated cuteness and sentimentalism. This complex blend of 'soothing images from an earlier age' and 'emerging' trends (Watts 1997: 452) is key to understanding Disney animation.

The studio's adoption of technological innovations brought notable transformations to its developing animation aesthetic. The use of the multiplane camera, for example, led to more elaborate depictions of perspective and depth, and 'a more convincing illusion of three-dimensional space' (Mihailova 2019: 48). As Donald Crafton explains, these evolutions have been discussed from a specific perspective: whether or not these were beneficial, 'leading to progress in cartoon art, or a detriment, causing producers and consumers to lose sight of the essence of the animated art form' (2013: 148). Criticisms focused on a perceived loss of 'early animation's verve, jazzy spontaneity, and ludic surrealism', with cartoons becoming 'less imaginative, less rubbery, more realistically inclined' (ibid.: 149). Paul Wells, for example, argues that Disney's emphasis on 'verisimilitude', with an increasing investment in anatomical and environmental 'authenticity' – as epitomised in *Bambi* (David Hand et al., 1942) – seemed to dilute the ability of the medium to 'challenge the parameters of live-action illusionism' (2002a: 9; 1998: 23). Building on Watts's concept, Disney animation was perceived as becoming more 'sentimental' than 'modernist', prioritising naturalism over fantasy.

Authors such as J. P. Telotte qualify such clear-cut understandings, observing that the studio's aesthetic remained a 'caricature of realism, combining believability and exaggeration' (2010: 134). It is precisely this aesthetic 'balancing act between faithfully recreating the physical world and embellishing it for stylistic and narrative purposes' which became 'the studio's house style', and had a 'lasting and international impact on commercial animation' (Mihailova 2019: 48). Such a balancing act, consolidated throughout the development of feature-length animation, also impacted the narrative worlds of the films. While fantasy and magic remained important influences, they were 'rationalised', governed by 'more stringent rules' in order to become plausible (Summers 2020: 15, 18). As Sam Summers explains, narrative techniques such as the obtrusive intervention of a narrator or animator, references to contemporary culture – Hollywood stars, for example – and anarchic visual tropes very rarely disrupted Disney's 'diegetic reality' and viewers' suspension of disbelief (ibid.: 18). By contrast, these became Warner Bros.' trademark, forming the 'antithesis' to Disney's prevailing 'hyperrealism' and cohesive narrative spaces (ibid.: 19).

Throughout the 1940s, the idea of a narrative and aesthetic Disney formula started to consolidate through various mechanisms of production.

The studio's new reliance on audience research helped assess and to some extent maintain viewers' expectations about Disney animation. As Susan Ohmer observes, 'opportunities for innovative narrative forms and image . . . required management and measurement', especially after the mixed success of *Fantasia*: subsequent films were expected to 'meet carefully defined corporate goals' (2011: 123). The formula was then supported by the studio's industrial growth and synergistic strategies. As Christopher Holliday notes, Disney's expansion as a global corporation throughout the 1950s and into the 1960s placed the perceived 'formulaic consistency' of animated features 'at new points of intersection with alternate multimedia enterprises', including television series, live-action films, consumer products and theme parks (2019: 117). The tremendous scope of these new marketing opportunities, with stories and characters circulating and being promoted through various platforms, widened the 1930s merchandising ventures initiated around characters such as Mickey Mouse and Snow White (Watts 1997: 372). Disney was so successful that, according to Watts, the company played a key role in the 'explosive growth of consumer capitalism after World War II' (ibid.: 362). Arguably, it was during those decades that notions of commercialism and consumption were being entrenched in the perception of the Disney formula.

This process notably accelerated between the late 1980s and the mid-1990s under Michael Eisner's impulse. Possibilities of synergy expanded dramatically with the addition of cable holdings (most notably Disney Channel), home video, Disney stores, and partnerships with other studios and technology companies.[2] As Chris Pallant observes, animation was only the first piece 'in a larger corporate jigsaw', perpetually generating merchandisable commodities which continuously promoted each other (2013: 82–3). This phase coincides with what is commonly referred to as the peak of Disney's Renaissance, a period of 'aesthetic and industrial growth' after the 'creatively stagnant' and financially difficult 1970s and early 1980s (ibid.: 78, 89). In this context, the success and most notably the visibility and scope reached by Disney animated films released in the late 1980s up until the mid-1990s were unprecedented: these consolidated further the idea of the Disney formula as producing a canon with a cohesive generic identity.

The films released during this period – namely *The Little Mermaid* (Ron Clements and John Musker, 1989), *Beauty and the Beast* (Gary Trousdale and Kirk Wise, 1991), *Aladdin* (Ron Clements and John Musker, 1992) and *The Lion King* (Roger Allers and Rob Minkoff, 1994) – all achieved critical recognition and box-office success.[3] Such popularity was reinforced via Disney's expanding synergistic machine. For example, *Beauty and the Beast* was the first animated feature to be adapted into a Broadway musical in 1994; it spawned two direct-to-video sequels in 1997 and 1998; since 1991, it has grossed $218,967,620 in the United States, thanks in part to its IMAX re-release in 2002 and a 3D reissue in 2012; its title character, Belle, has featured prominently throughout Disney merchandising; and its live-action remake (Bill Condon, 2017) grossed $504,014,165.[4] The other Renaissance animated films have followed a similar trajectory.

In the 1990s, such phenomenal success was perceived as Disney's return to its 'roots': 'films based on fairy tales, structured around musical set-pieces' (Summers 2020: 20). Admittedly, throughout the studio's history, the musical had been a pervasive generic influence, but only a small number of animated films had been fairy-tale adaptations: *Snow White and the Seven Dwarfs*, *Cinderella* (Clyde Geronimi and Wilfred Jackson, 1950) and *Sleeping Beauty* (Clyde Geronimi, 1959). The Renaissance fairy-tale musicals – three releases within three years – built on the earlier enduringly popular trio, and initiated 'a highly concentrated genre cycle' throughout the 1990s (Summers 2020: 172). As feature animation started to expand during that decade with the Bluth, Rich and Warner Bros. studios, competing with Disney meant releasing films which imitated the latter's aesthetic and narrative tropes, and most strikingly its generic approach – in Summers's term, the 'Renaissance formula' (ibid.: 20). By replicating this formula, animated features like *Thumbelina* (Don Bluth and Gary Goldman, 1994) and *The Swan Princess* (Richard Rich, 1994) not only reinforced Disney's position as a model to follow within the animation industry but also strengthened the studio's identification with fairy-tale musicals.

Throughout marketing and promotion, the Disney company itself insisted on and consolidated such a generic association. A striking example is the use of what I term the 'retrospective trailer' for the promotion of *The Little Mermaid* and *Aladdin* (Benhamou 2017). Animation studios, and especially Disney, particularly rely on this type of trailer, which opens with clips from past films before introducing the latest release. It constructs and sustains a cohesive studio identity through the recurrence of specific genres and themes. The retrospective trailer often aims to highlight an aura of prestige by showcasing clips from critically acclaimed hits, ultimately providing a specific interpretative framework for the studio's newest release. The trailer for *The Little Mermaid* opens with short clips from *Snow White* (the latter being carried away by her prince), *Pinocchio* (Hamilton Luske and Ben Sharpsteen, 1940), *Cinderella* (in her magic dress), *Bambi* and *Sleeping Beauty* (Aurora and Prince Phillip waltzing together). As the clips smoothly succeed each other through dissolves, transforming the Disney canon into a seamless series of successes – notably omitting 1970s and early 1980s films – the voice-over announces, 'for over fifty years, Walt Disney has turned classic stories into classic animated motion pictures. Now the tradition continues, as one of the world's greatest stories becomes the newest Disney motion picture classic.' While the label 'fairy-tale musical' is not explicitly used, this genre permeates the trailer, with references to 'magical new songs' and 'wonder and magic', along with the introductory presence of Snow White, Cinderella and Aurora. From the perspective provided in the trailer, *The Little Mermaid* is indeed a return to Disney's roots. *Aladdin*'s retrospective trailer showcases Disney's more recent Renaissance films, still framing the studio's newest release as the continuation of these successes. It opens with clips from *The Little Mermaid*, while the voice-over announces, 'three years ago, we took you on a magical journey under the sea'. As the trailer cuts from the underwater castle to the Beast's, and the soundtrack switches from 'Part of Your World' to 'Beauty and the Beast', the voice-over continues, 'last year, we took you to a place where a beautiful girl looked into the heart of a beast and found the man of her dreams. Now come with us and enter a whole new world beyond your imagination.' Through these carefully selected introductory clips, notions of fairy-tale romance and magic are directly associated with *Aladdin*: the latter's first shot is another 'castle' (Agrabah's palace), and the love story between Aladdin and Jasmine is particularly foregrounded. With an additional emphasis on songs ('from the Academy Award-winning composer of *The Little Mermaid* and *Beauty and the Beast*'), this retrospective trailer constructs the contemporary cycle of Renaissance films as representative of the Disney canon through their adherence to a cohesive fairy-tale/musical formula.

While throughout the marketing and promotion of the 1990s the Disney formula had overly positive connotations – success, classics, magic, romance, enchantment – it had widely different implications within critical and academic circles, and was studied as part of a process of 'Disneyfication'. This term, coined during that decade, corresponds to the studio's approach towards adaptation, namely its perceived 'bowdlerisation of literature, myth and history in a simplified, sentimentalised, and programmatic way': adapted material becomes sanitised, trivialised, standardised and 'instantly recognisable as being from the Disney stable' (Bryman 2004: 5). Due to the growth of the Disney company in the 1990s, critics often described Disneyfication as grounded in consumerism and commercial imperatives (Holliday 2019: 126–7). Disney's reappropriation of European fairy tales has been at the core of such debates. The traditionalist approach to gender constructions and promotion of elitism have been recurring issues, as exemplified by Jack Zipes's numerous accounts on Disney's versions, which he has described as 'hollow and fluffy narratives' (2011: 87). Due to the wide circulation of Disney films supported by the company's synergistic machine, several scholars observed that American audiences were mainly familiar with the studio's adaptations, while other authorial voices and stories featuring more complex characters were relatively unknown (Warner 1995: 207; Whelan

2014: 172–3). Pauline Greenhill and Sidney Eve Matrix similarly argue that 'the fairy tale as interpreted by Disney has … saturated mainstream Euro-North American culture' (2010: 7). Paradoxically, one could argue that academics' and critics' focus on Disney fairy tales, which only represent a small portion of the studio's releases, also contributed to some extent to their heightened visibility and emphasised Disney's identification with this genre, consolidating the idea of a fairy-tale/musical formula. Such an emphasis within Disney studies echoes observations from children's media experts and educators. As children are understood as Disney's primary – and easily influenced – target audience, a plethora of works have explored the potentially damaging effects of the Disneyfication process, and what the studio's animated films were actually 'teaching' these viewers (Giroux and Pollock 2010: 91). For example, Annalee Ward examined whether 'Disney films contribute positively to children's moral education' and include 'prosocial' messages (2003: 3, 134); Julie Garlen and Jennifer Sandlin argued that Disney operated as a 'curriculum' (2016: 16). These accounts added another potentially pejorative layer to the idea of the Disney formula.

Following the Disney Renaissance, a highly successful merchandising initiative arguably sealed the generic identity of the Disney formula and crystallised aspects that had come to define it, namely its commercial and sanitising dimension, as well as its potentially harmful teaching powers. Created in 2000, the 'Disney Princess' franchise extracted the protagonists of every Disney fairy tale – Snow White, Cinderella, Aurora, Ariel, Belle and Jasmine – and the heroines of *Pocahontas* (Mike Gabriel and Eric Goldberg, 1995) and *Mulan* (Tony Bancroft and Barry Cook, 1998) from the diegesis of their animated films and gathered them into an extremely lucrative brand to sell a wide range of consumer products. In 2001, Disney earned $300 million thanks to this franchise; in 2006, that number rose to $3 billion, globally (Orenstein 2006). The franchise has featured media products such as books and music, and a wider array of merchandise such as 'dolls, toys, clothes, jewellery, shoes, luggage, dishware, furniture, cosmetics, bath products, party supplies', and even wall paint (Wasko 2020: 86). This assemblage of varied heroines added another layer of Disneyfication to the literary sources, and reinforced the perception that fairy tales depicting dated constructions of gender were representative of Disney. As Jonathan Gray argues, film 'peripherals' such as merchandise and toys play 'a key role in refining and accentuating certain meanings' from their related films (2010: 181). The specific image selected in 2000 to represent each 'princess', subsequently replicated on consumer products, throughout Disney's theme parks and on the company's websites, showcased their prettiness and marriageability. They featured dressed in the sparkling outfits worn when they meet and/or waltz with their prince, like Cinderella, Aurora and Belle, and appeared demure, smiling, carefully holding their ball gowns. Even Pocahontas and Mulan, characters framed in notably more action-oriented narratives, underwent a fairy-tale makeover in subsequent variants. This involved glittery dresses and jewellery, and the striking disappearance of Mulan's soldier outfit, creating a more homogeneous vision of the Disney heroine despite generic variations, cultural specificities, and 'more nuanced portrayals' (Wasko 2020: 87). The promotion and wide circulation of this copyrighted construction of femininity prompted a 'wave of anti-Disney sentiment' (Whelan 2014: 184). For example, authors such as Peggy Orenstein found fault with the 'retrograde role models' of characters 'interested only in clothes, jewellery and cadging the handsome prince' (2006). Considering the phenomenal success of the Disney Princess franchise, such criticisms only corresponded to small sections of the mainstream audience. Yet, along with the numerous contemporary academic studies on Disney, they added to the growingly pejorative connotations of the Disney formula.

Whether circulated by the Disney company, or discussed in scholarly circles or popular accounts, the idea of the formula has often involved a degree of selection, omission, interpretation, and varying emphasis regarding what defines Disney animation aesthetics, narratives and characters. By 2000, it was part of Disney's 'mission statement for success, becoming carefully co-ordinated capital within the studio's manufacture of fantasy'; throughout critical and popular discourses, it denoted the 'perceived uniformity of Disney products' and testified to 'Magic Kingdom hegemony' (Holliday 2019: 118). Inevitably, this concept uneasily applied to a significant part of Disney's output, especially animated films other than the highly successful, continuously marketed, regularly analysed and commented upon fairy-tale musicals. Janet Wasko's description of the Disney formula, namely 'Classic Disney' and its 'Revised Classic Disney' variant, exemplifies the generic, aesthetic and thematic limits of this label (2020: 121). While conceding that 'not all Disney's films adhere as perfectly' to a 'standard formula', Wasko's focus remains on those that smoothly do (ibid.: 121). Admittedly, many authors have since re-examined the complexity of the Disney canon. For example, shifting the focus away from fairy-tale romance, Whitley has investigated Disney's numerous 'animal stories', identifying the pivotal role of the pastoral genre in early feature films, and the theme of the journey and buddy relationships as core aspects of subsequent releases such as *The Jungle Book* (Wolfgang Reitherman, 1967) (2012: 8, 16). While other authors have approached these films from the perspective of the musical (Smith 2011) or analysed the company's other generic experiments on television including nature documentaries, historical films and westerns (Brode 2010: 145), the idea of Disney as perceived through the lens of the fairy-tale/musical formula has persisted. It is precisely this specific construction of Disney that has been reappropriated, parodied, subverted, and ultimately reinforced by the company's competitors from the mid-1990s onwards.

Rise of Competitors: Pixar, DreamWorks and the Challenges to the Disney Formula

As Wells observes, 'Disney's prominence has only prompted other practitioners to view themselves in opposition to or, at the very least, different from, the Disney form' (2002b: 49). Such a differentiating impulse framed the production, marketing and reception of the output from two major animation studios which rose to prominence while Disney's Renaissance popularity was starting to wane: Pixar and DreamWorks.

When Apple founder Steve Jobs purchased the Graphics Group from Lucasfilm in 1986, it was a small hardware company, soon renamed Pixar, with ambitions to become a filmmaking studio (Herhuth 2017: 3). Founded by Ed Catmull and Alvy Ray Smith, Pixar produced animated shorts throughout the late 1980s, all directed by John Lasseter, relying on evolving computer-generated imagery (CGI). One of the studio's most notable developments was the Renderman software, which was licensed to other visual-effects and animation companies (Furniss 2016: 375). In parallel, Pixar provided Disney with the Pixar Image Computer (PIC) and the Computer Animation Production System software (CAPS), which 'radically changed the methods of 2D production', encompassing digital cel-painting and post-production (ibid.: 376). In 1991, Disney and Pixar signed a contract for a three-picture deal (initially), beginning with the development of *Toy Story* (John Lasseter, 1995), the very first computer-animated feature film. Its success and influence were considerable. While, under Disney's impulse, cel animation had been the dominant production technique in mainstream feature-length animation for over sixty years, *Toy Story* 'almost single-handedly' established computer animation 'as a central pillar of the contemporary Hollywood cinema and announced Pixar as a major creative force' (Brown et al. 2017: 1). As Helen Haswell observes, the film set 'a new standard by which subsequent animated films were measured' (2017: 186) – a position once firmly held by Disney films such as *Snow White* or *Beauty and the Beast*. The continued growth of Pixar's success, from *A Bug's Life* (Andrew Stanton and John Lasseter, 1998) and *Toy Story 2* (John Lasseter, 1999) to the critically acclaimed hits *Monsters, Inc.* (Pete Docter, 2001), *Finding Nemo* (Andrew Stanton, 2003) and *The Incredibles* (Brad Bird, 2004), arguably 'displaced hand-drawn traditions within mainstream American animation' (Haswell 2019: 95). New animation studios, such as Blue Sky Studios and Illumination

Entertainment, were set up and 'geared specifically towards computer animation', while others entirely retooled their 2D animation departments (Haswell 2017: 191). Summers underlines that the 2000s 'would prove to be the computer-animated feature's formative decade in the USA', with Pixar playing a pivotal role in crystallising its aesthetic conventions (2020: 1).

While Pixar worked towards a goal of 'high-quality, intricately shaded, photorealistic imagery' (Furniss 2016: 375), the studio followed core animation principles that were not that different from Disney's. Unlike the 'straight photorealism' of computer-animated films such as *Final Fantasy: The Spirits Within* (Hironobu Sakaguchi, 2001) and *The Polar Express* (Robert Zemeckis, 2004), Pixar relied on 'stylised realism', combining cartoonish characterisation with highly precise simulation of natural phenomena (Herhuth 2017: 37). Bending, but rarely breaking, the rules of physics, Pixar films represented a balance between the technologically enabled, 'accurate reproduction of light, shading, texture, perspective and movement and the distortion of these same parameters for aesthetic or narrative reasons' (Mihailova 2019: 52). Mediating the digital and 'disembodied context of computer-based production', they relied on 'believability', with protagonists that were often anthropomorphic and caricatured (Herhuth 2017: 22, 37). Summers observes that this specific 'mode of realism' was 'the three-dimensional equivalent of Disney's' (2020: 22). Even at the narrative level, Pixar films, like Disney films, maintained a 'discrete, consistent diegesis' without any incongruous intertextual references or narrator intrusions (ibid.: 22). In spite of these convergences, Pixar's paratexts often emphasised the studio's differences from Disney, and most interestingly from the generic components of the latter's formula.

An important aspect of the Disney formula, consistent throughout the studio's history, has been the presence of the musical. Such centrality was reinforced during the Renaissance period, as *The Little Mermaid*'s 'Under the Sea', 'Beauty and the Beast', *Aladdin*'s 'A Whole New World' and *The Lion King*'s 'Can You Feel the Love Tonight' were awarded the Oscar for Best Original Song, and Disney was starting to adapt its canon on Broadway. By contrast, production discourses widely reported Pixar's decision 'not to make *Toy Story* in the manner of a Disney musical', and to avoid diegetic numbers and songs (Smith 2017: 106). Yet, what resulted was actually – again – a 'compromise', with the use of underscoring to 'convey and amplify' the emotions of leads Woody and Buzz (Price 2009: 128). Admittedly, they did not break into song like Disney's Ariel or take part in elaborate ensemble performances like Simba. Still, Susan Smith argues that *Toy Story* was 'covertly a musical at heart', with pieces like 'You've Got a Friend in Me' giving outlet to 'the otherwise imprisoned feelings' of mute characters, namely toys in the presence of humans (2017: 112). From that perspective, *Toy Story* echoed sequences from Disney musicals such as *Dumbo* (ibid.: 112).[5]

While there were some convergences between Pixar's use of the musical and Disney's, an undeniable difference was the disappearance of its romantic potential, an aspect essential to the idea of the Disney formula. Some of the most popular, Oscar-nominated Disney Renaissance songs accompanied or expressed the courtship of the leading couple, whereas songs in the *Toy Story* franchise such as 'You've Got a Friend in Me' or 'When She Loved Me' conveyed toys' long-lasting devotion to 'their' child and friendship with each other. This reflected a wider generic shift away from romance, perceived as Disney territory.[6] Pixar's late 1990s and early 2000s films mostly focused on buddy and father–son relationships – Woody and Buzz, *Monsters, Inc.*'s Mike and Sully, Marlin and Nemo – following from the generic 'formula' of the buddy movie which was highly popular throughout late 1980s and 1990s American cinema (Holliday 2018b: 215–16). Although Disney did feature such male-centred narratives throughout its history, from *The Jungle Book* to *The Fox and the Hound* (Ted Berman and Richard Rich, 1981) and *The Great Mouse Detective* (Ron Clements and John Musker, 1986), these animated films did not enjoy the popularity and visibility of female-centred fairy-tale romances such as *Snow White*, *Cinderella* or *The Little Mermaid*. In other words, they were not representative of the Disney formula from which emerging animation studios needed to differentiate themselves.

Filmmakers' reported resistance to the musical, reflected through the disappearance of this genre from the majority of 2000s Pixar animated films, was also due to fears of a potential generic clash: Lasseter initially believed that 'musical numbers' would take *Toy Story* 'out of its reality' (Price 2009: 128). The 'reality' of Pixar films consisted indeed of contemporary or futuristic worlds which, although often presenting nonhuman characters and allegorical narratives, were 'more technological than magical' (Herhuth 2017: 11). In these contexts, the rules of the musical, closely associated with the fantasy world of fairy tales, could not explicitly be applied. As Holliday observes, initial critical responses to *Toy Story* 'immediately' established a link between Pixar's avoidance of these genres and its computer animation, opposing the studio's 'science and high-powered technology' to 'the tradition of Disney's artistry' (2018b: 215). *Toy Story* not only imitated more closely natural environments and physical phenomena, thanks to ground-breaking techniques, but also featured 'real-life toys' such as Mr Potato Head and Slinky Dog, depicting a world that looked and felt more 'familiar' to contemporary audiences than Disney's enchanted kingdoms (Summers 2017: 128–9). Arguably, Pixar's most striking and significant departure from the Disney formula was precisely the studio's combination of pioneering computer animation with genres beyond fairy-tale romance.

Unlike Pixar, newcomer animation studio DreamWorks most effectively challenged Disney's central position within mainstream animation by reappropriating its formulaic generic template. From its inception, DreamWorks was 'positioned to rival Disney, in particular through its Katzenberg-helmed animation division' (Summers 2020: 22). While the studio's first films – computer-animated *Antz* (Eric Darnell and Tim Johnson, 1998), cel-animated *The Prince of Egypt* (Brenda Chapman and Steve Hickner, 1998) and *The Road to El Dorado* (Bibo Bergeron and Don Paul, 2000) – met limited success, *Shrek* (Andrew Adamson and Vicky Jenson, 2001) was both a blockbuster and critical hit. As the first instalment of a franchise of four films spanning the 2000s, *Shrek* not only redefined the animated fairy-tale musical with its irreverent, critical parody of the Disney formula but also had a major influence on computer animation.

Focusing on the film text, *Shrek* swiftly mobilises the tropes of Disney's formulaic fairy-tale from its very start, drawing on pre-Renaissance films. Imitating the opening of *Snow White*, *Cinderella* and most strikingly *Sleeping Beauty*, *Shrek* starts with a book, lit from above, magically opening. As pages turn themselves, gilded illuminations and colourful illustrations are revealed, while a mysterious narrator solemnly reads in voiceover: a 'lovely princess . . . had an enchantment upon her . . . which could only be broken by love's first kiss. She was locked away in a castle guarded by a terrible fire-breathing dragon', waiting for a 'brave' knight to rescue her. The sequence, introduced by the typical phrase 'once upon a time' and accompanied by a soft non-diegetic melody, invites viewers to suspend their disbelief and enter the conventional world of a Disney fairy tale. Yet, as the digitally simulated camera zooms in on the knight drawn under the words 'true love's first kiss', kneeling before the princess and holding a bouquet of flowers, the narrator abruptly stops his reading. Incredulous and unimpressed, he exclaims, 'Like that's ever gonna happen, what a load of . . .', while a green hand tears the page (Figure 1.1). The ethereal music is replaced by the sound of a toilet flush, and Shrek (Mike Myers) is finally introduced. In one minute, the film not only irreverently mocked Disney's sentimental fairy-tale formula but also instantly rejected it as dated, setting the tone for its parodic take. Holliday argues that such generic irreverence is linked to computer animation itself: 'computer graphics and digital imaging software ultimately offer up a striking vision of modernity that does not quite gel with . . . the literary origins of fairy tales', making 'affectionate re-tellings' more difficult (2018b: 218). Replacing the two-dimensional, hand-drawn stock characters by the unexpected computer-animated ogre, *Shrek* introduced a new way to approach this central animated genre.

Throughout the narrative, the film shrewdly reconfigures the semantic tropes of the fairy tale. 'Traditionally good characters' are transformed into villains, and vice versa (Mollet 2020: 80): the expected knight is Lord Farquaad (John Lithgow), a tyrannical and self-obsessed leader; the fire-breathing dragon turns

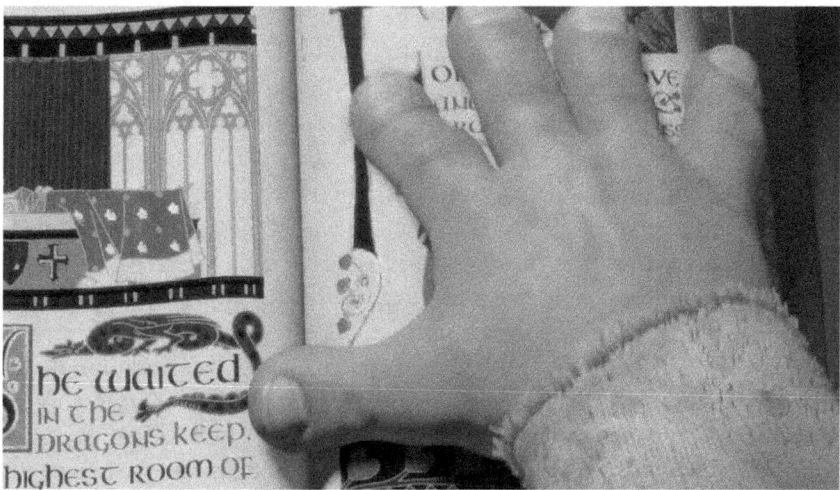

Figure 1.1 *Shrek tears the page of the formulaic fairy-tale book. Frame grab from* Shrek *(Adamson and Jenson, 2001).*

out to be a sensitive and loyal sidekick; grumpy ogre Shrek is the unlikely hero ordered by Farquaad to rescue the heroine, Princess Fiona (Cameron Diaz). These generic subversions are highlighted through playful self-reflexivity. As Summers points out, both Shrek and Fiona 'display an awareness of, and cynicism regarding the tropes of the genre they inhabit and the roles they are expected to play' (2020: 129). It is precisely the discrepancy between their – and viewers' – expectations and the unfolding events which creates comedy. For example, when Shrek comes to Fiona's rescue, she is frustrated and shocked that he does not kiss her, sweep her off her feet and onto his 'valiant steed', or even recite a poem: from a generic perspective, 'this isn't right'. What she expected corresponds to the demonstrations of 'courtly love and chivalric romance' introduced in the opening sequence and that have come to crystallise Disney's sentimental formula, from *Snow White*'s Prince serenading the heroine to Prince Phillip waltzing with Aurora in the forest (Bradford 2012: 180). *Shrek*'s irreverent take on 'Prince Charming' actually parallels Fiona's singular performance of the fairy-tale heroine. Although she is introduced as a damsel in distress, she single-handedly fights off Robin Hood and his Merry Men; far from possessing the admirable singing abilities of her Disney counterparts, she accidentally kills a bird which cannot compete with her high-pitched voice; far from being conventionally pretty, she transforms into an ogress every night. These challenges to the iconic and heavily marketed Disney Princess participate in *Shrek*'s wider subversion of the Disney formula.

Beyond these generic reconfigurations, which mostly satirise Disney's earlier, yet enduringly popular fairy tales, *Shrek* also critically parodies aspects of the studio's formula that were particularly commented upon in the 1990s: the sanitising aspect of and commercial impulses behind these adaptations, and Disney's overall 'dominance in the field of fairy-tale retellings' (Summers 2020: 131). Lord Farquaad's kingdom of Duloc epitomises this stance. Devoid of all fairy-tale creatures, which Farquaad describes as 'trash poisoning [his] perfect world', his kingdom appears cold, 'polished' and 'pristine': a metaphor for Disney's removal of 'grotesque', 'unrefined' and 'violent' elements when adapting its sources (ibid.: 133–4). The parody is made explicit through several anachronistic inclusions, transforming Duloc into Disneyland. At the entrance, the long queue formed from rope bollards and the souvenir shops hint at the consumerist underpinnings of Disney's formula, while the Farquaad mascot and high-pitched tune sung by animatronic puppets – reminiscent of Disneyland's 'It's a Small World After All' – convey a sense of forced cheerfulness which seems to permeate the studio's fairy-tale musicals.

The use of such explicitly anachronistic inclusions, numerous throughout the film, not only parodies the Disneyfication of fairy tales but also destabilises the diegetic world of the Disney formula. Disney animated films are 'internally consistent' and 'self-contained', as opposed to the 'temporal and generic anarchy of *Shrek*' (ibid.: 4, 135). From Fiona imitating Trinity's fighting style in *The Matrix* (Lana and Lilly Wachowski, 1999) to Donkey's (Eddie Murphy) final performance of the Monkees' 'I'm a Believer', these intertexts 'distance the diegesis from any sense of plausible reality' and create gaps in logic: they are what Summers terms 'contra-diegetic' (ibid.: 9–10). Challenging the type of narrative 'realism' established by Disney and perpetuated by Pixar, *Shrek* revived aspects of narrative-cartoonal comedy made popular by Warner Bros.' *Looney Tunes* shorts – a studio which also explicitly parodied and rejected Disney's model (ibid.: 4, 176–7).[7] Within the generic context of the fairy tale, *Shrek*'s consistent use of contemporary references consolidated the perception of the Disney formula as old-fashioned.

Paradoxically, by subverting and mocking so explicitly the Disney formula, *Shrek* also reintroduced the studio's sentimental fairy-tale romance within the contemporary animation landscape, and revived generic and gendered tropes that it initially aimed to parody. Although, at the time of *Shrek*'s release, Disney's fairy-tale formula was highly visible throughout paratexts and the company's synergistic machine, and examined within academic and critical discourses, there had not been a Disney fairy-tale release in almost a decade (*Aladdin*). The second half of the 1990s was characterised by action-oriented films such as *Mulan* and *Tarzan* (Chris Buck and Kevin Lima, 1999), but these failed to meet the success of Renaissance hits such as *Beauty and the Beast*. To some extent, DreamWorks further reinforced the association between Disney and the fairy-tale genre. Although *Shrek*'s approach was undeniably polemical, the film arguably did not solely 'explod[e]' – in Zipes's term – formulaic standards (2011: 244). Dan Harries observes that 'by evoking a genre to be spoofed, film parody . . . also reiterates and reaffirms the conventions that constitute the genre's structure' (2002: 283). The film correspondingly both consistently subverts Disney's sentimental fairy-tale formula and preserves some of its aspects, as epitomised in the closing wedding scene. After a misunderstanding which leads Fiona to accept Farquaad's marriage proposal, Shrek interrupts the ceremony and, unconventionally, the ogre declares his love for the princess, she turns into an ogress as the sun sets, and Farquaad gets eaten by the dragon. When Shrek and Fiona finally share 'true love's first kiss', she undergoes one last transformation. She magically rises up in the air, surrounded by sparkling light like *Beauty and the Beast*'s monstrous protagonist; unlike the latter, she does not turn into a human and remains an ogress. This transformation strikingly reconfigures the semantic tropes of Disney's formula and challenges its definition of female beauty; yet, the film adopts the same syntactic trajectory. As Shrek's friend Donkey joyfully exclaims, 'I was hoping this would be a happy ending', the couple kisses again and a match on action reveals Shrek and Fiona as newlyweds: the film celebrates, albeit knowingly, the same sentimental romance that it initially mocked. This smooth 'kiss transition' recalls *The Little Mermaid*'s ending, another film in which the appearance of the animated heroine is permanently altered for the couple to be reunited. Paradoxically, *Shrek*'s subversion of fairy-tale gendered tropes are not as radical as its self-aware approach may suggest. Fiona holds limited agency throughout the film, and her looks are still validated by her male suitor ('but you are beautiful'). As a whole, *Shrek* effectively satirised specific aspects of the Disney formula, yet its undeniable rejuvenation of the animated fairy tale still resuscitated some of its tropes.

The success of *Shrek* helped position DreamWorks not only as Disney's main rival but also as a significant player within the animation industry, exerting considerable influence on both the animated fairy-tale film and computer animation overall. *Shrek* became the highest grossing computer-animated film upon its release (Summers 2020: 190), and was awarded the first Oscar for Best Animated Feature in 2001. Critics consolidated the perception of *Shrek* as the 'antithesis of the passé Disney formula' (ibid.: 184). For example, reviewers praised the film for 'beating up the irritatingly dainty Disney trademarks . . . with demolition-derby zest' (Mitchell 2001), providing a 'full-scale parody of the Mousedom's chirpy ethic of old' (Nathan 2001), and using wit that 'transcends sentimentality' (French 2001). Yet, DreamWorks' irreverent satire and incongruous cultural references were also subject to criticism by some reviewers, hinting at the continued popularity of the Disney formula for some sections of the audience. *Shrek* was sometimes described as 'cynical' and 'hip', lacking 'the faintest glimmer of charm' (Lane 2001), and trying to 'have its cynicism and keep its daydreams, too' (Malcolm 2001). This perception of the two studios as representative of two opposite types of fairy-tale animation was paralleled in scholarly writing, with authors such as Clare Bradford contrasting 'Disney's reverential and nostalgic approach to fairy tales and the more brash sceptical style exemplified by *Shrek*' (2012: 174). As the *Shrek* franchise became the 'definitive alternative to the fairy tale/musical', DreamWorks also revived 'sarcastic, comedic and cartoonal' animation as a viable model against Disney's 'earnest, romantic and realist' mode (Summers 2020: 177). Summers points out that numerous 2000s computer-animated films relied on 'contra-diegetic cultural gags and modern pop songs' to distinguish themselves from Disney's previous output and that, most strikingly, computer-animated fairy tales like *Hoodwinked* (Cory Edwards and Todd Edwards, 2005) and *Happily N'Ever After* (Paul Bolger and Yvette Kaplan, 2006) reproduced *Shrek*'s parodic and 'anarchic twists' (2020: 137, 184). DreamWorks' 'tangible challenge' to Disney's formula (Downes and Madeley 2011: 75), added to Pixar's continuing success with its visually innovative computer-animated films beyond fairy-tale romance, seriously threatened Disney's leadership, forcing the studio to revise its approach to feature-length animation.

Disney's 2000s Generic Experiments: Diverging from, Mocking and Reclaiming the Formula

In the wake of the Disney Renaissance, the first half of the 2000s represented a challenging transitional period for the studio: the success of Pixar and DreamWorks reinforced by contrast the perception of Disney animation as dated and formulaic. It is precisely the idea of this formula, namely the studio's caricatured realism, sentimental cheerfulness and sanitised narratives crystallised by fairy-tale musicals, that Disney strove to rework within its feature animation. Pallant describes the period between 2000 and 2004 as Disney's 'most consistently experimental' era in terms of genre and aesthetic (2010: 114). Every 'Neo-Disney' cel-animated film attempted to distance itself from the Disney formula, starting with the studio's seemingly consistent 'hyperrealism' – the emphasis on 'artistic sophistication, "realism" in characters and contexts, and . . . believability within the hand-drawn medium' (ibid.: 105). For example, *Fantasia 2000* (Hendel Butoy and Eric Goldberg, 2000), a package feature inspired and accompanied by well-known pieces of classical music, included sequences such as 'Rhapsody in Blue' and 'Symphony no. 5' that were heavily stylised and anti-naturalistic, and which relied on an expressionistic use of colour. *Atlantis:*

The Lost Empire (Gary Trousdale and Kirk Wise, 2001) and *Lilo & Stitch* both departed from 'standard Disney physiognomy' and were underpinned by individual aesthetic visions: *Atlantis*'s uncommonly angular characters followed from Mike Mignola's style, while *Lilo & Stitch* adopted a more weighted and rounded aesthetic under co-director Chris Sanders's impulse (Pallant 2013: 116, 118). *The Emperor's New Groove* (Mark Dindal, 2000) developed and amplified the narrative-cartoonal comedy that had emerged in Disney feature animation with *Aladdin* and *Hercules* (Ron Clements and John Musker, 1997), relying on metareferential and anachronistic humour (Summers 2020: 175). As Summers explains, such a tonal and aesthetic shift was an attempt to diverge from the 'earnestness and sentimentality' identified with both Disney and its 1990s imitators (ibid.: 175). Another parallel strategy was the reappropriation of more 'mature' genres transcending the 'perceived childishness' of Disney's formula: fairy-tale magic and enchanted kingdoms were replaced by science-fiction 'technology' and 'futuristic settings' in *Atlantis* and *Treasure Planet* (Ron Clements and John Musker, 2002) (ibid.: 173). Unlike Renaissance features, most Neo-Disney films also foregrounded (substitute) father–son and buddy relationships over romance: *The Emperor's New Groove*'s Kuzco and Pacha, *Treasure Planet*'s Jim Hawkins and Silver, *Brother Bear*'s Kenai and Koda (Aaron Blaise and Robert Walker, 2003). In a move similar to Pixar's, such a focus on male-centred action-oriented stories was accompanied by a notable avoidance of the musical genre as consolidated throughout Disney's Renaissance. Despite such generic variety and experimentation, Neo-Disney films underperformed at the box office, and suffered from generally negative reviews, constituting 'a period of strategic uncertainty' (Pallant 2013: 125).

While such critical and financial failure can be explained by the overall box-office decline of cel animation in 2000s Hollywood (Summers 2020: 176), as reflected by the limited popularity of DreamWorks' early animated films, Disney's approach towards its own formula may also be in cause: *Lilo & Stitch* is a particularly insightful case in point. It was Disney's most successful post-Renaissance animated film in the early 2000s: according to Summers, this was due to its status as an 'anarchic' comedy as opposed to its contemporary science-fiction counterparts (ibid.: 176). As *Shrek* had demonstrated the previous year, the 'narrative-cartoonal mode' rather than the 'mature action genre' seemed to be an effective alternative to the 'traditional Disney formula' (ibid.: 177). Yet, *Lilo & Stitch*'s generic identity is a little more complex. Featuring science-fiction tropes typical of Neo-Disney, including space travel and alien creatures, the film still primarily focused on the story of a family and their – albeit unconventional – pet, echoing Disney narratives such as *One Hundred and One Dalmatians* (Clyde Geronimi and Hamilton Luske,

1961) and *Oliver and Company* (George Scribner, 1988). By also foregrounding the relationship between Lilo and her sister Nani, the film developed and updated Disney's 'legacy of family themes', an aspect that was particularly foregrounded in marketing and promotional interviews (Dean Deblois, quoted in Osmond 2002). In other words, the film drew on several motifs that permeated Disney's canon, but that the success and high visibility of fairy-tale musicals had somehow overshadowed.

While relying on familiar Disney components, *Lilo & Stitch* also more explicitly engaged with the idea of the Disney formula, adopting a dual approach which built on *Shrek*'s self-awareness and irreverence, and was pivotal in the studio's subsequent reclaiming of its formula: the film relied on a combination of parody and celebration. The very portrayal of Stitch crystallised such a dual approach. With his diminutive stature, big eyes and round, cuddly shape, Stitch displays the disarming cuteness typical of Disney's anthropomorphic characters. He is also a scientific experiment gone wrong, a blue alien who has crashed on Earth and is initially mistaken for a dog and an 'evil koala': mischievous, greedy and initially uncontrollable, he constantly wreaks havoc around him. While misleading cuteness is only briefly referred to in *Hercules* through the performance of villainous sidekicks Pain and Panic, who transform into helpless children and woodland animals, it is central to *Lilo & Stitch*.

Stitch's status as an unruly, hybrid, somehow monstruous yet endearing creature stands out within the context of the Disney formula: this contrast was at the core of the film's marketing, which presented Stitch as an intruder within a cohesive canon of enchanting stories with beloved characters. Posters depicted Stitch surrounded by protagonists from films representative of the studio's formulaic fairy-tale romance – *The Little Mermaid*, *Beauty and the Beast*, *Aladdin*, *Snow White* – and musicals – *Pinocchio*, *Peter Pan* (Clyde Geronimi and Wilfred Jackson, 1953) and *The Lion King*. These iconic characters express various levels of shock, disgust, fear and even anger at the sight of Stitch, who visually and generically clashes with their own magical and harmonious world. Such anger was echoed throughout a series of promotional teasers which operated as a twist to Disney's retrospective trailers. Each teaser started in the middle of a well-known musical sequence from Disney Renaissance films, playfully disrupted by Stitch. He is shown surfing behind Ariel, and his shouts of excitement interrupt her singing of 'Part of Your World': annoyed, she exclaims, 'I was singing here!', subverting the generic rules of the musical by foregrounding the artificial aspect of seemingly spontaneous and smooth performances. The romantic and courtly atmosphere of ballads 'A Whole New World' and 'Beauty and the Beast' is similarly spoilt, as Stitch wreaks havoc in the Beast's ballroom and flirts with Jasmine, taking her for a ride on his spaceship and leaving Aladdin alone on his magic carpet. Stitch's intrusions, obtruding into scenes that epitomised Disney's predictable fairy-tale sentimentality, reveal the studio's specific stance towards its own formula: embracing its perceived clichés as part of Disney's unique legacy, while knowingly subverting them. One year after *Shrek*, these teasers also effectively reminded audiences of Disney's unique positioning within the animation industry, showcasing the studio's biggest hits at a time when it was seriously challenged by Pixar and DreamWorks. One of *Lilo & Stitch*'s trailers specifically framed the Disney canon as a seamless succession of classics spanning several decades and possessing uniquely nostalgic and cross-generational appeal. The trailer opens as another celebratory retrospective, with clips from *Beauty and the Beast*, *Snow White*, *Bambi*, *Tarzan*, *The Little Mermaid* and *Aladdin*. The voice-over announces that 'for over seventy years, the Walt Disney Studio has won the hearts of audiences with the most enchanting, delightful, and lovable characters the world as ever known'. It is interrupted in the middle of *The Lion King*'s 'Circle of Life', when the animals realise in horror that Simba has been replaced by Stitch, leading to complete chaos in the savannah. Framing *Lilo & Stitch* as a departure, the trailer also nostalgically reclaims, mocks and perpetuates the idea of Disney's sentimental fairy-tale/musical formula.

By the end of the Neo-Disney period, computer animation had achieved ubiquity in Hollywood, while Disney's last cel-animated attempts – including *Home on the Range* (Will Finn and John Sanford, 2004) – led to critical and box-office failure: the release of *Chicken Little* marked Disney's shift to what Pallant terms its 'digital era' (2013: 127).[8] Not only adopting Pixar's stylised realism, the film also strikingly imitated DreamWorks' 'narrative-cartoonal mode', both in its continuous use of 'authorial intertextuality' and in its irreverent approach towards the idea of the Disney formula (Summers 2020: 167).[9] Reappropriating and expanding *Shrek*'s 'self-conscious, deconstructive' opening (Holliday 2019: 123), *Chicken Little* begins with three different introductions, which a narrator discards one after the other in voice-over. Each introduction crystallises a facet of the Disney formula: the sentimental fairy tale, signified by the words 'once upon a time', a soft orchestral melody and onscreen fairy dust; the hand-drawn hit musical, represented by the opening shot of *The Lion King*'s 'Circle of Life'; and the cheerful, childlike literary adaptation, depicted by a storybook opening by itself. Each time, an abrupt cut to black and a non-diegetic, incongruous sound (a door slamming, brakes screeching) interrupt these opening shots, while the narrator underlines their conventional predictability: 'How many times have you heard that to begin a story?', 'It sounds familiar. Doesn't it, to you?', 'How many have seen "opening the book" before?' Building on *Lilo & Stitch*'s text and paratexts, *Chicken Little* acknowledges perceived formulaic clichés, reappropriating DreamWorks' parodic critique. Unlike *Lilo & Stitch*, the film seems to equate its computer-animated departure to making a 'DreamWorks-esque, diegetically loose, essentially intertextual movie' (Summers 2020: 167). The film continuously relies on meta-humour and incongruous contra-diegetic intertexts to disrupt the cohesiveness of its diegesis. Settling on an opening presenting the main protagonist, Chicken Little, the film introduces a fictional anthropomorphic world mimicking our own in which animals wear clothes, use technology, go to school and have jobs – a world entirely devoid of humans. Despite this premise, there are many instances referring to live action and viewers' contemporary reality: animal cinemagoers watch a projection of *Raiders of the Lost Ark* (Steven Spielberg, 1981); duck Abby and pig Runt sing a karaoke cover of the Spice Girls' 'Wannabe'. These examples cannot be reconciled with the exclusively anthropomorphic and computer-animated setting of the story. Such DreamWorks tendencies, combined with an explicit, playful rejection of the idea of the Disney formula, did not lead to critical or box office success (Haswell 2019: 95). Not only did it add to the disappointing Neo-Disney performances, *Chicken Little* seemed also to further damage Disney's position within mainstream animation, which was already suffering following significant corporates changes.

In January 2004, Pixar revealed that it was severing ties with Disney, looking elsewhere to co-produce and distribute its films. This decision, resulting from heightened tensions between Eisner and Jobs, highlighted the growing gap between Pixar, considered the 'new Disney' thanks to its increasing prominence, and the Disney studio, the popularity of which was waning with the underperforming Neo-Disney films (Haswell 2017: 191). Between 1997 and 2004, Pixar had released critically acclaimed hits on which Disney was relying for box-office revenues, merchandise and theme-park attractions (ibid.: 188).[10] The loss of Pixar was perceived as a failure for Disney, with Eisner being mostly blamed for it (Wasko 2020: 38). As shareholders opposed Eisner's re-election to the company's board, he resigned and was replaced by Robert Iger in September 2005. The latter quickly approached Jobs: in January 2006, Disney acquired Pixar for $7.4 billion. Despite this corporate acquisition, Disney and Pixar were kept separate as animation studios. To restore the former's success, the course of action and rhetoric adopted by Ed Catmull (newly appointed President of Disney Animation) and John Lasseter (Chief Creative Officer) consisted in reviving and showcasing what was perceived as Disney's singularity, relying on two stylistic and generic pillars of the Disney formula. Catmull and Lasseter retooled the studio's hand-drawn animation department and announced the renewed production of fairy-tale musicals, including *The Princess and the Frog* (Ron Clements and John Musker, 2009) in July 2006 and *Tangled* (Nathan Greno and Byron Howard, 2010) in late

2007 (Holliday 2018b: 216–17).[11] This apparent new return to Disney's roots, contrasting with the approach of most Neo-Disney films and *Chicken Little*, was showcased in 2007 by the animation/live-action hybrid *Enchanted*.

Enchanted not only represented Disney's explicit response to Dream-Works' satirical attack but also updated and expanded on the idea of the studio's formula, reclaiming the sentimental fairy-tale musical for the post-Pixar era. Imitating Disney's earliest fairy tales, *Enchanted* opens with a storybook, leading to the hand-drawn animated world of Andalasia. The sweet and naïve heroine, Giselle (Amy Adams), sings to disarmingly cute woodland creatures her dreams of romance like Snow White, Cinderella and Aurora. She rapidly meets Prince Edward (James Marsden) after he rescues her from an ogre: Edward decides to marry her, they sing and ride away into the sunset. After having swiftly mobilised the tropes of the formulaic fairy-tale musical, *Enchanted* departs from its expected trajectory: evil queen Narissa (Susan Sarandon) casts Giselle away to live-action New York, where she is soon joined by Edward. The film then adopts a singular parodic stance. While *Shrek* relied on contra-diegetic intertexts, contemporary sarcasm and anachronisms to satirise Disney's sentimental formula, *Enchanted* somehow reverses this approach, bringing seemingly old-fashioned tropes into a contemporary context. Humorous incongruity is rooted in the perceived 'incompatibility' between fairy-tale fantasy and modern settings, from Giselle's massive glittery dress, impractical in New York's streets, to Edward's impulse to draw his sword against road workers (Mollet 2020: 83). Their belief in formulaic gendered and romantic tropes adds to their clichéd portrayal and clashes with their New York counterparts. For example, Giselle delights in household chores, and longs for Edward to come rescue her, as expressed in 'Happy Working Song', echoing Snow White's 'Whistle While You Work'. By contrast, single father and divorce lawyer Robert (Patrick Dempsey) is cynical about love; his girlfriend Nancy (Idina Menzel) is independent and has a career. Furthermore, Robert is stunned at Giselle's spontaneous singing, foregrounding and questioning the rules of the Disney musical, which seem artificial and incongruous in his live-action world (Figure 1.2).

Such self-reflexive and light-hearted teasing of the incongruity of the Disney formula leads to two parallel outcomes. Displaying the studio's efforts to reconsider some aspects of the Disney Princess, Giselle gradually transforms. Thanks to Robert, she starts doubting the 'happily ever after' she is supposed to live with one-dimensional Edward, she experiences anger and desire for the first time, and ultimately rescues Robert from evil queen Narissa – turned fire-breathing dragon – before setting up her own dress-making business in New York. At the same time, Giselle's and Edward's romantic belief in true love persists and influences both Robert and Nancy (Figure 1.3). In

Figure 1.2 Robert's incredulity challenges Disney's formulaic fairy-tale musical. Frame grab from Enchanted *(Lima, 2007)*.

Figure 1.3 Robert embraces sentimental fairy-tale romance, embodied by Giselle. Frame grab from Enchanted *(Lima, 2007)*.

a sequence echoing the setting and costumes from 'Beauty and the Beast', Robert waltzes with and finds himself – softly – singing to Giselle; later his kiss wakes her up from Narissa's curse. Nancy enthusiastically embraces the promise of a fantasy happy ending, and marries simple-minded yet sincere Edward in Andalasia. In other words, while *Enchanted* parodies and revises the gendered and generic tropes of the Disney formula, it also celebrates some of its core components.

Unlike *Shrek*, *Enchanted* stands out by its explicit reverence and nostalgia for the idea of the Disney formula, underlying its knowingly playful attitude: this duality is facilitated by the film's specific borrowings from the postfeminist romantic comedy. From a generic perspective, there is a 'meaningful and lasting connection' between romantic comedies and fairy tales (Brook 2015: 146). Heather Brook considers 'Cinderella', for example, to be 'a staple narrative of mainstream romance' (ibid.: 145). Some of its key semantic and syntactic tropes – rags to riches narrative, makeover transformation – have been reappropriated and reinvented in films such as *Pretty Woman* (Garry Marshall, 1990), *Maid in Manhattan* (Wayne Wang, 2002) and *Crazy Rich Asians* (Jon Chu, 2018). Frank Krutnik observes that, in the 1990s, the conventions of the romantic comedy permeated 'family-oriented fare' including fairy tales such as *The Little Mermaid* and *Beauty and the Beast* (2002: 137). Arguably, this generic dialogue between Disney and romantic comedies was developed further and amplified with *Enchanted*.

Throughout the film's paratexts and text, the worlds of hand-drawn fairy tale and live-action romantic comedy converge: New York functions as a 'magical gateway' between the two (Mollet 2020: 86). The city is not only an iconic romantic-comedy setting, showcased in *When Harry Met Sally* (Rob Reiner, 1989) and *You've Got Mail* (Nora Ephron, 1998), but also appears as an enchanted place in which fairy-tale characters can keep their extraordinary abilities, from Giselle talking to animals to Narissa turning into a dragon. In some posters, the two generic spaces mirror each other: the shape of the fairy-tale castle parallels that of the Empire State Building, and Robert is positioned as the contemporary counterpart to Edward's sword-wielding prince.[12] His portrayal as an alternative 'prince' for Giselle reveals how *Enchanted* reappropriates key romantic-comedy tropes to renew Disney's sentimental formula. His presence creates a love triangle, recurring in romantic comedies, which challenges 'the normative fairy-tale narrative' (ibid.: 83). Robert's cynicism and pragmatism contrast with and question Giselle's clichéd innocence: these differences precisely make them the 'typical romantic-comedy couple – opposed in almost every way, and yet clearly destined to be together' (Tasker 2011: 67). Through these oppositions, *Enchanted* playfully reinvents the dynamics of the Disney couple.

Another pivotal love triangle in the film, namely Giselle as an alternative to Nancy, reveals how *Enchanted* represents a 'quintessential expression of post-feminist ideology' (ibid.: 68). While Giselle's traditionalist performance of gender and firm belief in formulaic romance are initially mocked and framed as incongruously dated, she also embodies a fairy-tale fantasy that is ultimately welcomed in the generic space of 2000s romantic-comedy New York. For example, her candid observations and emotional response towards Robert's divorcing clients results in their reconciliation; her suggestion for Robert to invite Nancy to a ball is met with excitement by the latter – by the end, the only character finding fairy-tale romance 'nauseating' is the defeated evil queen. As Tracey Mollet observes, Robert and Nancy 'allow themselves to be enchanted by the allure of a fairy-tale ending, evidencing their embrace of nostalgia' (2020: 87). As will be developed in Chapters 2 and 3, it is precisely this deliberate return to traditionalist paradigms, combined with more empowering elements, such as the image of Giselle as a sword-wielding princess, that crystallises post-feminist sensibilities at the core of contemporary romantic comedies and subsequent Disney fairy tales.

Conclusion

Enchanted's critical and box-office success represented a turning point for Disney's approach towards its own perceived formula and associated generic identity.[13] Initially characterising the studio's 1930s hyperreal hand-drawn aesthetic and sentimental narratives, the formula gradually crystallised a limited set of tropes that had come to signify 'Disney' – tropes that were consolidated throughout films, critical discourses and an expanding synergistic machine. Becoming synonymous with hit fairy-tale musicals, sanitised literary adaptations and archaic constructions of gender, Disney faced significant competition from the late 1990s onwards. Pixar and DreamWorks challenged the studio's central position in the animation industry: despite some convergences with the Disney canon, their output was produced and received in opposition to Disney's old-fashioned formula. Such aesthetic, generic and tonal challenges fundamentally shaped Disney's 2000s releases. To face these new competitors, these films borrowed from science fiction and action adventure, and subsequently reappropriated Pixar's computer-animated aesthetic and DreamWorks' narrative-cartoonal mode. Yet, as illustrated by *Lilo & Stitch* and most strikingly *Enchanted*, the studio was arguably most successful when simultaneously mocking, celebrating and generically expanding its own formula. Under the impulse of Disney's new 2006 leadership, this approach framed the studio's subsequent animated features, interacting with two major generic strands: romance and action adventure.

Notes

1. For an analysis of the role and animated output of Blue Sky, Illumination and other studios such as Sony, see Holliday 2018a; Summers 2019, 2020 (esp. ch. 6); Brown 2021.
2. For a more detailed account of Michael Eisner and his team's strategy regarding partnerships, expansion and synergy, see Wasko 2020: 34–7.
3. The exception standing out in this series of successes is *The Rescuers Down Under* (Mike Gabriel, 1990), the first theatrically released sequel to a Disney animated feature, namely *The Rescuers* (John Lounsbery and Wolfgang Reitherman, 1977).

4. *'Beauty and the Beast* (1991)', *Box Office Mojo*, <https://www.boxofficemojo.com/title/tt0101414/?ref_=bo_gr_ti> (accessed 21 August 2021); *'Beauty and the Beast'*, *Box Office Mojo*, <http://www.boxofficemojo.com/movies/?id=beautyandthebeast2017.htm> (accessed 21 August 2021).
5. The songs 'Pink Elephants on Parade' and 'Baby Mine' convey the feelings of Dumbo and his mother, respectively – characters which do not utter any line of dialogue throughout the film. See Smith 2011: 173–4.
6. A notable exception is the later film *WALL-E* (Andrew Stanton, 2008), released after Disney's acquisition of Pixar, which introduces romance into the Pixar musical through the recurring use of excerpts from the live-action musical *Hello, Dolly!* (Gene Kelly, 1969). With characters re-enacting the latter's choreography and humming its songs to each other, *WALL-E* is Pixar's most conventional take on the musical genre from that era, until the late 2010s with *Coco* (Lee Unkrich, 2017). See Edney and Hughes 2010; Herhuth 2014.
7. Sam Summers identifies two types of 'cartoonal' conventions: visual tropes (warping of physical laws, impossibly malleable bodies, etc.) and narrative conventions (porous diegesis). The latter is specifically applied to *Shrek*. See Summers 2020: 17.
8. Disney's first computer-animated feature film was *Dinosaur* (Eric Leighton and Ralph Zondag, 2000), which adopted a photorealistic aesthetic more pronounced than Pixar's stylised realism. See Summers 2020: 163.
9. Authorial intertextuality 'denotes a reference consciously made by one text to another which is both deliberate and explicit, meant to be perceived and understood by a section of readers and interpreted in a certain way' (Summers 2020: 7).
10. In 1997, Pixar renegotiated the terms of its contract with Disney and signed a five-film co-production agreement. See Haswell 2017: 188.
11. *Tangled* was first announced in October 2003 as the computer-animated feature *Rapunzel Unbraided*. See Holliday 2018b: 217.
12. Posters also relied on Patrick Dempsey's star persona as romantic lead, from *Can't Buy Me Love* (Steve Rash, 1987) and *Sweet Home Alabama* (Andy Tennant, 2002) to *Grey's Anatomy* (Shonda Rhimes, 2005), to present him as a modern, 'real Prince Charming'. His character nickname in *Grey's Anatomy*, Dr Derek 'McDreamy' Shepherd, was directly referenced in one of the posters, with the tagline 'He's not Just Dreamy, He's Prince Charming'.
13. *Enchanted* grossed $127,807,262 domestically and three songs from the film were nominated at the Oscars for Best Original Song. See *'Enchanted'*, *Box Office Mojo*, <http://www.boxofficemojo.com/movies/?id=enchanted.htm> (accessed 21 August 2021).

Part 1

Disney and Romance

CHAPTER 2

Reanimating Fantasies of Fairy-tale Romance: Disney Nostalgia and The Princess and the Frog

> We're subject to huge scrutiny every time we come out with something new, especially a film like this, that is right in Disney's pocket . . . It's what we're supposed to do well – fairy tales, animation, and musicals. (Byron Howard, quoted in Kurtti 2010: 44)

Following the success of *Enchanted* (Kevin Lima, 2007), Disney's subsequent animated fairy tales represented a cohesive generic cycle which stood out within contemporary Hollywood animation. *The Princess and the Frog* (Ron Clements and John Musker, 2009), *Tangled* (Nathan Greno and Byron Howard, 2010) and *Frozen* (Chris Buck and Jennifer Lee, 2013) revived and renewed the studio's formula by engaging with contemporary genres of romance and with fairy tales beyond the Disney canon. As the studio's first post-*Shrek* hand-drawn animated fairy-tale musical, *The Princess and the Frog* was a spectacularly nostalgic reclaiming of the Disney formula. At the same time, these nostalgic impulses were accompanied and mediated by unprecedented semantic and syntactic reconfigurations: the film focuses on a black waitress who dreams of opening a restaurant in 1920s New Orleans, falls in love and marries a prince to whom she is initially opposed in every way. For this film, Disney was subject to 'huge scrutiny' not only because it released an animated fairy-tale musical but also and especially because of its history of racial and gender representation.

As Mike Budd observes, 'critiques of Disney's representations of African Americans and other racial groups are almost as old as the company's habit of caricaturing such groups' (2005: 20). Numerous authors have examined Disney's recurring association of anthropomorphism and racial stereotypes regarding Chinese people, African Americans and Native Americans in films such as *Lady and the Tramp* (Clyde Geronimi and Wilfred Jackson, 1955), *The Jungle Book* (Wolfgang Reitherman, 1967) and *Brother Bear* (Aaron Blaise and Robert Walker, 2003).[1] Writing on 1980s and 1990s animation, authors such as Natchee Blu Barnd argue that Disney applies racial attributes to 'clearly marked Others', while whiteness remains invisible yet privileged (2013: 69). Celeste Lacroix particularly notes that non-white heroines in films such as

Aladdin (Ron Clements and John Musker, 1992) and *The Hunchback of Notre-Dame* (Gary Trousdale and Kirk Wise, 1996) 'embody the exoticised Other woman – one whose sexualised presence is privileged above all else' (2004: 222). Scholars analysing more contemporary portrayals of race observe that, 'in response to a general increase of cultural sensitivity surrounding political correctness', Disney has adopted a 'philosophy of avoidance rather than engagement' (Parasher 2013: 45). Although animated features from the mid-1990s onwards have featured diverse ensemble casts, Sarah Turner notes that these films both address and 'erase race' (2013: 83). Critics and academics have often approached *The Princess and the Frog* from this standpoint and have investigated the persistence of Disney's problematic portrayal of race, from its perceived appropriation of contemporary colour-blind racism to its reviving of past stereotypes through anthropomorphised black characters (ibid.: 84).[2] Moving beyond approaches solely based on representational politics, I suggest that adopting a generic perspective leads to the reconsideration of Disney's racial constructions. Genre makes it possible to recontextualise and better grasp both the ambivalent perpetuation and, at times, the potential for subversion of Disney's past portrayals of race and gender in *The Princess and the Frog*. Writing on the Disney musical, Susan Smith explains that one needs to 'be alert to ideological issues while at the same time remaining open to the possibility of the films offering pleasures rooted in their animation' (2011: 176). From a parallel generic perspective, approaching *The Princess and the Frog* as a fairy tale engaging with the romantic comedy and the 'memory film' (Cook 2005: 4) reveals the ways it ambiguously reframes the American past and racial relations via nostalgic fantasies of romance, while at the same time notably reinterpreting Disney's generic and gendered configurations.

Throughout paratexts, *The Princess and the Frog*'s borrowings from the romantic comedy were presented and received as a move away from Disney's predictable formula. For example, reviewer Justin Chang observed that

> unlike most tales of its type, in which the heroine spends the whole movie in pursuit of Prince Charming, *The Princess and the Frog* follows the modern romantic-comedy template, granting its amphibious duo plenty of shared screen time and making them polar opposites. (Chang 2009)

Similarly, supervising animator Randy Haycock explained that,

> for once, we have a girl that meets a guy and it follows a romantic-comedy idea where the couple meets and they really don't like each other. And it takes them a while to warm up ... because they are such opposites. (Randy Haycock, quoted in Kurtti 2009: 32)

From its start, the film foregrounds these generic and gendered departures, while embracing key fairy-tale components. Tiana (Anika Noni Rose) is an ambitious waitress who, employed at the masquerade ball of her friend Charlotte La Bouff (Jennifer Cody), meets self-confident but gullible Prince Naveen (Bruno Campos), who has been transformed into a frog by a voodoo sorcerer. The unexpected outcome of Tiana and Naveen's kiss – she is also turned into a frog – leads the unlikely couple to venture into the Louisianan bayou to reverse the spell. Building on Celestino Deleyto's approach to the romantic comedy, our understanding of *The Princess and the Frog* and its construction of romance and gender dynamics 'changes significantly when we take on board the crucial presence of this genre in its narrative structure' (2009: 54). The centrality of the leads' antagonistic then romantic relationship, which corresponds to a major romantic-comedy convention, is key to Disney's contemporary reworking of the animated fairy tale.

More specifically, *The Princess and the Frog* interacts with two major strands of the romantic comedy: the screwball comedy and what Tamar Jeffers McDonald describes as the 'neo-traditional' romantic comedy (2007: 85). Throughout this chapter, I observe how the tropes of the former re-energise, to some extent, the formulaic Disney fairy tale, and are enhanced and expanded via the anthropomorphic framework adopted in the film. The influence of the more contemporary neo-traditional romantic comedy (late 1980s–2000s) contextualises and amplifies *The Princess and the Frog*'s more conventional sensibilities. As Michele Schreiber describes, this generic strand purveys a sense of '"post-feminist nostalgia": a relapse into an ostensibly outmoded desire for romantic fulfilment as a reassuring escape from the contradictions between feminist ideals and the realities of the labour and mating markets' (quoted in San Filippo 2021: 8). Balancing between the empowering impulses of the screwball and the generic constraints of the neo-traditional romantic comedy, *The Princess and the Frog* reveals how unstable the positioning of Disney's contemporary animated fairy tales is on the post-feminist spectrum.

Beyond the influence of post-feminist cinema, the idea of offering a 'reassuring escape' has always been at the core of Disney films: the studio's texts, paratexts and wider synergistic machine rely on several layers of nostalgia. Pam Cook defines nostalgia as 'predicated on a dialectic between longing for something idealised that has been lost, and an acknowledgement that this idealised something can never be retrieved in actuality, and can only be accessed through images' (2005: 4). Disney animated features overflow with such 'images' that allow the mediation between the audience's irretrievable past and their present. Svetlana Boym particularly describes nostalgia as 'a yearning for . . . the time of our childhood' (2001: xv). The studio's contemporary cycle of animated fairy tales, and most specifically *The Princess and the Frog*, provide the fantasy of accessing that past. They appeal to a wide intergenerational audience partly because they recreate the feel, tone and atmosphere of the animated features from their childhood – and their idealised romantic fantasies.

I argue that, situated at the intersection of post-feminist nostalgia and Disney nostalgia, *The Princess and the Frog* deploys nostalgia at the aesthetic, generic and paratextual levels to revive, or rather reanimate, the seemingly old-fashioned romance of the Disney formula, borrowing from and interacting with romantic comedies in the process. At the same time, these interactions allow the film to reinvent and subvert the generic framework of the Disney fairy tale, along with its gendered and racial constructions. Adopting the lens of the memory film, I examine the more ambiguous, problematic reverberations of nostalgia within *The Princess and the Frog*'s idealised fantasy world, which reveals Disney's and Hollywood's wider issues with cinematic constructions of the American past and race.

Reclaiming Disney Nostalgia: Hand-drawn Animation, Animated Fairy Tales and Fairy-tale Romance

The Princess and the Frog was produced, advertised and received as a throwback to the past of Disney's hand-drawn animation, framing the film's reviving of fairy-tale romance. As Disney's first hand-drawn animated fairy tale released since *Aladdin*, it represented a throwback not only in terms of genre but also to the pre-digital era of mainstream animation. Paratextual discourses focused on *The Princess and the Frog*'s singular aesthetic in the context of the contemporary mainstream animation market. Such nostalgic appeal is particularly foregrounded in *The Princess and the Frog*'s trailer. Remobilising the tropes of the retrospective trailer, it opens with a succession of iconic scenes from Renaissance hits *Aladdin*, *Beauty and the Beast* (Gary Trousdale and Kirk Wise, 1991), *The Little Mermaid* (Ron Clements and John Musker, 1989) and *The Lion King* (Roger Allers and Rob Minkoff, 1994). For each scene, lines pencilled on brown paper converge to form the lead characters, which are then replaced by their finished version with coloured settings and costumes. The transition from preparatory drawings to animated character is signified by sparkling pixie dust and blue lightning. This retrospective is accompanied by the following text: 'After 75 years of magic, Walt Disney Pictures brings a classic tale to life.' 'Magic' not only evokes the fairy-tale wonders of these films but also directly refers to animators' skills of bringing 'life' to still drawings: their invisible hand functions like the magic wand of Disney's many fairies and sorcerers. Implicitly, this trailer nostalgically alludes to the displacement of traditional hand-drawn techniques in mainstream animation, foregrounding the unique positioning of Disney and its iconic hand-drawn canon by contrast. Such displacement was more explicitly addressed in *The Art of the Princess and the Frog*. Jeff Kurtti noted that, in addition to the directing duo behind hand-drawn hits *The Little Mermaid* and *Aladdin*, the production included 'veteran animation artists . . . talents overlooked since the advent of computer animation' (2009: 1). Supervising animator Eric Goldberg described the former style of animation as 'Disney Magic', emphasising the specific 'warmth coming from hand-drawn films' (quoted in Kurtti 2009: 154). In such paratexts, prestige and appeal are associated with hand-drawn animation: these provide a strikingly nostalgic approach. From this perspective, *The Princess and the Frog* can draw on a largely successful and beloved canon going back to the 1930s. Jason Sperb argues that the exceptional popularity and longevity of such films is 'aided by the oft-noted ontological timelessness of the animation itself' (2016: 118). Critics' and Disney's own discourses on the studio's aesthetic have framed the latter as relatively cohesive and consistent, contrasting with the perceived dramatic changes brought about by computer-animated studios.

Reviews for *The Princess and the Frog* reveal the extent to which hand-drawn animation represents a powerful vehicle for nostalgia. Critics repeatedly expressed both their surprise at what they considered an anomaly in the digitally saturated animation market, and their admiration for it. For example, Catherine Shoard (2010) described the animation as 'shamelessly retro . . . all the more startling in an age of pixels'; Lisa Schwarzbaum (2009) affirmed that the 'old-fashioned charmer holds its own beside . . . the wonder of 3D technology'; Chang (2009) noted that it was 'an unmistakable pleasure to behold an old-school, hand-drawn toon . . . at a time when CG, 3D . . . are all the rage', and Ann Hornaday (2009) that the film 'evokes the most cherished Disney classics'. In these accounts, nostalgia for Disney films is intrinsically linked with nostalgia for hand-drawn animation, a style perceived as belonging to the past. In parallel, such praise is sometimes framed as a rejection of the current monopoly of computer animation. Cook observes that, 'as reality becomes increasingly virtual, the desire to find some form of authenticity has intensified' (2005: 4). In the context of animation, such 'authenticity' can be found in the 'warmth' of hand-drawn features described by Eric Goldberg, as opposed to the perceived coldness of their digital counterparts. Reviewer Kirk Honeycutt (2009) particularly elaborated on this aesthetic contrast: 'hand-drawn and painted animation has a richness to its textures, brilliance in its colours and humanity in its characters that digital 0s and 1s can't quite hack'. Honeycutt's argument reflects a wider reaction among some critics and artists against mainstream computer animation and its associated photorealism. At the time of *The Princess and the Frog*'s release, Pixar's stylised realism had become the norm: critically acclaimed hits such as *Up* (Pete Docter and Bob Peterson, 2009) showcased spectacularly sophisticated representations of vegetation and skin textures. At the same time, paratexts of computer-animated films such as *A Christmas Carol* (Robert Zemeckis, 2009) focused on the use of performance capture to imitate even more faithfully live-action aesthetics. By contrast, Oscar-nominated independent filmmakers such as Marjane Satrapi emphasised their avoidance of such techniques, which produce cold and 'perfect' images, in favour of hand-drawn animation: 'there's a vibration in the human hand which brings the image to life'.[3] Such discourses, framing hand-drawn animated films as conveying both expressiveness and warmth precisely because of their perceived imperfections, are key to contextualising *The Princess and the Frog*'s aesthetic positioning.

Compared with its mainstream counterparts, *The Princess and the Frog* seems indeed almost anachronistic: characters and settings are deliberately caricatured and stylised, with simple blocks of colour and a few expressive lines. For example, the design of Louis the alligator and Ray the firefly is closer to Disney's 1940s and 1950s animal characters, such as the crocodile in *Peter Pan* (Clyde Geronimi and Wilfred Jackson, 1953) and *Pinocchio*'s Jiminy Cricket (Hamilton Luske and Ben Sharpsteen, 1940), than Pixar's more contemporary computer-animated insects and reptiles. In *The Good Dinosaur* (Peter Sohn, 2015), the detailed texture and tone of the dinosaurs' reptilian skin strikingly differs from Disney's bicoloured crocodiles. The latter's numerous scales, which would be extremely difficult to depict through cel animation, are replaced by a few straight lines suggesting the body shape. Similarly, the expressive and painterly design of the night sky at the start of *The Princess and the Frog*, echoing the iconic early sequences from *Peter Pan* and *Pinocchio* with its couple of bright shining stars, is at odds with *The Good Dinosaur*'s photorealistic, almost live-action equivalent. Such an aesthetic may explain critics' nostalgic praise of *The Princess and the Frog*'s animation style. As Sperb argues, 'nostalgia is always more intense during periods of dramatic cultural and technological upheaval' (2016: 2). Disney's hand-drawn animation is constructed and perceived as a more authentic and simple alternative to computer animation: a timeless, nostalgic refuge from the spectacular photorealistic revolution that has taken place since the late 1990s.

Yet, such a clear-cut distinction between hand-drawn and computer animation is misleading: in *The Princess and the Frog*, the latter seamlessly enhances sequences through various visual effects such as water, fire and pixie dust, and is used in the design of backgrounds via 3D layout reference (Kurtti 2009: 100, 122). In *The Art of the Princess and the Frog*, visual effects supervisor Kyle Odermatt explains that, although 'special attention was given to keeping the visual styling strictly two-dimensional in appearance and feel', there is a 'sprinkling of things that change perspective . . . 3D assets that are the underlay to that world' (quoted in Kurtti 2009: 100). Such toning down of digital intervention ('sprinkling of things') harks back to Disney's use of

CGI in the late 1980s and adoption of the CAPS program in 1990. The Renaissance fairy tales showcased as hand-drawn classics in *The Princess and the Frog*'s retrospective trailer all benefitted from this state-of-the-art software, yet they 'still looked quite conventional – deliberately so' (Telotte 2008: 162). As J. P. Telotte underlines, Disney's marketing framed these films as consistent with the studio's long and popular tradition of 'craftsman-like animation' (ibid.: 162). When computer animation was foregrounded, it tended to be in relation to spectacular sequences within more action-oriented films such as *The Lion King*, *Hercules* (Ron Clements and John Musker) and *Mulan* (Tony Bancroft and Barry Cook, 1998).[4] Therefore, hand-drawn animation was arguably strongly associated with Disney's fairy-tale formula: paratexts diluting the use of computer animation for *The Princess and the Frog* perpetuated this link, combining aesthetic and generic nostalgia.

This strong connection between nostalgia for hand-drawn animation and nostalgia for fairy tales underlies a wider of level of nostalgia: Disney's self-reflexive nostalgia. In parallel with the approach adopted within *The Princess and the Frog*'s retrospective trailer and the wider marketing of the film, the animated text overflows with references to Disney's fairy-tale intertext and paratext, drawing on the aura of the Disney brand itself. As Kristen Drotner points out, because Disney 'for so long has been associated with children's culture, nearly all ages have met the brand's narratives, characters, and merchandise' (2004: 109). From its opening, the film correspondingly frames its fairy-tale tropes through the prism of childhood, and sets to revive viewers' memories of watching films and consuming products related to Disney. Creating a familiar atmosphere, its first shots reproduce Disney's opening logo.[5] *The Princess and the Frog* opens on the night sky, in which a bright star is singled out, before revealing a majestic mansion imitating Disney's iconic fairy-tale castles with its high turret. The lyrics of the accompanying soundtrack echo *Pinocchio*'s 'When You Wish Upon a Star', an iconic theme heard with the opening logo since the 1990s.[6] The film then introduces young Tiana and Charlotte while the former's mother is reading the end of Brothers Grimm's *The Frog Prince* to them in the pink decor of Charlotte's room, overflowing with dolls and costumes heavily reminiscent of the Disney Princess franchise. The illustrated fairy-tale book depicts an expectedly predictable formula: a beautiful princess kisses a frog which is transformed into a handsome prince; 'they were married and lived happily ever after'. The enthusiastic reading of Tiana's mother Eudora (Oprah Winfrey), along with the little girls' naïve and childlike sense of wonder while listening to the tale, effectively illustrates Disney's self-reflexive nostalgia (Figure 2.1). This sequence borrows from a type of prologue characteristic of Disney's pre-Renaissance animated films, revived in *Enchanted*, which includes an

Figure 2.1 *Eudora reads* The Frog Prince *to young Tiana and Charlotte. Frame grab from* The Princess and the Frog *(Clements and Musker, 2009).*

illustrated book, sometimes accompanied by a voice-over narrating early elements of plot as pages are magically turning.[7] These prologues replicate potential childhood experiences of fantasy storytelling and invite viewers' suspension of disbelief. Unlike *Shrek* (Andrew Adamson and Vicky Jenson, 2001) or *Chicken Little* (Mark Dindal, 2005), *The Princess and the Frog* stages this recurring trope without irreverent rejection or critical parody, explicitly positioning itself within the tradition of Disney animation, and emphasising its relationship to the fairy-tale genre and the world of childhood innocence.

Such an emphasis on the construction of 'sincere, classic Disney fairy-tale storytelling' (Peter del Vecho, quoted in Kurtti 2009: 153) is accompanied, however, by a degree of self-awareness. Unlike the opening of *Snow White and the Seven Dwarfs* (David Hand, 1937) or *Cinderella* (Clyde Geronimi and Wilfred Jackson, 1950), the fairy-tale book is directly integrated within *The Princess and the Frog*'s diegesis: the pages do not turn on their own, but are turned by Eudora, the diegetic narrator replacing the disembodied voice of Disney's fairy-tale prologues. The book plays a pivotal role, providing the overall syntactic structure of the film. Later on, it is used as evidence by frog Naveen to convince Tiana to kiss him, expecting the literary plot to correspondingly unfold in their animated world. By foregrounding the fairy-tale book and story, *The Princess and the Frog* eases the audience into a nostalgic and familiar world while directly acknowledging its own generic status and explicitly establishing a dialogue with Disney's wider fairy-tale canon. Young Tiana's strong yet pragmatic rejection of the proposed fairy-tale happy ending ('There is no way in this whole wide world I would ever, ever, ever, I mean never kiss a frog. Yuck!') self-reflexively expresses, to some extent, a sense of disbelief towards this same formula and echoes Shrek's incredulous 'Like that's ever gonna happen.' *The Princess and the Frog* aims at reviving the appeal of this sentimental fairy-tale fantasy, for both the extra-diegetic contemporary audience and the initially sceptical diegetic heroine. Disney's self-reflexive nostalgic approach in its opening sequence prepares viewers for both significant semantic changes and a predictable syntax – in other words, for a post-feminist fairy-tale romance.

The Princess and the Frog's multilayered deployment of nostalgia – at the aesthetic, intertextual and paratextual levels – frames and amplifies its reclaiming of Disney's idealised sentimental formula: the film borrows from the neo-traditional romantic comedy in the ways it restores the heteronormative fantasies associated with Disney fairy tales. This specific strand of the romantic comedy came after 'a period of turbulence' for the genre, following second-wave feminist movements in America (San Filippo 2021: 8). The romantic comedies of the 1970s and 1980s, exemplified by *Annie Hall* (Woody Allen, 1977), 'discredited monogamy and romantic idealism' (Krutnik 2002: 138). By contrast, the subsequent neo-traditional strand re-embraced sentimental fantasies, nostalgically referencing 'classic romances' such as *Casablanca* (Michael Curtiz, 1942) and *An Affair to Remember* (Leo McCarey, 1957) as models of passion and romanticism. As Annie (Meg Ryan) laments while re-watching the latter in *Sleepless in Seattle* (Nora Ephron, 1993), 'those were the days when people knew how to be in love. . . . It was right. It was real.' In these neo-traditional romantic comedies, love is constructed as 'something from a long-lost era that needs to be rediscovered in the modern world' (Krutnik 2002: 140). This idea manifests literally in films such as *Kate and Leopold* (James Mangold, 2001) – another neo-traditional Meg Ryan vehicle – and *Enchanted*, in which a character from a (fantasy) past is thrust into 2000s New York, and brings dreamy romance to cynical and pragmatic professionals. As such examples make explicit, neo-traditional nostalgia is linked to nostalgia for childhood stories and fairy tales: magic – both literal and metaphorical – associated with fate or destiny, is a pivotal component of these romantic comedies. Referencing a fantasised past when, 'it is assumed, romance was more straightforward' (Jeffers McDonald 2007: 86), these films favour chivalrous and formulaic types of courtship. Yet, as Maria San Filippo points out, these films maintain 'the fantasy of women's fulfilments through heteronormative coupling . . . while simultaneously displaying feminist revisionism, or at least an awareness of the wish-fulfilling nature of the fantasy' (2021: 8). It is precisely this typically post-feminist doubleness, this oscillation between 'generic unconsciousness and self-consciousness' (Alberti 2013: 4), that is at the core of *The Princess and the Frog*'s relationship with Disney's sentimental formula.

Responding to *Shrek*'s irreverent – yet not syntactically radical – take on fairy-tale romance, *The Princess and the Frog* knowingly acknowledges Disney's past tropes while nostalgically reclaiming them: the opening fairy-tale book and its formulaic plot lead to consistent references to the studio's own 'classic romances'. Both pre-Renaissance and Renaissance fairy tales, evoking viewers' childhood past and associated stories depicting love as simple, straightforward and formulaic, are repeatedly called upon. For example, intertextual hints are sprinkled throughout the dialogue – Snow White's song 'Someday My Prince Will Come' is often echoed in Charlotte's description of Naveen ('tonight my prince is finally coming') – and tropes such as 'true love's kiss' and magical transformations play a central narrative role, echoing *Snow White*, *Sleeping Beauty* (Clyde Geronimi, 1959), *The Little Mermaid* and *Beauty and the Beast*. As in neo-traditional romantic comedies, characters such as Eudora and most notably Charlotte approach love through a nostalgic prism, relying on 'classic' fairy-tale courtship and romance to map out desirable heteronormative paths. For Eudora, Tiana's future consists in meeting her 'Prince Charming' and dancing off into her 'happily ever after', which necessarily involves children ('I want some grandkids!'). Charlotte takes a more literal approach, using Prince Naveen's visit to New Orleans as an opportunity to organise a ball, in the hope of a marriage proposal. In typical neo-traditional, post-feminist fashion, *The Princess and the Frog* often self-reflexively acknowledges the wish-fulfilling nature of these sentimental fantasies: most characters, at some point, cynically or pragmatically point out their unrealistic dimension in a twentieth-century context. For the villains, namely voodoo sorcerer Dr Facilier (Keith David) and his accomplice, Naveen's servant Lawrence (Peter Bartlett), love and marriage only represent an economic transaction ('you need to marry a little honey whose daddy got dough'); for Tiana, these are an obstacle that would 'slow [her] down' on her way to becoming a restaurant owner; for Naveen, these are an inconvenient hindrance to his freedom. Yet, villains are ultimately proven wrong, while Tiana and Naveen learn to embrace fairy-tale nostalgia and sentimental fantasies. This process is best conveyed through another iconic Disney trope: the love ballad.

Performed by Ray the firefly (Jim Cummings), 'Ma Belle Evangeline' is a naïve, sincere and straightforward declaration of love, which asks both diegetic characters and extra-diegetic viewers to suspend their disbelief and indulge in the pleasures of fantasy fairy tales. The song is addressed to what Ray mistakes for a firefly, but that is actually a bright shining star, precisely the one introduced in the opening sequence. At first surprised and sceptical, Tiana and Naveen (turned into frogs at this point in the film) decide not to tell Ray the truth, contributing to the illusion of this idealised, fantasy romance. They are charmed by Ray's childlike innocence, and his sentimental performance inspires Naveen to start a waltz. Initially hesitant and self-conscious, Tiana lets herself go to this improvised dance, participating in another romantic fantasy: she becomes a dreamy Disney heroine, realising she has feelings for Naveen. The fact that they harmoniously dance together while acknowledging that they are falling in love is a standard motif of the Disney fairy tale, recalling *Cinderella*'s 'So This Is Love' and 'Beauty and the Beast'. Both genuine and formulaic, such an expression of true love is also staged as an elaborate *mise en scène*, facilitated by Ray and Louis's (Michael-Leon Wooley) intervention. When the couple starts dancing, Louis joins Ray's performance with his trumpet, and the latter lights up some waterlilies around the couple. When Tiana and Naveen get under the water, Ray projects his firefly light through pink and green leaves. This makeshift spotlight, with its rosy and natural hues, both reinforces the romantic cosy setting of the waltz, and its constructed aspect. 'Ma Belle Evangeline' both nostalgically idealises fairy-tale fantasies of nascent true love and sincere romance, and hints at the fact that these are indeed stagings. Seeing Naveen and Tiana laughing and waltzing, Ray and Louis exchange a knowing look, functioning like an implicit generic comment: they know that the 'magic' is about to happen. Adding a nostalgically familiar layer, the sequence replicates the romantic *mise en scène* of 'Kiss the Girl' in *The Little Mermaid*, in which Sebastian the crab actively creates 'the mood' with the help of numerous animals. Oscillating between self-awareness and wish-fulfilment, 'Ma Belle Evangeline' exemplifies Disney's post-feminist approach in reclaiming its own sentimental formula.

Such reclaiming takes a further dimension through *The Princess and the Frog*'s final sequences, both reflecting and amplifying a trend notable in 2000s romantic comedies: the staging of a spectacular wedding. Admittedly, in most romantic comedies, from the 1930s and 1940s screwball to the neo-traditional strand, the representation of a wedding is 'strongly associated with romantic closure': this expected narrative trajectory seals the expected reunion of the lead couple (Brook 2015: 150). Correspondingly, Clare Bradford observes that the set-piece finales of Disney fairy tales 'comprise weddings, celebrations, and scenes in which newly married lovers depart for their new lives' (2012: 180). Only a few of these fairy tales, namely *Cinderella* and *The Little Mermaid*, actually depict the wedding ceremony – most often its ending.[8] Yet, the combination of 'wedding' with 'happily ever after' is recurringly essential in all of them, from *Snow White* closing with the sound of wedding bells to its onscreen representation in Disney's many straight-to-video sequels, such as *Aladdin and the King of Thieves* (Tad Stones, 1996). Developing the generic parallels between romantic comedy and fairy tale, Heather Brook argues that the heroine's anxieties and difficulties are magically settled with her wedding, which signifies the 'promise of happiness ever after' (2015: 150). What has changed since the 2000s is the increasing importance of the event itself: from the planning to the day of the ceremony, the wedding constitutes not only the syntactic endpoint but also the semantic fabric of many contemporary romantic comedies. Weddings are often integral to the lead's life, as in *The Wedding Planner* (Adam Shankman, 2001), *Wedding Crashers* (David Dobkin, 2005) and *27 Dresses* (Anne Fletcher, 2008). Lengthy sequences or montages are dedicated to the choice of the dress, with dreamlike couture try-outs in *Sex and the City* (Michael Patrick King, 2008) and *Bride Wars* (Gary Winnick, 2009). In parallel, the 'wedding film' has become a 'significant strand of the chick flick genre' (Negra 2009: 52). As Diane Negra points out, these generic evolutions parallel the intensification of the bridal industry, along with the expansion in ancillary 'rituals' like bridal showers and bachelorette parties (ibid.: 52). Within this context, the wedding becomes an affluent and grand spectacle, and the bride is portrayed as a fairy-tale princess. These 'very traditional' tropes are nostalgically reclaimed within post-feminist romantic comedies as 'treasured pleasures' inextricably linked to femininity; pleasures supposedly taken away by the seemingly 'censorious' politics of second-wave feminism (McRobbie 2009: 20–1). This post-feminist stand is at the core of *The Princess and the Frog*'s ending.

Tiana and Naveen's love story culminates in not one but two weddings, borrowing from and expanding the aforementioned post-feminist romantic-comedy trope through the prism of fairy-tale nostalgia. The first ceremony, sealing the union of the couple as frogs, is inherently magical. The otherworldly quality of its setting, with the couple surrounded by anthropomorphised animals, bathed in sunlight and framed by beautiful flower beds, nostalgically echoes *Snow White*'s happy ending. In the latter, the prince's kiss magically awakens the sleeping princess, while the dwarves and various forest animals jump and dance out of joy. This exhilarating and enchanted atmosphere is reproduced in *The Princess and the Frog*: Tiana's kiss, as a princess, turns both protagonists back into humans, while all the bayou animals cheer. The smooth transition between the 'frog' ceremony and its royal 'human' counterpart preserves the former's enchanted aura. The two are linked through a match on action, namely Naveen holding Tiana in his arms, and a dissolve: the tall trees framing the couple are magically replaced by the pillars of a church, their foliage by chandeliers, and the animals by cheering human guests. This second ceremony develops further *The Princess and the Frog*'s wider intertextual web, imitating the ending of *Cinderella* with newly-weds Tiana and Naveen leaving the church in a horse-drawn carriage, waving at the crowd (Figure 2.2). It also explicitly connects fairy-tale nostalgia with post-feminist romantic comedies. During this grand and spectacular display,

Disney Nostalgia and The Princess and the Frog 63

Figure 2.2 *Tiana and Naveen's fairy-tale wedding is infused with post-feminist nostalgia. Frame grab from* The Princess and the Frog *(Clements and Musker, 2009).*

Tiana throws her wedding bouquet to a group of single women: Charlotte enthusiastically catches it, like the heroines of *27 Dresses* and *Bride Wars*. This double wedding is immediately followed by the magical resolution of Tiana's difficulties, depicted through a montage including Tiana buying her restaurant, renovating it with Naveen's help, and successfully opening it. The last shot of the film features Evangeline shining over the dancing couple, next to another bright shining star which, as the film suggests, is Ray: the fantasy quality of this celestial couple and Disney's wider self-reflexive nostalgia reinforce the magical and sentimental aura of the film and its reclamation of the studio's romantic formula.

Beyond the nostalgically romantic aspects of *The Princess and the Frog*'s film text, its merchandising and paratexts develop further Disney's embrace of post-feminist wedding culture. Bride Tiana, in her glittering green wedding dress complete with flowery pattern and a tiara, can be purchased as a doll, plush toy or figurine; she features on children's pyjamas, T-shirts, birthday invitations and phone cases; her dress has inspired both costumes for kids and wedding gowns. The latter are part of Disney's 'Fairy Tale Weddings Dress Collection': this bridal line, initiated in 2011, repackages the tenets of the Disney Princess franchise and the nostalgic appeal of the studio's animated films for the female adult audience, 'turning fairy-tale dreams into reality for today's brides'.[9] Beyond the bridal line, Disney has provided wedding services and organised ceremonies at most theme parks since the 1990s.

From the wedding invitations to the cake, every detail borrows from Disney's fairy tales, inviting the bride to perform the role of the princess for a day: she can even be escorted in a carriage drawn by white horses and greeted by uniformed trumpeters, just like Cinderella and Tiana. As Chrys Ingraham observes, Disney has become a major player in the wedding-industrial complex and the more recent intensification of bridal culture: animated fairy-tale weddings and 'happily ever afters' represent the 'foundation' of such success (2008: 87, 103). This intrinsic connection stands out through semantic tropes and the general tone used throughout Disney's Fairy Tale Weddings and Honeymoons website, building on Disney nostalgia and post-feminist sensibilities: the enchanted aura of animated fairy tales and the studio's sentimental formula are transformed into a spectacular purchasable experience. Accounts of ceremonies inspired by *The Princess and the Frog* benefit from another layer of nostalgia. Couples plan 'Mardi Gras inspired weddings' and pose for portrait sessions in Disneyland's New Orleans Square in order to re-enact their 'favourite love story'.[10] Conflating Disney's animated version of 1920s New Orleans and its nineteenth-century inspired theme-park counterpart, inspiration boards represent the city as a fantasy space rich with balls, jazz music, sweet treats and bayou adventures.[11] These descriptions reveal the more problematic aspects of Disney's nostalgic prism: in *The Princess and the Frog*, nostalgia for hand-drawn animation, animated fairy tales and fairy-tale romance is linked to idealised constructions of the American past.

Reframing Nostalgic Memories: Disney's New Orleans Kingdom and the Paradoxes of the Black Princess

The Princess and the Frog is unique within Disney's wider fairy-tale canon in the way it nostalgically reframes American history and past racial relations: it relies on strategies typical of the company's theme parks and similar to what Cook describes as the memory film to transform New Orleans into an uncomplicated and appealing fairy-tale world. At the same time, Tiana's portrayal qualifies such explicitly nostalgic impulses, subverting to some extent past constructions of the Disney Princess, particularly in relation to Charlotte's and Naveen's characterisation. In order to understand this complex nostalgic web, it is important to first consider the generic link between Disney fairy tales and theme-park experiences.

Both Disney's fairy tales and theme parks are designed to create a reassuring and enchanting atmosphere: the latter expand the former's nostalgic potential. Writing on Walt Disney World (Florida), Susan Willis argues that the theme park is 'an immense nostalgia machine whose staging and specific attractions are generationally coded to strike a chord with the various categories of its guests' (1995: 10). For example, the Fantasyland rides at the Magic Kingdom Park span several decades of the studio's animated fairy-tale history, potentially appealing to all ages. Visitors can step inside the castle from *Cinderella*, 'become part of' *The Little Mermaid* at the 'Under the Sea' attraction, or 'get a glimpse of' (an actress performing) Rapunzel from *Tangled* during the 'Royal Princess Processional'.[12] These examples hint at the particularity of the Disney theme parks: their 'overall narrative character' (Bukatman 2003: 16). As Shelton Waldrep explains, the visitors' 'experience is of a three-dimensional cinematic event that includes processions, sets, costumes, sound effects, and props': they are made to feel as if they were walking into a Disney animated fairy tale (1995: 81). Such an impression is conveyed at the very entrance of the park, from which the iconic Magic Kingdom fairy-tale castle can be spotted. Martha Bayless observes that the castle 'provides a cue that the visitor is about to enter the filmic narrative of the park. It is the focus of the establishing shot . . . that sets the scene for the story' (2012: 46). Correspondingly, the fairy-tale castle is a key semantic trope throughout Disney's intertext and paratext: it features prominently within the studio's opening logo and the opening sequence of fairy tales, from the book illustrations of *Cinderella* and *Sleeping Beauty* to the first animated shots of *Snow White* and *Beauty and the Beast*. The fact that *The Princess and the Frog*'s first shot includes Charlotte's home – a large mansion with an elaborate turret evoking that of a fairy-tale castle – invites viewers not only to suspend their disbelief in order to enter the world of fairy tales but also to step into an animated version of Disney's Magic Kingdom.

The Princess and the Frog does not solely draw on Fantasyland and its reconstruction of the imaginary, vaguely European setting and past of most Disney fairy tales: it repurposes their magical and nostalgic aura and combines it with a more specific, yet comparably idealised theme-park construction of the past, namely that of American history. From its start, the film explicitly signposts its temporality and location: it references President Wilson's election and the end of World War I – Tiana's father appears in a picture in soldier uniform, a medal hanging on the frame – and presents the life of various sections of the population 'Down in New Orleans'. This song invites viewers to look nostalgically at this city in a specific period of American history: New Orleans in the 'Jazz Age' (Kurtti 2009: 1), introduced with 'music . . . always playin'' and 'some sweetness goin' round'. Henry Giroux and Grace Pollock explain that some Disney theme-park attractions are constructed as an 'unproblematic celebration of the American people', experienced through sentiment and nostalgia (2010: 36). For Giroux, this approach is representative of the wider company's view of national identity, as Disney films and products 'aggressively' rewrite American history for 'stylised consumption' (1995: 45–6). As noted by numerous critics and academics, Disney's past canon includes many such examples, from *Song of the South*'s (Harve Foster and Wilfred Jackson, 1946) depiction of late nineteenth-century plantation life as an 'anachronistic', 'white musical utopia' (Sperb 2012: 1) to *Pocahontas*'s (Mike Gabriel and Eric Goldberg, 1995) significant downplaying of colonialist violence.[13] In Disneyland, areas of the Magic Kingdom Park such as 'Main Street, USA' and 'Frontierland' reconstruct similarly idealised versions of an American golden age, inviting visitors to 'travel back in time . . . in a charming turn-of-the-century vehicle' or through attractions such as an 'old-time Wild West shoot-out'.[14] There, not only can the past be experienced as entertainment but it can also be tasted and purchased. From a genre perspective, these theme-park lands function in the same way as what Cook terms the 'nostalgic memory film'. The latter includes heritage cinema, period melodrama and westerns, and 'reconstructs an idealised past as a site of pleasurable contemplation and yearning' (2005: 4). Cook notes that memory films tend to put on display 'an array of period artefacts . . . to satisfy the audience's desire to consume, rather than engage critically with history' (ibid.: 201). The Disney parks remarkably concretise such an uncritical desire to consume the past – or rather, a fantasised version of it – as illustrated in Disneyland's New Orleans Square. The latter is a nostalgically romanticised nineteenth-century depiction of New Orleans, functioning as a theme-park parallel to its 1920s animated counterpart in *The Princess and the Frog*. Both versions of New Orleans include local architectural and culinary ingredients: for example, Tiana cooks gumbo and bakes beignets, and Disneyland's 'French Market Restaurant' serves jambalaya and Cajun specialties.[15] *The Princess and the Frog* also features allusions to 1920s fashion and music, quoting iconic jazz musicians such as Louis Armstrong and Sidney Bechet. The design of the film was reportedly inspired by the 'ethnic American art from Harlem renaissance artists such as Aaron Douglas', especially notable in Tiana's dream sequence 'Almost There' (Kurtti 2009: 50). Such an appealing reconstruction of New Orleans, overflowing with memory film semantic tropes, arguably diverts viewers' attention from more problematic historical aspects.

Disney's animated version of New Orleans functions as a fantasy land: it appears as a joyful melting pot, a continuous celebration where both African Americans and whites dance and play jazz music in the streets, and a rich southern belle (Charlotte) can be best friends with the daughter of her seamstress (Tiana). This representation, showcasing 'an oasis of . . . ethnic accord', is seductive yet 'historically dubious' (Brown 2021: 123). The 1920s were marked by the re-establishment of the Ku Klux Klan, Jim Crow segregation laws, race riots and lynching (Gehlawat 2010: 420; Aza Missouri 2015: 173). Disney's perspective on this troubled past is typical of the memory film:

The Princess and the Frog relies on motifs signifying '1920s New Orleans' and 'Louisiana' to viewers, while glossing over the more sensitive aspects of the period. Segregation laws, for example, are only hinted at: the resulting racial order is recreated in a way which suggests that it was the unquestioned norm, and that both races lived harmoniously under these laws. A particularly representative example is Tiana's journey from the La Bouff estate to her own home. When she and her mother Eudora step into a streetcar, the white driver's wordless salutation, followed by their silent walk to the back, hints at the 'mutually recognized – and respected – colour line' (Gehlawat 2010: 420). Tiana gazes out the window, amazed at the opulence of the mansions in the white Garden District, which gradually dissolve into the significantly more modest houses in the black Ninth Ward. Such a transition admittedly reveals the economic discrepancies between the two districts, and the strict separation between the two communities. Yet, the smooth dissolve also prevents viewers from lingering on such stark differences, and from subsequently interrogating the causes and implications of African Americans' living conditions. The only character who represents a voice of dissent in the film by explicitly pointing out such disparity is Dr Facilier: 'aren't you tired of living on the margins while all those fat cats in their fancy cars don't give you so much as a sideways glance?' The fact that he refers to Charlotte's wealthy father, 'Big Daddy' La Bouff, who is associated with 'sugar barons' and 'cotton kings' in the song 'Down in New Orleans', actually seems to provide 'historically and racially accurate motivations' for his anger and frustration (Barker 2010: 494). La Bouff, alongside his spoilt daughter and the biased real estate agents Tiana must deal with (the Fenner Brothers), could be considered the 'real' villain of the film, helping perpetuate rigid racial stratification and a deep economic divide (ibid.: 494). Still, as observed by Jennifer Barker, such characters are portrayed as harmless, 'mildly' ridiculed, while 'the brunt of villainy' is put on Dr Facilier (ibid.: 494).[16] Such depictions exemplify how *The Princess and the Frog* avoids directly engaging with the economic inequalities and racial tensions underlying 1920s New Orleans' problematic social order. Instead, the animated film transforms the segregated city into an enchanting fairy-tale world where dreams can come true.

Through such a transformation, the magical power of the Disney fairy tale and the mythical power of the American Dream converge, framing Tiana's successful narrative trajectory: thanks to her determination and strong work ethic, she ultimately manages to buy her own restaurant. Tracey Mollet observes that, in *The Princess and the Frog*, the 'endless' possibilities of the American Dream are amplified by those of the nostalgic Disney fairy tale: Tiana's generic magical journey is 'inherently linked' to 'the entrepreneurial spirit of the American Dream' (2020: 113, 117). Although she learns early on from the Fenner Brothers that she has been outbid ('a little woman of your background would have had her hands full trying to run a big business like that'), there are few social and economic obstacles impeding her subsequent upward mobility. As Montré Aza Missouri points out, *The Princess and the Frog* affirms that 'even the most disadvantaged of the socio-economic stratification (young poor black women) should be capable of achieving the American dream', since 'racial injustice and economic struggle are non-existent' (2015: 169) – or rather, glossed over and heavily downplayed. Tiana's success contributes to Disney's idealised picture of 1920s segregated New Orleans. Through *The Princess and the Frog*'s nostalgic vision, the latter becomes another magic kingdom, an idealistic fantasy place where, as the introductory song describes, 'anything can happen'. Bayless notes that 'to enjoy oneself requires precisely that horrors and oppressions be overcome and effaced. The fairy-tale world of Disney narrative is a dream vision in which all can end happily' (2012: 54). Therefore, the notable disjunction between *The Princess and the Frog*'s enchanting multicultural and jazzy 1920s New Orleans and the bleak prospects of African Americans in the Jim Crow era is fundamental to Disney's nostalgically reassuring fairy-tale atmosphere.

While such an idealised, fantasy reconstruction points to the superficiality of Disney's engagement with the past, borrowing from the nostalgic memory film, *The Princess and the Frog*'s relationship with contemporary events in 2000s America further complicates its positioning. The animated film was released four years after Hurricane Katrina, which mostly impacted African American and low-income earners in Louisiana, primarily in New Orleans. As the population was still suffering from the aftermath of this disaster, Disney's vivid and magical depiction of the city and the fairy-tale success of its heroine led to strong local 'attachment' to the movie (Kennedy Haydel 2020: 145). Sheryl Kennedy Haydel argues that Tiana's portrayal

> represented a connection to place and space for New Orleans residents who had lost their home, city, community, culture, and heritage . . . To separate . . . the experiences of African Americans to [sic] the story of Tiana is an erasure of Blackness in mainstream discourse. (Kennedy Haydel 2020: 138, 145)

The various essays included in the prologue to Shearon Roberts's *Recasting the Disney Princess in an Era of New Media and Social Movements* similarly emphasise the cultural significance of a film which 'animated the city back to life' and was inspired by iconic local figure Chef Leah Chase (Walker 2020: 15; Shareef 2020: 17). The admittedly 'conflicted' nature of such perspectives – in the words of Prinsey Walker (2020: 15) – echoes the wider debates and criticisms surrounding *The Princess and the Frog*'s portrayal of its first African American heroine.[17] Going from this specific context of reception to the positioning of the film within Disney's wider fairy-tale canon, it appears that Tiana's portrayal as a black princess/entrepreneur in the kingdom of New Orleans has multifaceted implications. Considering the subversive potential of her characterisation – and the limits of such potential – through the converging generic lenses of the romantic comedy and the fairy tale reveals the ambiguities and paradoxes of both Disney's relationship with its own formula and of the studio's post-feminist constructions of race and gender.

Tiana's portrayal self-reflexively engages with the process of nostalgia for the Disney Princess, especially in relation to Charlotte's characterisation: aspects of formulaic fairy-tale femininity and its associated heteronormative framework are first challenged through the latter's parodic depiction. Appearing as the animated embodiment of the introductory fairy-tale book's princess – similarly blonde and white – Charlotte's portrayal represents a comically excessive version of the Disney Princess. It expands *Enchanted*'s gentle caricature by targeting and questioning most stereotypical tropes associated with this formulaic character, especially that of Disney's early cycle of fairy tales. Charlotte does not solely dream about fairy-tale princes, she actively – exuberantly – chases Naveen. When the latter arrives at her masquerade ball, she meticulously stages herself in a *mise en scène* that notably deconstructs Disney's formulaically gendered fairy-tale courting. Unlike the uncalculated, innocent way Cinderella attracts the Prince's attention, Charlotte whistles for a spotlight to follow her, spreads glitter around her, hides behind a fan, and bats her eyelashes while staring at Naveen (Lawrence disguised as Naveen). Her explicitly seductive behaviour contrasts with the naïve demureness of past princesses: she sees courting as a playful 'fray'. Her very appearance challenges Disney Princesses' innate and effortless beauty, a quality often signified in the very name of the heroines, and/or enhanced through enchanted transformations. Charlotte's portrayal reveals that Disney prettiness is hard work: she is repeatedly seen powdering her face, reproducing Snow White's perfect complexion. In her bedroom, functioning as the wings of princess performance, she is shown putting on mascara and rearranging her bustier. Her overly large and glittery pink dresses represent caricatures of the elaborate ball attire of protagonists such as Cinderella and Belle. The film notably matches such excessive and contrived princess behaviour with Lawrence-as-Naveen's performance of the courtly enamoured Disney prince: two outdated fairy-tale characters revised, to some extent, through Tiana's and Naveen's portrayal.

The Princess and the Frog challenges the characterisation of and dynamics between the formulaic Disney Princess and Prince by borrowing from a syntax developed throughout several strands of the romantic comedy: the protagonists go from initial mutual antipathy to subsequent accord. This generic 'hallmark' (Jeffers McDonald 2009: 147) contributes to the subversion of Disney's sentimental fairy-tale formula. While the former's conventional components involve 'love at first sight' followed by 'chivalric romance' (Bradford 2012: 180), *The Princess and the Frog* stages a parody of such idyllic encounters. Tiana and Naveen's meeting at the masquerade ball is based on a series of misunderstandings leading to frustration, confusion and anger. Dressed in a princess costume, Tiana stares at the night sky, while a frog amphibian silently stares at her. She jokingly asks if the amphibian wants 'a kiss', re-enacting the story from the fairy-tale book introduced in the opening sequence. She is horrified when the frog actually replies to her as Prince Naveen, and expresses further disgust when he pleads for his cause: she must kiss him for him to be human again. She accepts only when he mentions the wealth of his family and the possibility of a reward: she needs money to secure the down payment on her restaurant. This deal is of course quickly compromised when Tiana turns into a frog herself. This first encounter light-heartedly subverts Disney's romantic tropes, including – at first – the aura of magical kisses. It also introduces the antagonism that will characterise Tiana and Naveen's initial relationship. Tiana angrily blames Naveen for her unexpected metamorphosis, while the latter accuses her of lying to him. Such animosity is stirred up further through the opposite characterisation of the protagonists. Tiana is introduced as ambitious and hardworking, but sometimes too stern, while frivolous Naveen is more irresponsible and nonchalant. Both must overcome their differences to cross the bayou and find a way to reverse the spell. *The Princess and the Frog*'s initial syntactic reconfiguration of Disney's fairy-tale formula directly impacts its portrayal of the couple's dynamics: the protagonists become playful adversaries who vie with each other while striving to reach a common goal.

Such a playfully adversarial relationship is developed further through tropes from the screwball strand of the romantic comedy in order to destabilise the gendered hierarchy underlying Disney's fairy-tale formula. In this 1930s–40s strand of the genre, 'the energy of the couple's friction and mutual frustration', often motivated by class snobbery or 'reverse class snobbery', drives the narrative forward (Jeffers McDonald 2007: 20, 23). As exemplified in films such as *It Happened One Night* (Frank Capra, 1934) and *Bringing Up Baby* (Howard Hawks, 1938), this notably manifests through the use of dialogue. Correspondingly, Tiana and Naveen's sustained discord is conveyed through clever banter and teasing, as in this example:

> Naveen: You know, waitress, I have finally figured out what is wrong with you.
> Tiana: Have you now?
> Naveen: You do not know how to have fun. There. Somebody had to say it.
> Tiana: Thank you, because I figured out what your problem is, too.

Naveen:	I am too wonderful?
Tiana:	No, you're a no-'count, philandering, lazy bump on a log.
[. . .]	
Naveen:	Stick in the mud.
Tiana:	Listen here, mister. This stick in the mud has had to work two jobs her whole life while you've been sucking on a silver spoon chasing chambermaids around your ivory tower!
Naveen:	Actually, it's polished marble.

This sequence foregrounds Tiana's pluck and repartee, unlike past coy and gullible fairy-tale princesses. The latter are often silenced within their own narrative – falling into a deadly sleep or trading their voice for a pair of human legs, for example – or rely on the male lead's verbal indications to navigate new surroundings, like Ariel, Jasmine or Rapunzel. By contrast, Tiana asserts herself verbally, relying on humour and irony to challenge Naveen's expected authority ('oh, poor baby') and scare away some frog hunters ('and we talk too!'). As Frank Krutnik observes, screwball comedies

> define love as a kind of creative gamesmanship with lovers engaging in duels of wit to secure the terms of compatibility. Testing, teasing and teaching one another . . . protagonists reveal their ability to love by avoiding the banalities of sentimental love-speak to communicate through indirection. (Krutnik 2002: 140)

Borrowing from this generic dynamic, Tiana and Naveen's fast-flung insults and wordplay demonstrate their intellectual compatibility – Naveen subsequently praises Tiana for being 'secretly funny'. Their screwball skills put them on the same footing, subverting the portrayal of the Disney fairy-tale couple and its formulaic sentimental courting.

The Princess and the Frog further parodies the sentimental aspect of Disney's nostalgic fairy-tale romance by reappropriating and amplifying the physical humour typical of screwball comedies through the use of slapstick combined with anthropomorphism. Up until 'Ma Belle Evangeline', numerous sequences comically restage formulaic demonstrations of love: kisses and embraces actually lead to swift physical actions and chases. For example, once Tiana realises the first kiss has turned her into a frog, she throws herself onto Naveen out of anger, as if she were trying to strangle him. Later on, Naveen momentarily embraces Tiana to protect her from a threatening alligator: when it is revealed to be harmless trumpet-playing Louis, Naveen lets go of her body and she falls down, flat on her back, her twisted legs over her head. As Jeffers McDonald explains, 'the screwball comedy, fuelled by animosity, can direct its aggression into the humorous incidents it invents to punish the beloved whether by embarrassment, insults . . . [or] real violence' (2007: 19).

In *The Princess and the Frog*, slapstick violence literalises Tiana and Naveen's dynamic antagonism. Paul Wells observes that early animated shorts such as Mickey Mouse cartoons similarly featured a succession of accidental and random events of a mostly slapstick and destructive nature (1998: 161). These purely comic devices bring no harm but destabilisation and disorder: bodies are impossibly fragmented and stretched (ibid.: 189). This phenomenon is epitomised with Tiana and Naveen's second 'kiss' (Figure 2.3). Both are hungry and their stretchy amphibian tongue is uncontrollably drawn to a bug: their tongues accidently intertwine, and when they retract both frogs are thrown into each other's arms, their tongues completely stuck in a knot. Trying to separate them, Louis the alligator only aggravates their predicament, pressing their bodies against one another and turning them around as if playing with a Rubik's Cube. The couple ends up as one entangled mass standing on one leg, with their tongues endlessly wrapped around their bodies. Such a treatment of the prince and princess destabilises the well-defined order of the Disney fairy tale. While slapstick is integral to earlier animated films such as *Snow White* or *The Little Mermaid*, it is principally focused on secondary characters and animal sidekicks, such as the dwarves or Sebastian the crab. By having both protagonists turned into frogs and being the vehicle for most cartoon comedy, *The Princess and the Frog* remarkably and playfully trivialises the idealised aura of Disney fairy-tale couples. Chivalrous grand gestures are replaced by both verbal and physical fighting; the magical power

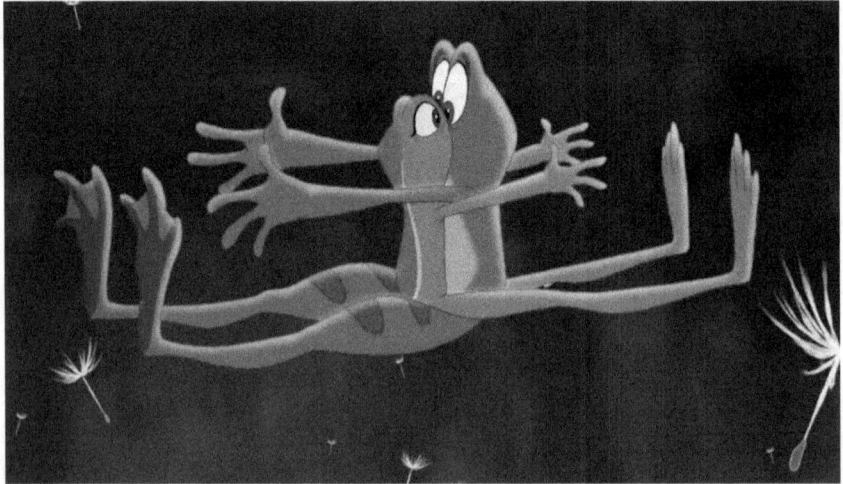

Figure 2.3 *Tiana and Naveen's unexpected second 'kiss'. Frame grab from* The Princess and the Frog *(Clements and Musker, 2009).*

of the couple's amorous kisses is parodied through their anthropomorphic reframing – animal instincts replace sentimental courting.

Such an anthropomorphic transformation also allows further freedom in the depiction of the couple's relationship. Wells observes that the representation of animals in cartoons 'in some ways reconciles the problems of representing "adult" behaviour in animated human beings, especially in relation to sex and violence' (2002a: 56). To some extent, the violence involved in *The Princess and the Frog*'s slapstick sequences is therefore comically mitigated through the animal form of the protagonists. Such anthropomorphising also facilitates the comedy of the second kiss sequence: the way Tiana's and Naveen's bodies are intertwined would have been impossible to represent if the characters had still possessed their human form. The knowing comment of Ray the firefly underlines the risqué potential of such a scene: 'Girl, I guess you and your boyfriend got a little carried away, am I right, am I right?' The live-action equivalent of such sequences is mostly found in 12-rated romantic comedies such as *The Proposal* (Anne Fletcher, 2009), in which the protagonists accidentally bump into each other naked in the bedroom.[18] Deleyto notes that the comic space of the romantic comedy 'generally affords the characters a franker confrontation with their sexuality' (2009: 34). This confrontation has a more literal and humorous manifestation in *The Princess and the Frog*, thanks to the freedom allowed by animated slapstick and anthropomorphism.

While Tiana's anthropomorphic portrayal allows her further physical – and to some extent, sexual – freedom, adding to her screwball pluck and assertiveness, it erases to some extent her racial identity, complicating the role of some generic and gendered tropes from the romantic comedy. Introduced as an ambitious, hardworking, independent young woman, Tiana's portrayal initially recalls the depiction of career women in post-feminist romantic comedies: in these films, heroines are constantly reminded of 'all the personal and romantic goals their labouring might put in jeopardy' (Leonard 2007: 103). From a generic perspective, the 'emotional void' created when jobs take precedence, as for the female leads in *The Proposal* and *The American President* (Rob Reiner, 1995), is 'unacceptable' (Deleyto 2009: 42). Correspondingly, Tiana's single focus on opening her restaurant leaves her little time for love or even entertainment, as her friends and mother regularly complain. It is only when she is turned into a frog that she gradually realises what she 'needs': romantic 'love'. In a syntactic turn reminiscent of *Enchanted* and *Kate and Leopold*, in which the career woman wilfully abandons her modern life to blissfully jump into an animated fairy-tale wedding or join her future husband in a fantasy past, Tiana happily chooses to remain a frog if it involves staying with and marrying Naveen. The notion of 'choice' is a 'central term within post-feminist cinema', although acceptable options remain relatively limited for female characters: they can use their 'feminist freedom to choose to re-embrace traditional femininity' (Tasker 2011: 75; Gill 2007: 243). Similarly, Tiana chooses a heteronormative happy ending including a grand wedding and a princess title. In a typically post-feminist combination, this traditionalist decision is rewarded: she regains her human form and subsequently buys her restaurant. However, the use of this gendered romantic-comedy trope combined with Disney's anthropomorphic framework, namely Tiana expressing her 'choice' while still a frog, glosses over the incentives that necessitated that she work so much in the first place. Kathleen Karlyn notes that work outside the home has rarely been a 'lifestyle choice' for American women of colour but instead 'an economic necessity' (2011: 193). While the majority of mainstream post-feminist romantic comedies feature affluent white women who make a conscious decision to prioritise their career, the few which focus on heroines of colour directly acknowledge the structural inequalities that heavily frame such a choice. For example, in *Something New* (Sanaa Hamri, 2006), Kenya (Sanaa Lathan) regularly points out to her white partner that, as a black woman, she must 'work extra hard just to stay in the game'.[19] In *The Princess and the Frog*, anthropomorphism contributes to Disney's wider nostalgic reconstruction of New Orleans as another Magic Kingdom, allowing such historical and generic racial inequalities to be magically dissolved.

Considering Disney's wider canon of fairy tales, Tiana's portrayal plays a pivotal role in *The Princess and the Frog*'s unstable positioning on a wider post-feminist spectrum. With her specific syntactic trajectory, the film displays 'nostalgia for the traditional princess narrative' (Mollet 2020: 117). Her semantic traits could, to some extent, be applied to most Disney heroines: 'industrious, gentle, kind, loyal, empathetic, dreamy, romantic . . . and – by the end of the film – ready to take her place as wife and mother' (Brown 2021: 123). Yet, she demonstrates resourcefulness and problem-solving skills, which allows her to keep herself and Naveen safe; she takes the lead in some action-oriented sequences – escaping from the alligators, navigating through the swamp – and single-handedly defeats Dr Facilier. Both embracing and subverting some aspects of the formulaic Disney Princess character, Tiana's portrayal notably differs from the latter's explicit caricature as embodied by Charlotte – yet she also fulfils Charlotte's dream, ultimately marrying a prince and becoming a princess. In a typically post-feminist way, the film preserves and starts disrupting aspects of the studio's formulaic gender portrayals, an approach that will be developed in subsequent animated fairy tales.

Conclusion

The Princess and the Frog inaugurated Disney's contemporary cycle of animated fairy tales and revived the studio's fantasies of old-fashioned sentimental romance through a multifaceted deployment of Disney nostalgia. Relying on and sustaining nostalgia for traditional hand-drawn animation, childhood memories of Disney fairy tales, and the wider experience of the Disney brand, the film establishes an ideal framework for reclaiming key tropes of the studio's formula. The latter's heteronormative trajectory, from romantic duet to declarations of true love culminating in a grand spectacular wedding, is reclaimed and amplified through the prism of neo-traditional post-feminist nostalgia. *The Princess and the Frog* crystallises not only the appeals of contemporary romantic comedies but also the contradictions of the genre. The parallel influence of screwball comedies, especially in the first half of the film, subverts the portrayal of the sentimental fairy-tale couple and of the Disney Princess, at times qualifying the overall nostalgic approach of the film and moving its positioning towards the empowering end of the post-feminist spectrum. Transposing its fairy-tale romance to the American past, *The Princess and the Frog* also transforms 1920s New Orleans into another Fantasyland, reproducing the problematic tendencies of the memory film and dissolving less enchanting aspects of history and racial relations. Such ambiguities point to enduring issues around some facets of the Disney formula that persist in a post-*Shrek* fairy-tale universe.

Notes

1. See the works of, respectively, Akita and Kenney (2013); Miller and Rode (1995); Parasher (2013).
2. Neal Lester argues that 'making the first African American princess a frog dusts off some painful and racially insensitive associations of black children with wild animals' (2010: 307).
3. See the documentary clip on *Persépolis* (Vincent Paronnaud and Marjane Satrapi, 2007) available at <http://www.filmeducation.org/persepolis/production-process.html> (accessed 17 March 2022).
4. This will be discussed further in Chapter 5.
5. This logo, introduced after the company's acquisition of Pixar, will be discussed further in Chapter 3.
6. The opening lyrics are: 'The evening star is shining bright / So make a wish and hold on tight'.
7. Examples of animated features opening with such prologues include *Snow White and the Seven Dwarfs*, *Pinocchio*, *Cinderella*, *Sleeping Beauty*, *The Sword in the Stone* (Wolfgang Reitherman, 1963), *The Jungle Book* and *Robin Hood* (Wolfgang Reitherman, 1973).
8. Prior to *The Princess and the Frog*, animated wedding scenes are also featured in *One Hundred and One Dalmatians* (Clyde Geronimi and Hamilton Luske, 1961), *Robin Hood* and *Enchanted*.

9. 'Gowns', *Disney's Fairy Tale Weddings and Honeymoons*, <https://www.disneyweddings.com/disney-boutique/bridal-gowns/> (accessed 30 May 2021). While Disney Fairy Tale Weddings and Honeymoons does cater to couples that do not include brides (homosexual male couples), the website 'overwhelmingly' focuses on the straight female bride (Maier 2019: 191). For further information, see also Wasko 2020: 228.
10. 'A Mardi Gras Inspired Wedding at Disneyland', *Ever After Blog – Disney's Fairy Tale Weddings and Honeymoons*, <https://www.disneyweddings.com/ever-after-blog/a-mardi-gras-inspired-wedding-at-disneyland/> (accessed 30 May 2021).
11. Korri, 'Disney Princess Look #09 – Tiana', *Ever After Blog – Disney's Fairy Tale Weddings and Honeymoons*, 13 June 2017, <https://www.disneyweddings.com/ever-after-blog/disney-princess-look-09-tiana/> (accessed 30 May 2021); Korri, 'Disney Princess Wedding Inspiration: Tiana', *Ever After Blog – Disney's Fairy Tale Weddings and Honeymoons*, 1 August 2016, <https://www.disneyweddings.com/ever-after-blog/disney-princess-wedding-inspiration-tiana/> (accessed 30 May 2021).
12. 'Under the Sea ~ Journey of The Little Mermaid', *Walt Disney World* <https://www.disneyworld.co.uk/attractions/magic-kingdom/under-the-sea-journey-of-the-little-mermaid/> (accessed 30 May 2021); 'Magic Kingdom Entertainment', *Walt Disney World*, <https://www.disneyworld.co.uk/entertainment/magic-kingdom/new-mk-entertainment/> (accessed 30 May 2021).
13. On Disney's approach to American history in *Pocahontas*, see for example Naidu Parekh 2003; Connor 2015: 234–7.
14. 'Frontierland Shootin' Exposition', *Disneyland Resort*, <https://disneyland.disney.go.com/attractions/disneyland/frontierland-shootin-exposition/> (accessed 30 May 2021); 'Main Street Vehicles', *Disneyland Resort*, <https://disneyland.disney.go.com/attractions/disneyland/main-street-vehicles/> (accessed 30 May 2021).
15. 'French Market Restaurant', *Disneyland Resort*, <https://disneyland.disney.go.com/dining/disneyland/french-market-restaurant/> (accessed 30 May 2021).
16. For a further analysis of the characterisation of Dr Facilier, see Davis 2013: 218–23; Ferguson 2016 (esp. pp. 1233–4 and 1236–7).
17. For a detailed account of the popular and critical reception of *The Princess and the Frog* at the time of release, see Lester 2010. Numerous authors also drew a parallel between the construction of race in the film and Barack Obama's first presidential campaign, during which race was 'simultaneously ever-present as a subtext and yet never invoked'. See Gehlawat 2010: 429.
18. '*The Proposal*', *British Board of Film Classification*, <https://www.bbfc.co.uk/release/the-proposal-q29sbgvjdglvbjpwwc00mjy4nzy> (accessed 30 May 2021).
19. When *The Princess and the Frog* does touch upon such structural inequalities, it is only through a few oblique references, including Tiana's father's advice to his daughter: 'that old star can only take you part of the way. You got to help it along with some hard work of your own, and then, yeah, you can do anything you set your mind to.'

CHAPTER 3

The DreamWorks Formula and the Post-feminist Disney Couple: Tangled's *Romantic Parodies*

> No one would have guessed that an ogre named Shrek, whose roar was feared throughout the land, would save the beautiful Princess Fiona. True love's kiss led to marriage and ogre babies . . . And they lived happily ever after. (The opening fairy-tale book of *Shrek Forever After*, Mike Mitchell, 2010)

In May 2010, DreamWorks released *Shrek Forever After*, the fourth opus of the ogre's adventures, which closed a decade of irreverent, cartoonal computer-animated fairy-tale parodies. In its opening, the film self-reflexively acknowledges the impact of its own fairy-tale blueprint: it starts with a revised version of the iconic storybook introduced in the first film, now featuring unlikely hero Shrek, Princess Fiona and their ogre family, all living 'happily ever after' in the highly intertextual, contra-diegetic kingdom of 'Far Far Away'. Recalling the main events of the three previous instalments, the opening book also highlights the central position *Shrek* (Andrew Adamson and Vicky Jenson, 2001) has acquired within fairy-tale cinema, replacing Disney as a reference point. A few months later, Disney released *Tangled* (Nathan Greno and Byron Howard, 2010), its first computer-animated fairy tale and arguably the studio's most direct attempt to both imitate DreamWorks' take on the genre and reclaim its own generically iconic territory. While *The Princess and the Frog* (Ron Clements and John Musker, 2009) initiated the late 2000s revival of the Disney formula through a strikingly nostalgic prism, *Tangled* represented an overtly more parodic approach. This chapter focuses on the parodic frameworks employed in *Tangled*, and most particularly the ways in which Disney's film reappropriates DreamWorks' specific type of tonal and generic parody.

The film focuses on Rapunzel (Mandy Moore), a princess whose long golden hair has magical healing powers. Kidnapped as a baby by villainous Mother Gothel (Donna Murphy), she is kept hidden in a tower, far from her kingdom – not unlike Princess Fiona. Fascinated by the lanterns released every year on her birthday, she decides to finally venture out when she is about to turn eighteen years old, with the help of a cunning thief known as Flynn Rider (Zachary Levi). Not unlike Shrek, he reluctantly agrees to act as her guide on her way to the kingdom.

Positioning DreamWorks' *Shrek* as a major influence on *Tangled* contrasts with most scholarly studies of contemporary animation, which prioritise the pivotal role of Pixar (Holliday 2018b; Archer 2019: 94; Haswell 2019). Disney's 2006 acquisition of Pixar has played an undeniably pivotal role in the reworking of the studio's formula, as will be discussed in subsequent chapters. Still, Disney's contemporary cycle of fairy tales was also notably framed in opposition to DreamWorks, highlighting its influence at the same time: as discussed in Chapter 2, *The Princess and the Frog*'s multilayered Disney nostalgia acted as a counterpoint to *Shrek*'s irreverent take on fairy-tale tropes and sentimental romance. By contrast, Disney seemed to embrace DreamWorks' 'disruptive influence' with *Tangled*: as Sam Summers observes, the film 'resemble[s] less a straight fairy tale and more a *Shrek*-style parody' (2020: 137). In the first part of the chapter, I analyse Disney's reappropriation of what can be described as the 'DreamWorks formula', combining contra-diegetic intertextuality and critical parody. This reappropriation stands out throughout the paratextual and textual portrayal of Flynn Rider, and is particularly notable in the first half of the film. In parallel with Flynn's double act, I examine how *Tangled* gradually reveals its formulaic identity, mediating its DreamWorks-style performance through tropes typical of the studio's sentimental fairy tales and idealised romance.

Such a delicate balance between parody and idealisation also characterises the construction of gender and coupledom. In the second part of this chapter, I investigate the typically post-feminist sensibilities characterising Rapunzel's and Flynn's portrayal both in *Tangled* and in the subsequent short *Tangled Ever After* (Nathan Greno and Byron Howard, 2012). I particularly look at the influence of 'genres of gender' from contemporary strands of the romantic comedy, including that of the 'rom com player' (Alberti 2013: 3; Gill and Hansen-Miller 2011: 44), and the ways these interact with other aesthetic and generic tropes, notably from the musical.

From a wider perspective, this chapter uses *Tangled* as a case study to reflect upon the influence of an animation studio beyond Disney's cinematic universe (DreamWorks) on the former's contemporary output and its formula. In parallel, this chapter examines further the interactions between genres of romance and Disney fairy tales, and the ways these impact on the positioning of the former on a wider post-feminist spectrum.

DreamWorks-style Parody: Disguising the Disney Fairy Tale

Disney's efforts to replicate DreamWorks' parodic approach in *Tangled* were notable even before the release of the film: paratexts adopted a dual strategy consisting in both separating the film from Disney's canon of formulaic fairy tales and replicating the tone and style of *Shrek*. The very generic identity and source of the film was deliberately reframed, starting with its title. In the words of producer Roy Conli, the title was 'broadened' – from *Rapunzel* to *Tangled* – to make

> sure that people understood that this is not simply a rote telling of a fairy-tale they think they already know everything about . . . The story is more than a simple princess tale, it has elements of thrills, comedy and magic that are new and unexpected. (Roy Conli, quoted in Kurtti 2010: 45)

The choice of a potentially vague, notably gender-neutral title seemed not only to open up the generic identity of the film but also to avoid the perceived predictability and sentimentality of the Disney formula. Such divergence contrasted heavily with the studio's promotional strategies for *The Princess and the Frog*, presented as a familiar tale in the tradition of the studio's 'classics'. With box office grosses of $104,400,899 domestically, the latter was considered a financial disappointment: President of Pixar and Disney Animation Studios Ed Catmull partly attributed this lack of success to the presence of the word 'princess' in its title (quoted in Chmielewski and Eller 2010).[1] *Tangled*'s paratexts erased not only such fairy-tale semantics but also the pivotal romantic narrative of the film, central to the Disney formula. The main promotional poster featured all characters as a team, ready for action, particularly foregrounding anthropomorphic comic protagonists Pascal the chameleon and Maximus the palace horse. Unlike Tiana and Naveen, singled out as a romantic couple in most *Princess and the Frog* paratexts, Rapunzel and Flynn appear far from potential love interests, not even making eye contact.

Tangled's trailers similarly shifted the generic focus of the film, while particularly reinforcing the tone and style borrowed from the DreamWorks formula. The soundtrack of the first official trailer displays DreamWorks' 'obtrusive and contra-diegetic intertextuality' throughout (Summers 2020: 155). Instead of relying on *Tangled*'s diegetic songs, it features Pink's 2003 popular rock song 'Trouble'. Such a DreamWorks-style borrowing is notably misleading: the film itself actually follows from Disney's previous musicals, with an original score by Alan Menken, the composer behind most Disney Renaissance hits. The trailer also misleads audiences in positioning Flynn Rider, introduced as the kingdom's 'fearless', 'dangerous' and 'greatest thief', as the lead, foregrounding swashbuckling action and comedy. Following Disney's logic, 'downplaying the princess and fairy-tale narrative improves *Tangled*'s chances of reaching a wider audience' (Haswell 2019: 100–1). Yet, fairy-tale tropes are present – but solely through the prism of the DreamWorks formula, as conveyed via Flynn's character. For example, the trailer closes with a scene, absent from the film, in which Flynn grandly shouts 'let down your hair' from the bottom of Rapunzel's tower. This well-known fairy-tale line is interrupted when, to Maximus's joy, Flynn is knocked down by an enormous mass of hair, undermining the sentimental potential of the request. Toning down some formulaic tropes and calculatingly subverting generic expectations, the trailer replicates *Shrek*'s take on the fairy tale.

Within the film, Flynn's portrayal is pivotal to *Tangled*'s DreamWorks-style critical parody of Disney's fairy-tale formula, and more specifically of the character of the Disney male romantic lead. From the classic 'handsome princes' of *Cinderella* (Clyde Geronimi and Wilfred Jackson, 1950) and *Sleeping Beauty* (Clyde Geronimi, 1959) to Renaissance 'dashing heroes' and 'action men', male characters most representative of Disney's formula tend to maintain a dignified aura: they are 'charming', with stunning good looks often sentimentally remarked upon by the heroines (Davis 2013: v, 109, 122). In *The Little Mermaid* (Ron Clements and John Musker, 1989), for example, Ariel is often shown lovingly gazing at Prince Eric. After having rescued him from a shipwreck, she lies next to him on the beach, and gently removes a strand of hair from his face, whispering 'he's so beautiful' before singing her longing to be with him. While this sequence represents a notable gender reversal – a sleeping prince rescued by the heroine – it preserves Disney's formulaic display of idealised nascent romance, and the fantasy of otherworldly handsomeness attached to fairy-tale masculinity. In typical DreamWorks fashion, *Tangled* parodically restages this sentimental encounter, only to mock the charming hero as embodied by Flynn. When the latter climbs into Rapunzel's tower to escape from the palace horse chasing him, she is terrified of the intruder, and knocks him out with a frying pan before he notices her presence. She observes him while he lies unconscious on the floor, slowly leans closer and removes the hair hiding his closed eyes with the handle of her frying pan. Amazed, she gazes at his face, like Ariel gazing at Eric: framed in a medium close shot, Flynn's handsome features are idealistically highlighted through a ray of sunlight. Such a sentimental moment is cut short when, as Flynn wakes up, Rapunzel hits him again with her frying pan. Throughout the rest of the sequence, the charming fairy-tale hero undergoes a surprising amount of violence, mitigated through slapstick comedy. As Rapunzel struggles to hide Flynn in her closet, pushing his unconscious body with a broom and throwing it away while tied to her hair, he repeatedly falls down on the floor like a rag doll. These comic manipulations recur throughout the film, relying on 'broad cartoon motion': Flynn's body squashes and stretches when fighting with Maximus, and receives overall numerous shocks, bumping into planks and bending into impossible shapes (Carter 2013: 15).

Expanding the playful approach adopted towards the figure of the male romantic lead in *Enchanted* (Kevin Lima, 2007) and *The Princess and the Frog*, *Tangled* preserves his dashing human looks only to consistently mock and undermine them, relying on the power of animated slapstick.

Developing further the parody of what Jack Zipes describes as the formulaic 'prince-meets-princess encounter' (2011: 88), *Tangled* also restages Disney's male-centred love-at-first-sight trope, only to consistently undermine its romantic potential. When Flynn finally catches a glimpse of Rapunzel, he is tied to a chair, positioned as a threatening suspect to be interrogated. She slowly steps out of the shadows, revealing her long blonde hair bathed in the sunlight, which gives her an angelic glow. A harp chord, followed by a grand crescendo in the orchestral soundtrack, parallels Rapunzel's movement, while Flynn remains voiceless, staring at her beauty in surprise and admiration. His stunned expression evokes Aladdin's first amorous look at Jasmine as he sees her at the market, or Prince Phillip's wonder at watching Aurora dancing in the woods. Initially unable to formulate an answer to her question ('Who are you, and how did you find me?'), he quickly replaces courteous, chivalric dialogue ('I know not who you are, nor how I came to find you') by more contemporary, informal flirting: 'Hi. How ya doin'? The name's Flynn Rider. How's your day going?' Flynn's unexpected switch from formal to informal register, leaving Rapunzel annoyed and confused, undercuts the sentimental atmosphere of the scene. Repeatedly, he mocks Rapunzel's reliance on fairy-tale tropes: when she mentions 'fate' and 'destiny' to explain Flynn's presence in the tower, recalling the numerous chance encounters of past Disney couples, Flynn dismisses the sentimental reference by just stating that 'a horse' brought him there. Despite such tension, Rapunzel and Flynn agree on a 'deal', which further tones down any remaining hint of formulaic romance – a syntactic reconfiguration replicated by all of Disney's contemporary fairy tales. Having been secluded all her life, Rapunzel asks Flynn to act as her guide to the kingdom before he can reclaim his loot, hidden inside her tower. The terms of the deal reflect the contrasting characterisations of the two characters: Rapunzel is a naïve, sheltered young princess while Flynn is a cunning, cynical and more experienced thief – not only is such a contrast pivotal for *Tangled*'s romantic narrative but it also crystallises its positioning towards the Disney formula.

The couple's initially antagonistic relationship represents, to some extent, a clash of fairy-tale formulas: while Rapunzel embodies Disney's pre-DreamWorks sentimental and cheerful innocence, Flynn corresponds to *Shrek*'s irreverent and sarcastic self-awareness, often functioning as *Tangled*'s main vehicle for its DreamWorks-style narrative-cartoonal mode. His flirting is not only informal but also highly anachronistic, relying on contemporary language and a 'demotic style' (Brown 2021: 129): he calls Rapunzel 'blondie', and randomly uses foreign words ('gesundheit', 'simpático') and shortened sentences ('No can do'). Although, as Noel Brown points out, *Tangled* does not reproduce *Shrek*'s consistently explicit 'interrogative irony', which underlines the 'perceived absurdity of generic conventions' (ibid.: 129), I argue that it provides notably self-reflexive moments mediated through Flynn's character. As the opening and closing narrator, his voice-over highlights the constructed nature of the fairy tale: it is a 'story' with some degree of predictability. In his closing monologue, he concedes that viewers 'could imagine what happened next'. Throughout the narrative, his character is used to point out and deconstruct other formulaic tropes, most strikingly the musical nature of the Disney fairy tale. When thugs spontaneously burst into song to perform 'I've Got a Dream', Flynn appears baffled, sceptically raising his eyebrows, and quickly bored (Figure 3.1). Moments later, he refuses to join them ('Sorry boys, I don't sing'), and when forced, initially struggles to take part: his dance steps are at first awkward and clash with the others', and he talks rather than sings. Questioning the integrity of the diegetic musical, Flynn's portrayal parallels that of *Enchanted*'s Robert, made to contrast with the naturally gifted Disney Princess. The song itself displays several contra-diegetic intertexts, with characters describing their anachronistic passions: one ruffian does 'interior design', another specialises in 'sublime' 'cupcakes'.[2] Reviewers particularly deplored such a reappropriation of the DreamWorks

Figure 3.1 *Flynn questions the integrity of the diegetic musical. Frame grab from* Tangled *(Greno and Howard, 2010).*

formula, perceived as unnatural for Disney: Richard Corliss (2010) argued that *Tangled* 'wades into the DreamWorks-style of sitcom gags and anachronistic sass'. Unsurprisingly, most criticisms were directed at Flynn's portrayal, described as a 'refugee from a *Shrek* sequel' (Turan 2010) and a 'crude commercial calculation, a sign ... to Disneyphobes that the studio can bring some DreamWorks-style attitude' (Scott 2010). Yet, it is revealed halfway through the film that self-aware and sarcastic Flynn Rider is part of a persona, hiding the more sensitive and sincere Eugene Fitzherbert: similarly, *Tangled* consistently, sometimes only subtly, reminds viewers that it remains a Disney fairy tale under a DreamWorks disguise.

Alternating between 'pulling away' from and embracing the studio's generic formula, *Tangled* 'occupies a place of negotiation' (Holliday 2019: 128): this is best illustrated in the opening sequence, which initially foregrounds DreamWorks' self-reflexiveness before reverting to more familiar Disney tropes. The film does not feature an introductory fairy-tale book: instead, *Tangled* opens with a 'Wanted' poster of Flynn Rider, and the latter's voice-over: 'This is the story of how I died. Don't worry, this is actually a very fun story and the truth is, it isn't even mine. This is the story of a girl named Rapunzel ...' His falsely dramatic tone and the poster overtly mislead the audience, who may expect the swashbuckling adventure-comedy showcased throughout *Tangled*'s paratexts. Introducing the film as a 'very fun story' also dismisses the solemn and sentimental aura of the Disney fairy tale and its predictability – DreamWorks-style. Yet, the formulaic phrase 'once upon a time', followed by the mention of typical semantic tropes ('kingdom', 'a beloved King and Queen', 'a princess'), quickly restores the fairy-tale genre after its apparent dismissal. Considering Disney's intertext beyond DreamWorks' storybook parody, Flynn's introductory voice-over actually imitates another strand of Disney fairy tales, calling upon the folkloric origins of the genre in the process. Flynn does not solely tell a story: he directly involves the audience in his narration, drawing their attention to specific elements: 'Oh, you see that old woman over there? You might want to remember her', 'all right, you get the gist', 'I'll give you a hint.' What Kristian Moen describes as the link between fairy tales and the spoken word of the storyteller, surrounded by a circle of listeners (2013: 182), is made explicit through Flynn's lines. This folkloric dimension was embraced in Disney animated fairy tales such as *Pinocchio* (Hamilton Luske and Ben Sharpsteen, 1940), in which narrator Jiminy Cricket, standing near a storybook, directly asks viewers, 'I'll bet a lot of you folks don't believe that ... about a wish coming true ... do you? Well, I didn't, either ... but let me tell you what made me change my mind. One night a long time ago ...' Similarly, in *Aladdin* (Ron Clements and John Musker, 1992), after the musical prologue 'Arabian Nights', a peddler addresses the audience: 'This is no ordinary lamp! It once changed the course of a young man's life . . . Perhaps you would like to hear the tale? It begins on a dark night. . . .'' In these three instances, *Pinocchio*, *Aladdin* and *Tangled* all start by misdirecting the viewer/listener, taking their disbelief into account and gradually drawing them into the tale. Although *Tangled* dismisses formulaic storybook openings parodied in *Shrek*, it revives the tradition of oral storytelling present in many Disney fairy tales: intertextual references are subtly reclaimed, hidden under DreamWorks-style self-aware narration.

After Flynn has revealed his true identity to Rapunzel, the film reclaims more explicitly its formulaic identity, not only as a Disney fairy tale but also as a Disney product: the depiction of the kingdom's village strikingly revives the enchanting aura of Disney theme parks, in opposition to Dream-Works' critical parody. As observed in Chapter 1, *Shrek*'s Duloc appears as an imposing and cold kingdom, directly referencing Disney's sanitised reappropriation and commercialisation of the fairy-tale genre through numerous contra-diegetic intertexts. By contrast, *Tangled* cheerfully invites viewers into a computer-animated version of Disneyland. Drawing on Disney's intertextual web, the production team took research trips to the theme park: the film imitates the architecture and stylised look of Fantasyland, especially the Pinocchio Village Haus (Kurtti 2010: 40). *Tangled* also replicates the sense of harmony, safety and cosiness that *Shrek* explicitly satirised. The parks' fairy-tale castles are conceived to be 'inviting play spaces': Disneyland's castle is both large and small, avoiding the intimidating effect of real-life medieval fortresses, which were, by contrast, 'martial displays of power . . . not palaces but fortifications, emblems of authority and intimidation' (Bayless 2012: 39, 41) – not unlike Duloc's strikingly tall castle. Jeff Kurtti observes that *Tangled*'s world 'has been scaled to feel charming, cosy, and inviting . . . surfaces and environments curve to envelop the viewers' (2010: 31). Production designer Douglas Rogers describes the kingdom's village as 'friendly, accessible, intimate . . . you would have a great afternoon exploring it' (quoted in Kurtti 2010: 136). When Rapunzel enters the kingdom, she is correspondingly delighted, gazing at the castle in admiration and excitedly pointing at it while uttering an enthusiastic 'wow' – just like a child visiting Disneyland for the first time (Figure 3.2). Innocent fun and friendly play seem to prevail in *Tangled*'s animated theme park, as Rapunzel takes part in several activities that recall Disneyland's attractions. She has her long hair beautifully braided with colourful flowers, evoking the princess makeovers little girls can enjoy at the Bibbidi Bobbidi Boutique,[3] and spontaneously starts dancing on hearing a band playing music, inviting the inhabitants to join her in a parade of sorts. The emblem of the kingdom itself, a stylised sun, recalls Disney's omnipresent logos, such as

Figure 3.2 *Rapunzel's excitement at visiting the theme-park inspired kingdom. Frame grab from* Tangled *(Greno and Howard, 2010).*

Mickey's silhouette: it is featured everywhere, from the village's banderols to the miniature flags that Eugene buys as a souvenir, just like the countless Disney items purchased by the parks' customers. This consumerist dimension, which *Shrek* explicitly mocked with the multitude of Lord Farquaad's toys displayed at 'Ye Olde Souvenir Shoppe', is not layered with shrewd parody in *Tangled*: the film encourages viewers to suspend their disbelief instead of critically engaging with their environment, like real-life visitors to the parks. Overall, the sequence conveys a sense of childlike wonder and nostalgic innocence at odds with DreamWorks' irreverent formula.

The tonal differences between the two studios' formulas are more explicitly articulated and foregrounded in paratexts competing with the approach adopted in the trailer and poster, revealing *Tangled*'s particularly ambiguous relationship with Disney's own formula. While the trailer dissimulated both the generic and studio identity of the film, fan-targeted products such as *The Art of* series of books, functioning as extended 'making of' documents with carefully selected conceptual artwork and interviews, positioned Disney fairy tales as a central influence. In *The Art of Tangled*, co-directors Greno and Howard describe themselves as Disney fans with a 'deep love of classic Disney', referencing *Cinderella* and *Sleeping Beauty* as inspiration, and therefore explicitly situating *Tangled* within the studio's fairy-tale canon (Greno and Howard 2010: 7). Striking a consistent yet delicate balance between nostalgia and novelty, their accounts throughout the book underline the enduring, inescapable weight of Disney's fairy-tale intertext. The latter, spanning more than seventy years, was still extremely popular at the time of *Tangled*'s release due to its central presence throughout Disney's synergistic machine, and notably the Disney Princess franchise, which had expanded the year before to include *The Princess and the Frog*'s Tiana. Inherent to constructions and perceptions of the Disney formula, it seems that Disney fairy tales could not be fully discarded or mocked throughout all of *Tangled*'s paratexts. Arguably, *Tangled* had less leeway in terms of subversion than DreamWorks' *Shrek*.

Yet, *Tangled*'s filmmakers notably reclaimed this potentially constraining intertextual heritage, reappropriating the perceived contrast between Disney's and DreamWorks' formulas in the process. *The Art of Tangled* includes several oblique references to DreamWorks' output, opposing Disney's 'commitment to sincerity' and 'classic', timeless stories to more contemporary parody (Kurtti 2010: 158). Greno argues, for example, that 'it's easy to do cynical, to look down your nose and create fairy-tale satire . . . and that's the exact opposite of what we set out to do' (quoted in Kurtti 2010: 45). Greno's insights on *Tangled*'s preproduction reaffirm this tonal opposition:

> There was an attempt to enliven the story with contemporary attitudes, titled *Rapunzel Unbraided* . . . When Glen Keane [*Tangled*'s animation supervisor] first pitched *Rapunzel*, he really wanted it to be a sincere fairy tale; because he is a heartfelt, sincere guy who believes in things such as love and true emotion . . . The company had tried to push the film in a satirical direction that made fun of fairy tales. But Glen, rightly so, said 'I can't do this kind of movie.' (Nathan Greno, quoted in Kurtti 2010: 12)

By continuously emphasising 'sincerity', Greno reappropriates criticism of Disney's fairy-tale formula: the studio's trademarked sentimentality and cheerfulness are reframed as a reassuring, nostalgic and more generically authentic alternative to DreamWorks' sarcastic irreverence: 'true emotion' versus 'satire'. Such fan-targeted paratextual discourse coexisted with more self-aware and ironic promotional texts aimed at a wider audience. This illustrates Disney's more ambiguous relationship with its much criticised and parodied, yet still very popular and lucrative formula, and uneasy positioning towards its main competitor's approach.

Such an apparent, yet sometimes unstable discursive differentiation between Disney and DreamWorks was consolidated in other categories of *Tangled*'s paratext, most notably reviews developing the opposition articulated by Helen O'Hara (2015) when writing on *The Princess and the Frog* – the contrast between the 'cynicism of *Shrek*' and Disney's typical sincerity. Many reviewers praised the Disney film behind the DreamWorks' disguise, describing *Tangled* as 'a traditional romance at heart' (Robey 2013), a 'basic, and very enjoyable, Disney princess musical' (Corliss 2010) with 'essential sweetness' (Turan 2010).

As Helen Warner notes, while reviews do not directly determine audiences' responses, 'they do offer an insight into how [they] are cued to understand texts' (2013: 223). In this case, *Tangled* is framed as another successful example of the Disney formula, perpetuating the association of Disney with tradition, romance, sweetness and princess musicals in the process. Such a formula possessed some appeal to sections of the mainstream audience; still, *Tangled*'s explicit DreamWorks-style disguise undeniably contributed to its box-office success, with twice the domestic grosses of *The Princess and the Frog*.[4]

Tangled's complex and ambiguous positioning towards its formulaic identity, both throughout its paratext and within its text, is arguably paralleled by its embrace of post-feminist sensibilities. With a DreamWorks-style romantic lead (Flynn Rider) transforming into a Disney hero (Eugene Fitzherbert), and a princess whose narrative was initially conceived as fairy-tale satire (from *Rapunzel Unbraided* to *Tangled*), the film occupies a 'place of negotiation' (Holliday 2019: 128), not only in generic and narrative terms but also in terms of gender constructions. Such ambivalence is further illustrated by the romantic trajectory of the film, and the specific aesthetic and musical tropes selected to convey such a narrative.

Post-feminist Parody: Disguising the Disney Couple

In order to reconfigure the formulaic Disney couple, *Tangled* borrows from a binary framework typical of romantic comedies, and developed for a substantial part of the film. Kathleen Karlyn defines romantic comedies as 'comedies of equality',

> establishing a conflict along a male/female line. For such a conflict to be dramatic, the sides must be well matched, at least temporarily. Women must be allowed more power, or men less, than they are allowed in conventional forms of representation. (Karlyn 1995: 118)

In the context of Disney, 'conventional forms of representation' refer to the formulaic gender portrayals from the studio's past fairy tales. Correspondingly, *Tangled* remobilises the trope of the formulaically passive and dreamy Disney Princess, so that its subsequent subversion particularly stands out, rebalancing the Disney couple. Throughout the early musical number 'When Will My Life Begin', almost eighteen-year-old Rapunzel is introduced trapped within a domestic and restrictive space, singing about her dream to see the lights released on her birthday while being subjected to what Tracey Mollet describes as 'classical era chores' (2020: 118). Like Snow White, Cinderella and Aurora, Rapunzel sweeps and mops the floor of her tower, cooks, sews dresses, all while interacting with a cute anthropomorphic animal (Pascal the chameleon). Far from such 'normatively feminine' activities (Langsdale and Myers 2018: 254), Flynn Rider first appears outside, in an action-oriented sequence including a theft, fast-paced chases and horse riding. Such a generically gendered divide is gradually challenged throughout the film through the narrative repositioning of Rapunzel. At first scared and confused by Flynn's presence and behaviour, she manages to assert her authority, impose a deal on him, and actively take part in chases and other male-dominated fast-paced adventures outside of her domestic space. This shift is epitomised through *Tangled*'s shrewd subversion of Rapunzel's stereotypical props of femininity. She uses her frying pan as a weapon that Flynn enthusiastically adopts; her beautiful magical hair also functions as a lasso, swing and rope. Her skilful mastery of its power and strength, added to her agility and athleticism, gradually transforms the formulaic Disney Princess into a competent action heroine.

However, a degree of traditionally gendered hierarchy persists throughout the film, leading to another shift in power dynamics and throughout the post-feminist spectrum. Unlike the humorously excessive portrayal of Charlotte in *The Princess and the Frog*, Rapunzel's performance of fairy-tale femininity is devoid of parody. Her disarming enthusiasm, kindness and innocence charm all the characters she encounters, from thugs at the Snuggly Duckling tavern to the kingdom's inhabitants. Not only is she 'conventionally beautiful' but she corresponds to the ideal of femininity perpetuated throughout Disney's fairy-tale canon (Brown 2021: 130). As designed by animation supervisor and executive producer Glen Keane, she closely resembles *The Little Mermaid*'s Ariel: his preparatory notes specifically point to Rapunzel's curvy breasts, narrow waist, wide hips, big eyelashes and radiating hair (quoted in Kurtti 2010: 69). Her thin silhouette and demure look on Keane's sketch echo some of her merchandising alter egos. Rapunzel's very body maintains a sense of gracefulness and fragility, typical of the formulaic Disney Princess. She may gently hit herself with the handle of her frying pan or even athletically jump off a cliff, but she is not consistently and explicitly mocked through broad cartoon motion or subjected to humorously repetitive yet violent episodes of slapstick comedy: unlike the figure of the Disney hero (Flynn), she maintains her dignified aura. Such a 'hyper-feminine', traditionalist portrayal uneasily coexists with the empowerment conveyed throughout action sequences – or rather, is a 'solid example' of post-feminist tensions (Langsdale and Myers 2018: 255–6). Her portrayal arguably shifts back to the traditionalist end of the post-feminist spectrum when Flynn, then revealed as Eugene, cuts her hair. Framed as Eugene's romantic self-sacrifice, saving Rapunzel from Mother Gothel's grasp at the cost of his own life, this act also leads to Rapunzel's 'disempowering loss of magical agency' (Hui 2019). As Christine Hui points out, the heroine is not ultimately allowed to explore the 'disruptive potential' of her hair (ibid.). In typically post-feminist fashion, this loss is legitimised through a formulaic heteronormative outcome: Rapunzel's narrative ends with romance and the promise of a wedding.

Such a formulaic repositioning of the Disney Princess is made explicit in the closing sequence. While Eugene jokingly steals Rapunzel crown, she grabs it back and kisses him, while his voice-over comments, 'I know what the big question is. Did Rapunzel and I ever get married?' Although his knowing tone adds a degree of playfulness, suggesting an unexpected gender reversal ('I am pleased to tell you that after years and years of asking . . . I finally said yes'), Rapunzel's inclusion within the voice-over restores a more traditional closure:

Eugene: All right, I asked her.
Rapunzel: And we're living happily ever after.
Eugene: Yes, we are.

As the final lines of the voice-over accompany the final kiss, the shot of Rapunzel and Eugene dissolves into that of the kingdom's castle. This recurring, framing image, both brand logo and generic signifier, consolidates the association between Disney formula and matrimony, fairy-tale happy endings and heteronormative closure, Disney Princess and Disney bride. Admittedly, the wedding is referred to only off-screen, seemingly in a side note. Still, it participates in Disney's wider post-feminist impulses, nostalgically reviving its gendered fairy-tale formula.

This nostalgically traditionalist repositioning is developed further in the animated short *Tangled Ever After*, notably expanding *The Princess and the Frog*'s post-feminist romantic staging. The animated short premiered in theatres with *Beauty and the Beast 3D* in January 2012, and was featured on the *Cinderella* Diamond Edition Blu-ray and DVD set in October 2012. These pairings explicitly framed the short within Disney's fairy-tale canon, contributing to the studio's wider reclaiming of its formula, and the latter's enduring popularity. The parallel between *Tangled Ever After* and *Cinderella* particularly stands out through their idealised depiction of a grand fantasy wedding, a pivotal, magical happy ending called upon in many post-feminist romantic comedies. Although *Tangled Ever After* focuses mainly on animal sidekicks Maximus and Pascal and the series of comic mishaps following their loss of the wedding rings, it is framed by the staging of a traditional and impressive ceremony. Rapunzel's voice-over reinforces the enchanted, idyllic aura of the wedding: 'Everything was perfect, just like I always dreamed it would be', 'it was a magical day'. The staging of her entrance into the church especially emphasises the marvellous aspect of the ceremony: as she steps into the light, all the guests turn around to admire her, astonished by her bridal beauty.

A similar *mise en scène* is featured in the wedding ceremonies of many contemporary post-feminist romantic comedies, as exemplified in the long wedding finale of *27 Dresses* (Anne Fletcher, 2008). As for *The Princess and the Frog*, Disney expanded this nostalgic romantic fantasy through merchandise, such as the 'Rapunzel Wedding Soft Toy Doll', adding to a multitude of existing wedding-themed children's and adults' products.[5] This image of Rapunzel as a smiling, silent bride contrasts not only with her portrayal in *Tangled* as an action heroine but also with that of Flynn/Eugene: framing the narrative of both films through voice-over, his post-feminist character revives other aspects of Disney's gendered fairy-tale formula.

With a hero shifting identities, from Flynn Rider to Eugene Fitzherbert, *Tangled*'s portrayal of its male lead fluctuates – like that of Rapunzel – throughout a post-feminist spectrum, borrowing from contemporary romantic comedies to both challenge and restore the gendered dynamics of the formulaic Disney couple. Flynn's DreamWorks-style sarcasm and self-confidence echoes the portrayal of what Rosalind Gill and David Hansen-Miller describe as the romantic-comedy 'player' (2011: 44). This gendered trope, exemplified by Matthew McConaughey's Connor in *Ghosts of Girlfriends Past* (Mark Waters, 2009) and Ryan Gosling's Jacob in *Crazy Stupid Love* (Glenn Ficarra and John Requa, 2011), characterises self-centred, rich male leads 'living a seemingly enviable life of parties' and 'casual sex with beautiful women' (ibid.: 44).[6] Gill and Hansen-Miller note that such a construction of 'virility is externally imposed upon an emotionally vulnerable boy' who ultimately 'lets go of his self-interest, rejects his foolishness, and engages in adult responsibilities' (ibid.: 41, 44). These responsibilities involve the embrace of monogamy with a female character who is portrayed as a suitable partner according to the genre – a future wife and mother. Within the framework of a Disney fairy tale, such a characterisation is evoked through Flynn's self-assurance and seductive behaviour towards Rapunzel. Like *The Princess and the Frog*'s Naveen, who brags about his dating experience and skills to Tiana ('all women enjoy the kiss of Prince Naveen', 'I've dated thousands of women') and whom Dr Facilier calls a 'playboy', Flynn confidently flirts with Rapunzel, applying techniques he initially believes to be infallible. Attempting to cajole Rapunzel into letting him leave her tower, he performs what he describes as 'the smoulder' ('I didn't want to have to do this, but you leave me no choice'): raised eyebrows, half-closed eyes, seductive pouting, complete with contra-diegetic saxophone soundtrack. Rapunzel's unimpressed look, added to her accidentally dropping Flynn's chair ('you broke my smoulder!'), playfully mocks his performance of player masculinity, contrasting with the archaic courtliness of formulaic Disney princes. Like his live-action counterparts, Flynn's player façade, relying on contrived lines and calculated behaviour, hides his vulnerability. His very name is based on a swashbuckling hero from a storybook he read as a child: his sincere confession to Rapunzel, revealing himself as orphan Eugene, contrasts with his knowing performance as Flynn. While Flynn is a self-aware DreamWorks-style player, somehow unproper for a Disney romance, more authentic Eugene appears as a satisfyingly traditional Disney leading man.

Flynn's transition to Eugene is accompanied by a metamorphosis into a nostalgically chivalric hero, the embodiment of a typically post-feminist fantasy which the first part of *Tangled* and some of its paratexts explicitly mocked and subverted. Initially positioned as a guide to younger and less experienced Rapunzel, he also provides her with 'frequent comfort and reassurance' (Langsdale and Myers 2018: 254). As Flynn, his advice is highly ironic: he falsely praises Rapunzel's rebellious escape from her tower, actually making her feel guilty for abandoning Mother Gothel, so that he can return and retrieve his loot. As Eugene, however, he becomes genuinely helpful and sincere, accompanying her through her discovery of the kingdom and reassuring her while she anxiously waits to see the lanterns. This gendered behaviour is celebrated in some post-feminist romantic comedies through the presence of a character type that Amy Burns labels the 'new hero' (2013: 133). Exemplified by Jude Law's Graham in *The Holiday* (Nancy Meyers, 2006), Ryan Reynolds's Andrew in *The Proposal* (Anne Fletcher, 2009) and Colin Firth's Mark Darcy in the *Bridget Jones* trilogy (2001, 2004, 2016), this character acts as a 'teacher', 'benefactor' or 'guardian angel', performing a metaphorical rescue of the heroine thanks to the 'rationality', 'strength' and 'stability' he brings to her life (ibid.: 141–3). Restoring traditionalist gender binaries, this character embodies post-feminist nostalgia for constructions of chivalric masculinity: an old-fashioned conception of the male romantic lead that contemporary romantic-comedy heroines often long for. In *Bridget Jones's Baby* (Sharon Maguire, 2016), for example, the lonely pregnant protagonist, locked outside her house, wonders whether 'knights in shining armour' still exist: the appearance of her love interest Darcy, who carries her to the hospital, magically answers her question. Correspondingly, in *Tangled*, it is thanks to Eugene's intervention that Rapunzel not only experiences the outside world for the first time but also finds a new purpose. His rescuing of the sheltered young woman becomes literal towards the end of the film. In a spectacular action sequence, Eugene is revealed as a formulaically courageous and fearless Disney hero, mounting his powerful steed like *Sleeping Beauty*'s Prince Phillip in order to reach Rapunzel, trapped back in her tower by Mother Gothel. As he enters, the latter fatally stabs him. While Rapunzel tries to save Eugene with her magical healing powers, he uses a shard of glass to cut her hair, breaking the enchantment that kept Gothel alive, but sacrificing himself as a result. Such a sequence foregrounds the hero's bravery, selflessness and complete devotion to the heroine: his post-feminist shift from romantic-comedy player to new hero, from DreamWorks lead to Disney prince.

The tensions and contradictions at the core of *Tangled*'s post-feminist refashioning of the formulaic Disney couple are crystallised when comparing two pivotal musical sequences: 'I've Got a Dream' and 'I See the Light'. These takes on a staple of Disney fairy-tale romance, the love ballad, are situated at opposite ends of the post-feminist spectrum. The DreamWorks-style, playfully self-reflexive song 'I've Got a Dream' not only deconstructs some tropes of the Disney musical but also gently mocks its sentimental framework. The staged aspect of the song, more explicit than in *The Princess and the Frog*'s 'Ma Belle Evangeline', stands out as the Snuggly Duckling tavern is transformed into a theatre. As the threatening patrons attempt to capture Flynn to obtain a reward, Rapunzel pleads his cause with a heartfelt description of her dream, seeing the lanterns at the kingdom: won over, each thug reveals his own secret dreams. Hook (Brad Garrett) sings about his wish to become a concert pianist, stepping onto a stage, under a spotlight, while Rapunzel enthusiastically listens. The upbeat tempo of his tune leads all of the other patrons to dance and sing the chorus, to Flynn's surprise. In this explicitly staged configuration, another thug, Big Nose (Jeffrey Tambor), confesses his longing for romance: although he describes himself as a 'disgusting blighter', he expresses his dream to 'make a love connection'. The comedy of the song is based on the discrepancy between the romantic lyrics, and what is shown onscreen. As Big Nose sings 'can't you see me with a special little lady, rowing on a rowboat down the stream', Disney love ballads such as *The Little Mermaid*'s 'Kiss the Girl' are called upon, as well as a specific conception of the Disney couple: heterosexual romance displayed through normative performances of gender. Yet, the *mise en scène* subverts to some extent this sentimental and formulaic configuration: Big Nose places himself in a barrel that he uses as a boat, and rows with Shorty (Paul F. Tompkins), a little old patron dressed as a cherub and holding a pink umbrella. This staging hints, to some extent, at romantic configurations beyond Disney's heteronormative framing of fairy-tale couples, and foregrounds the artificial construction underlying several Disney love ballads. Yet, it also presents a familiar, old-fashioned romantic cliché. Big Nose explicitly acknowledges how naïve this romantic dream is, conceding that it is 'grotesquely optimistic'; when forced to reluctantly join the song, Flynn insists that his own dream is 'less touchy-feely'. Still, in typically post-feminist fashion, this self-reflexive song prefigures several heteronormative happy endings: Big Nose is shown finding 'true love' with a 'special little lady', while initially sceptical Flynn ultimately performs a straightforward, sincere love ballad.

Performed while the lanterns are released over the kingdom, 'I See the Light' discards the playful self-awareness underlying 'I've Got a Dream', representing a straightforwardly romantic display of love instead. The song can be positioned at the other end of the post-feminist spectrum on which *Tangled* oscillates, revealing how the film crystallises the duality of post-feminism. Post-feminist 'doubleness' corresponds to the 'contradictory play of ironic knowingness on one hand, and the seemingly sincere presentation of ideas of true love on the other' (Tasker 2011: 68). Applied to *Tangled*, 'I See the Light' appears as a genuine celebration of Disney's fairy-tale romance and formulaic display of coupledom, contrasting with the humorous and knowing artificiality of 'I've Got a Dream' (Figure 3.3). Following from *Cinderella*'s 'So This Is Love' and *Aladdin*'s 'A Whole New World', 'I See the Light' functions like a predictable Disney love ballad, allowing Rapunzel and Flynn-revealed-as-Eugene to acknowledge and express their feelings for each other. Their realisation is expressed first individually, in voice-over. Happily gazing at the night sky, Rapunzel ponders on her 'new dream': to be with Eugene ('All at once, everything looks different. Now that I see you'). Similarly, Eugene becomes aware of his romantic feelings while observing Rapunzel ('Now she's here, suddenly I know'). As he concludes his verse, he takes her hand, she looks back at him joyfully, and both diegetically declare their love by singing in unison the chorus, amorously gazing at each other. This shift, from voice-over to diegetic performance, and from solo to duo,

Figure 3.3 *'I See the Light' celebrates Disney's formulaic display of coupledom. Frame grab from* Tangled *(Greno and Howard, 2010).*

is conducted particularly smoothly: within the context of the musical, this spontaneous, irresistible expression of their emotion is expected. It notably contrasts, however, with the emphasis on the contrived and staged aspect of romantic duets as mocked in 'I've Got a Dream'. While Flynn struggled to join the latter musical performance, adding self-reflexivity and sarcasm to his part, he effortlessly harmonises with his partner in 'I See the Light': as Eugene, he becomes a conventional Disney hero. The song represents a pivotal moment of straightforward, sentimental, sincere romance, permitted through the intimate and enchanting setting: a genuine environment after the mock staging of 'I've Got a Dream'. Strikingly, Eugene is, like Big Nose, floating down the stream with a 'lady'; yet Eugene's rowboat is real, and the spotlight has been replaced by the muted glow of a multitude of paper lanterns floating around the kingdom's castle, which nostalgically evokes Disney's wider fairy-tale paratext and intertext. Approached alongside 'I've Got a Dream', 'I See the Light' represents the persistence of Disney's seemingly naïve and authentic yet notably normative depiction of romance and coupledom: *Tangled*'s inclusion of the two songs allows the film, in typical post-feminist fashion, to both mock and idealise the formulaic Disney couple.

As *Tangled* renegotiates elements of the DreamWorks and Disney formulas, and embraces post-feminist sensibilities, combining ironic knowingness with sentimental sincerity, and empowerment rhetoric with traditionalist gender paradigms, another important aspect of the film impacts on, or rather frames, its refashioning of fairy-tale romance: its aesthetic. Visually, Disney's first computer-animated fairy tale is closer to *Shrek* than *The Princess and the Frog*. Still, *Tangled*'s film text and paratexts rely on nostalgia for the style of hand-drawn animation – but in a notably different way than its hand-drawn predecessor. State-of-the-art computer technology is consistently framed in relation to, and as drawing on traditional animation, and is at times used within the film to evoke its feel and look, performing an aesthetic compromise paralleling its generic post-feminist doubleness. Such a compromise is at the core of Disney's contemporary aesthetic, as the studio consistently reminds its audience in its opening credits. Since 2006 – after the acquisition of Pixar – the opening credits for Disney animated features have included two parts: first, the computer-animated 'Disney' opening, preceding every Disney animated film as well as live-action productions, franchises, remakes and Pixar features.[7] It depicts the iconic fairy-tale castle circled by pixie dust, often accompanied by the reorchestrated theme of 'When You Wish Upon a Star'. It is followed by the 'Walt Disney Animation Studios' opening, featuring sheets of gold paper quickly flipped, on which the silhouette then body of Mickey Mouse is gradually drawn. This *mise en scène* explicitly calls upon the production process of past, hand-drawn animated features.⁸ The paper finishes flipping as the outline of Mickey turns into an animated scene from the first Disney cartoon with synchronised sound, *Steamboat Willie* (Ub Iwerks, 1928). The pairing of these two opening credits – the computer-animated fairy-tale castle and hand-drawn Mickey Mouse – epitomises Disney's contemporary aesthetic approach: reviving nostalgia for hand-drawn animation, and mediating such nostalgia through the digital. In *Tangled*, Disney translates the nostalgic appeal of hand-drawn animation, undeniably central to *The Princess and the Frog*'s positive critical reception, to computer animation. Chris Carter explains that the latter was presented as 'an extension of the traditional 2D Disney aesthetic': animators applied the theoretical principles of hand-drawn animation to the digital (2013: 3). This specific type of mediation represents the continuation of Disney's gradual integration of digital techniques and software into its hand-drawn animated output since the late 1980s, culminating in *The Princess and the Frog*, and is representative of a wider phenomenon within mainstream animation and contemporary Hollywood.

In the late 2000s, while independent filmmakers such as Marjane Satrapi and studios like Cartoon Saloon made the seemingly anachronistic choice to continue to rely primarily on hand-drawn animation, resisting a perceived pull towards photorealistic computer animation, Disney and Pixar adopted a hybrid approach particularly notable in their short output. Such an approach was echoed in other sections of mainstream Hollywood. Jason Sperb notes that, in the early 2010s, films such as *Hugo* (Martin Scorsese, 2011) and *The Artist* (Michel Hazanavicius, 2011) 'toyed with the idea of nostalgia for earlier periods of media history at the dawn of the digital transition': these films 'do not attempt to conceal ... anachronistic differences between old and new as much as celebrate their hybridity in reassuringly nostalgic ways' (2016: 3, 6). Within the context of animation history, 'earlier periods' and 'reassuring nostalgia' distinctly evoke hand-drawn animation. Pixar correspondingly experimented with traditional 2D animation techniques, as exemplified by Oscar-nominated short *La Luna* (Enrico Casarosa, 2011), in order to achieve a 'look that is altogether non-artificial, analogue, and nostalgic' (Haswell 2014). Disney's 2010s short films were heavily influenced by Pixar, similarly blending the flat, expressive aesthetic of hand-drawn animation with the 'stability and refinement of computer animation' (ibid.). Oscar-nominated *Get a Horse!* (Lauren MacMullan, 2013), for example, recreates the look of a 1920s black-and-white hand-drawn Mickey Mouse short film, with iconic characters propelled into the computer-animated coloured world of a cinema room. As Helen Haswell argues, Pixar and Disney's application of the most advanced computer-animation techniques to experiment with an organic aesthetic can be interpreted as a clever strategy, making 'digital animation marketable to wide-ranging, intergenerational audiences, including to age groups that could be potentially alienated by the perfection of CG animation' (Haswell 2014). Disney shorts, such as *Paperman* (John Kahrs, 2012) and *Get a Horse!*, could also be seen as nostalgic vehicles for the studio's hand-drawn animated past. Released in theatres with computer-animated *Wreck-It Ralph* (Rich Moore, 2012) and *Frozen* (Chris Buck and Jennifer Lee, 2013) respectively, they function as introductions facilitating the transition to the more recognisably digital, three-dimensional look of the main feature-length films. The pairing of *Paperman* and *Wreck-It Ralph* is particularly remarkable in that sense. *Paperman* is characterised by a flat hand-drawn aesthetic, featuring a black-and-white love story set in the 1940s, in which sheets of paper play a pivotal role in reuniting the two leads. The short is then followed by colourful 3D computer-animated feature-length *Wreck-It Ralph*, which includes contemporary racing and first-person shooter video games. The choice of these pairings suggests that hand-drawn and computer-animation styles can happily coexist and complement each other; the shift to the digital is nostalgically framed and mediated.

In *Tangled*, Disney's shift from the familiar traditional hand-drawn to the state-of-the-art computer-animated fairy-tale is mediated in parallel ways. The film is framed by references to traditional animation: at the start, the 'Walt Disney Animation Studios' opening is altered to include the mention that *Tangled* is Disney's '50th Animated Motion Picture', with black-and-white Mickey happily whistling within the zero of '50th'. Unlike the playfully irreverential opening of computer-animated *Chicken Little* (Mark Dindal, 2005), *Tangled* seems to embrace and celebrate Disney's canon, being explicitly positioned within a long recognisable tradition of hand-drawn animated films. The end credits display a golden sheet of paper unrolling, with animated etchings by character designer Shiyoon Kim: a paratextual *mise en scène* echoing the introductory *Steamboat Willie* clip. These nods to Disney's hand-drawn roots permeate *Tangled*'s promotional materials: the role of co-producer and supervising animator Glen Keane, who had worked as a Disney animator since 1974, was particularly emphasised in *The Art of Tangled*, most significantly in relation to Rapunzel's design.

Within the film text, Disney's nostalgic impulse leads to the subtle reappropriation of hand-drawn principles displayed throughout the studio's animated canon: the 'stylised' movement of hand-drawn characters is replicated through strategic moments of 'broad cartoon motion' (Carter 2013: 15). This aesthetic can be noticed specifically in sequences including slapstick and functioning as comic relief, as exemplified by Flynn's encounters with

Maximus: as they wrestle and push each other, Flynn's body stretches, falls and is squashed down, before returning to its initial shape (ibid.: 13, 16). Such instances of squash and stretch are paired with other comic manipulations of the animated body – most often Flynn's – which rely on hand-drawn animation style and contrast with the photorealistic depiction of the body associated with computer animation. Christopher Holliday notes that computer-animated features generally 'avoid the physical comedy of stretching, splintering, crumpling, discoloration and squashing', depicting motion and bodily violence in ways similar, to some extent, to live-action cinema (2018a: 180). Films such as DreamWorks' *How to Train Your Dragon* (Dean DeBlois and Chris Sanders, 2010) and Pixar's *Up* (Pete Docter and Bob Peterson, 2009) 'frequently make spectators aware of the frailty and fragility of characters' bodies' (ibid.: 180). *Tangled*'s moments of cartoon slapstick challenge to some extent such a computer-animated aesthetic, building on the distinctive style and history of Disney's hand-drawn animation. Such an aesthetic referencing is also noticeable in the backgrounds and settings of the film: 'to create a more organic feel . . . artists adopted a shape language that reduces the use of parallel lines by "wedging" straight shapes against curves' (Carter 2013: 5). The design of the Snuggly Duckling and the kingdom exemplifies the imperfect, expressive aesthetic found in Disney's past animated fairy tales – absence of symmetry, curvy architecture – which was subtly recreated via computer animation.

Tangled's aesthetic recreation was particularly praised by reviewers: interestingly, the musical sequence 'I See the Light' was one of the most commented upon, crystallising Disney's multiple nostalgic impulses at the aesthetic, generic and tonal levels. This sequence not only represents *Tangled*'s shift from playful and knowing fairy tale to sentimental and sincere romance but also strikingly foregrounds effects reminiscent of pre-digital animation through the very use of computer-animated techniques – an instance of aesthetic and post-feminist doubleness. As directors Greno and Howard point out, 'I See the Light' takes advantage of the expressive lighting made possible thanks to computer animation: countless dots in muted shades of orange and pink are gradually spread across the screen (2010: 7). The lighting strikingly echoes *La Luna*, Pixar's short produced the following year, which explicitly draws on analogue aesthetics. In the latter, a multitude of stylised shimmering stars gently fall in slow motion around the characters, who are amazed by the spectacle. The scope of *Tangled*'s similarly dazzling show of lights is revealed by the computer-generated imitation of a tracking shot, with the 'camera' circling Rapunzel and then showcasing the illuminated kingdom through a long shot. This sequence was described as 'uncommonly pretty' thanks to its 'dazzling colour palette', reminiscent of Maxfield Parrish's works

(Hornaday 2010). Dan Kois (2010) argued that *Tangled*'s visuals, although 'generated inside a computer . . . [were] as warm and rich as a painting'. Such an emphasis on the artistry and appeal of the 2D look of 'I See the Light' was further developed by A. O. Scott: 'it departs from the usual 3D insistence on deep focus and sharply defined images, creating an experience that is almost tactile in its dreamy softness' (2010). Considering these accounts, it seems that what makes 'I See the Light' a particularly remarkable sequence is the way computer animation successfully imitates and magnifies the organic aesthetic of pre-digital art and animation. Such praise echoes reviewers' admiration for the 'retro' aesthetic of *The Princess and the Frog* (Huddleston 2010). Paradoxically, it was thanks to the latest developments in computer animation that it was possible to create *Tangled*'s particular aesthetic, perceived as distanced from the coldness and artificiality of the digital. Such an aesthetic functions as a unique framework for Disney's post-feminist refashioning of fairy-tale romance.

Conclusion

Following the highly nostalgic, neo-traditional *Princess and the Frog*, and closing a decade of self-referential, parodic *Shrek* films, *Tangled*'s multifaceted, sometimes contradictory generic identity points to Disney's ambiguous relationship with its generic and gendered formula. Paratexts oscillate between DreamWorks-style irreverence and nostalgic celebration of the studio's fairy-tale canon. The film text itself reappropriates the self-awareness, parodic critique and contra-diegetic humour of *Shrek* films, most notably mocking the figure of the Disney Prince and his romantic encounter with the Princess. Nevertheless, the Disney formula gradually re-emerges throughout the film, paralleling the post-feminist trajectory and portrayal of its animated couple. Flynn/Eugene's characterisation particularly draws upon post-feminist romantic-comedy tropes to both subvert and re-establish Disney's formulaic gendered configurations. The double identity of the male lead crystallises the competing generic, tonal and aesthetic influences at work in the film: at times disguising, refashioning and nostalgically celebrating the Disney fairy tale and its formulaic construction of coupledom.

Although *The Princess and the Frog* and *Tangled* draw on multiple influences, within and beyond Disney's cinematic universe, it seems that their primary generic identity as fairy tales represents a constraining framework. Portrayals seem to naturally shift back to the traditionalist end of the post-feminist spectrum, culminating in 'idealistic' fantasies of heterosexual romance (Brown 2021: 129). To what extent can a Disney fairy tale maintain an empowering trajectory?

Notes

1. '*The Princess and the Frog*', *Box Office Mojo*, <http://www.boxofficemojo.com/movies/?id=princessandthefrog.htm> (accessed 1 August 2021). Ed Catmull justifies the title change further, explaining, 'based upon the response from fans and critics, we believe [global ticket sales] would have been higher if it wasn't prejudged by its title' (quoted in Chmielewski and Eller 2010).
2. This song is highly reminiscent of a similar sequence in *Shrek the Third* (Raman Hui and Chris Miller, 2007), in which fairy-tale villains are also convinced by a royal lead (Arthur) to be who they 'want to be', which leads them to confess passions and aspirations that are highly contra-diegetic. For example, the Wicked Witch from *Snow White*'s fairy tale is longing to 'open up a spa . . . in France'. The Snuggly Duckling tavern itself recalls *Shrek*'s The Poison Apple, with its collection of various villains and thugs – one of the many convergences between *Tangled* and the *Shrek* franchise.
3. See 'Bibbidi Bobbidi Boutique at the Disneyland Resort', *Disneyland Resort*, <https://disneyland.disney.go.com/shops/disneyland/bibbidi-bobbidi-boutique/> (accessed 1 August 2021).
4. '*Tangled*', *Box Office Mojo*, <http://www.boxofficemojo.com/movies/?id=rapunzel.htm> (accessed 1 August 2021).
5. 'Wedding', *Disney Store*, <http://www.disneystore.co.uk/search?q=wedding> (accessed 18 February 2018).
6. The screenplays of *Tangled* and *Crazy Stupid Love* were both written by Dan Fogelman, which might point to generically gendered similarities between the two films through the characters of Flynn and Jacob.
7. Examples include *Enchanted* and *Pirates of the Caribbean* (2006, 2007, 2011, 2017) up to *Cruella* (Craig Gillespie, 2021) and *Jungle Cruise* (Jaume Collet-Serra, 2021). Pixar animated films include the Disney fairy-tale castle opening, and are then followed by the studio's own 'Luxor' opening credits.
8. Artists working with hand-drawn animation also created a series of movements in pencil outline on separate sheets of drawing paper, and then flipped through them to ensure that the action moved as desired (Furniss 2016: 18).

CHAPTER 4

Brave New Tale? Reframing Love and Romance in Frozen

> Who will save the day? The ice guy? The nice man? The snowman? Or no man? (Disney's *Frozen*, Chris Buck and Jennifer Lee, 2013, Official Trailer)

Building on the successful marketing strategy for *Tangled* (Nathan Greno and Byron Howard, 2010), Disney's initial trailers and posters for the studio's third contemporary animated fairy tale showcased a thrilling action-adventure comedy seemingly far from Disney's sentimental formula. Nevertheless, like its two fairy-tale predecessors, *Frozen*'s film text actually draws on familiar fairy-tale and musical tropes, while interacting with several strands of the romantic mode, to revisit and renew the studio's iconic formula. The official trailer hinted at two aspects revealing to be pivotal in such a renewal: the central role of female characters and sisterhood ('Who will save the day? . . . no man?'), and the presence of an alternative to the conventional Disney male lead ('The ice guy? The nice man?'). These two aspects form the basis for *Frozen*'s generic revision. Focusing on the original 2013 film, this chapter explores how *Frozen* questions the primacy and plausibility of fairy-tale romance as displayed throughout Disney's canon; how it challenges and reframes its foundation, namely the concept of 'true love', and, to some extent, its associated heteronormative trajectory.

The film focuses on two orphaned princesses, naïve but resourceful Anna (Kristen Bell) and more distant Elsa (Idina Menzel), who was born with extraordinary ice powers. On the latter's coronation day, Elsa and Anna have an argument following Anna's hasty engagement to chivalric Prince Hans (Santino Fontana). Upset, Elsa unwittingly traps Arendelle in an eternal winter and flees her kingdom, which drives Anna to set off on a perilous journey to the North Mountain to bring her sister back. She is reluctantly helped by ice harvester Kristoff (Jonathan Groff), whose personality and conception of romance initially clash with hers, and an endearing snowman named Olaf (Josh Gad).

Foregrounding two heroines and two heroes, *Frozen* develops the approach initiated in neo-traditional and nostalgic *The Princess and the Frog* (Ron Clements and John Musker, 2009) and DreamWorks-inspired *Tangled*. The contrasting portrayals of Tiana and Charlotte in the former, and Flynn/Eugene in the latter, allow a degree of subversion, parody and self-awareness, which *Frozen* takes strikingly further. This chapter examines the scope of *Frozen*'s reinvention of Disney's fairy-tale formula, illuminating specifically two layers of generic influence and reappropriation.

The first part of the chapter analyses the converging points between *Frozen* and another contemporary animated fairy tale, which notably diverges from both the Disney and DreamWorks canons: *Brave* (Mark Andrews and Brenda Chapman, 2012). As a princess-centred narrative released by Pixar after its acquisition by Disney, *Brave* operates a shift within a familiar framework, relying on the 'courtship-marriage plot' to explore the bond between a mother and her daughter (Brown 2021: 128). Using a similar starting point, *Frozen* calls into question the syntactic structure of Disney's fairy-tale formula. This chapter examines the extent and implications of such a self-reflexive impulse.

In typically post-feminist fashion, these radical generic departures are mediated through the presence of character and narrative 'doubling'. The second part of the chapter analyses how *Frozen* draws on multiple strands of romance, from the chick flick to the screwball, as well as different genres of gender, in order to accommodate both ends of the post-feminist spectrum. I argue that the inherent semantic and syntactic doubleness of the film, namely the tensions between sister plot and romantic plot, traditional and challenging performances of gender, allows both the update and expansion of the fairy-tale formula, without its complete dilution. The portrayal of Elsa epitomises *Frozen*'s more subversive impulse towards Disney's own formulaic framework.

Studying how *Frozen* interacts with Hollywood's genres of romance, Disney's cinematic universe, as well as post-feminist sensibilities allows us to reconsider the studio's highest grossing animated feature of the 2008–18 decade beyond potentially reductive binaries – feminist or anti-feminist, 'improving' constructions of gender or not (Mollet 2020: 123). In parallel, the chapter illuminates *Frozen*'s pivotal role in Disney's wider re-envisioning and expansion of its fairy-tale formula.

Frozen, *Brave* and the Revised Fairy Tale: Female Bonds vs Formulaic Romance

Released one year apart, Disney's and Pixar's Oscar-winning animated fairy tales converged first through their respective production discourses: paratexts emphasised the studios' efforts to diverge from the fairy-tale formula as constructed, popularised and reiterated by Disney. In *The Art of Brave*, co-director Brenda Chapman repeatedly insisted that she was aiming for a 'unique' fairy tale: 'there was no room for a prince or another love interest to come along and save the day – or even be part of the day', 'I purposely didn't want a love story' (Chapman 2012: 8; Chapman, quoted in Lerew 2012: 15). Such an emphasis explicitly positioned *Brave* outside of the romantic framework of Disney fairy tales, while implicitly hinting at criticisms surrounding the studio's formula and its constructions of passive femininity. In *The Art of Frozen*, co-director Jennifer Lee foregrounded the same perspective: 'we'd talk about classic fairy tales and princess movies, but those stories are dominated by this sense of romance . . . we didn't want the boy to drive Anna and Elsa apart or save the day' (quoted in Solomon 2013: 14). As *Brave* ultimately focused on a 'love story between mother and daughter' (Chapman 2012: 8), *Frozen* operated a similar shift from romantic love to female bond: 'it's about the two sisters . . . their broken relationship, and how they repair it' (Jennifer Lee, quoted in Solomon 2013: 14). Such a focus was reportedly initiated by Chapman and Lee, both the first women to co-direct an animated film at their respective studios. Chapman explained that her 'predominant inspiration' for *Brave* was her own daughter (2012: 8), while Lee drew on her relationship with her own sister for *Frozen* (Solomon 2013: 14). This correlation between an emphasis on 'supportive female relationships' and the 'significant female creative forces behind the scenes' was noted by numerous critics and scholars (Lester 2019: 197). The syntactic structures of the films correspondingly mirror themselves in their departure from romantically centred classic and Renaissance-era Disney fairy tales, or even more contemporary films like *The Princess and the Frog* and *Tangled*.

Both *Brave* and *Frozen* open with the depiction of a harmonious female relationship: a dangerous threat to this harmony triggers the plot, which is only resolved once the relationship is repaired. In the former, Queen Elinor (Emma Thompson) is introduced happily laughing and playing with her young daughter Princess Merida (Kelly Macdonald), until they are attacked by a dangerous beast, Mor'du; in the latter, young Anna and Elsa similarly joyfully spend time together, until Elsa inadvertently hurts her sister with her ice powers. Throughout the years, both pairs grow apart: Merida rejects the restrictive gendered rules associated with her princess status and imposed on her by Elinor, while Elsa avoids her sister, fearing her powers. The prospect of betrothal for each red-haired princess – a diplomatic necessity forced upon Merida, a villainous manipulation passing for romance in the case of blissfully unaware Anna – causes a rift in the relationship. Merida refuses to be married and flees the kingdom to Elinor's despair, while Elsa disapproves of Anna and Prince Hans's hasty engagement, losing control of her powers before also fleeing her castle. Both Merida and Anna face challenges and trials, including encounters with magical beings – a mischievous witch in *Brave*, trolls in *Frozen* – which share riddles of sorts that will help the princesses reconsider their relationships. In *Brave*, Elinor is transformed into a bear through a spell: she and Merida solve the witch's riddle together and break the spell, 'mend[ing] the bond torn by pride'. Merida rescues her mother from her father's and the lords' capture, before Elinor defends her daughter from and defeats Mor'du. They heal their rift, and agree to change the ancient patriarchal law regarding betrothals. In *Frozen*, Anna is hurt a second time – her heart is frozen – by Elsa while she attempts to bring her back to the kingdom: her sacrificial rescue of her sister from villainous Prince Hans, who reveals that marriage was a ruse to access Arendelle's throne, heals her frozen heart. Anna and Elsa reconcile after declaring their love for each other in a way that recalls Merida's emotional speech to her mother before the latter transforms back into a human. In both films, female relationships then become the motor of the narrative, while marriage and patriarchal figures appear as obstacles to overcome. Despite such radical syntactic changes from the perspective of the formulaic Disney fairy-tale, its heteronormative underpinning is not entirely discarded: the way *Brave* and *Frozen* ultimately deal with this narrative prospect, however, represents a key difference between the two studios' generic take.

In *Brave*, the prospect of betrothal is presented as a political necessity, strengthening the alliance supporting the kingdom: romance is irrelevant, almost redundant in this ancient patriarchal tradition. In Disney fairy tales such as *Sleeping Beauty* (Clyde Geronimi, 1959) and *Aladdin* (Ron Clements and John Musker, 1992), the imperative of marriage is made more palatable because the princess happens to fall in love with the suitor chosen or ultimately approved by her father: it is precisely the development of this romantic plot which is at the core of Disney's fairy-tale formula. *Brave*, however, focuses on the diplomatic and familial implications of such narratives. Thanks to her remarkable archery skills, Merida mocks and surpasses the three suitors who compete for her hand, but her challenging act causes unrest among the kingdom's clans and angers the Queen, who is aware of the dangerous consequences of such a challenge. Admittedly, to maintain peace, marriage is only delayed: Elinor, convinced by her daughter, agrees to let her find love in her 'own time'. For authors such as Annette Furo and colleagues, this postponing maintains the 'restrictive' structure of the Disney fairy tale: such 'heteronormative policing provides the illusion of choice in whom to marry, while continuing to bind Merida to the social norm of marriage' (Furo et al. 2016: 214). Still, the film de-romanticises this norm and calls it into question: early in the film, Merida admits that 'she might not ever be ready' for marriage. As Chapman explains, *Brave* portrays royalty as a 'job', even for princesses (Lowther 2012). Merida is represented as a competent ruler, exercising power and drawing on her mother's wisdom to reason with the clans' leaders. Up until its ending, as Merida and her mother watch the lords sail away, the film consistently discards romance as a plot pivot or conclusion.

Brave's further challenge to Disney's fairy-tale formula consists in the deconstruction of desirable fairy-tale femininity: for Merida, it becomes a difficult, alienating and restrictive gendered performance. The overwhelming list of skills and qualities described by Elinor that Merida must adopt hints heavily at the formulaic features of earlier Disney Princesses: a princess 'doesn't chortle' or 'stuff her gob', is 'compassionate, patient, clean, cautious' – in other words 'strives for perfection'. While *The Princess and the Frog* playfully parodies such fairy-tale femininity through the portrayal of Charlotte, *Brave* explicitly rejects it, foregrounding instead Merida's resourcefulness, spontaneity, physical skills and adventurous spirit. Reappropriating a familiar generic trope, the film includes a brief sequence during which Merida prepares to meet her suitors, with her mother's help. In Disney fairy tales, such sequences overflow with glamour and spectacle: Cinderella is magically 'made over', her hair perfectly tight in a bun and her dress beautifully sparkling in the night; Belle appears in a stunning off-the-shoulder ball gown to waltz with the Beast, to his delight. Even Rapunzel undergoes a brief makeover of sorts: when she enters her kingdom, her long hair is styled in an elaborate flowery braid – Eugene gazes at the result with admiration. In *Brave*, however, such a transformation becomes a painful exercise. In a rapid montage sequence, Elinor vigorously tightens Merida's corset, brushes her untidy hair, and makes her wear an extremely tight-fitting blue dress, with sparkling stones forming an elaborate golden design at its bottom: in other words, she is turned into a 'beautiful' – in her mother's words – Disney Princess. Far from delighted, Merida struggles to move and breathe, and ends up cursing and tearing up the dress to properly use her bow. In *Brave*, fairy-tale femininity as defined by Disney is framed as an artificial and difficult performance, and is ultimately discarded, like romantic courtship.

Nevertheless, since *Brave*'s release, Merida's design has been heavily altered to be added to the Disney Princess franchise, and her appearance has become closer to the homogenised, glittery look of her Disney counterparts: such a contradiction between text and paratext reveals tensions at multiple levels.[1] As a Pixar film appropriating Disney's iconic genre, *Brave* can be positioned at the border of Disney's fairy-tale canon, and is therefore submitted to semantic and syntactic constraints that are not as pronounced for non-fairy-tale films such as *WALL-E* (Andrew Stanton, 2008) or *Up* (Pete Docter and Bob Peterson, 2009). The film and its paratext crystallise 'discourses of continuity and rupture' on which Disney and Pixar's relationship has been predicated: with *Brave*, Pixar both capitalises on 'Disney's own return to fairy-tale storytelling' and indicates a desire to make the fairy-tale genre available to the studio after its acquisition by Disney (Holliday 2018b: 214, 218). Through this in-between status, *Brave* managed to initiate a generic shift that, not unlike DreamWorks' *Shrek* (Andrew Adamson and Vicky Jenson, 2001), notably impacted on Disney's own fairy-tale output.

Released one year after *Brave*, *Frozen* combines Pixar's generic revisions with the nostalgic intertextuality and humorous self-reflexivity characterising Disney's contemporary fairy-tale cycle: the film questions the primacy and authenticity of formulaic fairy-tale romance by reframing the concept of 'true love'. As Catherine Lester points out, the film does so by showcasing an 'intense awareness of Disney's back catalogue of fairy tales' (2019: 197). *Cinderella* (Clyde Geronimi and Wilfred Jackson, 1950) represents an important reference point in order to approach *Frozen*, especially in the way it hints at the implausibility of romance as conceived in fairy tales. In *Cinderella*, the King's plan to find a wife for his son by organising a ball is initially unsuccessful. The Duke gently mocks his scheme by relying on a generic template:

> You, sire, are incurably romantic. No doubt you saw the whole pretty picture in detail. The young prince bowing to the assembly. Suddenly he stops. He looks up. For, lo, there she stands. The girl of his dreams. Who she is or whence she came, he knows not, nor does he care, for his heart tells him that here, here is the maid predestined to be his bride. A pretty plot for fairy tales, sire. But in real life, oh, no. No! It was foredoomed to failure.

As the Duke speaks, the Prince actually notices Cinderella, walks towards her, greets her and starts a waltz, followed by the romantic duet 'So This Is Love'. Through this piece of dialogue, Disney both reiterates and mocks the seemingly conventional literary portrayal of fairy-tale romance which, ironically, will be repeated and consolidated as part of the studio's own fairy-tale formula in subsequent animated features. This generically knowing sequence represents a small self-reflexive parenthesis in a film which opens with Cinderella expressing her longing for romance in 'A Dream Is a Wish Your Heart Makes', and closes with an idealised fairy-tale wedding. This parenthesis is expanded and becomes the core of *Frozen*'s narrative, questioning foundational tropes of Disney's fairy-tale romance through the initially familiar portrayal of its princess lead.

Following the presentation of the sisters' growingly difficult relationship throughout the years, *Frozen*'s introduction of Anna as a young woman functions as a generic reminder of Disney's formula. Although, at first, her portrayal seems unconventional – she wakes up drooling and late for her sister's coronation, for example – it appears to rapidly fit the '"Disney Princess" mould' (Lester 2019: 197). In her song 'For the First Time in Forever',

Anna expresses her excitement at seeing the kingdom gates open and her enthusiasm at meeting new people – enthusiasm that quickly shifts from meeting 'everyone' to meeting 'the one' and finding 'true love'. This rapid shift echoes Ariel's transition from longing to be part of humans' world to longing to be part of Eric's world in the reprise of *The Little Mermaid*'s iconic song (Ron Clements and John Musker, 1989). Like earlier classical heroines such as Aurora, who are 'primed for heterosexual romance before they encounter their princes, manifesting desire through their imaginings of idealized partners' (Bradford 2012: 180–1), Anna describes her 'dream' to 'find romance' while singing to cute little ducklings and waltzing with the bust of a man. She also re-enacts idealised depictions of romance, superimposing herself onto courtship scenes from various paintings: she curtsies to a painted male suitor, presents her hand for another to kiss while continuing to dance and sing. As observed by Owen Weetch, Anna's desire is 'limited and constrained ... by traditional, two-dimensionally rigid expectations': the 'outmoded, restrictive representations' which hold her back contrast with the three-dimensional world she inhabits (2016: 137). These flat representations, like Charlotte's fairy-tale book in *The Princess and the Frog*, echo the predictable development of Disney's romantic formula. Such nostalgically idealised scenes are immediately repeated when, like Snow White's Prince, Prince Hans magically appears at the end of Anna's song – the 'beautiful stranger tall and fair' she was hoping for. After the coronation, they waltz and sing a romantic duet concluded by a marriage proposal, which Anna happily accepts. These familiar romantic stages, taking place within the first third of the film, seem to constitute an accelerated re-enactment of Disney's fairy-tale formula, reminiscent of *Enchanted*'s (Kevin Lima, 2007) animated opening: this nostalgic framework, however, is ultimately subverted.

Frozen shifts from playfully nostalgic re-enactment to dramatic generic revision by remobilising another formulaic trope, pivotal in numerous Disney fairy tales including *Snow White and the Seven Dwarfs* (David Hand, 1937), *Sleeping Beauty*, *The Little Mermaid*, *Enchanted* and *The Princess and the Frog*: 'true love's kiss'. In the latter two films, the spectacular magical power of such a kiss is only momentarily challenged: Prince Edward fails to wake up Giselle only because Robert is her 'true love'; similarly, only Tiana's kiss can transform her and Naveen back into humans. In *Frozen*, however, the very act of the romantic kiss is discarded as the 'true' manifestation of sincere love. Convinced by the trolls that her frozen heart will be healed through 'true love's kiss' – the logical manifestation, from a generic perspective, of an 'act of true love' – Anna returns to the kingdom to find Hans. However, he refuses to kiss her: he is revealed to be a traitor, marrying her solely to access the throne. Anna's naivety, reminiscent of the endearing romanticism of past princesses, is almost fatal for her. The 'act of true love' that actually saves her is her own sacrifice towards her sister Elsa: she throws herself between the latter and Hans, who was wielding his sword against her. Through this reimagining, namely replacing a romantic kiss by an act of sisterly love, *Frozen* rewrites the 'established conventions of the form' (Brown 2021: 133). Unlike the 'overtly comedic' approach of *Shrek*, *Frozen*'s generic shift is characterised by 'revisionism at the syntactic level', going further than DreamWorks' semantic parody (ibid.: 133). Arguably, such revisionism ultimately relies on *Frozen*'s consistent questioning of the generic plausibility of Disney's fairy-tale formula.

This questioning operates through a generic clash between Anna's portrayal as an idealistic Disney Princess, believing in romantic 'true love', courteous princes and love at first sight, and all the other main characters, who approach the fairy-tale genre they inhabit from a different perspective. The first challenge to Disney's sentimental formula is voiced by Elsa, who, shocked by Anna's precipitous engagement, refuses to bless her sister's wedding because she 'can't marry a man [she] just met'. Anna's convictions ('you can if it's true love') are further challenged by Kristoff, who repeatedly voices his disbelief at what he considers to be Anna's misplaced trustfulness ('You mean to tell me you got engaged to someone you just met that day?'). He opposes her conception of true love, especially the instant chemistry associated with love at first sight, with his down-to-earth, unromanticised vision of love, checking how much she actually knows about Hans through a series of questions. His quizzing ('What's his last name?', 'Foot size . . .?') trivialises the magical dimension of Anna's experience: like Aurora, she feels that her prince is no 'stranger'. As Michelle Law points out, 'Anna's idealism quite self-reflexively mirrors the romanticism of the Disney princesses of the past, whereas Elsa and Kristoff represent the modern voices of reason' (2014: 23). This opposition between past and contemporariness, idealism and reason are recurrent in analyses of Anna's characterisation. For example, Lester notes that that, 'like many other fairy-tale princesses . . . Anna has an idealistic and unrealistic view of . . . love' (2019: 198); similarly, Tracey Mollet explains that Anna eventually 'shakes off her dated views about true love', recognising that her 'idealism and fairy-tale views of romance are foolish' (2020: 124–5). These observations suggest that, in a post-*Shrek* and post-*Brave* landscape in which the Disney fairy tale has been repeatedly criticised, mocked and subverted, the studio's generic and gendered formula can no longer function. Instead, it is reappropriated by Prince Hans and transformed into a villainous scheme. Taking advantage of Anna's generic expectations, even he condescendingly points out, 'you were so desperate for love you were willing to marry me, just like that'. Steve Neale's concept of generic 'verisimilitude', which involves various systems and forms of 'plausibility, motivation and belief' varying from genre to genre, is particularly useful in this context (2000: 32). Anna's portrayal and what she knows about 'true love' crystallise a regime of verisimilitude that is no longer appropriate both diegetically and for contemporary audiences: the regime of Disney's fairy-tale formula. Elsa and Kristoff, by contrast, embody different norms and expectations, which rely on a generic framework that goes beyond the studio's fairy-tale intertext, with a slightly different regime of verisimilitude: the romantic comedy.

Frozen's generic revisionism and self-awareness echoes an important component of the romantic comedy, a genre particularly inclined towards self-reflexivity. Writing on 2010s romantic comedies, Maria San Filippo observes that,

> while the neotraditional romcoms that flourished in Hollywood in the 1990s and 2000s, from *Pretty Woman* to *The Ugly Truth* (2009), reverted to the genre's atavistic, idealizing strategies for representing romance, romantic comedy of the past decade has increasingly opted for a sobering appraisal of the labors and letdowns of love and the compromises involved in coupling. (San Filippo 2021: 16)

Numerous romantic comedies contemporaneous to *Frozen* self-reflexively display, to varying degrees, a sense of disenchantment regarding romance as portrayed within the genre, often voiced by the disillusioned and/or cynical female protagonist. In *(500) Days of Summer* (Marc Webb, 2009), for example, sceptical Summer (Zooey Deschanel) argues to hopeless romantic Tom (Joseph Gordon-Levitt) that 'there is no such thing as love. It's fantasy'; in *Friends with Benefits* (Will Gluck, 2011), Jamie (Mila Kunis) claims that she must 'stop buying into this bullshit Hollywood cliché of true love'; in *Trainwreck* (Judd Apatow, 2015), Amy (Amy Schumer) initially follows her father's mantra, 'monogamy isn't realistic'. In these examples, as in *Frozen*, the dominant regime of generic verisimilitude is called into question, hinting at alternative narrative trajectories. Still, the heroines of these romantic comedies are ultimately proven wrong: in typically post-feminist fashion, the films nostalgically reclaim the 'fantasy' or 'cliché' of sentimental romance, after having momentarily challenged the idealisation of familiar and predictable tropes. *Frozen* uses a similar strategy: unlike *Brave*, which entirely discards romantic love in its narrative, the film relies on syntactic and semantic doubling. By presenting two parallel story lines, two potential male partners for its princess, and two female leads, *Frozen* mediates its self-reflexive generic revision of Disney's fairy-tale formula, borrowing from multiple strands of the romantic comedy in the process.

FROZEN AND GENRES OF ROMANCE: UPDATING AND EXPANDING THE FAIRY-TALE FORMULA

The syntactic and semantic doubling characterising *Frozen* follows from a specific strand of the contemporary romantic comedy that particularly foregrounds female relationships: the chick flick. Admittedly, authors such as Hilary Radner argue that 'few' chick flicks are 'romantic comedies per se' (2011: 29). Using the label 'female friendship movies', Heidi Wilkins notes that chick flicks such as *Sex and the City* (Michael Patrick King, 2008), *Bride Wars* (Gary Winnick, 2009) and *Bridesmaids* (Paul Feig, 2011) foreground 'female relationships rather than male–female heterosexual partnerships' (2016: 151). Films including *Monster-in-Law* (Robert Luketic, 2005), *27 Dresses* (Anne Fletcher, 2008) and *Crazy Rich Asians* (Jon Chu, 2018) adopt a similar approach to explore familial bonds between women. Still, these films borrow heavily from the romantic comedy. Their explorations of female relationships are developed within a specifically heteronormative context, corresponding to the happy ending of many romantic comedies: the preparation of a wedding. The prospect of the ceremony and its associated range of standardised activities – from dress fittings to bachelorette parties and rehearsal dinners – tend to represent a source of conflict between the female characters, testing their friendship or sisterly bond. Therefore, the female-centred plot and the romantic plot are directly linked.

Frozen adopts a similar syntactic development: the sister plot, namely Anna and Elsa's relationship, and the romantic plot, namely Anna and prince Hans/Kristoff, alternate in their primacy and consistently clash, particularly after the announcement of Anna's engagement. As a Disney fairy tale generically subverting the studio's formula, *Frozen* dissimulates its female friendship film tropes, misdirecting the audience only to ultimately reclaim this strand of the romantic comedy. When Anna leaves to bring Elsa back to the kingdom after she has fled, her explicit goal, namely reaching her sister, is subtly juxtaposed with her romantic goal: marrying Hans. As she journeys to the North Mountain accompanied by Kristoff, the possibility of a new romantic relationship is gradually developed. The latter is put on hold when Anna finds Elsa in her ice palace: she attempts a reconciliation while they bond over a childhood memory. Still, she is unsuccessful at bringing her sister back: Elsa urges Anna to leave, fearing for her safety, and panics further when she learns that she has caused an eternal winter to fall over the kingdom. During the reprise of 'For the First Time in Forever', Anna shifts her initial focus from romantic love to sisterly bond ('you don't have to keep your distance anymore', 'we can work this out together'), but Elsa sings a different melody and, overwhelmed, strikes Anna again with her powers. Chased away by a gigantic snowman made by

Elsa, the group must follow a new narrative trajectory: instead of bringing Elsa back, they must find out how to heal Anna's frozen heart. The film then seems to relegate the sister plot to the background, misdirecting the audience. Following the encounter with the trolls, romantic conventions resurface: these characters insist that Anna's ideal partner is actually Kristoff, staging a troll-themed wedding for the pair during the song 'Fixer Upper', and that 'true love's kiss' will save her. While during this musical sequence the growing chemistry between Anna and Kristoff is apparent, the lyrics hint at and apply to the underlying sister plot: prefiguring Anna's final act, one troll sings to her that 'love's a force that's powerful and strange' and that 'true love brings out the best'. Even after Hans is revealed to be a villain, the romantic plot seems to predominate over the sister plot. When Olaf finds Anna alone in the castle, betrayed, weak and desperate, his observation on love, although interpreted as applying to Kristoff, actually announces Anna's actions: 'love is . . . putting someone else's needs before yours'. It is the following narrative shift, namely the positioning of the sister plot as replacing the romantic plot as syntactic resolution, that leads to *Frozen*'s most significant revision of the Disney formula, and parallel with the female friendship film.

This syntactic shift from romance to sisterly relationship is staged as a spectacular generic reversal in the final section of the film. Once Olaf notices Kristoff riding back to the castle, he and Anna rush to reach him: as they believe, 'there's [the] act of true love, right there'. The film cuts back and forth between them, struggling to leave the castle, and Kristoff, sprinting across the frozen fjord waters and into the snowstorm. The film relies on familiar tropes, intertextually echoing *Sleeping Beauty*, to frame the expected ending: Kristoff kissing Anna. The ice spikes initially blocking Anna and Olaf's path are reminiscent of the thick thorny bushes surrounding Aurora's castle. Like Prince Phillip, Kristoff bravely rides his steed to reach his princess, while obstacles arise: the white-out wind pushes him back, ships capsize in front of him, while ice cracks threateningly beneath him. Law observes that 'by drawing audiences in with familiar tropes and characters, we are lulled into a false sense of expectation, but are ultimately surprised by the outcome' (2014: 24). The couple calls each other's names, before Anna finally catches a glimpse of Kristoff. As they run towards each other, Anna hears Hans's sword being drawn from his scabbard, as he attempts to kill Elsa. Torn between romantic and sisterly love, Anna gives a final longing look at Kristoff, and throws herself in front of her sister. She freezes to solid ice at that instant, which causes Hans's sword to shatter completely, the force of which knocks him out. When Anna starts to thaw, and Elsa expresses her surprise and admiration at her bravery ('You sacrificed yourself for me?'), the former declares, 'I love you.' This affirmation, subversive within the context of Disney's sentimental formula, yet central to female friendship films, not only leads to the sisters' reconciliation but also helps Elsa bring back summer in Arendelle. *Frozen* ultimately 'discredit[s] romance with the formerly idealized prince and valorises sororal love and care as a more than fitting replacement' (Negra 2015). The final sequence, featuring the reunited sisters embracing each other and ice skating among their people, echoing their joyful play as children, reconfigures Disney's fairy-tale formula by positioning the sister plot and female relationships as central to the overall happy ending – as in contemporary chick flicks (Figure 4.1).

While *Frozen* operates a significant syntactic shift regarding Disney's fairy-tale formula, and challenges the regime of verisimilitude of its romantic framework, it does not entirely suppress the latter: as in many chick flicks, the romantic plot may not ultimately take precedence, but it does not disappear. Both in *Bride Wars* and *Bridesmaids*, for example, the heroines' reconciliation, conveying a powerful ode to female friendship, notably takes place on the day of the wedding ceremony. Even if the grooms and boyfriends remain secondary characters, they still play a pivotal role within the heroines' lives and the syntactic structure of the film: the friendship plot is directly impacted upon by the romantic plot. In ensemble chick flicks such as *Sex and the City* or *How to Be Single* (Christian Ditter, 2016), some of the female protagonists may strengthen their friendship while remaining happily single, but the others will necessarily marry or start new romantic relationships. In typically post-feminist fashion, the 'doubling of characters and/or the use of double narratives' highlights the 'profound ambivalence' that contemporary romantic comedies often exhibit about the role of romance and marriage

Figure 4.1 *The reunited sisters are central to* Frozen's *happy ending. Frame grab from* Frozen *(Buck and Lee, 2013).*

in a woman's life (Radner 2011: 37). Similarly, the tensions between Elsa and Anna, romantic and sisterly plot, point to Disney's wider balancing act throughout its contemporary fairy-tale cycle: to borrow Christopher Holliday's term, the nostalgically traditionalist formula can only 'stretch' so far on the post-feminist spectrum (2019: 127). In order to mediate this stretch, *Frozen* provides additional, individual happy endings for each sister.

Before *Frozen*'s sister-centred happy ending, a series of concluding sequences brings romantic resolution for Anna while consolidating Elsa's status as a single queen. After Hans is expelled from Arendelle, Anna is shown with Kristoff, offering him a brand-new sled. Out of joy and excitement, Kristoff sweeps Anna up high overhead and spins her around, in a gesture recalling many past princes with their princesses, exclaiming, 'I love it! I could kiss you . . .' Then, he drops her, suddenly embarrassed, and awkwardly asks for her permission, a notable generic subversion considering the hardly consensual first kisses in *Snow White* and *Sleeping Beauty*. Anna grants it, and they exchange a kiss, which co-director Jennifer Lee labels 'true love's kiss' in the script (2013: 111). This conventional romantic scene is followed by a sequence featuring Elsa accepted among her people. No longer isolating herself due to her powers, she creates an ice rink in the castle while the gates remain open. By using semantic and syntactic doubling, namely portraying a princess happily starting a relationship and a single queen in a position of leadership, *Frozen* presents a generic compromise which accommodates both ends of the post-feminist spectrum. The film combines a familiar romantic resolution with subversive generic revisionism foregrounding empowerment and sisterhood: it both preserves and challenges aspects of Disney's fairy-tale formula by reappropriating the ambivalent doubleness of chick flicks.

In addition to its narrative doubling, *Frozen* self-reflexively revises Disney's sentimental formula by including two potential male partners for Anna: the characterisation of Prince Hans represents a pivotal reconfiguration of Disney's gendered fairy-tale formula. With his formal attire and gentle manner, Hans strongly references *Cinderella*'s royal protagonist: his portrayal resuscitates the old-fashioned figure of the Disney Prince, nostalgically reclaimed in some post-feminist romantic comedies through the 'new hero'.[2] Introduced at the end of 'For the First Time in Forever', Hans courteously helps Anna to her feet after she has fallen bumping into his horse. He bows before properly introducing himself; when he learns that she is a princess, he drops to his knees and 'formally apologise[s]' for the incident. Regal, handsome and chivalric, he symbolises the epitome of the classic fairy-tale prince: Anna appears instantly smitten. His elaborate performance of fairy-tale masculinity is developed through additional intertextual references, mobilising several formulaic tropes of fairy-tale courtship: a spontaneous dance catching the princess by surprise, a romantic duet ('Love Is an Open Door') and a marriage proposal. As they dance, the couple casts shadows on the sails of ships in the docks, particularly recalling the way Cinderella and her Prince are framed throughout their romantic duet 'So This Is Love'. As a result, the image of past Disney Princes and the nostalgic aura of old-fashioned fairy-tale masculinity is superimposed onto Hans. His portrayal during the rest of the film further develops his status as the ideal fairy-tale hero. Left in charge of Arendelle by Anna, he supervises the distribution of food and clothes to the kingdom's subjects. When she goes missing, he leads a group to the North Mountain to find her and fights a gigantic snowman. However, as for the concept of true love as presented throughout Disney's fairy-tale canon, *Frozen* frames Hans's formulaic gendered performance as archaic and no longer plausible in a post-*Shrek* and post-*Brave* landscape.

Fairy-tale masculinity as performed by Hans, involving selfless bravery and courteousness, is revealed to be a treacherous disguise, the sinister underpinning of Disney's gendered formula. This dramatic shift occurs when Anna is brought back to the castle by Kristoff, and urges Hans to kiss her, as she desperately needs 'an act of true love' to heal her frozen heart. In a performance reminiscent of *Snow White*'s, *Sleeping Beauty*'s and *Enchanted*'s heroes, Hans gives the weakened princess a tender smile, gently and slowly leans in to kiss her, but stops an inch from her face. The unexpected nature of this act is echoed by the sudden halt of the soft romantic non-diegetic music. While Hans reveals his true motive, he puts out the candles and the fire of the room to accelerate Anna's 'freezing', notably taking off one of his gloves – or rather, part of his princely disguise. As the room gets darker and he delivers his threatening monologue, he gradually comes out as a villain. His aim was to marry Anna to access the throne; her potential death represents an opportunity to charge Elsa with treason and become the sole ruler of Arendelle. Anna's initial surprise and incomprehension is followed by anger at having been fooled by Hans's gendered performance, which represents a drastic departure in the way Disney has framed its formulaic construction of fairy-tale masculinity. One of Hans's final lines to Anna not only debunks further the aura of the Disney Prince but also reveals the gender imbalance behind such an idealisation of male heroism. Stating that Anna is 'no match for Elsa', Hans repositions himself as the formulaic fairy-tale rescuer, notably standing up and putting his glove back on: 'I, on the other hand, am the hero who is going to save Arendelle from destruction.' Framed in a low-angle shot, he appears in a position of power. Such an image of heroic masculinity, mirroring the initial low-angle shot introducing the character, appears nostalgically reassuring in the context of post-feminist romantic comedies and many Disney fairy tales including *Tangled*, in which Eugene ultimately becomes a chivalric hero. Yet, male heroism relies on the fact that the female protagonists are positioned, at some point in these narratives, as helpless and devoid of agency: this leads to romantic scenes of rescue. In *Frozen*, however, this gendered trope becomes threatening and sinister: weak and fragile Anna is left alone, lying on the floor, deceived by Hans's performance of courtly selflessness and romantic spontaneity.

Frozen's explicit rejection of the formulaically gendered trope of the Disney Prince builds on a wider trend of generic revisionism, both within and beyond Disney's cinematic universe. As part of its many semantic reconfigurations, the *Shrek* franchise portrays 'Prince Charming' as a self-seeking rogue who, like Prince Hans, is only interested in marrying Princess Fiona to become king. In *The Princess and the Frog*, the character of Prince Naveen consists partly of a masquerade: his servant, Lawrence, poses as the prince after Naveen has been transformed into a frog thanks to Dr Facilier's talisman. Lawrence-as-Naveen's romantic waltz with Charlotte, referencing the staging of similar musical sequences in *Cinderella* and *Sleeping Beauty*, similarly misleads the audience through nostalgic intertextuality. What differs in *Frozen*, however, is the overall tone adopted in relation to Prince Hans's portrayal: the film discards DreamWorks-style parody and the more playful approach of *The Princess and the Frog*. The debunking of Hans's initially courteous and chivalric performance is framed as a dramatic, radical generic twist. By featuring Anna punching him in the face at the end, and having him expelled from the kingdom, Disney explicitly distances its contemporary canon from such a portrayal of fairy-tale masculinity, which appears to be retrograde and harmful.

Instead of discarding the presence of a male romantic lead, as in *Brave*, *Frozen* introduces an alternative construction of masculinity through the character of Kristoff: his portrayal differs, to some extent, from Disney's fairy-tale formula through its reappropriation of gendered tropes at the core of several male-centred contemporary romantic comedies. Relying on examples such as *Swingers* (Doug Liman, 1996) and *Along Came Polly* (John Hamburg, 2004), Tamar Jeffers McDonald describes the 'homme-com' as a reaction against the sentimental and 'sexless' neo-traditional romantic comedy (2009: 152). Although these films preserve the conventional heteronormative narrative closure of the genre, they prioritise 'gross-out' humour, physical and sexual comedy as a semantic departure (ibid.: 147, 153, 158). Within a fairy-tale context, these semantic differences parallel *Shrek*'s generic approach in opposition to Disney's sentimental formula, with its ogre hero bathing in mud, using his earwax to make candles, getting hit in the groin and joking while making sexual innuendos. As a more moderate incarnation of the homme-com hero, Kristoff's portrayal concentrates *Frozen*'s physical and gross-out humour. Not only is he the victim of comedic slapstick like most anthropomorphic characters – for example, he runs into a pole blindfolded – but his behaviour and dialogue also actively draw on gross-out comedy. While he journeys with Anna to the North Mountain, he cleans the dash of his sled by spitting on it: the spit flies back and hits Anna in the face. His list of questions to Anna about Hans ends with the rather unexpected 'What if you hate the way he eats? What if you hate the way he picks his nose . . . and eats it?' To Anna's shock and disgust ('Excuse me, sir. He is a prince'), Kristoff casually replies that 'all men do it'. During the song 'Fixer-Upper', the trolls reinforce his gross-out characterisation, explaining that 'he always ends up sorta smelly' and that he 'only likes to tinkle in the woods'. In *Olaf's Frozen Adventure* (Stevie Wermers-Skelton and Kevin Deters, 2017), Kristoff introduces Anna, Elsa and Olaf to a troll tradition consisting in building a troll out of rocks, grass and fungus, licking its forehead and making a wish: the sight makes Elsa gag, while Anna exclaims, smiling, 'gross'. Through Kristoff's homme-com inspired portrayal, *Frozen* develops further the approach of *The Princess and the Frog* and *Tangled* regarding formulaic fairy-tale masculinity, explicitly trivialising and subverting the idealised aura of the male hero.

By opposing the portrayals of Kristoff and Hans, and ultimately favouring the former as Anna's romantic partner, *Frozen* frames formulaic fairy-tale masculinity as obsolete and artificial: Kristoff's initial failure to attain this idealised gender construction echoes the struggles of many homme-com heroes. These male characters, exemplified by Seth Rogen's performance in *Knocked Up* (Judd Apatow, 2007) and Jason Segel's in *Forgetting Sarah Marshall* (Nicholas Stoller, 2008), all wrestle with the 'personal inadequacy and social anachronism' of what John Alberti terms the 'the gender genre of the Alpha Male' (2013: 34). The latter is characterised by 'conventional' norms of 'male attractiveness, physical power and social status' (ibid.: 34), and could correspond to romantic-comedy types described in Chapter 3, such as the self-confident wealthy player and the nurturing new hero. By contrast, Seth Rogen's and Jason Segel's heroes are insecure and isolated, and struggle professionally, financially and romantically (ibid.: 35). Correspondingly, unlike Disney's 'Alpha' Prince Hans, Kristoff lives alone, with a reindeer as sole companion; he agrees to take Anna to the North Mountain because he cannot afford his new supplies. His rather unrefined manners and gruff attitude notably contrast with Hans's courtliness. As sung by the trolls, Kristoff speaks in a 'grumpy way' and is 'socially impaired'; in *Olaf's Frozen Adventure*, Olaf jokingly warns Anna that, as a princess, she does not 'have to settle' with such an unconventional man. Homme-coms foreground such portrayals in a 'claim for radical honesty', subverting the perceived 'fantasy and wish fulfilment' of conventional romantic-comedy masculinity (Alberti 2013: 36).

Frozen adopts a similar approach, renewing Disney's gendered formula by presenting a version of masculinity framed as more authentic and desirable, devoid of theatricality – unlike falsely courteous and dignified Hans. Less confident romantically, Kristoff appears awkward with Anna. Still, his behaviour relies on an understanding of romance as consensual and respectful – notably he asks whether he may kiss her (Figure 4.2). In typically post-feminist fashion, Kristoff ultimately becomes a truly chivalric hero, rushing to rescue Anna and braving a snowstorm. At the same time, he remains 'sensitive and sweet', described as the 'honest goods'. Through this semantic shift, namely prioritising homme-com hero Kristoff over fairy-tale prince Hans, *Frozen* revises the gendered imbalance underlying its romantic formula.

This semantic revision is framed by a similar shift from formulaic fairy tale to romantic comedy regarding the syntactic trajectory of *Frozen*'s romantic relationships: Anna and Hans's idealised encounter is discarded as implausible, while Anna's initially difficult yet more egalitarian relationship with Kristoff ultimately succeeds. Like *The Princess and the Frog* and *Tangled*, *Frozen* borrows from the syntactic 'hallmarks' of the romantic comedy, portraying a couple who reaches an accord despite a degree of 'initial mutual antipathy' (Jeffers McDonald 2009: 147). Unlike Anna and Hans's sentimental encounter, Anna and Kristoff's first meeting at Oaken's Trading Post is tense and awkward. Kristoff appears as a threatening and laconic character covered in snow, not really appreciating Anna's joke about his ice business ('that's a rough business to be in right now'). Their contrasting personalities add to their animosity: the talkative, friendly and naïve princess clashes with the solitary, down-to-earth, initially gruff ice harvester. Despite these differences,

Figure 4.2 Frozen *prioritises 'sensitive and sweet' homme-com hero Kristoff. Frame grab from* Frozen *(Buck and Lee, 2013).*

the couple reaches an accord – a ride to the North Mountain in exchange for new supplies and a sled. Their compatibility is gradually displayed, first through dialogue: like Tiana and Naveen, Anna and Kristoff's verbal battles and banter borrow from screwball dynamics, positioning the princess on the same footing as the male lead. Unlike Anna and Hans's relatively superficial demonstration of their compatibility or 'mental synchronisation' ('We finish each other's' / 'Sandwiches'), Anna and Kristoff's exchanges are witty, fast-paced – almost overlapping – and playful, as illustrated throughout their dynamic conversation about Hans:

> Anna: But Hans is not a stranger.
> Kristoff: Oh yeah? What's his last name?
> Anna: . . . Of-the-Southern-Isles?
> [. . .]
> Anna: Look it doesn't matter; it's true love.
> Kristoff: Doesn't sound like true love.
> Anna: Are you some sort of love expert?

This verbal compatibility is matched by their complementary action skills, or rather the physical manifestation of their swordplay, displayed during the rest of the sequence: when they are attacked by a pack of wolves, Kristoff kicks one out of the sled, then Anna knocks another away with a lute. The couple's slow realisation of their compatibility and romantic feelings for each other similarly highlights *Frozen*'s favouring of romantic-comedy conventions over those of the formulaic fairy tale. Hans no longer represents an idealised figure, but functions as the romantic-comedy 'unsuitable partner' (Jeffers McDonald 2007: 11), who reveals by contrast the rightness of the true romantic interest, namely Kristoff. Such a triangular configuration is at the core of numerous romantic comedies, from screwballs up to neo-traditional romantic comedies and Disney's own live-action output, including *Enchanted*.[3] These multiple semantic and syntactic borrowings reveal how *Frozen* consistently relies on the romantic comedy to revise and renew Disney's fairy-tale formula, from its narrative doubling and romantic framework to the portrayal of the male leads.

While Anna's character is at the core of *Frozen*'s syntactic and semantic doubling, positioned at the centre of two parallel romantic-comedy narratives – sister and romance plots – and romantically interacting with two different generic constructions of masculinity, Elsa's portrayal does not quite fit into such generic and heteronormative frameworks. She not only remains single throughout the film but also shows no interest in romance: her narrative arc 'solely focuses on her self-acceptance and assertion', epitomised by her triumphant song of 'self-actualization', 'Let It Go' (Mittermeier 2021). Such a syntactic departure from Disney's fairy-tale formula has led academics, critics and audience members to interpret her character as queer, and her iconic song as a coming-out anthem (ibid.). As Noel Brown points out, while there is sufficient evidence to sustain the possibility that Elsa is queer, lesbian or asexual, 'there is certainly not enough that viewers who prefer to believe otherwise are forced to accept it as fact', which corresponds to the strategy of 'deniability' characterising most Hollywood animation (2021: 136). Unlike some – isolated – animated films contemporaneous to *Frozen* like *ParaNorman* (Chris Butler and Sam Fell, 2012), the former does not include any explicit references to queerness or queer relationships.[4] The fact that *Frozen* can still 'project and appeal to' representations and identifications beyond the heteronormative 'mainstream' (Archer 2019: 94) is arguably tied to specific interpretation strategies. As Alexander Doty explains, queerness can be approached as a 'mass culture reception practice . . . a term with some ambiguity' (1995: 72). As a critical concept, queerness encompasses and illuminates 'resistance . . . to normative codes of gender and sexual expression' (Aaron 2004: 5). From this perspective, a queer reading does not require a film to have explicitly queer characters, but representations which challenge and question norms. In other words, the rest of this chapter does not investigate in detail Elsa's potentially queer identity: this would deserve a lengthier discussion, which may take into account fan readings and a wider analysis of the reception of the film, both of which lie outside the remit of the book.[5] I rely on this critical lens to examine how Elsa's portrayal resists norms within the context of Disney's specific genre of gender, namely how it queers the studio's formulaic constructions of fairy-tale femininity.

As developed throughout the pivotal musical sequence 'Let It Go', Elsa's characterisation is closer to the portrayal of fairy-tale villainesses than that of princesses, transgressing the semantic gendered binaries displayed throughout Disney's canon. Amy Davis observes that classic 'wicked women' such as *Snow White*'s Evil Queen and *Sleeping Beauty*'s Maleficent show a 'much higher proportion of agency' than the princesses: they shapeshift, 'actively seek to control' their lives, and are 'often very creative . . . mature, powerful and independent . . . everything that their female victims are not' (2006: 107). Subsequent villainesses such as *The Little Mermaid*'s Ursula also use their 'sexuality as a weapon', which is framed as part of their 'inherent wickedness', as opposed to the 'modest and virginal princesses' (Lester 2019: 203).[6] Living outside of heteronormative and patriarchal structures, these villainesses are ultimately destroyed. Throughout most of *Frozen*'s pre-production, Elsa's portrayal was directly drawing on these characters, initially conceived as a villainous '*femme fatale* or diva' (ibid.: 200). While she was ultimately reconceptualised as a sympathetic lead, her transformation in 'Let It Go' conjures up Disney's powerful and seductive villainesses. Elsa rejects the patriarchal constraints that have been imposed on her, notably discarding her father's mantra, 'conceal, don't feel': she shows agency by experimenting with her previously hidden ice powers. The song features both spectacular moments of creativity, during which she builds a snowman, an elegant staircase and an impressive ice castle, and more transgressive moments where she displays the sexual confidence of Disney's wicked witches: in the last chorus, she transforms her modest coronation dress into a revealing gown and high heels. While this transformation recalls the magical appearance and sparkling gowns of Cinderella and Ariel, it is notably self-directed – for Elsa's 'own benefit', not in the service Disney's formulaic heteronormative romance (Whitfield 2017: 229). Considering Elsa's overall narrative trajectory, namely that she is loved by her sister and accepted by her people, such a portrayal reclaims for a heroine the demonstrations of agency, power and independence formulaically associated with villainesses. As the song concludes and Elsa breaks the fourth wall, her look of defiance at the extra-diegetic audience reveals an additional layer of transgression in relation to Disney's gendered fairy-tale formula: femininity appears as an excessive performance.

In 'Let It Go', Elsa's glamorous metamorphosis also borrows from the campness of Disney's wicked witches, whose portrayal challenges the fixity of gender: femininity becomes a masquerade. While the formulaic Disney Princess possesses a 'natural beauty, one which conceals any effort taken in achieving' her look, evil women must 'construct' it: they employ 'obvious makeup and dramatic clothing in their doomed attempt to attain a desirable femininity' (Duffy 2019). *The Princess and the Frog* hints at such artificiality through Charlotte's portrayal, with her large pink gowns and elaborate makeup, while *Brave*'s younger Merida rejects it as constraining and restrictive. Lisa Duffy argues that the characterisation of villainesses goes further: witchcraft 'provides another layer of artificiality as the women harness unnatural forces to secure youth and attractiveness. It is this obvious falseness which marks these figures as camp, existing outside society's hegemonic ideals' (ibid.). Although such camp performances are associated with villainy and are ultimately erased, they queer fairy-tale femininity as displayed throughout Disney's canon, questioning the stability of its norms. In *The Little Mermaid*, camp witch Ursula notably teaches naïve Ariel about desirable femininity and heterosexual seduction, destabilising constructions of gender and exposing their inherent performativity (Sells 1995: 184). Elsa's sparkling transformation follows from these excessive portrayals: the initially reserved and modest queen adopts the smoky eye, darker lip and form-hugging dress of many fairy-tale villainesses (Duffy 2019). Her triumphant, flamboyant walk, accompanying the line 'that perfect girl is gone', reclaims the camp performance of the witches (Figure 4.3). Elsa becomes a transgressive site of contradiction: she displays the 'youthful beauty associated

Figure 4.3 *Elsa reclaims the camp performance of Disney's witches. Frame grab from* Frozen *(Buck and Lee, 2013).*

with goodness while layering a constructed image of glamour on top' (ibid.). Olaf's playful re-enactment of 'Let It Go' – notably Elsa's defiant walk – during a game of charades in *Frozen II* (Chris Buck and Jennifer Lee, 2019) retrospectively adds another layer of artificiality and excess to the original song, expanding the scope of Elsa's camp performance. All in all, the semantic and syntactic transgressions underlying her portrayal in *Frozen*'s musical sequence, added to her subversive camp performance of femininity, queer Disney's constructions of gender while pointing to alternative generic directions, ultimately expanding the studio's formulaic fairy tale.

Conclusion

As the third film in Disney's contemporary animated fairy-tale cycle, *Frozen* represents a pivotal step for the studio's reinvention and renewal of its formula. The film questions and challenges both the centrality and plausibility of romance as displayed throughout Disney's fairy-tale canon, and most particularly its underpinning, true love. Drawing on Pixar's *Brave*, *Frozen* foregrounds female relationships, namely Anna and Elsa's sisterly bond, as the most significant and empowering embodiment of 'true love', impacting on the syntactic configuration of the Disney fairy tale. In this context of revisionism and subversion, the idea of romance does not entirely disappear: it persists as the dominant mode, but its generic manifestation subtly shifts. *Frozen* revises and updates its sentimental formula by relying on multiple strands of the romantic comedy: semantic and syntactic tropes from the contemporary chick flick, the homme-com and screwballs alter and replace elements of the Disney fairy tale. Such a shift from fairy tale to romantic comedy as major generic influence stands out through the typically post-feminist use of double narratives, semantic doubling – two heroines, two male leads – and an important degree of self-reflexivity. *Frozen*'s spectacular box-office and critical success, and its enduring presence – four short films, one theatrically released sequel, a mini-series, attractions and merchandising – suggest that, after a decade of *Shrek*, Disney has managed to reconquer its central position within the animated fairy-tale landscape, while notably re-envisioning its romantic formula.

Beyond Disney's cinematic universe, *Frozen*'s considerable success reveals the profound generic influence and central position of the romantic comedy within the contemporary Hollywood landscape. Far from a niche genre, it actually surfaces in a multitude of films, including notable blockbusters. Animated features, and most specifically contemporary Disney fairy tales, reveal the wide-ranging presence of and illuminate changing trends within the romantic comedy. Studying *The Princess and the Frog*, *Tangled* and *Frozen* from this generic perspective, namely as non-canonical romantic comedies, illuminates semantic and syntactic hybridisations between the fairy tale and strands of romance: from the post-feminist fantasies of fairy-tale weddings to the screwball dynamics of animated couples. Such a generic perspective also reveals the scope of Disney's continuous dialogue with Hollywood, reappropriating tropes within and beyond its cinematic universe in order to renew the studio's formula, while preserving some aspects of its iconic identity.

Disney's contemporary cycle of animated fairy tales illustrates how the studio revived a genre which has come to signify Disney: *The Princess and the Frog*, *Tangled* and *Frozen* draw on a familiar canon to nostalgically celebrate, knowingly parody, and self-reflexively question the studio's formula, carefully maintaining a balance between preservation and subversion. Through its generic revisionism and the character of Elsa, whose portrayal particularly queers the gendered and romantic framework of Disney's formula, *Frozen* points to the significant influence of another mode characterising the 2008–18 decade, coinciding with Disney's expansion of its multimedia properties. The studio's contemporary output notably reappropriates a variety of action-adventure genres, interacting most consistently with tropes from Pixar and Marvel, and looking outside of Disney's animated intertext to renew and expand its generic formula. The following chapters turn to the centrality of Disney's generic dialogue with action-adventure cinema.

Notes

1. For further details on *Brave*'s merchandising, see Furo et al. 2016: 217–18.
2. See Chapter 3 for a discussion of these gendered tropes.

3. Examples of romantic comedies based on triangular configurations, namely featuring an unsuitable partner, include screwballs such as *Bringing Up Baby* (Howard Hawks, 1938) and *The Philadelphia Story* (George Cukor, 1940), neo-traditional romantic comedies like *Sleepless in Seattle* (Nora Ephron, 1993) and *You've Got Mail* (Nora Ephron, 1998), and more recent post-feminist chick flicks such as the *Bridget Jones* trilogy (2001, 2004, 2016) and *27 Dresses*.
4. In the penultimate scene of *ParaNorman*, seemingly stereotypical high-school jock Mitch is revealed to be gay: when cheerleader Courtney asks him on a movie date, he mentions that his 'boyfriend' is a 'chick-flick nut'.
5. For further discussion of queerness in relation to *Frozen*, see Langsdale 2014; Charania and Albertson 2018; Brugué and Llompart 2020; Mittermeier 2021.
6. It should be noted that the representation of female sexuality and seduction prior to the time period under study in this book is notably different in relation to non-white princesses and heroines. See Lacroix 2004.

Part 2

Disney and Action Adventure

CHAPTER 5

Animating the Digital Action-adventure Spectacle

During the 2008–18 decade, Disney not only notably revised the studio's formula of fairy-tale romance but also ventured into and re-envisioned action-adventure cinema. This chapter specifically illuminates how the studio reframed the digital action-adventure spectacle, expanding the generic scope of its constructed formula in the process. Relying on *Bolt* (Byron Howard and Chris Williams, 2008), *Wreck-It Ralph* (Rich Moore, 2012), *Big Hero 6* (Don Hall and Chris Williams, 2014) and *Moana* (Ron Clements and John Musker, 2016) as case studies, this chapter examines how Disney animation reproduced action-adventure visuals and thrills, self-reflexively questioned the *mise en scène* behind such a dazzling experience, and expanded the generic boundaries of the potentially empowering action spectacle.

The selected case studies reveal the breadth of Disney's generic explorations and reappropriations. *Bolt* focuses on a dog which is unknowingly the lead of an American television show. The latter features his fast-paced adventures as a 'super dog', helping his owner Penny (Miley Cyrus) to find her father, captured by villain Dr Calico (Malcolm McDowell). *Wreck-It Ralph* follows video-game 'bad guy' Ralph (John C. Reilly) on his quest to prove his worth, venturing into several games including first-person shooter 'Hero's Duty' and kart-racing game 'Sugar Rush'. *Big Hero 6* depicts a team of young superheroes led by teenage genius Hiro (Ryan Potter) and his robotic nurse Baymax (Scott Adsit), investigating the death of Hiro's brother in the fictional city of San Fransokyo. In *Moana*, the title character sets out on a perilous journey across the Pacific Ocean to find demigod Maui (Dwayne Johnson) and save her island from destruction.

These synopses hint at the multifaceted action-adventure influences observable in Disney's contemporary output in terms of narrative, character dynamic, aesthetics and gender constructions. *Bolt*, *Wreck-It Ralph*, *Big Hero 6* and *Moana* semantically and syntactically distance themselves from Disney's iconic fairy-tale genre: there are no enchanted kingdoms, no princes and princesses – both *Wreck-It Ralph*'s Vanellope and Moana explicitly refuse this generic label. These animated films generically look outwards to re-envision the Disney formula, while revisiting generic tropes and boundaries within the action mode. This chapter analyses how *Bolt*, *Wreck-It Ralph*, *Big Hero 6* and *Moana* rework the digital action-adventure spectacle in three interrelated ways. Disney animated films knowingly and playfully reproduce the visuals and thrills of the genre; they challenge the artifices of such action performances and displays; and they generically expand the empowering potential of the action-adventure experience for the protagonists. Relying on such a generic perspective reveals the extent of Disney's dialogue with contemporary Hollywood cinema, beyond the romantic mode, and opens up new areas for the study of the action-adventure genre.

Since the 2000s, the action-adventure mode has dominated contemporary mainstream animation, as exemplified by successful computer-animated franchises such as Pixar's *Toy Story* (1995, 1999, 2010, 2019), Blue Sky's *Ice Age* (2002, 2006, 2009, 2012, 2016), DreamWorks' *Kung-Fu Panda* (2008, 2011, 2016) and *How to Train Your Dragon* (2010, 2014, 2019), and Illumination's *Despicable Me* (2010, 2013, 2015, 2017, 2022). The action-adventure mode was initially prioritised by newer studios to differentiate their output from Disney's, which had been mostly associated with the hand-drawn fairy tale and the musical.

Yet, although not as iconic as *Snow White and the Seven Dwarfs* (David Hand, 1937) or *Beauty and the Beast* (Gary Trousdale and Kirk Wise, 1991), numerous Disney animated films have engaged with the action mode. They initially borrowed from genres such as the swashbuckling and pirate film, as in *Peter Pan* (Clyde Geronimi and Wilfred Jackson, 1953), *The Sword in the Stone* (Wolfgang Reitherman, 1963), and *Robin Hood* (Wolfgang Reitherman, 1973). With growing competition from other animation studios, Disney's generic influences started to diversify from the mid-1990s onwards, including sword-and-sandal in *Hercules* (Ron Clements and John Musker, 1997), war film in *Mulan* (Tony Bancroft and Barry Cook, 1998), and science fiction in *Lilo & Stitch* (Dean DeBlois and Chris Sanders, 2002) and *Treasure Planet* (Ron Clements and John Musker, 2002). Simultaneously, these animated features toned down their musical heritage, with films such as *Atlantis: The Lost Empire* (Gary Trousdale and Kirk Wise, 2001) including no diegetic songs. Disney also relied increasingly on CGI, as epitomised in *Mulan*'s Huns' charge sequence, particularly foregrounded in trailers.[1] However, as discussed in Chapter 1, the limited success of these films compared with the hits of Disney's Renaissance period, alongside the critical and academic focus on fairy-tale musicals, and the latter's continuous presence throughout Disney's synergistic machine, has arguably downplayed the presence and influence of the action mode throughout Disney's canon.

By contrast, since the mid-2000s, Disney has explicitly and largely adopted action-adventure as a recurring generic template with films such as *Bolt*,

Wreck-It Ralph, *Big Hero 6*, *Moana*, as well as generically hybrid *Frozen* (Chris Buck and Jennifer Lee, 2013) and *Zootopia* (Byron Howard and Rich Moore, 2016), which will be analysed in subsequent chapters. Such a predominance of the action mode within both Disney and mainstream animation partly comes from what Eric Lichtenfeld describes as the 'overlap of the aging-down action movie and the aging-up family film' (2007: 322). This phenomenon is exemplified by the multiplication of superhero live-action films based on comic books, and the growing number of animated features labelled as 'family films' but rated PG for 'action violence' (ibid.: 322–3). Accompanying this generic move, Disney has primarily shifted to computer animation, following the disappointing box office results of early 2000s hand-drawn animated features.[2] Within this saturated, digital action-adventure milieu, where does contemporary Disney animation stand?

Looking at the critical reception of *Bolt*, *Wreck-It Ralph*, *Big Hero 6* and *Moana*, it seems that the perceived identity of Disney animation has dissolved into a mode that is ubiquitous in mainstream cinema, yet clashes with the idea of the studio's formula. For example, reviewers underlined the conventional nature of films such as *Big Hero 6*, which relies too heavily on another ubiquitous formula belonging to action adventure: the Marvel superhero live-action film. Peter Debruge (2014) criticised the fact that the 'filmmakers felt obliged to resort to a final battle with a less-than-special villain' characterised by 'relatively generic . . . power hungry schemes'. Jordan Hoffman (2014) similarly described the 'interminable third act featuring a deadly, mayhem-causing portal to another dimension' as an unavoidable feature of this 'kid version of *The Avengers*'. Claiming that 'the Disney Marvel Universe is already filled to bursting with big heroes', Debruge questioned the very point of Disney's animated addition to the genre (2014).

Yet, the perceived originality of Disney's computer-animated version of the action-adventure film surfaced in specific ways, drawing on the studio's generic intertext and aesthetic. Reviewers particularly noted the comic and endearing friendship between young protagonist Hiro and his healthcare robot Baymax: Hoffman argued that this duo helps 'differentiate [*Big Hero 6*] from usual fare' (2014); Dan Jolin underlined that 'it's in the burgeoning . . . friendship between Baymax and Hiro that we find *Big Hero 6*'s most humorous moments' (2014); Michael Rechtshaffen particularly remarked that 'Baymax handily steals the show . . . to maximum comic effect' (2014). Such an emphasis on an unlikely human–anthropomorphic friendship echoes the structure of *Lilo & Stitch* and many other Disney animated films. Elements specific to Disney were also observed at the aesthetic level. Although critics praised *Moana*'s state-of-the-art computer animation, they also focused on how smoothly the style of hand-drawn animation was incorporated throughout the film. Debruge admired Moana's 'expressions . . . reflecting all the subtleties of performance possible in hand-drawn animation' (2016a); Robbie Collin particularly noted the design of the ocean wave: 'the effortless expressivity of that single, curved line . . . is an invisible triumph of tactile visual thinking' (2016a). All in all, what was repeatedly foregrounded was a fruitful balance between 'technological prowess' and a 'hand-drawn aesthetic that feels genuinely expressive and spontaneous', as Collin observed (ibid.). Such comments echo the praise surrounding *Tangled*'s computer animation: reviewers appreciated 'I See the Light' partly because the musical sequence skilfully rendered the organic quality of pre-digital animation. Reviewers also welcomed the presence in *Moana* of Disney's more familiar generic tropes. For example, A. O. Scott underlined that *Moana* included both 'visual and musical showstoppers' (2016), reminiscent of *The Little Mermaid* for Devon Coggan (2016) and *Frozen* for Nick De Semlyen (2016). This brief overview of the critical reception of Disney's action-adventure animated films reveals that, beyond fairy-tale romance and princesses, the presence of humorously lovable characters and endearing duos, musical sequences, and hand-drawn animation style are perceived and praised as essential components of Disney features – or rather, preserved aspects of the studio's formula. These specific visual and generic tropes form the basis for the studio's distinctive approach to the action-adventure film.

Yvonne Tasker describes the action-adventure genre as the combination of 'adventure', namely 'narratives of quest and discovery', and 'action', associated with 'scenes of combat, violence and pursuit' (2015: 2). Considering that such sequences and narratives are 'ubiquitous' within Hollywood cinema, Tasker approaches action adventure as an 'over-arching term' in order to acknowledge its multiplicity and hybridity: a central cinematic mode alongside romance (ibid.: 3, 19). Disney consistently incorporates the multiple characteristics and genres of action adventure throughout its contemporary output. For example, *Bolt*'s thrilling explosions and chases are combined with a narrative evoking the spy film and the road movie; *Wreck-It Ralph*'s interactions with the video-game film and gaming culture more generally allow for a wide range of action set pieces, from battles in the 'high-definition . . . futuristic, science-fiction world' of 'Hero's Duty' to kart chases on the colourful tracks of 'Sugar Rush' (Lee and Malone 2012: 51).[3] Tasker observes that, despite the varied iconography of action-adventure genres, they share a common emphasis on impressive set design and special effects, presenting an awe-inspiring cinematic spectacle (2015: 12).

The concept of spectacle is at the core of the action mode, based on visual displays 'at which we might wish to stop and stare . . . "larger than life" representations' (King 2000: 4). Digital effects favour such contemplation, from *Moana*'s breath-taking seascapes to *Bolt*'s stirring stunts. The action-adventure spectacle not only dazzles the audience but also strikes and impacts them. The high speed of perilous chases exemplifies the 'centrality of movement' in action-adventure films, creating a 'sensational' cinema (Tasker 2015: 49).

Larger-than-life representations and dynamic movement characterise another kind of spectacle: the musical. Geoff King notes that both the Hollywood musical and action adventure overflow with 'energy and intensity, on both the actions of the characters and the dynamics of cinematography' (2000: 102–3). Punctuating the films, action set-pieces and musical numbers have also been compared for the structural function they share: both play 'an important role in dramatizing the themes of a movie and drawing audiences in emotionally' (Tasker 2015: 16). Another key parallel is the concept of performance. Numerous musicals are 'about putting on a show', revealing their 'own inner gears to the film audience' (Feuer 1993: 23, 42). This self-reflexive dimension also applies to action adventure to some extent. Protagonists often knowingly comment on the impossibility of stunts, or on their breath-taking, over-the-top nature. For example, in *The Other Guys* (Adam McKay, 2010), Detective Allen (Will Ferrell) struggles after the explosion of a nearby shop, screaming, 'How do they walk away in movies without flinching when it explodes behind them? There's no way! I call bullshit on that!' This film is part of a wider trend of action films in the late 2000s and early 2010s which show a 'developed awareness of the conventions and tropes of action cinema' (Purse 2011a: 189). This trend includes 'mock or spoof action' films, such as *Tropic Thunder* (Ben Stiller, 2008) and *Red* (Robert Schwentke, 2010), alongside 'nostalgic remakes or homages', like *The A-Team* (Joe Carnham, 2010) and *The Expendables* franchise (2010, 2012, 2014) (Purse 2011a: 189).

It is in this context that *Bolt*, *Wreck-It Ralph*, *Big Hero 6* and *Moana* can be approached: action-adventure spectacle, or rather the performance of it, is at the core of Disney's generic reworking. This chapter focuses on the three most distinctive layers of this reworking. At the surface level, these films remarkably and humorously reproduce the dazzling visuals of live-action action-adventure through computer animation, as pioneered and influenced by Pixar. I pay attention to the way certain aspects of animation aesthetics typically associated with Disney are preserved, representing a potential selling point throughout Disney's discourses of promotion. I also examine how these films preserve the thrills of the genre, while mitigating its photorealistic violence and excesses.

Bolt, *Wreck-It Ralph*, *Big Hero 6* and *Moana* not only humorously reproduce impressive live-action action-adventure displays but also foreground and challenge their artificial nature. At a second level, I explore how they self-reflexively interact with the techniques of both computer animation and pre-digital animation to re-envision the action spectacle as an illusionistic *mise en scène*, depending on the performance of its actors and audience. After having unveiled the action-adventure staging and undermined the action hero's status, they reconstruct a more authentic, unmediated performance.

In parallel, some specific action spectacles are staged as exhilarating and empowering experiences for the protagonists. At a third level, I examine how Disney animated features expand the generic borders of action-adventure by drawing on the studio's musical roots. In the process, they reimagine and take further the relationship between the two spectacular genres, as epitomised in their explicit merging in *Moana*.

Exploring the multilayered reworking of the digital action-adventure spectacle in *Bolt*, *Wreck-It Ralph*, *Big Hero 6* and *Moana*, this chapter elaborates on two interrelated points: the extent to which the studio questions and re-envisions action-adventure genres, and how Disney updates and differentiates its generic and aesthetic approach in the process, while expanding the studio's formula.

From Live-action to Animation Milieus: Playfully Transposing the Dazzling Digital Spectacle of Action Adventure

Bolt, *Wreck-It Ralph*, *Big Hero 6* and *Moana* reproduce the dazzling digital spectacle of action adventure by relying on Pixar's state-of-the-art technological tools and aesthetic. At the same time, they foreground a particularly humorous approach towards the excesses, thrills and photorealistic impulses of the digital action spectacle. They build on and develop a sense of knowingness already at the core of some action-adventure films. The playful approach of *Bolt*, *Wreck-It Ralph*, *Big Hero 6* and *Moana* is also based on elements typically associated with Disney and its aesthetic style. As live-action action-adventure films rely more and more on computer-generated imaging, and computer-animated action-adventure films are multiplying, Disney's challenge is to preserve its singularity as an iconic animation studio, while relying on the same digital tools and generic framework.

In live-action cinema, digital imaging is mainly used to render 'impossible vistas and impossible bodies' onscreen, elements that would not have been convincing with analogue technology in earlier decades (Purse 2013: 25). Even when action adventure borrows from fantasy, protagonists' exploits are depicted in a photorealistic way, as if they had occurred in front of the camera (ibid.: 6–7). This implies credibility and seamlessness in the inclusion of visual effects (Halfyard 2013: 184). Such an effort to erase any trace of digital intervention is consistent with the style of mainstream live-action cinema. Lev Manovich observes that the latter 'pretends to be a simple recording of an already existing reality' while hiding the artifices of its construction (2001: 298–9). In this context, digital characters perceived as unbelievable may compromise the level of photorealism established within the rest of the film (Purse 2013: 60). For example, Lisa Purse explains that the negative reception surrounding early digital superheroes such as *Spider-Man* (Sam Raimi, 2002) and the *Hulk* (Ang Lee, 2003) came from their inconsistent depiction, which clashed with their readily recognisable urban setting (Purse 2013: 60). Incoherent character stretching and an unconvincing sense of body mass led some reviewers to describe the Hulk as an overly cartoonish character (ibid.: 58–61). The transition from the live-action actor to their digital alter ego was perceived as 'the central problem' of the genre for Scott Bukatman, as it severed the connection between the two and undermined the aesthetic fluidity of the film (2011: 121).

Computer-animated films, in which 'everything belongs to a shared level of reality' (Bukatman 2009: 116), provide an interesting contrast to live-action films which only partially rely on the digital. Unlike mainstream live-action cinema, animation principally foregrounds its artificial character: Manovich notes that 'its visual language is more aligned to the graphic than to the photographic' (2001: 29). Both depending on exaggeration and caricature, and building on the dazzling potentials of the digital, computer animation is particularly suited to adapt the larger-than-life spectacle of action-adventure, as exemplified by Pixar's computer-animated films. For example, *Toy Story*'s (John Lasseter, 1995) images and visual effects imitate the photorealism of live-action cinema: the toys' bodies and actions function 'plausibly' within a recognisable and familiar environment (Telotte 2008: 165). This 'reality illusion', produced through Pixar's Renderman software, was reinforced through the simulation of a mechanical camera and its accompanying effects, such as lens flares and motion blur (ibid.: 165). However, Pixar distinguished its aesthetic from live-action imagery by maintaining a certain degree of caricature, notably in character design: what could be described as 'stylised realism', as discussed in Chapter 1 (Herhuth 2017: 37). This approach came from initial technological limitations, but also from the 'uncanny effect' produced by images perceived as 'too clean and perfect' (ibid.: 160–1).[4] Later films such as *The Good Dinosaur* (Peter Sohn, 2015) do achieve photorealism, but the detailed rendering of the background landscapes – lush vegetation, glistening water – is still balanced with the heavily caricatured leads. Such a hybrid aesthetic, blending photorealistic backgrounds and camerawork with cartoon-like protagonists, has become mainstream both within and beyond Hollywood animation.[5]

Disney's computer animation follows on from Pixar's stylised realism. As Disney acquired Pixar in 2006, the subsequent internal reshuffling meant that it was actually 'Pixar's hierarchy' that would drive Disney animation forward, both at a boardroom level – John Lasseter became chief creative officer of both studios – and artistically (Pallant 2013: 130–1). Disney's computer-animated features released under the new leadership similarly replicate the photorealistic visuals and effects of live-action cinematography, while depicting caricatured protagonists and stylised worlds (ibid.: 137–8). *Big Hero 6*'s first flight sequence exemplifies such a state-of-the-art aesthetically hybrid animation. Protagonist Hiro flies on robot Baymax over the fantasy cityscape of San Fransokyo, which blends visual tropes from American and Japanese architecture and environments. The simplicity of the characters' design is epitomised through Baymax's minimalist facial features: two dots linked by a straight line. This stylised look stands out from the photorealistic cloudy sky in the background. The lighting convincingly and beautifully reproduces the late-afternoon rosy light of the sun, reflected on a virtual camera as the simulation of lens flares appears onscreen. This seamless combination of animation and live-action aesthetics, namely stylised and caricatured protagonists with photorealistic cinematography, echoes comparable sequences in Pixar's *The Good Dinosaur*. Arlo, a heavily caricatured young dinosaur, befriends a human child named Spot, who behaves like an animal. These two anthropomorphised characters run through the natural landscape: Spot sits on Arlo's back, and Arlo throws him upwards, into the clouds, soaring into the photorealistic sky like Disney's Hiro and Baymax.

Although contemporary Disney appears to have aesthetically converged with Pixar, the studio strives to foreground its persisting singularity. Disney has always subtly combined innovation and tradition regarding animation aesthetics, building on its long history of cel animation: this is what distinguishes the studio's approach to the digital action-adventure spectacle.

The discourses of promotion surrounding *Bolt*, the first computer-animated feature entirely supervised by Disney's new leadership, positioned the film within the continuity of Disney's past hand-drawn releases. *The Art of Bolt* particularly emphasised the 'painterly style' of the film (Cotta Vaz 2008: 11). Such an aesthetic was reportedly inspired by 'classic Americana painters' such as Edward Hopper, and rendered through the reproduction of a 'brushstroke effect' in the backgrounds (ibid.: 122). For example, as Bolt (John Travolta) and his animal friends Mittens (Susie Essman) and Rhino (Mark Walton) travel through the United States, the American landscape unfolds through a montage of painterly sequences featuring motorways, country fields and snowy mountains. *Bolt*'s painterly style is mostly noticeable in sequences evoking the road movie genre and characterising the real non-mediated world of the film. By contrast, art director Paul Felix underlines that the aesthetic of the action-adventure television programme shown within the film leans towards photorealism, borrowing more explicitly from the look of live-action cinematography (quoted in ibid.: 122).

The transition from the world of *Bolt* to the titular television show epitomises these generically dependent aesthetic variations. The film opens with the moving adoption of lovable puppy Bolt by young Penny (Chloë Grace Moretz) at an animal rescue centre. Naturalistic lighting and muted, painterly colours help create a warm, intimate atmosphere to depict the new happy family. A title card ('Five years later') introduces a shift to the action-adventure show 'Bolt'. Several cuts to black punctuate a phone conversation between Penny and her 'father', creating a disorienting sense of tension enhanced by saturated colours and a play on expressive shadows. Functioning as a credit sequence, it provides the synopsis for the television show: Penny's father is a scientist who has been mysteriously kidnapped, but managed to transform Bolt into a super-dog in order to protect Penny. This variation of aesthetic styles points towards the singularity of Disney's computer animation, framing the studio's generic commentary. *Bolt* alternates between two-dimensional styles and photorealistic digital effects to contrast specific genre moments in the film. Action-adventure sequences stand out as particularly dazzling, playful and ultimately parodic reproductions of the live-action action spectacle.

Disney most spectacularly demonstrates its parodic mastery of live-action action adventure later in the 'Bolt' episode, with a thrilling chase throughout the city and its beltway. It starts as a typically gripping and well-executed action sequence. The increasing speed of Penny riding her scooter and Bolt running along is enhanced by the accelerating digitally simulated camera movement: the camera tracks with them as they zigzag between cars and trucks and avoid a growing number of henchmen on motorcycles. This dynamic pace slows down at key moments of the chase to showcase Bolt's spectacular powers, most notably through a process called 'speed ramping'. Particularly popular in contemporary live-action action-adventure films, it enables an 'intensified focus on the body in motion' through the alteration of speed within a shot (Purse 2011a: 68). For example, it occurs when Bolt jumps high over a helicopter, a few inches from the rotor blades, in order to avoid a missile. As the action almost halts, the audience is encouraged to stare in amazement at Bolt's impressive feat. The pace accelerates again when Bolt successfully lands on his feet. The missile that was tracking him hits the helicopter instead, leading to a spectacular explosion displayed in a way that effectively reproduces the 'impact aesthetic' (ibid.: 59) of live-action action-adventure. The same exploding helicopter is shown four times in a row via multiple reframings. The four shots rapidly succeed each other, taking the audience closer to the smoke and fire which fill the screen in the third shot. However, this striking and staggering sight, typical of action-adventure spectacles, is humorously undermined through the fourth shot of the roaring explosion. Shown in an extreme long shot, it turns into a silent yellow dot lost between skyscrapers, its sole impact being the fall of a plastic cup in the foreground. These contrasting shots comically subvert the necessarily increasing scale of 'thrills and destruction' (King 2000: 100) typical of action film style, subverting their dramatic scope.

The last scene of the episode brings *Bolt*'s action-adventure parody further. The chase culminates when Penny and Bolt are trapped on a road with cars, SUVs and helicopters heading towards them. Bolt's 'super-bark' triggers a shock wave that throws all of these into the air. Smoke, debris and vehicles fill up the screen, hurled towards the digitally simulated camera and displayed from multiple angles, taking the audience both to the heart of and above the chaotic scene. Efficiently imitating the 'impact aesthetic' introduced earlier, the scene also stands out through its excess: the considerable number of vehicles, the disproportionate effect of tiny Bolt's 'superbark'. The scene becomes a genre joke, a nod to what Tasker describes as the 'gleeful and spectacular destruction of property' (2015: 186) which frames the climactic battle scenes of live-action action-adventure films such as *The Avengers* (Joss Whedon, 2012).

Throughout the film, Disney subtly yet consistently mocks the formulaic visual and aural tropes of live-action action adventure, as in the television programme that 'Bolt' fan Rhino is introduced watching. Although the television set remains off screen, a tough male voice ('Hey man, this time, we'll do it my way') and bullet sounds are heard. Mocking genre clichés such as the witty one-liner and the shoot-out, this sequence also hints at action-adventure excessive gun violence, notably absent from *Bolt*. When Bolt finds his way back to Hollywood, he passes in front of film posters, including one which points to the stock visuals of the stereotypical live-action action film. Entitled 'Blast Radius', it features a suited man unflinchingly walking ahead, gun in hand, with a fireball and explosions in the background. This poster mocks further the systematic reliance on violence and over-the-top destruction of live-action action cinema.

Bolt's multifaceted generic playfulness also characterises Disney's wider action-adventure animated canon. *Wreck-It Ralph*, for example, parodically repurposes the process of speed ramping, humorously defusing the tension underlying the live-action action spectacle and undermining the aura of the action hero. In the video game 'Hero's Duty', Ralph is attacked by a tiny Cy-Bug, a deceptively harmless creature that is half-cyborg, half-bug. He leaves the game in an escape pod, but fails to keep the vehicle under control, as the Cy-Bug clings onto his face and blinds him. The pace is slowed down at the very moment his pod flies at characters' eye level. Two characters (Felix and Calhoun) look up: Ralph appears in slow motion, struggling against the Cy-Bug. Instead of displaying the 'postures of mastery' described by Purse as typical of action adventure (2011a: 68), here speed ramping foregrounds Ralph's comical helplessness, as he grimaces and screams while being overpowered by a small Cy-Bug.[6]

Many live-action action-adventure franchises, such as *Lethal Weapon* (1987, 1989, 1992, 1998) or *Charlie's Angels* (2000, 2003, 2019), mock their own conventions at times, or knowingly foreground the impossible nature of digitally enhanced action feats (Romney 2000: 35; Purse 2013: 20). Other animated films reappropriate live-action digital effects like speed ramping, as exemplified in *Shrek*'s (Andrew Adamson and Vicky Jenson, 2001) parodic *Matrix*-style fight between Princess Fiona and Robin Hood's Merry Men. What further distinguishes Disney's approach is the addition of generic tropes specifically associated with early animation. *Bolt*, *Wreck-It Ralph*, *Big Hero 6* and *Moana* rely on episodes of cartoon comedy to both counterbalance and subvert live-action tension and violence. Echoing Chuck Jones's Road Runner gags, these sequences rely on repetition and present the animated body as indestructible – or rather, the slapstick as harmless.

In *Moana*, for example, some spectacular and potentially dangerous action feats are undermined through cartoon comedy. As Moana (Auli'i Cravalho) jumps from a cliff to reach Maui and get her boat back, she lands flat on her belly, a few inches from the boat. Finally on board with the help of the sentient ocean, she starts a prepared speech; Maui interrupts her by throwing her overboard. The same scene reoccurs straight away, then a third time later in the film. Its repetitive nature and harmless effect – recalling the multiple frying pan hits received by Flynn in *Tangled* (Nathan Greno and Byron Howard, 2010) – render the act more comic than potentially violent. The sequence of the Kakamora attack is another example of action-oriented tension counterbalanced with cartoon humour. The Kakamoras are silent, small pirates who wear coconut shells with static facial features drawn onto them as armour. Although Moana actively hits them with an oar, their diminutive stature and simplified, caricatured aesthetic – angry eyes, pointy teeth – lend a comedic tone to the action.

This cartoony, almost endearing appearance also gives the Kakamoras a particularly appealing look, which playfully defuses their threatening potential. They contrast significantly with the frightening skeleton pirates from the live-action Disney film *Pirates of the Caribbean: The Curse of the Black Pearl* (Gore Verbinski, 2003). Although both pirate crews are computer-animated, Verbinski's pirates tend towards a photorealistic rendition of decaying corpses, within the context of a live-action action-adventure film borrowing from the horror genre. By contrast, the Kakamoras' design exemplifies Disney's play with the conventions of action-adventure through the caricatured style of hand-drawn aesthetics.

Their appearance also represents a nod to the studio's own animation style: as Moana initially exclaims, 'they're kind of cute!' The addition of animated cuteness within an action-adventure context undermines further the threat posed by the digital villain or monster. Art director of characters Bill Schwab describes the Kakamoras as 'cute-scary' (quoted in Julius and Malone 2016: 114); in *Wreck-It Ralph*, the ravening Cy-Bugs were conceived as both 'creepy' and 'cute' (Lee and Malone 2012: 79). 'Disarming cuteness' has been a staple part of Disney animation since the 1930s (Watts 1997: 104) and the aesthetic underlying of the studio's formula, which has recurrently been satirised and subverted. From the introduction to *Red Hot Riding Hood* (Tex Avery, 1943) to the portrayal of Puss in Boots in *Shrek 2* (Andrew Adamson, Kelly Asbury and Conrad Vernon, 2004), harmlessly cheerful, big-eyed characters have functioned as parodic references to Disney's sentimental impulses. The studio's contemporary output acknowledges and reappropriates these parodies: cuteness is attributed not only to lovable sidekicks – such as Pua in *Moana* or Olaf in *Frozen* – but also to hordes of little villains, such as the Kakamoras and Cy-Bugs.

Playing with characters' and viewers' generic expectations, as illustrated through Moana's comment, Disney's aesthetic of cuteness also characterises unlikely action heroes, such as Bolt's hamster sidekick Rhino. Although he is small, fluffy – as a film extra exclaims, 'you're so cute with your little whiskers' – and rarely leaves his hamster ball, he single-handedly delivers Bolt from a dog catcher's truck. This efficiency comes from his passion for and knowledge of action-adventure genres. His recurrent comments on the ongoing action spectacle both help contextualise the narrative and mock predictable generic tropes, such as the 'pep talk' to the action hero and the importance of his sidekicks. Like Fred (T. J. Miller) in *Big Hero 6* ('We're under attack from a super-villain, people'), Rhino's characterisation represents one of Disney's many strategies for generic knowingness and self-reflexivity. Beyond their skilful reproduction of the dazzling spectacle of action adventure, *Bolt*, *Wreck-It Ralph*, *Big Hero 6* and *Moana* rely on animation as a form to foreground and challenge the illusory aspects of the digital action spectacle.

Questioning and Distancing the Action Spectacle: Animated *Mise en Scène* and Performance

Bolt, *Wreck-It Ralph*, *Big Hero 6* and *Moana* question the *mise en scène* behind the digital action spectacle, relying on Disney's unique status as a studio that both possesses a long history of hand-drawn animation and is now releasing successful computer-animated films. Disney's distinctive animation aesthetic does not solely serve a humorous purpose, parodically subverting the excesses and tension of live-action action adventure. *Bolt*, *Wreck-It Ralph*, *Big Hero 6* and *Moana* also self-reflexively build on both pre-digital and digital animation styles to deconstruct the elaborate yet artificial action-adventure performance.

In order to approach the specific kind of self-reflexivity at work in Disney's action-adventure animated films, the 'backstage musical' provides a useful generic framework. Such a perspective builds on and explores further the affinities between action films and musicals introduced earlier. Richard Dyer describes the backstage musical as an early trend of the wider Hollywood musical, including films such as *Gold Diggers of 1933* (Mervyn LeRoy, 1933) and *42nd Street* (Lloyd Bacon, 1933), in which narrative and number are kept clearly separated: musical performances occur independently, onstage or in cabarets (2002: 26). Jane Feuer applies this generic label more widely, considering later musicals such as *Easter Parade* (Charles Walters, 1948) and *The Band Wagon* (Vincente Minnelli, 1953), which adopt a more integrated approach towards numbers but also unveil and explore the 'backstage' world behind some of the performances. These films take the audience to places they would not have access to, such as the wings, detailing the elaboration and practice of musical productions (Feuer 1993: 42). The penchant of backstage musicals for revealing their 'own inner gears' demystifies the 'illusion' of the live performance: these films reveal the stage paraphernalia used to create the 'magic', and show the performers out of character (ibid.: 42). The overall effect is to reframe the production as 'an act of extreme calculation' and as a routine, a mere 'job' (ibid.: 42).

Disney animated films function as backstage action-adventure films, demystifying the digital action spectacle in ways which resonate with their live-action musical counterparts. *Bolt* is a *mise en abyme*, depicting the shooting of the eponymous action-adventure television programme. After Bolt's spectacular 'super bark', a bell rings: seemingly dead extras stand up and leave what turns out to be a television set, with a fake airport background being lifted and a film crew carrying surprisingly light car props. Cat-actors practise their 'evil laugh' and one-liners, while Bolt does not understand that their behaviour is a teasing performance. The subsequent episode deconstructs further the extreme calculation behind the display of Bolt's superpowers. For example, the bars he bends are made of rubber, and the weapon destroyed through his 'heat vision' is automatically dismantled at a distance by a crew member. The 'heat vision' itself cannot be seen – it was displayed in the earlier episode – which suggests that it would be digitally added in post-production.

This visual trick not only foregrounds the digital mediation at the core of the action spectacle and performance but also reveals the extent to which the viewer's gaze is manipulated. The second episode alternates between the 'wings' of the television show, namely the control room in which the director gives his instructions, and the television set, where hidden camera operators accordingly 'widen out camera 3' and 'track with' Penny and Bolt. Revealing the artifices of both live-action cinema and the action performance, this particular emphasis on the manipulation of the gaze also functions as a comment on the very act of watching the action spectacle. The first episode already hinted at such constructedness, beginning with Penny and Bolt spying on the villain through binoculars. The audience shares their viewpoint: a henchman is sitting with his back to the camera, in the foreground, looking at a screen on which Dr Calico (the show's villain) explains his plans. These multiple frames, including the frame of the binoculars and the frame on which Calico is projected, are accompanied by a multiplication of diegetic audiences, which sets the tone for the television episode: theatricality, explicit stagings, and more particularly digital mediation will be at the core of the action spectacle. Similarly, the subsequent display of Bolt's spectacular feats systematically includes characters watching: Penny looking up at the car thrown in the air by Bolt, the helicopter pilot looking up at Bolt jumping above him. Along with the use of speed ramping, this self-conscious display does not solely invite audiences 'to be amazed and to enjoy the spectacle', as Tasker notes of action movies (2015: 69). These meticulous stagings play a key narrative role, hinting at the constructedness of Bolt's world: like the latter, the audience must learn to decode the extreme calculation behind the action spectacle. Such decoding is permitted through incursions into the backstage world of the action-adventure television show.

Wreck-It Ralph and *Big Hero 6* also deconstruct the illusion on which the action spectacle rests, especially the digital component of its *mise en scène*. *Big Hero 6* takes the audience behind the scenes of digital production, showing Hiro designing the super suits of his friends on his computer screen before fabricating them. His 'pre-production' work for Baymax includes the transfer via motion capture of martial arts combat moves onto a chip he installs into Baymax's access port – not unlike like the digital filmmaking process itself (Figure 5.1). While the work of digital animator Hiro goes relatively

Figure 5.1 *Hiro's 'pre-production' work for Baymax. Frame grab from* Big Hero 6 *(Hall and Williams, 2014).*

smoothly, the illusionist dimension of the digital action performance is deconstructed more explicitly in *Wreck-It Ralph*, most strikingly through the depiction of video-game character Vanellope (Sarah Silverman). As a 'glitch', her digital representation is unstable: her animated body repeatedly breaks into dozens of pixels. Alan Meades notes that glitches subvert game spaces, exposing the incoherent inner workings of digital technology (2015: 281). Building on Meades's point, Vanellope's depiction challenges the seamless inclusion of digital effects within live-action cinema, foregrounding instead the constructedness, and potential anomalies, of the digital spectacle.

Digital mediation is central to *Wreck-It Ralph*, which opens with a computer-animated *mise en abyme*: the screen of an arcade game ('Fix-It Felix') inhabited by pixelated, 2D 8-bit characters, is framed by the more photorealistic 3D world of the arcade. The borders of the screen are reminiscent of a proscenium. On this 2D stage, 8-bit Ralph is introduced as the 'bad guy' who wrecks the building that 'good guy' Felix (Jack McBrayer) fixes, helping the 'Nicelanders'. As the digitally simulated camera passes through the screen of the arcade game console, the aesthetic shifts from 2D to 3D. This 'alternative reality behind the screen' (Wood 2015: 87) evokes the wings of the musical. As the audience is taken into the backstage world of 'Fix-It Felix', the game is revealed to be a performance, a mere routine for Felix and his friends ('Quittin' time . . . Good job everyone!'). Out of character, Ralph actually appears kind-hearted and suffers from his marginalised position: his 3D portrayal differs notably from his simplistic 8-bit stage persona.

This self-reflexive use of digital animation, and more particularly the ostentatious shifts from one animation style to another, are specific to Disney action-adventure films. Other animated features, such as Pixar's, develop a self-reflexive approach through animated *mise en abyme*. Christopher Holliday observes that computer-animated film narratives 'commonly grant spectators the intrigue of a puppet/puppeteer relationship . . . creatively "doubl[ing]" the kinds of interaction between animators and their digital objects' (2018a: 131). Examples include the *Toy Story* franchise, in which toys are acted upon by children, and *Ratatouille* (Brad Bird, 2007), in which Remy the rat controls Linguini's moves while he cooks by pulling on his hair. *Wreck-It Ralph*'s characters are also being acted upon by gamers. However, what is specific to Disney is that the explicitly different 2D aesthetic of Ralph's performance foregrounds the constructedness of the game and correspondingly of the action feats of 8-bit Ralph and Felix. Disney action-adventure films tend to imitate 2D or pre-digital animation for generic purposes, challenging the authenticity of the action performance.[7]

Disney's animated action-adventure output relies on self-reflexive *mise en scène* not only to demystify protagonists' feats but also to question the very definition of the 'action hero', revealing the importance of the diegetic audience in attributing this label. For example, in *Wreck-It Ralph*, the settings and characters of 'Fix-It Felix' are recreated through an elaborate cake for an anniversary party. Their malleable texture is reminiscent of plasticine stop-motion figurines: this pre-digital, pre-production version of the game reinforces the marginalised position of Ralph as a villain. While all the Nicelanders are found on the roof of their building with Felix receiving a medal, Ralph is found at the bottom, alone, in the (chocolate) mud. He is depicted as a deranged monster scarily waving his arms, with red eyes, an angry grimace, and missing teeth (Figure 5.2). Ralph tries to reappropriate this heavily mediated representation of himself by reshaping the cake figurine: he traces a smile on its face, places it on top of the building, and adds a medal to it. One Nicelander opposes this reshaped version by putting the figurine back into the mud, stating that Ralph is 'just the bad guy who wrecks the building'. While in the previous sequence Ralph was introduced as a sympathetic character with spectacular – though initially destructive – wrecking abilities, this little stop-motion staging reasserts his 'action villain' label. The sequence also shows that such denominations depend on a *mise en scène* staged and commented upon by an audience: the Nicelanders surrounding Ralph genuinely perceive him as a dangerous and scary character, correspondingly depicted through the cake figurine.

In *Moana*, the depiction of the audience assessing the exploits of action hero and demigod Maui is part of an elaborate, yet ultimately illusory re-enactment of his spectacular feats. During his song 'You're Welcome', his heroic deeds are animated on his skin, as his tattooed alter ego 'Mini-Maui' is shown lassoing the sun, harnessing the breeze, and pulling islands from the sea. Imitating the caricatured aesthetic and minimalist, expressive line of 2D hand-drawn

Figure 5.2 *Ralph represented as a plasticine-like deranged monster. Frame grab from* Wreck-It Ralph *(Moore, 2012).*

animation, this staging includes a cheering crowd – Mini-Maui's action-adventure spectators – lifting Mini-Maui up. In this re-enactment, the spectators actually reflect Maui's distorted perception of his own abilities and aura as an action hero. Later in the film, he struggles and needs Moana's help, learning to work within an action team.

The second half of the song pushes the *mise en scène* further through an aesthetic more strikingly and explicitly contrasting with the computer-animated style of the film: 3D Maui pulls a tapestry down, creating a flat decor resembling cut-out animation, in which he is shown fighting various monsters. This fantasy staging, including ornamented backgrounds and stylised characters, acts as a diversion, fooling Moana while Maui attempts to steal her boat. The discrepancy between the flat cut-out 'illusion' and the 3D, more recognisably computer-animated 'reality' is revealed at the end of the song. The colourful cut-out stage is replaced by a dark cave in which Maui traps Moana, and the cut-out flower garlands and fruit she had been offered turn out to be photorealistic rocks and algae. This aesthetic clash underlines the heavily mediated aspect of the action hero performance, and parallels the contrast between Maui's idealised action persona, invincible and admirable, and his true character, self-centred and brash.[8]

Throughout Disney animated films, the artifices behind the protagonists' action feats are gradually deconstructed, leading to a more authentic performance. When Bolt finds himself out of the set by mistake, he is at a loss to know why his superpowers do not work. His heroicness is comically undermined: for example, his head gets stuck between fence bars he cannot bend. His abilities become ridiculously unbelievable out of a heavily mediated action context. When he uselessly stares at the lock of a truck door, stating that it will 'burst into flames and melt', alley cat Mittens is more 'concerned' than impressed. Such instances are numerous in *Bolt*, humorously furthering the demystification of action stunts and effects initiated throughout the backstage sequences of the television programme.

Feuer argues that, in backstage musicals, 'demystification is always followed by a new mystification': performers are placed back on their pedestal and the seamless final live show is celebrated (1993: 43–4). In the context of the action performance, the same process takes place: *Bolt*, *Moana*, as well as *Big Hero 6* and *Wreck-It Ralph* all end with a spectacular action sequence. Yet, these final performances are devoid of most of all the digital and/or pre-digital artifices that constituted the action *mise en scène*: characters are not onstage any more. Bolt saves Penny as the television set burns into flames: his action stage and the wings are literally destroyed. Although he has realised by then that he does not possess super strength or speed, he still manages to lead her to safety (near a vent). His bark is realistically amplified through the vent, creating an echo that helps firemen locate them. His performance is closer to a rescue dog than a 'super' dog. Action films such as *Mission: Impossible: Ghost Protocol* (Brad Bird, 2011) and *Iron Man 3* (Shane Black, 2013) include such sequences in which the protagonist is successful despite missing his high-tech gadgets or super suit, but they are only temporary. In fully abandoning the props and effects of the digital action *mise en scène*, *Bolt* deliberately avoids the remystification characterising live-action performances. The film provides a genre lesson, reframing its regime of verisimilitude by discarding the artifices of the action spectacle.

Moana also moves towards a more genuine and unmediated action performance. When Moana ultimately confronts Te Ka, a threatening lava monster, Maui stands back and acts only as a helper. Yet, although 2D Mini-Maui and other tattoos remain motionless, Maui is still self-consciously performing. He uses his magical fish hook not only as a weapon, slicing Te Ka's arm and hand, but also to transform into a giant hawk, a bug, a whale and a man–shark hybrid. His playful transformations bring comedy to the violent action fight, functioning as the animated visual equivalent of a live-action one-liner ('Shark head!'). This shift from humorous verbal asides to visual gags relies on the transformative abilities of the animated form.[9] When his hook is broken by Te Ka, he loses his action prop and must adapt his performance: he starts a haka, ready to selflessly sacrifice himself. This traditional war dance functions as a diversion, while Moana attempts to restore the 'heart' of 'Mother Island' Te Fiti. When she realises that Te Ka and Te Fiti are one and the same goddess, the violent action spectacle ceases, and Maui goes from actor to spectator. The ocean between Te Ka and Moana parts; Te Ka threateningly crawls towards Moana, but she calmly walks ahead, in slow motion, and starts singing. Her soft, clear, angelic voice contrasts sharply with both Maui's aggressive chant and Te Ka's shrieks. When the latter faces Moana, she stops, soothed by Moana's empathetic song. This peaceful and dreamlike sequence redefines the action spectacle. It not only puts violent displays aside but refocuses attention on the core of Moana's performance, namely her voice, which leads to her unmediated communion with Te Ka/Te Fiti. In this particular sequence, the type of action feat privileged in live-action cinema is put in the background – or rather, *Moana* reconfigures the action sequence into a musical piece.

This sequence from *Moana* ultimately distances the violent and heavily mediated action spectacle which previous Disney action-adventure animated films have questioned and deconstructed. Functioning as backstage action films, *Big Hero 6* and more particularly *Bolt* demystify the digital *mise en scène* behind action stunts and spectacular effects. *Wreck-It Ralph* and *Moana* reproduce animation styles and aesthetics that explicitly differ from photorealistic computer animation – cut-out, plasticine, hand-drawn animation – to foreground the constructed aspects of the action performance and action labels. Disney animated action-adventure films self-reflexively draw on the multiple stylistic potentials of animation, both digital and pre-digital, to unveil the artifices of the digital action spectacle. Privileging an unmediated action performance, Disney's animated action heroes ultimately discard their illusory props. *Moana*'s alternative, more peaceful outcome explicitly and seamlessly merges action adventure and musical, re-envisioning genre boundaries.

Expanding the Spectacle: The Disney Action Musical

Moana's generic fusion, directly combining action adventure and musical, distinguishes Disney's animated output further within the wider digital action-adventure milieu. The musical is a genre that is intrinsically linked with the studio, an essential aspect of the Disney formula. Through the dynamic and communal impulses of the musical, *Wreck-It Ralph*, *Big Hero 6* and most notably *Moana* reframe the artificial and mediated action performance as empowering and expansive. By including action within the musical, Disney updates and expands its iconic formula; by foregrounding the musical within action adventure, and more specifically through the theme of space, the studio also brings forward and re-envisions the affinities between the two genres.

The analogy between the action film and the musical works to foreground the importance of bodily movements in such genres: often violent action gestures and moves can be reframed as 'choreography' (Tasker 2015: 49). In Disney's earlier hand-drawn action-adventure musicals such as *Hercules* and *Mulan*, diegetic songs accompany the leads' often rough action practice, testing their strength, agility and resilience. In *Mulan*, for example, Captain Shang (BD Wong) uses a staff to demonstrate combat moves and martial arts while singing 'I'll Make a Man Out of You'. This weapon, expertly handled by his recruits at the end of the song, evokes the cane used by Fred Astaire in his tap-dancing routines: the action prop (staff) becomes a dancing prop.

While *Moana* ultimately discards violence, it preserves and develops such merging of action-adventure and dancing moves. Sailing is represented as an elaborate choreography introduced in the song 'We Know the Way', repeated by Maui during and after the Kakamoras' attack, and later by Moana. This includes, for example, raising one's hand to the sky as a compass, jumping to one end of the boat and using one's body weight to shift its direction, and holding and swinging on the mast – the action-adventure equivalent of the musical protagonist swinging on a lamp post in *Singin' in the Rain* (Stanley Donen and Gene Kelly, 1952).

Moana's sailing lessons, during which she learns this choreography, also notably take place during a musical montage. The latter develops further the generic convergences between action adventure and musical, namely between sailing and dancing: while Maui teaches Moana, the lyrics of 'Logo Te Pate' – the song used as the soundtrack – describe 'the sway / the energy / expressed in the dance' (Te Vaka n.d.).[10] Such musical montages point to the importance of the soundtrack in contemporary Hollywood action sequences more generally, both reflecting and enhancing their affective quality (Purse 2011a: 69). For example, writing on the highly popular *Fast & Furious* films (2001, 2003, 2006, 2009, 2011, 2013, 2015, 2017, 2019, 2021), Todd Decker argues that 'beat-driven' soundtracks are employed as 'constituent parts of the franchise's cinematic topics of chases, races and street racing sociability' (2017: 171). Chases specifically function as 'tightly integrated musical numbers', 'kinetic spectacles' of bodies – and cars – in motion (ibid.: 162). The inclusion of Rihanna's 'Shut Up and Drive' in *Wreck-It Ralph*, Fall Out Boy's 'Immortals' in *Big Hero 6* and Te Vaka's 'Logo Te Pate' in *Moana* plays a similarly pivotal narrative and generic function in Disney's contemporary output. These songs frame action practice as an empowering physical and musical performance, following the protagonists' progress as they familiarise themselves with their elaborate costumes and props. 'Shut Up and Drive' foregrounds Vanellope's excitement at her racing progress and her thrill at her kart's speed; 'Immortals' accompanies Hiro's team as they enthusiastically try their new gear, gliding around in circles and jumping high in the air. Mutually enhancing one another, action adventure and musical merge in other ways throughout *Moana*. Moana's song 'How Far I'll Go' revisits Disney musical tropes through its exploration of the concept of space, following from both musical and action genres.

Dyer explains that musicals are 'discourses of happiness': the musical set pieces offer solutions to or respite from the problems set up within the narrative (2012: 101). In this sense, they are utopian: they express hopes, wishes, alternatives, '"something better" to escape into' (Dyer 2002: 20). Dyer points out that one manifestation of this musical bliss is 'the motif of expansion . . . the way a number develops outwards from its moment in the narrative, opening up spatially and temporally' (2012: 101). Spatial expansion often gradually involves more people and movement, and therefore more energy throughout the performance (ibid.: 28).

Expanded space and movement are often at stake within Disney musical set pieces, especially during the protagonists' solos. Throughout these songs, Disney heroes and heroines express their utopian yearning for 'a better world beyond the confinements of [their] present situation' (Byrne and McQuillan 1999: 24). This constraining environment, such as Belle's 'provincial life' in

Beauty and the Beast, often manifests explicitly and physically. For example, in *The Hunchback of Notre-Dame* (Gary Trousdale and Kirk Wise, 1996), Quasimodo longs to be 'out there', accepted by and living among Parisian people, outside the confines of the cathedral. Similarly, *Tangled*'s 'When Will My Life Begin?' introduces Rapunzel trapped in her lonely tower; in *Frozen*'s 'For the First Time in Forever', Anna excitedly waits for her castle's gates to be opened. Disney protagonists' desire for another life corresponds to a generic longing for spatial expansion. Their static, constrained position – both metaphorically and literally – is made all the more unbearable considering the musical context of the films. In 'Part of Your World' from *The Little Mermaid* (Ron Clements and John Musker, 1989), Ariel longs for the human world partly for the physical freedom she associates with it. She wishes to 'walk', 'run', sings that 'legs are required for jumpin', dancin'': she desires to be part of a liberating musical performance.

Similarly to the musical, the cinematic construction of action-adventure space depends on physical expansion. Tasker notes that adventure narratives frequently 'involve a journey into uncharted, unfamiliar or dangerous terrain' (2015: 52). The journey itself is at the core of the sea-adventure subgenre described by Brian Taves. With its open settings – the 'high seas' – and naval iconography, it particularly develops themes of exploration, widening the borders of action-adventure space (Taves 1993: 30).

Moana's narrative conflict, initially between Moana and her father, manifests in opposite generic interpretations of space, as introduced in the first musical piece 'Where You Are'. Moana longs to sail and explore the ocean beyond her island's reef: as a toddler, then a little girl and a teenager, she tries to go on a boat against her parents' wishes. Her sea-adventure approach to space clashes indeed with her father's, who always brings her back to the village, among the harmonious singing and dancing of her people. His conception of space – 'the village of Motonui is all you need' – prevents the spatial expansion inherent in sea-adventure films, and notably limits that of the musical as well. 'Where You Are' praises the virtues of tradition, stability and ultimately – metaphorical – stasis: 'no one leaves'. While the song gradually involves more villagers joining in the singing and dancing, preserving the sense of 'belonging' and 'togetherness' also intrinsic to the musical (Dyer 2002: 24), their dynamic performance remains spatially limited.

Moana's solo 'How Far I'll Go' epitomises this generic conflict between the action-adventure space, potentially isolating for her, and the musical space, associated with community but unbearably restrictive at the start of the film. She starts singing 'at the edge of the water', which represents the physical barrier that confines the Disney heroine. As she stands still, the digitally simulated tracking camera momentarily features her village in the background, representing her duties on the island as the daughter of the chief. The anaphoric second verse of the song ('every turn I take, every trail I track, every path I make, every road leads back') reinforces this sense of immobility. As Dyer points out, repetition and redundancy within song sequences tend towards 'a sense of temporal stasis, of not going anywhere' (2012: 24): this parallels Moana's spatial limitations. Indeed, as she walks away from the shore, backgrounds succeed each other, featuring woodlands, the village, and her starting point, namely the shore: she appears to be spatially stuck. This sense of entrapment is reinforced in the first chorus as she steps onto a boat. Although she is swinging from the mast, looking towards the horizon, the boat remains on the ground: sea adventure remains a fantasy (Figure 5.3). Momentarily giving up this dream of expansion, Moana walks back again to the village, surrounded by her people: adults harvest coconuts while children happily play around. Within this community, her role as a future chief is symbolised by a mountain towering over the village, on which she is expected to put a stone. Arriving at the top and about to perform this ritual, she holds back at the spectacular view from the mountain: the endless, glistening seascape.

This stunning, limitless panorama leads her to return excitedly to the shore: time seems to accelerate as the musical sequence moves firmly into action adventure. Moana vigorously jumps up, loops a leaf over a horizontal palm tree, and slides along the trunk. This athletic, energetic stunt foregrounds Moana's action-adventure potential – or rather, dancing skills. This move is indeed spectacularly repeated when she retrieves the heart of Te Fiti from the Kakamoras' ship. In order to escape, she throws an arrow attached to a rope towards Maui's boat: as it stretches, she uses her oar to slide away down the rope. 'How Far I'll Go' continues as Moana races towards the ocean: she runs

Figure 5.3 Sea adventure initially represents a fantasy for Moana. Frame grab from Moana (Clements and Musker, 2016).

past the village's cabins, and reaches the shore where geysers erupt along her path. This sense of physical dynamism, matched by the energetic singing performance of Auliʻi Cravalho, allows the musical and sea-adventure subgenre to converge. The song concludes as she sails towards the distant horizon: the musical space has finally expanded, and the sea adventure can begin.

Moana's first attempt at sailing is unsuccessful not only because she lacks practice but also – and mostly – because she is isolated: *Moana* recurrently frames sailing and its associated journeys of exploration and adventure as a communal activity. This sense of togetherness is epitomised in the subsequent song, 'We Know the Way'. This musical 'flashback' introduces Moana's ancestors as 'voyagers', sailing across the ocean and discovering new islands. Throughout their journey, they are shown singing in harmony, performing the dance/sailing moves that Moana learns during 'Logo Te Pate'. In the latter, navigating is also represented as a collaborative activity, based on the team effort of both Moana and Maui. While in the song 'I Am Moana' – partly reprising the melody of 'How Far I'll Go' – the heroine considers abandoning her quest, it is the presence of both her grandmother's spirit and the voyaging ghosts of her ancestors that helps her overcome her self-doubt. In the final sequence, reprising 'We Know the Way', she leads, teaches and sails amongst her people, reviving a tradition of communal exploration. The sense of togetherness and energy conveyed through the musical and sea adventure are finally merged. The final shot features the Disney heroine looking ahead, while her island stands far in the background: the generic expansion taking place in *Moana* parallels the expanding borders of the Disney musical.

Conclusion

Building on, reframing and expanding Disney's musical and aesthetic formula, *Bolt*, *Wreck-It Ralph*, *Big Hero 6* and *Moana* re-envision the digital action-adventure spectacle. They parodically reproduce its dazzling visuals and effects, subverting and counterbalancing its excess and violence; as backstage action films, they question and deconstruct the *mise en scène* behind such thrilling displays; and they generically expand the liberating potentials of the action performance, developing further existing affinities between the action adventure and the musical. Through this distinctive, three-layered reworking, Disney's contemporary computer-animated films stand out within the action-adventure milieu, foregrounding a playful, knowing and challenging approach which specifically draws on Disney's visual style and generic identity. The digital action-adventure spectacle appears as a humorously excessive, artificial and heavily mediated performance, gradually replaced by a more genuine and empowering musical alternative.

From a wider perspective, studying Disney animated features through an action-adventure lens reveals some of the studio's recurring approaches towards both genre and its own formula. Despite notable semantic and syntactic differences between animated fairy tales and action adventures, the concept of a comedic and self-aware generic performance, from the staging of the action spectacle to that of the sentimental love ballad, is key throughout the studio's contemporary canon. As pointed out in Chapter 4, the performance of gender, from Prince Hans's villainous masquerade to Elsa's subversive campness, represents also a central component of Disney's self-reflexive revision of its formula.

Dyer wrote in 2000 that action-adventure heroes had mostly been white males, and asserted that any alternative would 'still . . . feel exceptional for some time to come' (2000: 20). The multiplication of cinematic action heroines from the 2000s onwards has challenged to some extent this statement. The mainstreaming of the action heroine has led to generic revisions and tensions, altering the performance of the action spectacle. In parallel, since the 2000s, another type of performance has developed within the action mode, bringing its spectacular dimension further: the superhero film. The following chapter explores another facet of Disney's dialogue with the genres of action adventure, focusing on the gendered implications of the studio's generic reworking of the superhero film.

Notes

1. In the film, the considerable number of computer-animated Huns is emphasised through long shots and crane shots. A digitally simulated camera tracks across the landscape, giving an impressive, vertiginous feel to the scene.
2. *The Princess and the Frog* (Ron Clements and John Musker, 2009) and *Winnie the Pooh* (Stephen Anderson and Don Hall, 2011) remain notable exceptions. At the time of writing, the Disney studio has not communicated any plans to release a new hand-drawn animated feature in the foreseeable future.
3. *Wreck-It Ralph*'s creative team was inspired by 'first-person shooter games like Halo, Gears of War, and Mass Effect' for the game 'Hero's Duty'. For further information on its design, see Lee and Malone 2012: 51–85.
4. A sensation known as the 'uncanny' occurs when 'a viewer senses an odd disconnect between the images seen and his or her expectations of how they should appear – a subconscious warning that what we see is "not right"'. This idea is based on the concept of 'the uncanny valley'. See Furniss 2016: 372.
5. Such a hybrid aesthetic also characterises contemporary anime, as illustrated by films such as *Wolf Children* (Mamoru Hosoda, 2012), *Your Name* (Makoto Shinkai, 2016) and *A Silent Voice* (Naoko Yamada, 2016). These films include 2D characters drawing on the aesthetic style of manga, within computer-animated

Animating the Digital Action-adventure Spectacle 149

environments. Cityscapes and rural scenery are showcased through sweeping camerawork, the presence of which is signalled through numerous digitally constructed lens flares.

6. This sequence also parodically references the science-fiction film *Alien* (Ridley Scott, 1979), in which a member of the crew is similarly attacked by a face-hugging alien creature.
7. Disney's reliance on a 2D, non-photorealistic aesthetic for the 1980s-inspired game 'Fix-It Felix' in *Wreck-It Ralph*, imitating *Pac-Man*'s visuals (featured in the film) also echoes contemporary video-game films such as *TRON: Legacy* (Joseph Kosinski, 2010) and *Scott Pilgrim vs. the World* (Edgar Wright, 2010). These films reappropriate 'anachronistic gaming aesthetics' in order to generate 'nostalgia for earlier periods of media history' (Sperb 2016: 142). For a further analysis of *Wreck-It Ralph* within this specific context, see Sperb 2016: ch. 6. For further information on the relationship between *Wreck-It Ralph*, video-game aesthetics and digital technology, see Davis 2014; Wagner and Jang 2016.
8. This aesthetic clash serves other functions. The hand-drawn aesthetics of Maui's tattoos, like the stylised tapestries present in the opening sequence and 'You're Welcome', also denote the specific inspiration for the film, namely Polynesian and Pacific Island cultures (Anjirbag 2018).
9. The transformative and fluid potential of the animated form will be developed further in the following chapter, focusing on the protagonists' powers.
10. These lyrics are the English translation of 'Logo Te Pate', a song released in 2011 by the South Pacific band Te Vaka.

CHAPTER 6

Disruption/Containment: Gender, Marvel and Disney's Superheroes

> Look, the code may say I'm a princess, but I know who I really am, Ralph, I'm a racer with the greatest superpower ever! (Vanellope in *Wreck-It Ralph*, Rich Moore, 2012)

At the end of *Wreck-It Ralph*, Vanellope is revealed as the 'Rightful Ruler' of the kart-racing game 'Sugar Rush'. While she had been marginalised and excluded from racing, her crossing of the finish line resets the game, and the other characters finally remember that she is a princess. This restored status is conveyed through the magical appearance of a pink sparkling dress and a crown, which she quickly discards. She then excitedly 'glitches' around, quickly appearing and disappearing throughout the frame. This short scene encapsulates the central generic influences characterising the portrayal of Disney's contemporary animated characters. Vanellope shifts from the fairy tale ('princess') – the iconic underpinning of the Disney formula – to the action-adventure mode ('racer') and a genre more unusual for the studio: the superhero film ('superpower').

This chapter explores how *Wreck-It Ralph*, *Frozen* (Chris Buck and Jennifer Lee, 2013), *Big Hero 6* (Don Hall and Chris Williams, 2014) and *Moana* (Ron Clements and John Musker, 2016) reappropriate and rework constructions of gender characteristic of the superhero genre, revising and expanding Disney's gendered formula in the process. Disney animated films rely on the comic potentials and aesthetic freedoms of the animated medium to challenge contemporary portrayals of superheroes and superheroines. This distinctive animated prism reveals, and at times magnifies, contrasts between male and female characters' exertion of their extraordinary powers and heroic feats.

By the late 2000s, the superhero genre was becoming 'undeniably dominant' within mainstream action-adventure cinema (Brown 2017: 1): the first *X-Men* trilogy (2000, 2003, 2006) and Sam Raimi's *Spider-Man* trilogy (2002, 2004, 2007) had enjoyed significant success, while Christopher Nolan's *Batman* films (2005, 2008) and Pixar's *The Incredibles* (Brad Bird, 2004) also received widespread critical acclaim. Films based on Marvel comic books have been 'at the forefront of this trend' (Kent 2021: 2), which spectacularly grew with the first phase of the Marvel Cinematic Universe, launched in 2008 with *Iron Man* (Jon Favreau) and *The Incredible Hulk* (Louis Leterrier). In this context, Disney's purchase of Marvel Entertainment in December 2009 represented an extremely profitable deal, and an opportunity for the company to significantly expand its brand and appeal to a wider market, following on from the acquisition of Pixar in 2006 (Pallant 2013: 144). Having access to a large library of new characters, Disney could also release in-house films based on Marvel comics, directly stepping into superhero territory.

Big Hero 6 is the direct product of this acquisition. The film features a super-team of college students, led by teen Hiro and robotic nurse Baymax. They investigate the death of Hiro's brother Tadashi (Daniel Henney), facing a dangerous masked villain in the process. This Disney animated superhero film not only follows on from Marvel tropes but also foregrounds issues surrounding the construction of gender within the genre. Through the portrayal of Hiro and Baymax, *Big Hero 6* questions the relationship between masculinity, femininity, superpowers and control.

These themes actually run through most of Disney's contemporary animated releases, engaging with core aspects of 2000s superhero cinema. The studio's recent output features characters endowed with extraordinary but potentially unruly and/or dangerous abilities, including Ralph and Vanellope, Elsa in *Frozen*, and Maui in *Moana*. In *Frozen*, Queen Elsa's extraordinary but dangerously strong powers trap her kingdom in an eternal winter, which drives her sister Anna to set off on a perilous journey to bring her back. In *Wreck-It Ralph*, Vanellope also possesses uncontrollable abilities: as a 'glitch', her body can dematerialise and 'teleport' itself, and potentially disrupt the appearance of props and characters she touches. As a result, she is marginalised and banned from racing in 'Sugar Rush', which leads her to team up with Ralph. Like Vanellope, Ralph is feared and rejected in his own video game ('Fix-It Felix') because of his 'bad guy' persona, and more particularly due to his wrecking powers and uncontainable angry outbursts. Determined to prove his worth as a hero, he leaves his game to win a medal that he loses in 'Sugar Rush'. Vanellope agrees to assist him if he helps her enter a race. Moana makes a similar deal with Maui. The imposing brash demigod agrees to accompany her on her journey to restore the heart of Te Fiti. In return, she agrees to help Maui find his magical fishhook, the source of his spectacular but – at first – unreliable shapeshifting abilities.

This chapter focuses on the gendered performance of such overflowing, potentially disruptive superpowers, specifically throughout the portrayal of Ralph, Vanellope, Elsa, Hiro, Baymax and Maui. These 'super' gender constructions take Disney's reworking of the digital action-adventure spectacle, discussed in Chapter 5, in new directions. Relying on the distinctively comic and expressive potentials of animation, Disney's gender portrayals re-envision constructions of masculinity and femininity as displayed within the superhero film. These animated features foreground underlying tensions in the gendering of live-action super-heroism, pointing to the more problematic framing of empowered live-action heroines in action-adventure cinema.

Although *Wreck-It Ralph*, *Frozen*, and *Moana* were not explicitly marketed as superhero films, the protagonists' depiction was often approached from this generic perspective – *Frozen* being the most striking example. As developed in Chapter 4, *Frozen* extensively relies on and subverts the tropes of the Disney fairy tale, notably through the portrayal of and couple dynamics between Anna/Hans and Anna/Kristoff, borrowing from genres of romance. Elsa particularly stands out within this romantic fairy-tale configuration: lacking a love interest, her portrayal is also characterised by other generic influences. Her magical abilities were directly described as 'superpowers' by co-director Jennifer Lee, and effects supervisor Marlon West compared them to Frozone's from *The Incredibles* (quoted in Solomon 2013: 11, 127). Reviewers also referred to the superhero genre: Peter Bradshaw similarly noted that Elsa's powers were 'the most impressive since Frozone' (2013); Anne Billson described them as coming 'straight out of a superhero movie, not unlike that of . . . Iceman . . . in the *X-Men* franchise' (2013); Scott Foundas likened her ice castle to 'Superman's Fortress of Solitude' (2013). The presence of the superhero genre within *Frozen*'s paratexts is not as incongruous as it may seem. Marvel comic-book writer and publisher Stan Lee explained in an interview that the popularity of superhero films is partly due to audiences' fondness for fairy tales: 'fairy tales are all about things bigger than life: giants, witches, trolls, dinosaurs and all sorts of imaginative things . . . Superhero movies are like fairy tales for older people' (quoted in Cavna 2011). Considering Tamar Jeffers McDonald's parallel description of romantic comedies as 'fairy tales for adults' (2007: 14), Disney's *Frozen* can be situated at a converging point between superhero films and romantic comedies. Both genres are reappropriated to subvert and expand Disney's formulaic underpinning: the fairy tale. In the same way as *Frozen*'s playful reworking of fairy-tale coupledom can be better understood from a romantic-comedy perspective, Elsa's fairy-tale characterisation can be reassessed through the generic lens of superhero cinema. The semantic manifestation and syntactic development of her 'magic' or 'sorcery' is particularly close to that of the overflowing, 'bigger than life' powers of superheroes.

Such a reading of Elsa's character, and Disney animated features more generally, is more unusual within the context of genre studies. Contemporary works on the superhero film tend to include analyses of animated features that are only explicitly labelled as such, such as Pixar's *The Incredibles*.[1] As in studies on romantic comedies, some authors omit animated films altogether.[2] Jeffrey A. Brown, for example, passes them over because 'animated children's superhero movies are already a distinct genre' – he does not elaborate further on this 'difference' – not as 'wide-reaching' as their live-action counterpart (2017: 8, 161). Such positioning emphasises the recurring marginalisation of animated films within live-action focused genre studies, as well as potential preconceptions about animation audiences.

Yet, studying *Frozen*, *Wreck-It Ralph* and *Moana* as superhero films, alongside more straightforward manifestations of the genre like *Big Hero 6* and Marvel's live-action output, opens up new perspectives on both the superhero genre and Disney's contemporary canon. This approach relies on an expanded conception of genre, uncovering the fluid boundaries of the superhero film. Superhero tropes resurface in a wide variety of works, and most unexpectedly – and strikingly – in contemporary Disney animated features. These films, actually wide-reaching in box-office terms, transcend potentially reductive categorisations such as 'children's films'. Following on from Janet Staiger's observations on the male melodrama, using a different generic lens in order to approach specific aspects of a film allows one to 'see things perhaps not otherwise visible' (2008: 86). In the context of *Wreck-It Ralph*, *Frozen*, *Big Hero 6* and *Moana*, the gendered construction of the protagonists' extraordinary bodies, their relation to issues of power and control, and their syntactic trajectories are better understood from the illuminating perspective of the superhero film, as exemplified by Elsa's portrayal.

The empowered body is an essential component of the spectacular action-adventure mode (Purse 2011a: 2). Semantically, the action-adventure body is strong, agile and resilient, enhanced through or functioning as a weapon (ibid.: 3). Syntactically, the protagonist's trajectory towards this physically empowered body is articulated through a 'narrative of becoming', often involving training in new skills (ibid.: 33). The display of the extraordinary capacities of the action body, its exertion of powerful movement and mastery of violence, depends notably on its gender. The woman in action-adventure films has often been positioned as a 'romantic or sexual object of interest for the hero and . . . a figure in peril' (Tasker 2015: 65). The greater prominence of the action woman from the mid-1980s onwards – with her notable mainstreaming since the 2000s – has challenged action-adventure semantics and narratives (Tasker 1998: 143–4). For instance, the protagonists in *Thelma and Louise* (Ridley Scott, 1991) and *Terminator 2: Judgment Day* (James Cameron, 1991) access technologies such as cars and guns, traditionally associated with male characters, as semantic 'means of empowerment', signifiers of freedom and power (Tasker 1993: 139). They leave the restrictive space of their homes and become proactive in violent sequences, challenging the role of victim usually performed by the female character. However, these images of strength are complicated throughout the narratives: characters' generic subversion tends to be contained, to some extent, as they are repositioned into more conventional roles – mother, helper – or killed off. Therefore, gendered reconfigurations create potential tensions between semantics and the syntactic structure of a film.

Reprising 'in spectacular form' the semantics of the action mode, superhero films emphasise the extraordinary dimension of protagonists' powers and bodies, able to fly or transform effortlessly (Tasker 2015: 180–1). Syntactically, the 'prominence of origin stories' expands the scope of the action-adventure 'narrative of becoming', positioning the acquisition and mastery of superpowers as central to the plot (ibid.: 180). The superhero genre also spectacularly reprises the male-centred blueprint of action adventure. Since the original *X-Men* (Bryan Singer, 2000), the past two decades have been marked by a significant rise in superhero films – or rather, 'manifestations of (predominantly) male heroism' (Purse 2011a: 204). Numerous authors have noted that female characters have been 'present yet oddly peripheral to superhero cinema' (Tasker 2015: 189), tending to be 'secondary characters' in ensemble narratives (McSweeney 2020: 58) – as illustrated by the first two phases of the Marvel Cinematic Universe (2008–15).[3] By contrast, they play a pivotal role in Disney's animated superhero films, as exemplified by *Frozen*.

Disney's super characters struggle with remarkable, but often unpredictable and dangerous faculties: Shahriar Fouladi's concept of 'monstrosity' (2011: 161), describing the uncontrollable aspect and destructive potential of superheroes' powers, is particularly useful here. The way Disney's protagonists exert and ultimately master such extraordinary abilities – or rather, channel their monstrous potential – varies significantly depending on their gender. This chapter explores how *Wreck-It Ralph*, *Frozen*, *Big Hero 6* and *Moana* negotiate tensions underlying the portrayal of both super masculinity and femininity within contemporary superhero cinema through the specific lens of Disney animation.

This chapter first focuses on *Big Hero 6*'s Hiro and Baymax. I explore how the portrayal of teenage Hiro playfully subverts the coming-of-age narrative as depicted in Marvel live-action superhero films, such as the original live-action *Spider-Man* (Sam Raimi, 2002) and *Captain America: First Avenger* (Joe Johnston, 2011). Hiro's relationship with Baymax and their collaborative performance of super-heroism complicates gendered binaries as constructed within the superhero genre. The characterisation of robotic superhero/nurse Baymax epitomises *Big Hero 6*'s hybrid construction of gendered superheroes. Staging super-heroism as a balancing act, the film provides a primary framework through which to understand Disney's gendered approach to super-heroic performance.

The chapter then examines the parodic construction of male super-heroism characterising the portrayals of Ralph and Maui. Relying on the comic potential of animation aesthetics, especially caricature and metamorphosis, *Wreck-It Ralph* and *Moana* knowingly mock superheroes' excessive and unruly performance of masculinity, as showcased through the portrayals of the Hulk and Thor throughout the Marvel Cinematic Universe. I also explore how these films reframe superheroes' narrative of becoming, as protagonists' trajectories towards the mastery of their extraordinary but overflowing bodies, superpowers and emotions – especially anger – result in selfless superhero acts.

Lastly, this chapter investigates Disney's starkly different treatment of female super-heroism. The portrayals of Vanellope and Elsa are not characterised by such a light-hearted approach, foregrounding instead a more ambiguous and typically post-feminist narrative of becoming. The figure of Elsa particularly crystallises Hollywood's uneasiness towards the construction of the empowered superheroine. I focus on Disney's use of the specifically creative and disruptive power of animation to translate the artistically expressive and liberating, yet dangerously transgressive potential of superheroines.

By looking closely at the performance of super-heroism in Disney's contemporary animated output, this chapter aims to illuminate the gendered implications of such performances as constructed within contemporary Hollywood, and more specifically the uneasy negotiation of power with male/female anger. I examine how Disney relies on the comic, creative, as well as disruptive power of animation to magnify and challenge such gendered performances, while differentiating its animated superhero output and expanding its gendered formula in the process.

Disney Does Marvel: *Big Hero 6*'s Teen and Hybrid Superheroes

When *Big Hero 6* was released in 2014, the superhero genre had become particularly prominent throughout mainstream live-action cinema. Major animation studios such as Pixar and DreamWorks had already reappropriated some tropes of the genre with the former's *The Incredibles* and the latter's *Megamind* (Tom McGrath, 2010). With *Big Hero 6*, Disney differentiated its superhero output in two significant ways: the film playfully subverts the formulaic male-centred super coming-of-age narrative, and challenges the gendered divide associated with the performance of super-heroism.

As for Disney's post-*Shrek* fairy tales and post-Pixar computer-animated action adventures, the marketing and discourses of promotion surrounding *Big Hero 6* strove to foreground the studio's singularity – or rather, the preserved aspects of its successful formula. *Big Hero 6*'s source material is a relatively unknown comic-book series, which critic Graeme McMillan described at the time as 'the most obscure Marvel property to make it to the big screen' (2014). This gave Disney a significant level of freedom: as head of animation Zach Parrish explains, they 'could adapt it to whatever direction [they] wanted to go' (quoted in Kamen 2015). In other words, filmmakers could easily impose the Disney label onto the Marvel text. As the 'American–Japanese cultural mix of the series' was 'retained', co-directors Don Hall and Chris Williams also underlined the influence of anime in press interviews, from Katsuhiro Ôtomo's *Akira* (1988) to Hayao Miyazaki's *Laputa: Castle in the Sky* (1986) and *My Neighbour Totoro* (1988) (Lui 2014). This blend of 'comic books and anime with fantasy' was channelled through a distinctive 'Disney lens': filmmakers repeatedly referred to 'the heart and humour that Disney is known for', specifying that the relationship between Hiro and Baymax was 'the core emotional thread of the movie' (Hall and Williams 2014: 7; Hall, quoted in Julius 2014: 10). These were also aspects that reviewers precisely pointed out, as noted in Chapter 5. Disney's marketing also relied heavily on the presence of the two protagonists in order to foreground *Big Hero 6*'s singularity within the superhero milieu. The teaser trailer, for example, focuses on Hiro fabricating Baymax's high-tech costume, and the latter's difficulties in putting it on: his large, curvy, inflatable body cannot fit into the imposing and sophisticated armour. This teaser trailer – consisting mostly of footage not included in the final film – parodically references Tony Stark (Robert Downey Jr) making his Iron Man suit in the 2008 film. Such explicit intertextual referencing, building on Marvel live-action films, seems to ultimately downplay Disney's potentially singular approach to the superhero genre.

Admittedly, from a syntactic perspective, *Big Hero 6* appears as a rather conventional example of Marvel superhero cinema: the narrative trajectory of fourteen-year-old Hiro can be understood as a male coming-of-age narrative juxtaposed with a superhero origin story. His portrayal echoes the original *Spider-Man*'s Peter Parker (Tobey Maguire), a teenager who 'possesses an extraordinary talent . . . yet lacks the mature capacity to channel . . . that power for the common good' (Flanagan 2007: 150). Both Peter and Hiro initially rely on their skills in order to earn easy money: Peter joins in an amateur wrestling competition, while robotics prodigy Hiro takes part in illegal 'bot fights'. Like Peter's Uncle Ben (Cliff Robertson), Hiro's elder brother Tadashi acts as a mentor. Aware that his little brother is wasting his potential, he urges him to use his 'gift for something important' – words reminiscent of Uncle Ben's 'with great power comes great responsibility'. Claire Jenkins notes that the traumatic death of mentor figures is a recurrent superhero trope: it is the 'catalyst' for the male protagonist's transformation into a true superhero (2015: 73). This is the case after both Uncle Ben's and Tadashi's death: Peter's and Hiro's motivation evolves from mere revenge into a drive to protect the citizenry. By the end of each film, they have proved their worth as selfless heroes, successfully saving lives. Hiro's final voice-over echoes Peter's, revealing their maturation as superheroes and confirming the determining influence of their late mentors. Flying around the city with his teammates, Hiro proudly recalls that his 'brother wanted to help a lot of people, and that's what we're gonna do'. Similarly, Peter's final voice-over reiterates his mentor's phrase and his importance in guiding his superhero performance: 'whatever life holds in store for me, I will never forget these words, "with great power comes great responsibility"'.

Beyond these many syntactic similarities, Hiro's super coming-of-age narrative differs from Peter's through the very nature of his 'extraordinary talent', or rather its semantic, physical manifestation. Following a bite by a genetically engineered 'super spider', Peter does not just become stronger: his transformation is signified by a dramatic body change. Staring at his reflection in disbelief, Peter is delighted to discover his new muscular physique. This humorous display is reprised in more spectacular proportions in *Captain America: First Avenger*. At the beginning of the film, Steve Rogers's (Chris Evans) potential as a superhero is seriously limited. He is repeatedly unsuccessful in enlisting in the US Army due to his numerous health problems; when he is finally enlisted, Colonel Phillips (Tommy Lee Jones) doubts his abilities, describing him as a 'skinny', '90-pound asthmatic'. Yet, Dr Erskine (Stanley Tucci) chooses Steve to test his 'super-soldier' serum precisely because 'a weak man knows the value of strength'. When injected with the serum, the digitally shrunk 'little guy' body is replaced by actor Chris Evans's tall and muscular one. The audience is invited to gaze up at his post-transformation shirtless torso, first showcased in a low-angle shot, which elicits the admiration of both male and female characters.[4] Such films then equate the acquisition of impressive, eye-catching muscles with being the essential tool of the superhero. They literalise what Terence McSweeney describes as the 'wish-fulfilment fantasy' at the core of the genre, or rather the fantasy to be 'stronger, faster, smarter, more virile' (2020: 39–40). As Brown points out, this type of male-centred physical transformation is 'so conventional now that it has almost become a joke' (2017: 43).[5] *Big Hero 6* playfully acknowledges then discards this muscular trajectory.

Big Hero 6 represents superheroes' spectacular physical transformation as a rather ridiculous masculine fantasy of empowerment. After Hiro and his friends' first encounter with the villain, they take refuge in Fred's house. The bedroom of this superhero fan is overflowing with comic books and collectibles, along with a portrait of himself as an exaggeratedly burly warrior, showing off enormous bulging muscles (Figure 6.1). The contrast between

Figure 6.1 *Superheroes' spectacular muscular physique as a ridiculous fantasy. Frame grab from* Big Hero 6 *(Hall and Williams, 2014).*

the animated representation of Fred – the 'grungiest, slacker-est member of the team' in the words of writer Dan Gerson (quoted in Julius 2014: 124) – and the painting is so striking and excessive that it becomes comical, leaving his friends more perplexed than impressed: Wasabi (Damon Wayans, Jr.) complains that his 'brain hates [his] eyes for seeing this'.

The superhero 'upgrade' that follows contrasts sharply with Fred's parodic comic-book transformation: no member of *Big Hero 6*'s team undergoes a spectacularly muscular metamorphosis. Contrary to Peter Parker and Steve Rogers, Hiro remains the same 'gangly' teenager (John Lasseter, quoted in Julius 2014: 81). The source of his extraordinary masculinity is his remarkable scientific precociousness, especially his robotics skills, as displayed in the opening 'bot fight' sequence. Hiro and his inoffensive-looking, smiley robot are not taken seriously by his imposing and threatening opponent, Yama (Paul Briggs): he contemptuously calls Hiro 'little boy'. Hiro turns this to his advantage, catching Yama off guard: the tiny but actually highly sophisticated robot beats the latter's. This opening sequence sets the tone of the film: appearances are not what they seem in *Big Hero 6*'s superhero world, and its masculine coming-of-age narrative semantically relies on brains, not muscles. Hiro becomes indeed the main engineer of both his team's and his own superhero 'upgrade'. He is the one turning his friends' science projects into super suits and props. He also becomes an efficient team leader, elaborating a plan that his friends follow, and advising them to 'think [their] way around the problem' when they struggle against the villain. This approach to superhero teamwork exemplifies *Big Hero 6*'s intellectualised version of superhero performance, challenging super masculine coming-of-age narratives in the process.

Big Hero 6's move away from Hollywood's construction of male superheroism is reinforced through a questioning of violence as an inherent component of such a performance, as epitomised in the climax of most superhero films. The latter typically end with the brutal, male-centred fight between superhero and villain, or even between the two leads, as in *Captain America: Civil War* (Anthony and Joe Russo, 2016) and *Batman v Superman: Dawn of Justice* (Zack Snyder, 2016). *Big Hero 6*'s repositioning of robotic healthcare companion Baymax in a superhero role significantly subverts such a configuration. Although voiced by a male actor (Scott Adsit), this roundly shaped, inflatable anthropomorphic character strikingly lacks the clear gender markers characterising male superheroes – Hiro first describes him as a 'walking marshmallow'. Introduced as a 'non-threatening, huggable' 'robotic nurse', Tadashi's robotics project is characterised by a complete lack of aggressiveness: his voice is particularly soft and high-pitched, his moves are slow, cautious, almost childlike. Co-director Chris Williams explains that Baymax draws on *My Neighbour Totoro*'s titular lead: like the large furry creature, Baymax is 'quiet, girthy, but with a sense of goodness, selflessness . . . warmth', 'innocence and gentleness' (quoted in Walker 2014; Lui 2014). Such a description considerably differs from the 'super' robots of contemporary superhero cinema, such as Tony Stark's sophisticated and deadly hard-shelled creations, evoking their muscular human counterparts. Character designer Shiyoon Kim notes that the minimalistic design of Baymax's face – two dots joined by a straight line – allows the audience to 'project onto him whatever they need in that moment' (quoted in Julius 2014: 90). From a gender perspective, this also provides, to some extent, a blank canvas from which to construct a uniquely hybrid superhero performance.

Robotic nurse Baymax initially seems out of place within a superhero context: this apparent generic unsuitability comically stands out when he and Hiro first encounter the villain. While being chased, Baymax gets stuck in a window, bumps his head, stumbles over, and is at a loss when Hiro urges him to 'kick down' and 'punch' locked doors to escape. However, at the end of the chase, he successfully rescues Hiro from a fall by acting as a protective shield, enveloping him with his body, which bounces back on the ground. This type of performance, grounded in Baymax's caring skills, tends to be associated with female characters within superhero cinema. For example, *The Incredibles*' Violet repeatedly encloses both herself and her family in force fields to protect them from bullets and explosions, visually paralleling Susan Storm in the *Fantastic 4* films (2005, 2007, 2015); in *Iron Man 3* (Shane Black, 2013), Pepper Potts's first superhero act when donning Tony Stark's suit is to shield him from a falling roof.

In order to catch the villain, Hiro decides to 'upgrade' Baymax for him to perform a fiercer, namely more masculine, version of super-heroism. He first transfers the moves of a martial arts film character onto a chip, which he installs into Baymax's access port. He then builds a suit inspired by samurai and ninja costumes. Although Baymax worries that this new warrior appearance may undermine his 'non-threatening, huggable design', he diligently rehearses a violent but highly controlled choreography relying on his new 'fighting database'. His second suit includes a rigid red armour, rocket fists and thrusters, echoing Iron Man's spectacular Hulkbuster in *Avengers: Age of Ultron* (Joss Whedon, 2015). Such a shift towards this new superhero persona does not go entirely smoothly: Hiro struggles to make Baymax's big soft body fit into the new armour; Baymax's still naïve and childlike nature comically contrasts with his newly imposing look, as he chases butterflies while Hiro wants him to show off his new gear. Yet, Baymax adapts quickly, convinced that these upgrades will help catch the villain and improve Hiro's emotional state as a result. However, Baymax's performance takes a dangerous turn when Hiro and his friends finally apprehend the villain. Turning out to be Tadashi's former professor (Callaghan), he reveals that he escaped from the explosion that killed Tadashi, while the latter went to save him. Holding Callaghan (James Cromwell) responsible for his brother's death, Hiro furiously orders Baymax to 'destroy' him, removing his initial healthcare chip. With only his fighting chip left, Baymax becomes an excessively aggressive killing machine, determinedly aiming his rocket fist at Callaghan, and brutally pushing away the other team members trying to stop him.

While such a performance may be conventional superhero fare, evoking for example the fight between Tony Stark's Hulkbuster and a mind-controlled Hulk in *Age of Ultron*, *Big Hero 6* quickly interrupts this violent display. When his healthcare chip is restored, Baymax shows Hiro Tadashi's test videos, reminding him of his brother's original, non-violent purpose when designing the robot: 'help' people. Convinced, Hiro ultimately manages to catch Callaghan with the help of Baymax and his friends, neutralising his 'microbots' without resorting to force. The action sequence concludes when Hiro satisfyingly tells Callaghan that 'our programming prevents us from injuring human beings', while Baymax's clenched fist appears only a few inches from Callaghan's face. *Big Hero 6* thus suggests that it is only when Baymax's healthcare and martial arts abilities are combined, namely both his protective and combative skills, that he can be an efficient, exemplary superhero. This balance between qualities that tend to be coded as feminine and masculine in superhero cinema subverts the strict gender binary underlying the genre. Similarly, Baymax's relationship with Hiro contributes to *Big Hero 6*'s generic subversion. Hiro is indeed the only member of his team not to possess

Figure 6.2 Baymax as a hybrid superhero. Frame grab from Big Hero 6 *(Hall and Williams, 2014).*

any high-tech prop: his super suit is Baymax, functioning as an extension of his own body. The duo harmoniously blends Hiro's intellectual skills with Baymax's both powerful and caring character, epitomised in their rescue of Callaghan's daughter. Baymax's suit is partly destroyed as he shields them from debris, but he uses his rocket fist to get them both to safety. Visually combining his soft, huggable appearance with what remains of his hard-shelled superhero armour, his portrayal provides a hybrid gendered version of super-heroism, both protective and proactive (Figure 6.2).

Through the semantic reworking of Hiro's super coming-of-age narrative, the hybrid portrayal of Baymax, and the complementary relationship between these two protagonists, *Big Hero 6* re-envisions contemporary constructions of male super-heroism beyond muscular and violent demonstrations of strength, and challenges the gender binary characterising superhero cinema. *Big Hero 6* also points to underlying tensions surrounding these gendered constructions. Fred's parodic superhero portrait, reimagining the fanboy as a hyper-muscular, godlike figure, comically hints at the knowing excesses of superheroes' physical portrayals; Baymax's 'destroy' mode reveals the potential danger of such excessive, unrestrained demonstrations of power. The move towards a more stable and mastered performance of male super-heroism is at the core of *Wreck-It Ralph* and *Moana*.

EXCESSIVE MASCULINITY, PLAYFUL KNOWINGNESS AND THE UNRULY SUPERHERO IN *WRECK-IT RALPH* AND *MOANA*

Through the portrayal of *Wreck-It Ralph*'s lead and *Moana*'s Maui, Disney mocks the construction of contemporary live-action male super-heroism. These films rely on parodic intertextual Marvel references and the comic potentials of animation to magnify the playfully excessive performance of superheroes' masculinity. They also both foreground and subvert the threatening potential of overflowing male anger. Throughout the films, these portrayals evolve towards a more mastered, controlled and selfless performance of masculinity.

Male superpowers tend to be rooted in superheroes' spectacular physical abilities, as exemplified by characters such as Captain America, Thor or the Hulk. In comics, this super strength is visually conveyed through superheroes' extreme muscularity: 'bulging muscles . . . impossible abs, biceps and chests highlighted by . . . skin-tight costumes' (Brown 2017: 42). Fred's fantasy portrait in *Big Hero 6* comically foregrounds the absurd nature of such muscular excess. On screen, the camera lingers on the correspondingly athletic bodies of actors Chris Evans (Captain America) or Chris Hemsworth (Thor), often showcasing their nude, muscled torsos. The excessively sturdy comic-book superhero body is also enhanced through computer animation when impossible to replicate in live action, as is the case for the Hulk, or is reproduced on characters' protective armours and costumes, as for Iron Man or Batman.

However, Lisa Purse argues that a degree of 'playful knowingness is also evident' in these depictions (2011a: 103). In comparison with other action-adventure genres, including blockbuster epics such as *Gladiator* (Ridley Scott, 2000), superhero films display a 'less serious and more knowing attitude' towards the construction of the male body, featuring 'ironic dialogue about gender performativity alongside their hyperbolic declarations of machismo' (ibid.: 98). Excessive muscularity and aggressiveness not only represent the core components of masculine performance, as in the final battles of most superhero films, but can also become a source of comedy, as in *Hancock* (Peter Berg, 2008) and *Thor* (Kenneth Branagh, 2011). In the latter, for example, female characters jokingly comment on the superhero's physique ('For a crazy . . . person, he's pretty cut') or his rather unrefined manners ('No more smashing. Deal?').

Such playfulness towards the extraordinary male body is also noticeable throughout Disney's late 1990s action-adventure animated features, as epitomised in *Hercules* (Ron Clements and John Musker, 1997). Parodically reworking sword-and-sandal gendered tropes, the film comically overemphasises the attractiveness of the brawny protagonist. In the opening scene, one of the muses excitedly calls him 'hunkules'. The song 'Zero to Hero', illustrating his rising fame, features a 'Hercules Store' in which a multitude of Hercules action figures showcase overly large pectorals: the muse's singing line, referring both to the toy and its inspiration, describes a 'perfect package pack[ing] a pair of pretty pecs'. *Hercules* also underlines the *mise en scène* associated with such a muscular construction. As the muses sing that

Hercules's 'daring deeds are great theatre', he is shown attending a theatrical re-enactment of his defeat of the Hydra. The latter and the play parallel each other, featuring a strong hero performing his spectacular feat surrounded by a cheering audience.

Disney's contemporary animated films build on *Hercules*'s humorously theatrical portrayal of extraordinary masculinity and expand the playful knowingness of live-action superhero films. They particularly point to the constructedness of the excessively brutal and muscular performance of super-heroism. As pointed out in Chapter 5, *Wreck-It Ralph* and *Moana* self-reflexively rely on animated stagings that explicitly clash with the overall computer-animated aesthetic of the films to demystify the action-adventure spectacle. *Wreck-It Ralph*, for example, mediates the protagonist's feats through the two-dimensional 8-bit frame of his video game, and later represents these with plasticine-like characters and settings. Such a *mise en scène*, foregrounding the contrived and illusory aspects of the action-adventure spectacle, also relates to the gendered performance of action. *Wreck-It Ralph* repeatedly pokes fun at representations of brutally violent performances of masculinity, as illustrated in the Bad-Anon sequence. It features a support group of video-game villains including powerfully built male characters from games such as *Mortal Kombat* and *Street Fighter II*. Although they play very violent roles – as Zangief (Rich Moore) puts it, 'crushing man's skull like sparrow egg between [their] thighs' – their excessive brutality is mediated and contained within the staged setting and 2D world of their own games. In the 3D wings, they reveal a more sensitive, caring character, empathically listening to each other's problems. In the opening scene, *Street Fighter* characters stop beating each other as soon as the arcade closes, and happily go for a drink at Tappers: brutal muscular masculinity appears as a staged performance.

Moana's portrayal of Maui further develops Disney's playfulness and knowingness towards superheroes' version of masculinity, emphasising its excess through the specific aesthetic of animation. This 'Oceanic superhero', in the words of co-director Don Hall, possesses godlike strength (quoted in Julius and Malone 2016: 86). Voiced by former wrestler and action-adventure actor Dwayne Johnson, he is correspondingly powerfully built – but in a highly caricatured, almost parodic way. Production designer Ian Gooding explains that Maui is constructed as a 'square', with disproportionately short legs (quoted in ibid.: 87). His muscles are less marked and focused on than those of his live-action superhero counterparts, or even animated predecessors such as Hercules and *Tarzan*'s lead (Chris Buck and Kevin Lima, 1999). While the latter's musculature elicits the admiration and often desire of the female leads, Maui's physique mainly functions as the canvas for his past exploits and as the two-dimensional stage of his alter ego Mini-Maui, tattooed onto his skin.[6]

During the song 'You're Welcome', Maui's extraordinary masculinity is rendered as a highly theatrical performance, foregrounded through the presence of Mini-Maui. The latter is animated as a sentient, independent character who mimics and interacts with Maui. At the start of the song, Maui confidently sings 'I know it's a lot: the hair, the bod! When you're staring at a demigod', while flexing his pectorals in rhythm with the music. Mini-Maui accompanies his dance move, repeatedly jumping from one pectoral to the other. This comical instance of 'Mickey Mousing' – when animated movement and music parallel each other – reveals that Maui's flamboyant performance of masculinity is inseparable from his energetic musical performance. Showing off his muscles is one of his many dance moves, drawing attention to Mini-Maui's re-enactment of his extraordinary feats at the very same time. For example, while Maui sings 'Also I harnessed the breeze', he flexes his biceps: a digitally simulated zoom in showcases his muscle, on which Mini-Maui is shown 'harnessing' the breeze (Figure 6.3). This theatrical display, juxtaposing Mini-Maui's action-adventure spectacle with Maui's musical rendition, knowingly foregrounds the excessiveness and artificiality of superheroes' muscular performance.

This excessive display also characterises Maui's conceited and cocky behaviour, reminiscent of Marvel superhero Thor. In addition to semantic similarities in the representation of both superheroes' powers – jumping high in the air while wielding their hammer/fish hook – their narrative trajectory is also comparable. Maui is first introduced stealing the 'heart' of 'Mother Island' Te Fiti, which leads to the destruction of the island and the birth of demon Te Ka. In the 2011 Marvel film, Thor trespasses on the realm of the Frost Giants, confronting their leader and breaking the truce between his

Figure 6.3 *'Mini-Maui' re-enacts Maui's spectacular feats. Frame grab from* Moana *(Clements and Musker, 2016).*

kingdom and theirs. Maui's and Thor's arrogance, challenging superhuman entities more powerful than them, not only has dangerous consequences for their people but also results in the loss of their super props: Thor's hammer is confiscated by his father Odin (Anthony Hopkins), and Maui loses his fish hook when hit by Te Ka. Their self-confidence is further undermined when they try to retrieve their super prop. Thor subsequently fails to wield his hammer, as it is protected by an enchantment. As for Maui, he cannot properly shapeshift – turning into a tiny fish instead of a giant hawk – and is quickly overpowered when faced by villain Tamatoa (Jemaine Clement). Appearing vulnerable and weak, he is dragged along the ground and thrown against the walls of Tamatoa's cave, while the latter sings 'what a terrible performance... you don't swing it like you used to, man', deconstructing Maui's elaborate staging of male super-heroism.

Maui's shapeshifting struggles echo the issues faced by the protagonists of films such as *Spider-Man 2* (Sam Raimi, 2004) and *Iron Man 3*, in which superheroes experience difficulties with or lose their powers. As Purse points out, the 'superhero movie permits a particular mode of heroic masculinity that is explicitly uncertain, one that brings playful knowingness with a sense of the powerful male body as unruly' (2011a: 105). In the aforementioned examples, the superhero cannot rely on his superpowers any more; they escape from his control. The construction of superpowers as difficult to master, unpredictable and unstable has characterised Marvel Comics' protagonists from the 1960s onwards, and has been predominant in live-action adaptations with franchises such as *X-Men*, *Fantastic 4* and *Spider-Man* (Fouladi 2011: 163). Fouladi uses the term 'monstrosity' to refer to the latent danger of these superpowers, which constantly threaten to overflow (ibid.: 176). While Fouladi's term refers to both genders, it seems that male 'monstrosity' stands out through its spectacular manifestation, rooted in the protagonist's rising anger and resulting in his loss of control over his powers. This phenomenon is epitomised through the cinematic portrayal of the Hulk, the 'super' alter ego of scientist Bruce Banner who, due to exposure to radioactive rays, transforms into a green-skinned, hyper-muscular giant during bouts of uncontrollable rage.

Ralph's portrayal evokes the threateningly monstrous Hulk: similarly massive, he is also often depicted with his huge fists clenched. Beyond these visual similarities, Ralph struggles with his role as a powerful but destructive video-game super-villain. Like Bruce Banner at the beginning of most of his cinematic appearances,[7] his anger easily overwhelms him, which leads his super strength to overflow. During *Wreck-It Ralph*'s anniversary party scene, the cake 'staging' described in Chapter 5 makes Ralph threateningly furious, and paves the way for an overflowing performance. Seeing himself represented as a deranged monster, isolated from all the other characters, he places his little cake alter ego on the top of the cake, instead of that of Fix-It Felix. A Nicelander protests, putting the figurine back into the chocolate mud, arguing that Ralph is 'just the bad guy who wrecks the building'. Ralph repeats that he is 'not', getting so angry that he ends up slamming his fist down on the anniversary cake. At that moment, Ralph appears particularly frightening, revealing the underlying danger and instability of his extraordinary strength.

Yet, overall, Ralph's portrayal functions as a parody of the Hulk. Contrary to the latter's terrifying appearance, Ralph's potentially scary outlook is often defused. While the Hulk's massive body furiously destroys S.H.I.E.L.D's plane in *The Avengers* (Joss Whedon, 2012), Ralph's clumsily bumps into ceilings and walls. While Bruce's growing muscles spectacularly tear through his clothes when he transforms into the Hulk, Ralph noticeably lacks the latter's well-built physique. His large belly only deforms the tight soldier outfit he puts on when entering 'Hero's Duty': the well-defined abdominals reproduced on the suit comically bulge out, echoing Baymax's first attempts at 'suiting up'. The parody becomes more explicit when Ralph first enters 'Sugar Rush': he falls into a green gooey taffy pool, and when he comes out, he wreaks havoc in the game. Covered in green taffy with twigs and candy stuck to him, this Hulk figure is more amusing than terrifying: he struggles to walk, waves his arms in the air while shouting, and finally gets trapped in a giant cupcake.

Beyond Ralph's caricatured physique – recalling Maui's 'square' shape – *Wreck-It Ralph*'s parodic approach towards the Hulk's spectacular masculinity also applies to the manifestation of his anger and aggressiveness. Both Bruce Banner and Ralph humorously use euphemism to describe their monstrous behaviour and its consequences: in *The Avengers*, Banner (Mark Ruffalo) recalls that the 'last time [he] was in New York [he] kind of broke Harlem'; in his introductory voice-over, Ralph explains that he has 'got a little bit of a temper' on him, while his 8-bit alter ego furiously shouts and beats his fists against the ground. Yet, whereas Banner's angry transformations are often both terrifying and spectacular, revealing the scope of his super strength, Ralph is rather prone to temper tantrums – Vanellope calls him 'diaper baby' – which leads him to wreck anything that comes to hand. After an argument with Vanellope, for example, incensed Ralph starts smashing candy trees and stubbornly punches a giant jawbreaker until it cracks.

Moving beyond the initially parodic aspects characterising Ralph's super performance, *Wreck-It Ralph* foregrounds the gradual transformation of the comically strong, childishly quick-tempered protagonist into a real superhero: his narrative of becoming. Fouladi observes that superheroes' monstrous, overflowing powers are 'subsequently put under control' (2011: 176). In the case of male 'monstrosity', anger and its disruptive effects are then steadily mastered. For example, while the first parts of *The Incredible Hulk* and *The Avengers* feature Banner as a passive victim of his horrendous metamorphosis, he is seen to spark and channel his rage actively by the end of each film, which allows him to properly perform his superhero role. *The Incredible Hulk* notably includes sequences in which Banner (Edward Norton) trains with an instructor to mindfully 'control' his body, and correspondingly his anger; in the final shot, he calmly sits cross-legged, then smiles at the camera while his eyes turn green.[8] Ralph goes through a similar process, striving to use his powers in a more focused and productive manner: he scares away 'Sugar Rush' racers who bully Vanellope, builds a race track for her to practise on, and frees her and Felix from King Candy's 'fungeon', all thanks to his wrecking abilities. The 'mini game' sequence, in which Ralph helps Vanellope 'bake' a kart, particularly illustrates Ralph's efforts to moderate and adjust his super strength, alternating between breaking the equipment and fixing his mistakes.

In the final action sequence, Ralph efficiently destroys harmful Cy-Bugs that threaten 'Sugar Rush', and is willing to sacrifice himself, finally acting as a proper superhero. With his angry grimace and shouting, his clenched fists and gigantic smashing arms, he is highly reminiscent of the Hulk ultimately fighting alongside the Avengers, having both mastered their rage and channelled their power. Ralph's overall portrayal resonates with what Friedrich Weltzien describes as 'the successful performer of masculinity, as displayed in the superhero genre ... one who is able to stay in control throughout his transformation' to superhero form (2005: 244). In other words, by the end of the film, Ralph is able to smoothly shift from his regular self to his 'Wreck-It Ralph' superhero performance, without being overwhelmed by his overflowing anger. He successfully overcomes the monstrosity of his superpower, and peacefully returns to his 'job' as a wrecker. At the end, he is also recognised and valued for his demonstrations of anger/power and is fully involved within his video-game community. He welcomes homeless characters who help him with his wrecking within the game. The Nicelanders are 'actually being nice' to him, offering a cake on which he finally features with everyone else. By the end of the film, Ralph has mastered his overflowing anger and associated power, and embraced what Fouladi terms superheroes' 'prosocial and selfless' function (2011: 161): the ultimate performance of super-heroism.

Maui's more literally transformative trajectory also consists in a move towards selflessness, as well as cooperativeness. Like Thor, he slowly distances himself from his earlier arrogant super persona, providing the more authentic action-adventure performance described in Chapter 5: he gradually lets go of his elaborate *mise en scène* of masculinity. It is only after he confides his 'origin story' to Moana, revealing that he actually stole Te Fiti's 'heart' for the humans, that he successfully regains mastery of his superpowers, namely his shapeshifting abilities. At the end of his musical training sequence – 'Logo Te Pate', as seen in Chapter 5 – during which he successfully turns into various creatures, including a shark, a giant hawk and a whale, he notably agrees to let Moana sail. From this moment on, the self-centred superhero becomes a helper, leaving space for Moana's action feats.

Blending a parodic take on Marvel superhero tropes and the comic potential of animation aesthetics, Disney's contemporary animated features mock the cinematic depiction of male super-heroism and exertion of power. Despite the playfulness of these portrayals, *Wreck-It Ralph* and *Moana* maintain a core aspect of super masculinity: for superheroes' performance to be effective, they must master their excessive and overflowing, namely 'monstrous', superpowers. Although not as threatening and dangerous as those of their live-action counterparts, Ralph's and Maui's unstable powers are similarly intrinsically linked to their uncontrollable anger and/or arrogant self-confidence. Once their powers are channelled, they become proper superheroes. In *Moana*, the powerful superhero not only revises his performance but also lets the action heroine take centre stage.

Disney's contemporary portrayals of fairy-tale femininity build on and subvert a formulaic gendered template that the studio has developed throughout a large and easily identifiable canon; by contrast, the portrayals of *Wreck-It Ralph*'s Vanellope and *Frozen*'s Elsa borrow from a genre unusual for Disney – the superhero film. This generic influence re-envisions the characterisation of the post-feminist Disney heroine, beyond romantic frameworks and into new empowering spheres. The studio generically looks outwards in terms of gender construction. Considering the relative paucity of live-action leading superheroines within contemporary Hollywood, how do Disney animated films negotiate female superpower? To what extent does the narrative of becoming differ when uncontrollable abilities are possessed by a spectacularly powerful superheroine?

'MY POWER FLURRIES THROUGH THE AIR INTO THE GROUND': THE SUPERHEROINE AS A CREATIVE AND TRANSGRESSIVE FIGURE

In Disney's contemporary animated superhero features, female superpower is constructed as both a creative and disruptively powerful force. From a self-reflexive perspective, the narrative of becoming of Vanellope and Elsa parallels their practice and mastery of super animating skills. While the depiction of their superpowers shares similarities with Ralph's and Maui's – initially causing havoc, out of control, and driven by extreme emotions – the development and outcome of their superhero performance is at times more ambiguous. Disney's depiction of female superpower does not share the parodic impulses of male super-heroism, nor the playful construction of the super lead's body.

As a 'glitch', Vanellope's body uncontrollably breaks into dozens of pixels when she experiences strong emotions, such as joy, sadness or fear. Her digital image is momentarily blurred as a result, her movements become jerky and her voice is artificially modulated. Such 'glitching' affects the props and characters she touches, which correspondingly break down into a multitude of pixels, or even disappear and reappear in slightly different locations. This powerful but visually disruptive figure, threatening the aesthetic cohesiveness and stability of the arcade game she inhabits, is considered a 'freak', 'an accident waiting to happen': other racers bully and reject her, following King Candy's (Alan Tudyk) orders. This patriarchal authority figure is responsible for Vanellope's marginalised position, forbidding her from racing seemingly to protect both herself and the other game members. Although Vanellope finds support with Ralph, who encourages her to practise racing, he also urges her to 'get that glitching under control'. While she trains, her excitement at her progress makes her glitch, and she loses control of her kart. Later on, during the final race, some 'cherry bombs' hit her kart and make her glitch, which affects the trajectory of her vehicle, making it disappear and reappear throughout the race track. Although she ends up in front of her opponents, her disruptive superpowers are still highly unstable. She repeats to herself that she must keep them 'under control, no more glitching'.

Such a theme of control through concealment and marginalisation of female superpower is intrinsic to Elsa's narrative trajectory in *Frozen*. She is introduced as a little girl, playing with her younger sister Anna: they slide on an ice rink and off snowbanks Elsa creates, and build a snowman. This joyful display is interrupted when Elsa accidentally strikes Anna with her powers. Her parents take them to a community of trolls for help, who warn them that 'there is beauty . . . but also great danger' in Elsa's powers: she 'must learn to control' them. While speaking, the troll chief conducts the Northern Lights to show the silhouette of an adult Elsa creating magical snowflakes, surrounded by an admiring crowd. The snowflakes quickly morph into sharp spikes; the human figures panic and attack Elsa's silhouette. This animated staging prefigures the reaction of Arendelle's inhabitants after Elsa's coronation, alternating between fear – calling her a 'monster' – and wonder at her powers. Echoing *Wreck-It Ralph*'s animated cake sequence, this representation of Elsa's superpowers is heavily mediated, imitating pre-digital techniques such as silhouette animation and shadow play: a highly theatrical, nightmarish staging which aesthetically clashes with the colourful and more photorealistic world of the film. Like Ralph, Elsa is being 'animated'; unlike him, she has no control over this artificial construction of her super performance. She is a helpless viewer in front of a threatening *mise en scène* which emphasises the menace that her powers seem to represent. Such a sequence contrasts sharply with the humorous tone of *Wreck-It Ralph*'s sequence, in which the cake version of the protagonist looks more ridiculous than genuinely dangerous.

Such a contrast between the depictions of the superhero and superheroine is further developed throughout *Frozen*. Unlike Ralph, the Hulk and Maui, Elsa does not initially train and master her overflowing powers. She becomes afraid of her unstable abilities, which get stronger as she grows older, so that she cannot touch anything without turning it into ice. Her father – another patriarchal authority figure – decides to 'limit her contact with people', and encourages her to wear gloves: a metaphor for her hidden powers and correspondingly suppressed emotions. Later in the film, on her coronation day, the young woman is shown rehearsing her father's lessons of restraint: 'conceal it, don't feel it, don't let it show'. Repeating his mantra, her 'super' performance consists in dissimulating her superpowers, appearing reserved and distant as a result – an illusion of control.

Wreck-It Ralph's and *Frozen*'s diegetic characters then perceive female exertion of superpowers as particularly harmful and disruptive: the control of female power is equated with its containment and erasure. By contrast, in the context of Disney's diegetic worlds, it is suggested not that the masculine performance of wrecking, shapeshifting or super strength should be hidden or interrupted, but that it should be mastered. From that perspective, *Wreck-It Ralph* and *Frozen* seem to reproduce the tendency of mainstream cinema to 'undermin[e] female potency as it becomes threatening' (Bruzzi 1997: 180) – in other words, when women's powers become too great.

However, Elsa eventually embraces and explores the scope of her extraordinary abilities through an exhilarating musical sequence. After having fled Arendelle, she sings the empowering song 'Let It Go', notably throwing away her glove. The song follows on from the superhero genre in the way it reveals Elsa's growing mastery of her powers and enthusiasm in the process. Justin Schumaker observes that superhero films tend to dedicate a significant amount of time to the protagonists' testing and exploration of their superpowers, foregrounding the 'majesty' and 'delight' these bring (2011: 134). Such thrilling training sessions can be found at the beginning of both *Spider-Man* and its 2012 reboot *The Amazing Spider-Man* (Marc Webb), during which Peter Parker tries out his new superpowers by climbing walls, jumping between buildings, and spinning webs.

The empowering dimension of such sequences is conveyed through the physical manifestation of Elsa's powers. In her hands, snow becomes a three-dimensional fluid and changeable material taking the shape of small snowflakes, then long arabesqued lines stretching into the sky: her creations reveal the 'plasmatic' freedom of animation (Figure 6.4). Sergei Eisenstein uses the term 'plasmatic' to describe characters from Disney's early shorts, such as *Hawaiian Holiday* (Ben Sharpsteen, 1937) and *The Moth and the Flame* (Burt Gillett, 1938), specifically their 'freedom from ossification' and 'ability to assume dynamically any form' (quoted in Taylor 2006: 101, 103). Metamorphosis and 'plasmaticness' are also intrinsic to the superhero genre. Scott Bukatman argues that 'plasmatic fantasy . . . underlies the entire superhero genre with its transformative bodies' representing 'the central fascination of the superhero film' (2012: 19; 2011: 121). Correspondingly, the malleable, endlessly stretching bodies of Sandman and Venom in *Spider-Man 3* (Sam Raimi, 2007), as well as Groot in *Guardians of the Galaxy* (James Gunn, 2014), are rendered through computer animation. Considering the central aesthetic role of 'plasmaticness' both in the superhero genre and within animation, Elsa's superhero practice takes a self-reflexive turn, foregrounding and developing the affinities between animation and the superhero film: she becomes the super-animator of superheroes' 'plasmatic fantasy'. Her line 'it's time to see what I can do, to test the limits and break through' translates her status both as a superheroine gradually mastering her powers and as an animator artistically exploring the limitless potentials of animation. Her creative flurry comes to a crescendo with an impressive ice castle rising before viewers' eyes. Ice beams, archways and a sparkling chandelier gradually take shape onscreen: the sequence 'métaphorise' the process of computer animation ('becomes a metaphor for', Chion 2020: 155; my translation). As Michel Chion observes, Elsa manipulates snowflakes and crystals like pixels to build her creations: 'nous voyons quelqu'un créer à toute vitesse et sans machine des images de synthèse selon sa fantaisie'

Figure 6.4 *Elsa's powers reveal the 'plasmatic' freedom of animation. Frame grab from* Frozen *(Buck and Lee, 2013).*

('we watch someone creating digital images without a computer, at top speed, following her imagination', ibid.: 156; my translation). Elsa's awe-inspiring demonstration of her animating skills parallels her thrilling superhero practice. The finale of this spectacular sequence, consisting of a long shot of the completed ice castle at the top of the mountain bathed in sunlight, establishes the artistry and scope of Elsa's superpowers, and foregrounds her limitless agency as a super-animator.

Not only does this sequence demonstrate that animation is the most ideally suited medium to translate the 'plasmatic fantasy' of the superhero film, but the animated form also enhances the sense of liberation expressed within the musical. In 'Let It Go', Disney develops and expands generic affinities between the superhero film and the musical through the specific qualities of animation. As Elsa's animated creations become more and more elaborate, her face lights up in amazement at the scope of her extraordinary abilities, and she experiences a growing sense of freedom that she expresses in the chorus. Singing 'can't hold it back anymore', she designs a snowman, which takes shape out of swirling snow (Olaf). Her enthusiastic singing at that moment resonates with what Susan Smith describes as the 'self-conscious delight in animation's capacity for bringing things to life', which constitutes the specific pleasures of the animated musical (2011: 172). Such expression of joy, heightened by the 'physical vitality and emotional intensity' (ibid.: 172) characteristic of the musical genre, peak at the end of the song, when Elsa's spectacular abilities as a super-animator culminate in the creation of the castle. Surrounded by archways resembling icy prosceniums, she moves throughout what looks like a stage, projecting sparkling snow all around. Her large and graceful arm gestures echo the 'spiralling . . . frozen fractals' described in her song. This superhero ballet is concluded by a more explicitly theatrical performance. Standing at the centre of her stage, Elsa energetically takes down her hair, transforms her royal attire into an eye-catching sparkling dress made of ice, and confidently struts out onto the balcony of the castle, singing 'here I stand in the light of the day'. 'Let It Go' becomes a thrilling song of multilayered empowerment: what Jane Feuer describes as the 'liberating vision . . . at the heart of the musical genre' (1993: 84) intensifies the empowering nature of superhero practice. This elaborate *mise en scène*, crystallising the generic convergence of the superhero film and the musical, is notable because it is self-directed. Contrary to *Wreck-It Ralph*'s cake animation and *Frozen*'s earlier silhouette sequence, 'Let It Go' features Elsa as her own animator, designing her own set and costume. Unlike Maui in 'You're Welcome', she does not rely on a two-dimensional double or a mediated, illusionistic environment. Such cohesiveness in direction and animation style allows Elsa's superhero practice to become, through the musical, a strikingly liberating and empowering experience: her musical performance spectacularly amplifies her artistic and expressive mastery of her superpowers.

Nevertheless, the specific *mise en scène* accompanying this self-directed liberating experience reproduces to some extent the tensions surrounding the contemporary depiction of the powerful superheroine. When Elsa walks towards the castle balcony and faces the audience at the end of her song, the revelation of her glamorous appearance, emphasised through her off-the-shoulder sparkling dress and transparent stilettos, echoes the last stage of a makeover. Sarah Gilligan explains that the makeover narrative, most noticeable in romantic comedies and teen movies, works 'to establish the parameters of acceptable feminine appearance, while also offering viewers the vicarious visual pleasure of witnessing the protagonist's transformation from frump to bombshell' (2011: 167). At the end of 'Let It Go', the digitally simulated camera first shows Elsa's blurred reflection on the icy floor, then gradually tilts up, following the slit of her dress to reveal her leg, knee and whole body. Such camerawork, constructing Elsa's body as the object of the gaze, emphasises the contrast between her earlier demure, maidenly appearance – dark clothes, long turtleneck dress – and her new confidently attractive demeanour. Elsa's makeover is notably self-directed; unlike romantic-comedy and teen-movie makeovers, or fairy-tale transformations as displayed in *Cinderella* (Clyde Geronimi and Wilfred Jackson, 1950), heterosexual romance is not its goal. Still, *Frozen* conflates Elsa's new-found empowerment as a super-animator, and the culmination of her spectacular abilities, with the inscription of a more glamorous, objectified and sexualised construction of femininity. A similar makeover – or 'super makeover' – occurs in superhero films such as *Batman Returns* (Tim Burton, 1992) and *Catwoman* (Pitof, 2004). Shy, childlike and clumsy Selina Kyle (in the former) and Patience Phillips (in the latter) transition to Catwoman's assertive, powerful and sexualised persona when they don their hand-made black leather outfits. Disney replicates, to some extent, such self-orchestrated super makeovers at the end of 'Let It Go', portraying Elsa as both subject and object of her creative flurry.

Such merging of female empowerment and glamour foregrounds what Yvonne Tasker terms the 'doubleness of post-feminism' (2011: 70). Within the wider context of action-adventure cinema, it manifests through the combination of heroines' 'readily apparent strength and skill with a more traditionally feminine, and often emphatically sexualized, physique' (Purse 2011b: 187), as exemplified in early 2000s female-centred franchises such as *Charlie's Angels* (2000, 2003) and *Lara Croft: Tomb Raider* (2001, 2003). Superheroines tend to represent a hyperbolic manifestation of post-feminist doubleness: these spectacularly skilled women are both more powerful and equivalently more sexualised than their action counterparts. They are often scantily clad, and the camerawork and costumes reveal a physique both toned and curvaceous, a body that is both physically strong and constructed as sexually appealing. For example, blue-skinned Mystique principally appears 'naked' in the original *X-Men* franchise (2000, 2003, 2006) and is played by former model Rebecca Romijn; more recently, in *Wonder Woman* (Patty Jenkins, 2017), teammate Sameer (Saïd Taghmaoui) exclaims that he is both 'frightened and aroused' by the athletic Amazon. Purse argues that such sexual objectification, at times undeniably knowing as in the former example, is a representational trope which functions as a 'containment strategy', reducing the threat of female potency (2011b: 187, 189). By contrast, male-centred superhero films notably tone down the muscular attractiveness of the leads in pivotal sequences, refocusing on their extraordinary bravery and feats. For example, neither Spider-Man nor Captain America appears bare-chested in his climactic fight against the villain: such sequences foreground the dramatic scope and effects of superheroes' superpowers, not their bodies. In this context, Elsa's super makeover seems to dilute, to some extent, the spectacularly empowering demonstration of her superpowers. While 'Let It Go' showcased a crescendo of animated artistry, which stands out as a particularly striking – and rare – exploration of female superpowers, the use of the final makeover trope seems to reposition Elsa within a more conventional version and display of the superheroine. This shifts the attention from her spectacular powers to the spectacle of her glamorous appearance.

Admittedly, Elsa's makeover is also characterised by the transgressive campness of her performance of femininity – reminiscent of Disney's wicked witches – as discussed in Chapter 4; still, *Frozen* develops multiple containment strategies throughout the narrative, diluting to some extent the liberating effect of 'Let It Go' and Elsa's agency. The film repeatedly points to the danger of unbridled female power, especially when fuelled by strong emotions. While adult superheroes such as Ralph learn to master both their anger and their superpower, turning their childish temper tantrums into an efficiently channelled superhero performance, Elsa's powerful anger remains threateningly unruly and frightening, as exemplified in the following sequences. Early in the film, at her coronation party, Elsa inadvertently reveals her hidden powers by breaking from her composed performance. When Anna insistently questions her ('Why do you shut the world out? What are you so afraid of?') Elsa angrily shouts, 'enough!' Ice then shoots from her hand, forming spikes across the floor. Scared, she flees the kingdom. While singing 'Let It Go', she not only embraces her spectacular superpowers but also expresses her 'pleasure at being released from emotional regulation' (Negra 2015). Yet, this demonstration of limitless agency is short-lived: as Elsa later sings to her sister, 'I'm such a fool, I can't be free.' Later in the film, her powerful superhero performance is initially efficient and controlled, but ultimately contained, portrayed as threateningly dangerous. When thugs attack her castle, she manages to single-handedly defend herself: at first helpless and scared, she uses her powers defensively, creating an ice wall that protects her from the thugs' arrows. She then becomes more proactive and directly attacks the thugs, urging them to 'stay away' while shooting ice at them. The more self-assured and powerful she gets, the more menacing and angrier she appears. Her scared expression is gradually replaced by a determined, furious look; she ultimately traps one thug in a cage of spikes, and pushes back the other towards the edge of the balcony. Prince Hans arrives at that very moment, telling her not to be 'the monster they fear' she is. She stops herself, overwhelmed, and one thug takes advantage of her confusion by shooting an arrow at her; although rescued, she wakes up in chains, imprisoned in the castle.

This sequence reveals the extent to which contemporary superhero and action-adventure cinema still struggles to render the performance of the powerful superheroine, angry yet in control. Diane Negra observes that post-feminist popular culture foregrounds a version of femininity which stays 'emotionally within bounds' (2009: 139). While *Wreck-It Ralph*'s lead efficiently uses superpowers that are sparked and fuelled by anger, *Frozen* favours a more composed, palatable version of femininity, and correspondingly a less potentially dangerous performance. Elsa's superpowers are admired for their artistry – when Anna and Kristoff step into her castle, they are overwhelmed by its beauty – but feared when used in a more aggressive, or even defensive way. Contrary to her male counterparts Ralph and Maui, or the more hybrid duo Hiro and Baymax, Elsa is excluded from the performance of selfless rescues or non-violent but spectacular battles.

In *Frozen*, female super-heroism is then only permitted within specific limits and a harmless context. Like Ralph, Elsa ultimately returns to her people: as Owen Weetch points out, her acceptance of and by her community represents the 'only utopian element that was lacking' from her musical performance (2016: 152). However, Elsa has also become more 'tempered', using her powers in 'de-fanged' ways (Holmes 2014). While Ralph 'learns to embrace his destructiveness and use it for the good of others' (Davis 2013: 145), properly performing masculine super-heroism, Elsa's final display of her powers consist in the creation of an ice rink for Arendelle's inhabitants and ice skates for Anna, reproducing the way she used her powers as a little girl. While the male lead must abandon his childishness – self-centredness for Maui and tantrums for Ralph – to become an efficient, mature superhero, the dangerously assertive and powerful superheroine seems to syntactically regress to her playful, harmless childhood state. Most strikingly, her power as a super female animator is significantly toned down. During 'Let It Go',

Elsa spectacularly displayed the life-giving potential and expressive, plasmatic freedoms of animation. By contrast, in the concluding sequence, she creates icy ornaments on the castle walls and freezes fountains: water stops flowing and its movement, the very essence of animation, halts. Elsa's super performance becomes merely decorative, resulting in beautiful but still, static designs. The scope of her superpowers is similarly restricted in subsequent short films released within the timeframe of this book. In *Frozen Fever* (Chris Buck and Jennifer Lee, 2015), Elsa creates miniature ice sculptures and magically decorates dresses for Anna and herself. The musical culminating point of *Olaf's Frozen Adventure* (Stevie Wermers-Skelton and Kevin Deters, 2017) consists in diluted variations of 'Let It Go': the gradual appearance and design of Elsa's Christmas tree are strikingly reminiscent of the chandelier 'crystallising like an icy blast' in the former song. These short films contain traces of Elsa's lifegiving powers, yet the resulting magical creatures materialise independently from her will: in *Frozen Fever*, her sneezes spark mischievous tiny snowmen which Olaf calls 'little brothers'. All in all, most of the original 'Let It Go' sequence represents a 'temporary fantasy' (Holmes 2014), constructing the superheroine as an entirely autonomous, powerful, emotionally and artistically unrestrained woman.[9]

Elsa's ultimate childlike regression not only reveals a stark contrast between constructions of male and female super performance, but it also suggests that, as Brown observes, the super girl is a more 'palatable figure of strong femininity' (2011: 167). *Wreck-It Ralph*'s young Vanellope remains a visually disruptive character throughout the film, ultimately reappropriating and mastering her overflowing powers to perform super-heroism. When King Candy, revealed as the villain, traps her and calls her 'glitch', paralleling Elsa's 'monster' sequence, Vanellope decides to use her abilities, focusing to channel both her emotions and her superpowers. She then glitches, smoothly disappearing and reappearing away from King Candy's kart. When she sees Ralph sacrificially falling into a 'Diet Cola' volcano, creating a beacon that will destroy the Cy-Bugs, she runs to his rescue. Finding a kart, she speedily glitches towards the volcano, combining her racing skills with her newly mastered superpower. Once she catches Ralph, she glitches them both to safety, quickly teleporting with a single move of the head, and efficiently performing a selfless act of super-heroism in the process.

As opposed to *Frozen*, there is no syntactic closure containing the scope or quality of Vanellope's superpowers. Although less jerky and unpredictable, her glitching still represents a particularly disruptive force that she ultimately embraces: as she happily tells Ralph, she is not giving up 'the best superpower ever'. Unlike Elsa, she also remains an empowered 'super' animator. Successfully manipulating the pixels of her own digital image, she controls her movements and her own appearance, notably discarding the ready-made glittery pink dress that appears when she is revealed as the princess. Throughout the film, she stays bold, energetic and proactive; she is also a tiny and cute 'princess', representing a significantly revised and updated, yet persisting version of Disney's template for animated femininity – as Ralph claims, 'everybody loves an adorable winner'. Brown argues that girls 'can play out the most extreme fantasies of heroism in a liminal realm' (ibid.: 166). As a little girl, Vanellope's powers are not restrained. She is not yet as threateningly dangerous as the more powerful, older Elsa: she does not need to become more tempered or sexualised, and remains a visually disruptive, though childlike, figure.

Conclusion

Approaching *Wreck-It Ralph*, *Frozen*, *Big Hero 6* and *Moana* as superhero films opens up new perspectives on the ways Disney expands its animated formula: the studio engages with its own cinematic universe and reappropriates contemporary Hollywood genres through the lens of Marvel films. Disney animated superhero films foreground and question the gendered implications of and tensions within superhero performances as constructed within live-action cinema. They focus on characters endowed with spectacular yet overflowing, dangerous and monstrous abilities: the ways these are exerted, between mastery and containment, channelled abilities and restrained power, is arguably what defines the gendering of the super performance.

These animated films challenge the association of masculinity with violent demonstrations of strength; they mock and subvert superheroes' muscular narrative of becoming and unruly performance; and they further develop the sense of playful knowingness characterising Marvel portrayals through the comic potential of animation. In *Wreck-It Ralph* and *Moana*, Ralph's and Maui's mastering of their own extraordinary bodies, superpowers and emotions represents a move towards a balanced performance of super-heroism. Disney animated superhero films also self-reflexively rely on the expressive, plasmatic and disruptive power of animation to re-envision female super-heroism: Vanellope and Elsa are framed as artistic figures, super animators. At the same time, these films magnify tensions surrounding such constructions, ambivalently containing extraordinarily yet dangerously powerful superheroines.

In parallel, these animated portrayals generically broaden the figure of the post-feminist Disney heroine. They strikingly expand the empowering potential of princesses whose characterisation borrows from genres of romance, and who are placed on the same footing as their princes. Yet, Elsa's depiction points to Disney's notable tendency to position such challenging figures within more conventional frameworks. In the same way as witty and active fairy-tale women also become sentimental brides, embodying persisting aspects of Disney's gendered formula, Disney's superheroines possess extraordinarily powerful skills which tend to be contained and more harmlessly reframed by the end of the narrative – unless they are adorable girls. Such characterisations crystallise Disney's signature combination of tradition and empowerment regarding contemporary constructions of femininity, and foreground their unstable positioning on the post-feminist spectrum.

In *Big Hero 6*, the portrayal of the duo Hiro–Baymax re-envisions superheroism as a harmoniously hybrid performance, challenging the gender binary of superhero cinema; the film also points to the key role of anthropomorphic characters in Disney's contemporary generic reconfigurations. *Zootopia* (Byron Howard and Rich Moore, 2016) similarly features anthropomorphic leads, but in an unlikely generic environment for Disney: the action cop buddy film. The next chapter explores the gendered and racial implications of this anthropomorphic reimagining.

Notes

1. See for example the works of Bukatman 2009; Jenkins 2014; Flanagan et al. 2016.
2. See for example Gray II and Kaklamanidou 2011; Brown 2017; Yockey 2017.
3. Up until 2018, the end of the period under study in this book, only three mainstream superhero films had featured women as primary leads: *Catwoman*, *Elektra* (Rob Bowman, 2005) and *Wonder Woman*. Arguably, since 2018, this number has increased, including *Captain Marvel* (Anna Boden and Ryan Fleck, 2019), *Birds of Prey (and the Fantabulous Emancipation of One Harley Quinn)* (Cathy Yan, 2020), the sequel *Wonder Woman 1984* (Patty Jenkins, 2020), *Black Widow* (Cate Shortland, 2021), as well as the Netflix comedy *Thunder Force* (Ben Falcone, 2021). It remains to be seen whether these films are reflecting a developing trend, or remain 'rare exceptions' (McSweeney 2020: 60).
4. Vfx supervisor Edson Williams explains that the vast majority of shots featuring Steve Rogers before his transformation were done by 'digitally shrinking Evans's own face and body' (quoted in Cohen 2011).
5. In *The Flash*'s 'Pilot' episode (2014), for example, Barry Allen is astonished that 'lightning gave [him] abs'. See Brown 2017: 43.
6. The significant age gap between Moana and Maui, and the corresponding absence of romance narrative, also frames this excessively playful construction of masculinity.
7. This is especially the case in the cinematic 'origin story' versions of 'Hulk', namely in *Hulk* and *The Incredible Hulk*.
8. Bruce Banner's struggles to master his Hulk alter ego are reintroduced and developed throughout subsequent *Avengers* films, from *Age of Ultron* to *Thor:*

Ragnarok (Taika Waititi, 2017) and *Infinity War* (Anthony and Joe Russo, 2018), up to *Endgame* (Anthony and Joe Russo, 2019), in which Banner has managed to transform permanently into a hybrid Hulk/Banner, combining the 'brains and the brawn' and reaching a balance in his performance of super masculinity.

9. In that regard, *Frozen* contrasts with *Frozen II* (Chris Buck and Jennifer Lee, 2019), which features Elsa successfully using her superpowers to protect her kingdom.

CHAPTER 7

Animal Action Buddies: Disney's Anthropomorphic Reimaginings in Zootopia

> Nick: So, are all rabbits bad drivers or is it just you?
> (Judy slams on the brakes, Nick lurches forward.)
> Judy: Oops. Sorry.
> Nick: Sly bunny.
> Judy: Dumb fox.
> Nick: You know you love me.
> Judy: Do I know that? Yes. Yes, I do.
> (*Zootopia*, Byron Howard and Rich Moore, 2016)

As *Zootopia*'s officer Judy Hopps (Ginnifer Goodwin) smiles at her new cop partner Nick Wilde (Jason Bateman), she stomps on the accelerator, Nick puts on his sunglasses and hits the siren, and their patrol car speeds away for new adventures. This final sequence illustrates *Zootopia*'s multiple borrowings from a specific strand of action-adventure cinema, in which a police officer or 'cop' is typically paired with a dissimilar, initially antagonistic, and ultimately supportive and complementary partner: the cop buddy film. By the end of *Zootopia*, rabbit Judy and fox Nick swap banter expressing their affectionate partnership, knowingly flipping stereotypes associated with their colleague's species ('sly fox, dumb bunny'). Such a dialogue, primarily referring to their status as animals, has wider implications: Nick's lines echo stereotypes related to femininity ('are all rabbits bad drivers'), and the inter-species exchange evokes the configuration of numerous action cop buddy films. These parallels crystallise *Zootopia*'s wider generic strategy.

Zootopia stands out within Disney's contemporary animated canon through the exclusive presence of animal characters: the anthropomorphising of action cop buddy tropes forms the basis for *Zootopia*'s reworking and questioning of issues linked to gendered and racial identity. Such reworking can be noticed at three levels. *Zootopia*'s anthropomorphic reconfiguration functions as a lens magnifying and challenging the gendered imbalance of cop buddy films, and constructions of femininity within post-feminist action-adventure cinema. This generic reworking resonates, at times ambiguously, with wider social dynamics, including constructions and understandings of race within contemporary America. The anthropomorphising of action buddy tropes also frames a more self-reflexive revising. *Zootopia* qualifies and re-envisions to some extent Disney's contemporary portrayals of race relations, related to the studio's formulaic sentimental impulses and generic predictability. This chapter examines *Zootopia*'s anthropomorphic reimagining of the action cop buddy film, and how this reimagining impacts on generic gendered roles, wider issues of racial identity, and Disney's own representational and generic dynamics.

The buddy film functions for the most part as an 'all-male modelling of the conventional Hollywood romance' (Kuhn and Westwell 2012). Like romantic-comedy protagonists, the duo moves from 'antagonism to affection and support' (Tasker 1998: 85). The leads' opposite personalities are articulated through differences in 'taste, culture, costume': such contrasts are often juxtaposed with racial or ethnic differences (ibid.: 155). A particular strand of action-adventure cinema has light-heartedly explored such buddy partnerships. Popular franchises such as *Lethal Weapon* (1987, 1989, 1992, 1998) – rebooted as a television series in 2016 – and *Rush Hour* (1998, 2001, 2007) blend semantic tropes from the action cop film with the syntactic structure of the buddy genre. In these films, the unlikely pair must learn to cooperate despite their dissimilarities and dislike of each other in order to pursue their investigation.

Zootopia's generic dialogue with the action cop buddy film was explicitly acknowledged: co-director Byron Howard described it as a 'buddy movie' (quoted in Julius 2016: 28); reviewer John Nugent as a 'buddy-cop movie' (2016); Robbie Collin compared Judy and Nick to 'Nick Nolte and Eddie Murphy in *48 Hrs.*, albeit considerably cuter' (2016b). *Zootopia* directly follows on from this generic configuration: Nick's cynicism and 'hustler' ways – in Judy's words – clash with her professional zeal and naïve optimism. Despite their antagonism, they must work together: rabbit Judy wittily tricks initially uncooperative fox Nick into helping her, as he is a key witness in a case she is investigating.

Disney's incursion into the domain of action buddy films is a particularly notable generic move: the adoption of the buddy narrative allows the studio to move beyond the familiar romantic framework of its iconic fairy-tale formula. Like Ralph and Vanellope in *Wreck-It Ralph* (Rich Moore, 2012) and Moana and Maui in *Moana* (Ron Clements and John Musker, 2016), *Zootopia*'s primary relationship is characterised by a platonic partnership. *Zootopia* expands the playful adversarial dynamics of romantic-comedy influenced *The Princess and the Frog* (Ron Clements and John Musker, 2009), *Tangled* (Nathan Greno and Byron Howard, 2010) and *Frozen* (Chris Buck and Jennifer Lee, 2013), while challenging more distinctly their sentimental and nostalgic impulses.

Along with the studio's animated superhero films, *Zootopia* illustrates Disney's efforts to generically look outwards, interacting with its wider cinematic universe and Hollywood. Such reappropriation of the action buddy film allows Disney to take part in a genre that has been central to contemporary mainstream animation. In an initial effort to distance their output from Disney's fairy-tale romances, studios such as Pixar have relied on the buddy narrative, developed in films such as *Toy Story* (John Lasseter, 1995) and *The Good Dinosaur* (Peter Sohn, 2015). The former focuses on the rivalry between Woody, a vintage sheriff doll, and Buzz, a space ranger, who ultimately become friends through a series of perilous adventures; *The Good Dinosaur* follows unlikely pair Arlo and Spot, a dinosaur and a young boy who must travel together through hostile prehistoric lands. *Zootopia* specifically transposes the buddy narrative to an anthropomorphic framework: animals that are 'natural enemies' – a fox and a rabbit – partner up and overcome their differences through their action-oriented journey. Such a generic move was generally praised, yet met with surprise, as exemplified by the critical reception of *Zootopia*.

Reviewers emphasised two points stemming from *Zootopia*'s generic reworking and pointing to wider popular preconceptions about Disney animated films and mainstream animation more generally: *Zootopia*'s political and racial subtext, and the varied intertextual generic references within the film, transcending the Disney fairy tale. Critics repeatedly framed *Zootopia*'s approach to race and gender as unexpectedly bold and topical. Jen Chaney observed that 'the idea that a cartoon starring an adorable bunny, a slippery fox . . . might have something meaningful to say about race relations, especially in #BlackLivesMatter America, sounds pretty ridiculous. But it's true' (2016); Peter Travers stated that 'the last thing you'd expect from a new Disney animated marshmallow is balls . . . This baby has attitude, a potent feminist streak, a tough take on racism' (2016); Rebecca Keegan noted that 'the studio known for its fairy-tale castles and doe-eyed princesses has sneaked a tart, subtle examination of bias into . . . a talking-animals movie' (2016). Such critical surprise related to *Zootopia*'s contemporary relevance, and more particularly its topical portrayal of race relations, is framed by generic preconceptions surrounding both Disney and mainstream animation. These reviews point to the typical association of Disney with sentimental and retrograde fairy tales – or rather, perpetuate criticisms surrounding the studio's formula – and of animated films with lightweight and childish content. Animation scholars note the 'stigma' associated with children's audiences (Wells 1998: 175), deploring that animated films have been 'stereotyped' as an inane medium (Furniss 2014: 225; Denis 2020: 10). The presence of animal characters reinforces such devaluation, representing a semantic barrier separating juvenile 'cartoons' with 'adorable' creatures – in Chaney's words – from supposedly more serious, mature live-action film.

Yet, it is precisely the anthropomorphic nature of *Zootopia*'s characters which allows such a challenging, complex yet ambivalent depiction of gendered and race relations. Paul Wells notes that 'the animal is an essential component of the language of animation' (2009: 2): it also represents a key vehicle for caricature and social critique. Anthropomorphism functions as a lens which, as Christopher Holliday more generally observes, permits the 'dilution, exaggeration and satirising of the machinations of the human condition', including 'behaviour, socio-cultural hierarchies' (2016: 248). The representation of animals has itself a rich tradition in art and literature: Wells explains that the 'animal story' has proved attractive to animators 'because it inevitably works as part of a surreal, supernatural, or revisionist reinvention of human experience' (2009: 60). Such reinvention has characterised numerous Disney films featuring animal stories, from *Dumbo* (Ben Sharpsteen, 1941) and *Bambi* (David Hand et al., 1942) to *The Lion King* (Roger Allers and Rob Minkoff, 1994). *Zootopia* builds on this paradigm, relying on the very specificity of the central duo's animal status to explore human relations, and using the action cop buddy film as a way into issues of identity and social roles, including certain connotations of racial and gendered identity. These are explored through an anthropomorphic lens, transposing the antagonistic dynamics from live-action buddy films to an animated animal story featuring an inter-species partnership. *Zootopia*'s animated animals are endowed with humanlike qualities: they can talk, have jobs, walk on two feet, and use technology. Still, some species remain enemies, and some patterns of behaviour appear at first intrinsically linked with specific animals: prey or predator. This dichotomy resonates with generic and wider social dynamics: tensions between species evoke the impact and implications of racial bias, as well as the gendered imbalance underlying the live-action buddy film.

Beyond the buddy genre, reviewers noted and praised the wide range of intertextual references within *Zootopia* that led the film to generically transcend Disney's formula of fairy tales and sentimental romances and appeal to a wide audience as a result. Critics such as Collin described *Zootopia* as finding itself 'unexpectedly – but by no means unwelcomely – in the twilit domain of *film noir*' (2016b); Michelle Orange mentioned 'crime underworld movies, including *The Godfather* and *Chinatown*' (2016). Similarly, Peter Debruge argued that the film

> lends itself surprisingly well to a classic *L.A.*-style detective story, a la *The Big Lebowski* or *Inherent Vice*, yielding an adult-friendly whodunit with a chipper 'you can do it!' message for the cubs ... Genre-wise, the film couldn't be farther from the terrain of *Frozen* and other Disney princess movies. (Debruge 2016b)

Such comments not only point to persisting stereotypes surrounding audiences for mainstream animation – reduced to children and families – but also encapsulate wider preconceived ideas about animated features and genre. Reviewers still tend to approach animated films first as family films, a genre that suffers from 'perceived defects' such as excessive 'sentiment' and 'juvenility' (Brown 2012: 10). Disney's output epitomises such reductive generic categorisations, being mostly associated with innocence, childishness and sugar-coated 'marshmallow' – in Travers's words – fairy tales. *Zootopia*'s multifaceted generic identity calls into question such preconceptions, which is not entirely surprising considering Disney's wider contemporary output. As discussed in previous chapters, a fairy tale like *Frozen* reworks and converges with genres as varied as the romantic comedy and the superhero film. Through tropes from the action cop buddy film, *Zootopia* expands its formula and directly challenges the studio's perceived generic predictability, as well as other aspects of its contemporary output: the carefree and cheerful theme-park atmosphere of Disney's enchanted animated worlds, and issues related to the latter's social and racial cohesion.

This chapter elaborates on Disney's distinctive reworking of another facet of action-adventure cinema, beyond its cinematic universe of Marvel superhero films. I argue that, by relying on the specificity of the animation medium and the studio's canon and paratexts, *Zootopia*'s anthropomorphic reappropriation of action cop buddy tropes frames a three-layered questioning of issues linked to genre, gender and wider social dynamics. At a first level, *Zootopia*'s anthropomorphic lens reconfigures the gendered power dynamics within the buddy partnership. The portrayal of Judy and the difficulties she faces as a 'bunny cop', as labelled in the film, as well as her relationship with both Nick and her colleagues resonate with and challenge the typical positioning of women within the action cop buddy genre. Her very design and framing as an anthropomorphic action heroine also re-envision the post-feminist construction of contemporary action-adventure heroines.

Zootopia's subversive strategy not only impacts generic portrayals but also has wider implications: species identity is framed to evoke elements of gendered identity as well as certain aspects of racial identity. *Zootopia* repeatedly includes explicit references to discourses on and constructions of race, racial relations and racism in the United States, mediated through anthropomorphic language and aesthetics. Relying on Nick and Judy's antagonistic buddy relationship, and Zootopia's wider animal dynamics, the film challenges to some extent stereotypes associated with specific species. This chapter will examine the ways these constructions resonate with wider issues of racial identity.

Beyond generic and wider social dynamics, *Zootopia*'s anthropomorphising of action cop buddy tropes ambivalently frames Disney's self-reflexive revision of its own contemporary representational strategies. *Zootopia*'s antagonistic animal partners and anthropomorphic world contrast with the idealised and harmonious diegetic configurations of films such as *The Princess and the Frog* and *Big Hero 6* (Don Hall and Chris Williams, 2014). Yet, it is through this very lens that more ambiguous and problematic representations re-emerge. *Zootopia* challenges more effectively the wider generic tropes of the Disney formula. Sentimental innocence, idealism and reassuring predictability are conveyed through Judy's characterisation and humorously challenged by more sarcastic partner Nick. To some extent, the fantasy atmosphere of Disney animated films, reminiscent of the company's enchanting theme parks, is complicated by the wider depiction of Zootopia.

Zootopia's Anthropomorphic Lens and the Gendered Dynamics of the Action Cop Buddy Film

'You'll never be a real cop. You're a cute meter maid though.' Nick's line, concluding his first sarcastically witty but particularly confrontational conversation with Judy, crystallises some of the gendered tensions underpinning Disney's anthropomorphising of the action cop buddy film. Following Judy's failed attempt at apprehending him, this antagonistic, unlikely partner mocks her dream of becoming a police officer, belittling her by drawing on stereotypes related to her species: an inoffensive, 'cute' bunny. He also notably calls her a meter maid, ironically foregrounding her subordinate gendered job status. *Zootopia*'s anthropomorphic lens repeatedly magnifies the gendered imbalance characterising the action buddy film through the difficulties and prejudices that Judy encounters as a 'bunny cop'. Her positioning at the centre of the narrative and her portrayal as an athletic, strong bunny challenge the gendered dynamics of the buddy relationship and re-envision the construction of the post-feminist action heroine.

From the start, Judy's ambition appears decidedly unusual: as a child, young fox Gideon Grey mocks her ('What crazy world are you living in where you think a bunny could be a cop?'), her parents worriedly warn her that 'there's never been a bunny cop', and she secures her job thanks to a 'Mammal Inclusion Initiative'. Such insistence on her identity as a bunny might divert attention away from the fact that she is also a female recruit. This species-related exceptional status strongly resonates with the positioning of women within action cop films: Yvonne Tasker notes that, in this generic environment, the heroine most often 'stands alone' (1998: 83). This marginalisation parallels the absence of women within buddy films. Despite notable exceptions such as *The Heat* (Paul Feig, 2013), the Hollywood cop buddy genre – like the wider action mode – is still predominantly male-centred.

Tasker observes that the verbal banter characterising the male buddy dynamic 'becomes more transparently sexual when transposed onto the male/female pair': the inclusion of a woman very often leads the buddy relationship to turn into a romantic one (ibid.: 74–5). Many romantic comedies could indeed be approached as buddy films due to the initial syntactic parallel between the two genres: a mismatched pair forced to reach a deal. More generally, when female characters are featured alongside an action hero, they are rarely on the same footing as the latter: they tend to be positioned as supportive sidekicks and/or romantic interests, not as buddies/partners (ibid.: 85).

Zootopia acknowledges these marginalised positionings: its anthropomorphic lens first literalises and – light-heartedly – magnifies some typically gendered difficulties faced by women entering the male-centred cop narrative, then challenges these configurations through the characterisation of Judy and her integration into a buddy dynamic. Judy's role as Nick's partner is as syntactically important as her individual trajectory as an apprentice police officer. She is the one framing the narrative, from her traumatic yet foundational encounter with a fox to her joining the police force and her delivering the commencement address to the new Police Academy graduates at the end of the film. Yet, like the heroines of *Blue Steel* (Kathryn Bigelow, 1989), *The Silence of the Lambs* (Jonathan Demme, 1991) and *Fargo* (Ethan and Joel Cohen, 1996), Judy is isolated in *Zootopia*'s police force: she has no opportunity to bond with other women, and while other officers work in teams, she initially has no partner.[1]

Such syntactic isolation is highlighted visually and aurally. When Judy first enters the police 'bullpen', her portrayal is reminiscent of Clarice Starling (Jodie Foster) at the start of *The Silence of the Lambs*. The latter initially misleadingly suggests that this little, frail trainee may be out of place in the FBI: as she steps into the elevator, she is surrounded by taller and sturdier male colleagues, which makes her look particularly vulnerable. *Zootopia*'s anthropomorphic lens magnifies such a sense of perceived female fragility. Bunny Judy appears so tiny in comparison with her imposing male colleagues – large animals including polar bears, buffalos, tigers and rhinoceroses – that they actually struggle to see her: cheetah Clawhauser (Nate Torrence) needs to lean over his desk, buffalo chief Bogo (Idris Elba) to put on his glasses. When Judy interacts with these large male mammals, high-angle shots are mostly used, framing her as a minuscule, defenceless creature (Figure 7.1). The whole police environment looks hostilely intimidating: even sitting on a chair – or rather, climbing up onto it – requires an additional effort. As Kevin Chew points out, sound design reinforces Judy's identification by her colleagues as 'frail': in the bullpen, her high-pitched, cheery voice 'strains to be heard', as opposed to the 'wordless grunts of the larger animals' which 'fill and echo in the room', along

Disney's Anthropomorphic Reimaginings in Zootopia

Figure 7.1 Judy is framed as a minuscule, defenceless creature. Frame grab from Zootopia (Howard and Moore, 2016).

with the thuds of their fists on the tables or against each other (2019: 580). The emphasis on Judy's visual and aural cuteness isolates her further from her male counterparts: this aspect of her characterisation is particularly 'gendered' (ibid.: 579). She is not taken seriously because of her harmless, diminutive, soft bunny appearance. As illustrated by Clawhauser's inadvertent patronising and Nick's sarcastic mocking – 'there's a toy store missing its stuffed animal' – cuteness is associated with the realm of childhood and innocence: Judy's oversized eyes, highly expressive ears and fluffy tail crystallise disarming cuteness as associated with Disney's formula. This additional aesthetic clash with Judy's massive and gruff male colleagues underlines her apparent unsuitability for the tough and dangerous job of a police officer. Therefore, *Zootopia*'s choice of a bunny cop foregrounds the underlying gender imbalance of the action cop film: women are conspicuously rare or marginalised because of persisting generic stereotypes related to female fragility and helplessness.

Disney's specific animation style and *Zootopia*'s anthropomorphic lens question such generic preconceptions through Judy's characterisation as a 'tough bunny', in animation supervisor Kira Lehtomaki's words (quoted in Julius 2016: 35). As shown throughout the studio's contemporary action-adventure canon, animated cuteness is deceptive: from *Wreck-It Ralph*'s Cy-Bugs to *Moana*'s Kakamoras, it functions as a façade masking potential danger and/or mischief. In Judy's case, her undeniable, formulaic Disney cuteness is combined with a strong, active body. Art director of characters Cory Loftis specifically 'accentuated her muscle mass', 'giving her heavier thighs and arms than real rabbits have' (quoted in ibid.: 30). Lehtomaki's description crystallises the paradox of such a design: 'she's a tough bunny, but she's still feminine. She's sweet, but she's not weak' (quoted in ibid.: 35). This in-between characterisation particularly stands out in the Police Academy montage sequence, building on boot camp film tropes. Judy initially struggles to keep up with her rhinoceros and polar bear counterparts. However, she gradually makes progress both through intensive training – she is shown running and performing sit-ups – and by relying on her skills as a rabbit. Instead of imitating her massive and burly male colleagues to climb an ice wall, for example, she jumps off their backs; thanks to her agility and wit, she knocks a rhinoceros down by bounding over him and using his momentum, kicking his other hand into his face.

Through Judy's anthropomorphic portrayal, *Zootopia* transcends some containment strategies associated with the post-feminist heroine, including the tendency to combine action-adventure empowerment with sexual objectification, and to frame female effort and stunts as conventionally glamorous. In films such as *G.I. Jane* (Ridley Scott, 1997) and *Edge of Tomorrow* (Doug Liman, 2014), training sequences typically showcase both heroines' flexing muscles and sweating bodies. In *Edge of Tomorrow*, the camera zooms in on Sergeant Vrataski (Emily Blunt) as she finishes an 'air plank', and she is shown pushing on her arms in slow motion. By contrast, *Zootopia* does not include lingering shots of Judy while she works out; although she wears tight-fitting gym gear, there is no emphasis on her curves. The Police Academy sequence focuses instead on the results of her training, and how she outperforms her peers. Such absence of objectification is particularly notable considering the recurrent sexualisation of female rabbit characters, from the 'Playboy bunny' figure to Warner Bros.' Lola Bunny in the original *Space Jam* (Joe Pytka, 1997).[2] *Zootopia*'s portrayal of Judy challenges the depiction of the often-sexualised contemporary action woman.

Yet, Judy's in-between characterisation – a tough bunny – echoes other aspects of the post-feminist action heroine: on the surface, her portrayal epitomises the combination of traditionalist paradigms and empowerment typical of post-feminist constructions of femininity. Although athletic, Judy is more agile and graceful than visibly muscular and sturdy: she remains a conventionally 'feminine' cop (Kira Lehtomaki, quoted in Julius 2016: 35), a bunny version of frail Clarice Starling. Carol Dole argues that 'casting an actress of small stature' – like Jodie Foster – 'limits' the 'threat' posed by the subversive gun-wielding female cop (2001: 87). From an anthropomorphic perspective, Disney's choice of a bunny as *Zootopia*'s lead may contain this threat further: Judy would represent a palatable, non-threatening post-feminist image of female power. Yet, Judy's and Clarice's appearances are misleading, a semantic trope that emphasises both their isolation within the male-dominated police force and their exceptional status as a result. Judy's in-between characterisation as a tough bunny allows her to lead action scenes and plays a key role in her relationship with Nick: her naivety, fragility and helplessness, associated with her deceptively harmless cuteness, constitute pivotal performances in her buddy partnership.

While Judy's first encounter with Nick echoes the marginalisation of female cops and the gendered imbalance of action cop buddy films – 'You'll never be a real cop. You're a cute meter maid though' – she later challenges this configuration, relying on Nick's very preconceptions. When she apprehends him for the second time and asks him about a missing animal, he neither takes her seriously nor answers her questions, repositioning her as a cute, inoffensive, subordinate meter maid through anthropomorphic characterisations: he calls her 'Carrots' and 'fluff', and compares her to a 'stuffed animal'. Feeling unthreatened, he inadvertently reveals his earnings from illegally selling merchandise: Judy takes advantage of his carelessness, using a seemingly innocuous carrot pen to record his words. As he refuses to cooperate, Judy pretends to be sad and disappointed: losing her smile, she looks at him wide-eyed, her ears drooping slightly, mobilising the visual signifiers of Disney's formulaic cuteness. However, she suddenly abandons her performance of endearing harmlessness ('Then we'll have to do this the hard way'): she threatens to arrest him for felony tax evasion, tricking him into helping her with her investigation. With a smirk, she notably repeats Nick's earlier condescending one-liner 'it's called a hustle, sweetheart', reversing the power dynamics of their nascent partnership. Such reprise in the dialogue is typical of action cop buddy films like *48 Hrs.* (Walter Hill, 1982), in which both leads repeat 'you're gonna be sorry you've ever met me / I'm already sorry'. This humorous exchange of one-liners illustrates the fruitful potential of the collaboration between the two partners.

Zootopia's anthropomorphising of action buddy tropes, pairing a male fox and a female rabbit, gradually produces a homogeneous partnership: moving from playful antagonism to support and friendship, Nick and Judy's relationship challenges the gendered imbalance of power of the action cop buddy film. They possess complementary abilities which help them progress in their investigation and ultimately solve the case. Nick's insider knowledge leads them to key witnesses and helps them locate suspects avoiding surveillance cameras; Judy's competency as a trained cop ('top of [her] class at the academy') allows her to take the lead in action sequences, rescuing Nick and getting them both to safety. Their complementarity manifests further through an exchange of skills: Judy learns from, and knowingly imitates, Nick's criminal ways ('it's called a hustle, sweetheart'). As for Nick, he adopts Judy's action cop behaviour and logic: he interrogates a suspect and refuses to leave her behind during dangerous chases. Nick's cynicism leads Judy to become less naïve and more pragmatically sensible. Judy's ethics and dedication also inspire Nick, who starts acting as a supportive partner. Nick stands up for Judy when she is asked to quit and drop the case: like the buddy protagonists described by Jeffrey A. Brown, they 'achieve a level of trust that carries them past their initial antagonism' (1993: 82). Their platonic affection allows them to overcome a typical buddy break-up, with Nick jokingly using Judy's carrot pen recorder while she apologises to him – replicating the way she initially tricked him. Their efficiency as partners culminates when, towards the end, they catch the villain together. They succeed in part thanks to Judy's performance as a vulnerable, defenceless bunny, resonating with the recurrent positioning of women as victims to be rescued in action cop buddy cinema. Pretending to be helpless, she records the villain revealing her plans: she then breaks from her performance, standing arm in arm with Nick, and asserts her success by proclaiming to the villain, just before the latter gets arrested, 'it's called a hustle, sweetheart'.

Judy's performance of the defenceless bunny has wider implications, beyond generically gendered dynamics: she also performs the 'prey' as opposed to Nick's performance of the 'predator', a species division associated with underlying tensions and discriminations within the world of the film. From this perspective, *Zootopia*'s anthropomorphising of action cop buddy tropes does not solely challenge the gendered dynamics of the genre and the characterisation of the contemporary action heroine. The anthropomorphic lens of the film functions as a way into broader questions of identity, including certain connotations of racial identity, race relations and racial constructions.

'SLY FOX, DUMB BUNNY': ADDRESSING RACIAL IDENTITY AND DYNAMICS THROUGH THE ANTHROPOMORPHIC COP BUDDY FILM

> Judy: Y'know, it burns me up to see folks with such backward attitudes toward foxes. I just wanna say, you're . . . a real articulate fella.
> Nick: Ah, well, that is high praise. It's rare that I find someone so non-patronizing.

Before discovering Nick's illegal business and tricking him into working with her, Judy takes his defence against the hostile owner of an ice-cream parlour who refuses to serve foxes: her selfless action is followed by an awkward, problematic compliment, which Nick ironically welcomes. As reviewer Rebecca Keegan noted, the choice of the adjective 'articulate' is 'reminiscent of a cringe-worthy comment' President Joe Biden made about former President Barack Obama in 2007, before he became the first African American president of the United States (Keegan 2016): Biden described him as 'the first mainstream African-American who is articulate and bright and clean and a nice-looking guy' (Clemetson 2007). Writing on the incident, journalist Lynette Clemetson observed that 'when whites use the word ["articulate"] in reference to blacks, it often carries a subtext of amazement, even bewilderment . . . When people say it, what they are really saying is that someone is articulate . . . for a black person' (ibid.). This little adjective exemplifies *Zootopia*'s many references to racial tensions and micro-aggressions against minorities in America, from police profiling ('you think I'm going to believe a fox?') to misplaced appropriation of slang ('a bunny can call another bunny "cute", but when other animals do it, it's a little . . .') and unwelcome hair touching ('you can't just touch a sheep's wool'). As Sarah Nilsen points out, the film was in production during Obama's second term, the rise of the Black Lives Matter movement, 'along with a heavily racist backlash against the Obama administration, which then led to the presidential election of Donald Trump in November of 2016' (2019: 70). Relying on the initial generic antagonism between partners Judy and Nick, who belong to different species, *Zootopia*'s anthropomorphising of action cop buddy tropes functions as a tool to interrogate wider social dynamics during a period of 'inflamed racial divisions' within the United States (ibid.: 70). The film subverts some stereotypes related to specific animals, and reframes species as partly constructed and potentially constituting a performance. Through this anthropomorphic lens, *Zootopia* strives to evoke and re-envision issues of racial identity and race relations.

Some of the most high-profile action cop buddy films and franchises, including *48 Hrs., Lethal Weapon, Rush Hour*, and their science-fiction variant *Men In Black* (1997, 2002, 2012, 2019) notably paired actors from different races and/or ethnicities. In this configuration, such differences represent an additional aspect of the partners' dissimilar characterisation, adding to their clashing personalities and working style (Brown 1993: 80). Two interdependent narratives then unfold: the development of the leads' friendship despite their differences and potential prejudices, and their overcoming of action obstacles to solve a case and catch the villain. Annette Kuhn and Guy Westwell observe that such films acknowledge racial inequalities within contemporary America through the 'unequal status of the buddies' (2012), and that their ultimate friendship reconciles and smooths over such inequalities. Mainstream cop buddy films tend not to directly address racism as an issue: tensions are simplified and resolved by the end of the film, presenting audiences with what Philippa Gates describes as 'an escapist fantasy' (2004: 22). The comedic impulse of the buddy dynamic partly explains such bypassing, leaving a more explicit and thorough questioning of race relations to genres such as dramas, biopics and documentaries.

Transposing the buddy genre from live action to animation, and most notably transforming human protagonists into anthropomorphic characters,

Zootopia provides a unique space to play through such social complexities, including race relations and racial constructions. The antagonism of the partners and their initial distrust of each other due to their differing species – rabbit versus fox– is juxtaposed with the wider oppositions and tensions underlying the city of Zootopia – prey versus predator. These oppositions function as a way into wider explorations of social roles and identity. Disney's approach particularly stands out from other animated buddy films such as DreamWorks' *Shrek* (Andrew Adamson and Vicky Jenson, 2001) and *Shark Tale* (Bibo Bergeron and Vicky Jenson, 2004). The latter reproduce the black/white pairings of their live-action counterparts through voice casting – Mike Myers and Eddie Murphy in *Shrek*, Jack Black and Will Smith in *Shark Tale* – while *Zootopia*'s leads are voiced by white performers Jason Bateman and Ginnifer Goodwin. Such a choice distances Disney's portrayals from the stereotypes associated with both buddy performances and casting in these contemporary animated films. For example, Sam Summers argues that *Shark Tale* fails to 'reconcile the racial, ethnic . . . stereotypes and inequalities' it tangentially evokes, notably casting African American and Afro-Caribbean actors to play 'hustlers with a pronounced affinity for hip hop and reggae' (2020: 180–1). *Zootopia*'s clash of species and the prejudices and rivalry between the animated partners represent the primary tools to address and rework the representational politics of the genre, and question wider issues of identity.

Zootopia relies on Judy's perspective, and most particularly her unconscious bias and fear of foxes, impacting on her partnership with Nick, to weave challenging observations into its narrative, resonating with contemporary issues related to racial representation and race relations. Entirely devoid of humans, the basis for Zootopia's world is that animals have 'evolved': the division between 'vicious predator' and 'meek prey' has disappeared and all animals 'live in harmony', as Judy explains in the opening scene. Yet, as the film gradually reveals, significant distrust and ingrained fear of predators, which represent a minority of the animal population, persists. At first, such fear seems justified: it is young fox Gideon Grey who bullies sheep and attacks Judy, who tries to defend them. As he unsheathes his claws like a switchblade, he appears to be particularly dangerous. Although Judy ultimately outsmarts him, this violent event is foundational within her narrative trajectory; it also shows how the film uses anthropomorphism to point to derogatory preconceptions and bias against minorities, and more specifically the idea that one ethnic and/or racial group is naturally inferior to the other. In *Zootopia*'s world, this means more primitive and violent. Such presumed innateness is made explicit through direct references to the 'biology' of predators. While cop Judy does not explicitly discriminate against foxes ('Gideon Grey was a jerk, who happened to be a fox'), her deep-rooted prejudices stand out when she first meets Nick. Her initial impulse is to reach for 'fox repellent'; when she realises he is harmless, she unconsciously patronises him. At a press conference, she connects the violence of predators mysteriously going 'savage' to their 'biology... something in their DNA'. This not only hurts Nick and leads to their buddy break-up but also sends journalists into a frenzy, plunging the city into chaos. A montage sequence includes news reports of a peace rally marred by protest, where species-related slurs are exchanged ('Go back to the forest, predator!'); in the subway, Judy observes a female bunny who brings her child closer to her when a tiger sits nearby. This scene crystallises *Zootopia*'s magnification of the insidious effects and dangerous consequences of racial bias, based on irrational fear.

Zootopia particularly insists on such irrationality by consistently subverting stereotypes and preconceived ideas related to the supposedly innate qualities or tendencies of each species. This representational strategy not only is a source of comedy – an elephant lacks stereotypical memory skills, a sloth exceeds the speed limit – but also plays a pivotal role through the narrative. The characterisation of Bellwether (Jenny Slate) exemplifies such a strategy. The harmless-looking assistant, working for the more charismatic and imposing Mayor Lionheart (J. K. Simmons), is revealed to be the villain towards the end of the film, which operates as a major narrative twist since she represents the epitome of the 'meek prey'. Visual development artist Shiyoon Kim describes her as 'a timid lamb with a shy voice and huge eyes, so you'd never think she's actually the villain' (quoted in Julius 2016: 79). Like *Moana*'s Kakamoras and *Wreck-It Ralph*'s Cy-Bugs, the design of such a vulnerable and fluffy character builds on and subverts the formulaic Disney trope of cuteness, traditionally associated with adorable animal leads such as Bambi and Thumper. Along with Judy's 'cute bunny' appearance, Bellwether's characterisation destabilises any certainty related to species within *Zootopia*'s world.

Zootopia not only challenges species-related stereotypes, but it also foregrounds their constructed and artificial aspect. When grown-up Gideon Grey apologises to Judy, explaining that his 'unchecked rage and aggression' were the manifestation of 'self-doubt', it leads Judy to the real reason behind predators' inexplicable behaviour. They are not 'reverting to their primitive, savage ways', and are not even biologically predisposed to violence: they are hit with bullet-like pellets of toxic serum made from a poisonous flower, causing their uncontrollable aggressiveness. Such a sinister plot is elaborated by Bellwether: in targeting predators, she managed to replace Lionheart as mayor, sustaining a climate of paranoiac fear in Zootopia which allowed her to stay in power. Such a sinister *mise en scène*, building on fears against a specific minority of animals – predators – which are then fuelled by news media's careless circulation of Judy's misplaced claims, points to the constructed aspect of racial representations, and shows how prejudices are artificially instilled and perpetuated.

Zootopia particularly magnifies the violence of such preconceptions: the anthropomorphic lens of the film shockingly literalises the dehumanising effects of racism, turning marginalised and feared predators into feral creatures. Under the effects of the toxic serum, predators are transformed into wild animals: they run on all fours, grunt and roar – with their pupils vertically slit – and randomly attack their peers. In the context of the film, this behaviour is not natural: it is an artificially engineered transformation – even bunnies can suffer from the toxic effects of the poisonous flower. In the context of an anthropomorphic animated film, predators' aggressiveness is even more disturbing: they are thoroughly de-anthropomorphised, practically losing their animated characterisation. As Holliday explains, animation and anthropomorphism are both 'rhetorical strategies . . . invested in degrees of personification, the impression (and impassion) of consciousness, and the presumption of subjectivity' (2016: 249). To some extent, the unexpected de-anthropomorphising of predators in *Zootopia* breaks animation rules, preventing the audience from caring for and empathising with these protagonists: lacking their human characteristics, they correspondingly lose their associated animated appeal. From a wider perspective, such de-anthropomorphising also points to racist discourses associating specific races with animals.[3] *Zootopia* touches upon the social and political consequences of such discourses and constructions: the frightening images of predators purposely turned 'savage' circulated through television news sustains inhabitants' fears and helps Bellwether stay in power.

Zootopia not only shows that some ideas and representations related to specific species are constructed and have dangerous potential, but it also emphasises that racial identity itself is socially constructed and partly constitutes a performance. Numerous authors, such as Linda Williams, have relied on the terms of performance in relation to onscreen understandings of race to examine concepts of 'blackface' and 'passing' in late 1920s and 1930s melodramas and musicals (2001: 176). Williams particularly points to the degree of 'overacting' and 'artifice' as a pivotal aspect of such cinematic performances of race: use of makeup, presence of exaggerated gestures or restraint (ibid.: 176). More recently, Whoopi Goldberg's impersonation of a white man in *The Associate* (Donald Petrie, 1996) along with discourses surrounding the star personas of actresses and singers such as Jennifer Lopez and Nicki Minaj (Butler 2013: 51) have demonstrated the potential fruitfulness of this concept, foregrounding the unstable and multifaceted aspect of racial identities.

Zootopia's exploration of species' performance resonates with such discourses, as illustrated in the introductory scene, staging the bygone era of 'vicious predators' and 'meek prey'. The film opens in a dark jungle, where

Disney's Anthropomorphic Reimaginings in Zootopia

a cute, defenceless little bunny is stalked by a tiger. When it jumps at the bunny, the digitally simulated camera zooms out, revealing an amateur stage production: the 'vicious predator' is played by a young jaguar, wearing a tiger costume with huge paws and claws, pretending to maul young Judy. The latter's performance of the 'meek prey' is humorously exaggerated: she shrieks and screams, 'blood, blood, blood', using reams of red papier mâché and ketchup as fake blood. Judy then proceeds to explain the rules of *Zootopia*'s world: animals have evolved beyond such 'primitive savage ways', and predators and prey live in harmony. Beyond its expositional function, this scene subtly reveals that 'meek prey' and 'vicious predator' are archaic and artificial labels in *Zootopia*'s evolved age: these old notions are mere performances that are not founded on any tangible traits or characteristics any more.

Nick's characterisation and his evolving partnership and friendship with Judy particularly illustrate *Zootopia*'s reframing of species as a performance, resonating with wider issues of racial identity and representations: his behaviour is gradually revealed to be contrived, developed due to discrimination he has encountered. At first, he seems to conform to the cliché of the 'sly fox' – as he describes himself – the anthropomorphic equivalent to the stereotype of the street-smart 'hustler' – in Judy's term – found in action cinema ('I know everybody'). The hustler typically possesses a 'network of street contacts' and displays an 'ease and confidence' within urban environments that seems natural (Purse 2011a: 118). Yet, Nick's behaviour is revealed to be a performance, contextualised by numerous scenes in which he is prejudiced against, from a police officer dismissing his testimony to the recollection of a traumatic childhood memory of him being muzzled by young prey animals. His initial witty cynicism ('you can only be what you are: sly fox') contrasts with his subsequent heartfelt yet bitter confession to Judy: 'if the world's only gonna see a fox as shifty and untrustworthy, there's no point in trying to be anything else'. As she gradually realises, Nick is 'so much more than that', actually a loyal friend and efficient apprentice cop. Their partnership challenges the 'fox/bunny' configuration: Nick and Judy are placed on an equal footing, building on their complementary abilities and exchanging skills.

Nick and Judy's final *mise en scène*, demonstrating their efficiency as partners and supportive friendship, represents the culmination of *Zootopia*'s re-envisioning of species' behaviour as performance. When Bellwether and her accomplices corner them, Bellwether hits Nick with what she believes to be a capsule of toxic serum. While Bellwether reveals her scheme in a threatening monologue, Nick crouches, growls, stalks and attacks defenceless Judy. Yet, as he appears to bite her, her scream is followed by an over-the-top performance of death, miming blood spurting out of her body

Figure 7.2 *Judy's over-the-top performance of the attacked prey. Frame grab from* Zootopia *(Howard and Moore, 2016).*

(Figure 7.2). Nick playfully interrupts her ('all right, you're milking it'), putting an end to their improvised performance. This has allowed time for Judy to record Bellwether's confession, leading to her subsequent arrest. This staging directly echoes the opening amateur stage production. As these two stagings frame *Zootopia*'s narrative, they show that foxes and bunnies can easily get in and out of character, namely break out of their impersonation of stereotypes and preconceptions related to their own species: the dichotomies sly fox versus dumb bunny, and vicious predator versus meek prey, constitute mere performances in *Zootopia*'s world. Juxtaposed with Judy's knowing re-enactment, this sequence suggests that some aspects of gendered and racial identities can be also understood as performances.

Zootopia's anthropomorphising of action buddy tropes questions understandings and constructions of race and racial relations – issues that most live-action cop buddy films rarely address. Through the portrayal of initially antagonistic animal leads, as well as the wider underlying hierarchies of Zootopia, the film magnifies the dangerous potentials and dehumanising effects of racism and bias, crystallised through the city's sinister anti-predator paranoia and the de-anthropomorphising of some animals. Subverting some species-related stereotypes, Disney's anthropomorphic lens notably re-envisions species as a partly constructed, fluctuating and performative identity, which resonates with wider issues and understandings of social dynamics and racial identity. Such a commentary on identity politics appears to some extent to be a departure from Disney's contemporary constructions of race and racial relations. Paradoxically, the lens mediating this very commentary produces at times more ambiguous, even problematic constructions.

The Anthropomorphic Cop Buddy Film as a Self-reflexive Tool: *Zootopia*'s Revision of Disney's Representational and Generic Approach

> Nick: Tell me if this story sounds familiar: naïve little hick with good grades and big ideas decides . . . 'I'm gonna move to Zootopia, where predators and prey live in harmony and sing Kumbaya!' Only to find . . . we don't all get along . . . No one cares about her or her dreams.

As Judy first fails to apprehend Nick, a rather animated conversation follows between the two leads, during which Nick sarcastically describes Judy and her ambitions. Just before concluding that she will 'never be a real cop', he specifically mocks her idealistic vision of Zootopia, and her innocent belief that 'anyone can be anything'. Building on the dynamic between the two soon-to-be partners, this sequence playfully echoes and ridicules the cheerful naivety associated with Disney animated films, especially the studio's fairy tales: the predictable, 'fluffy' narratives and enchanting happy endings that Jack Zipes associates with the Disney formula (2011: 87). Judy's innocent optimism regarding Zootopia's social dynamics also resonates with Disney's contemporary portrayal of racial harmony, as illustrated in the fantasy worlds of films such as *The Princess and the Frog* and *Big Hero 6*. *Zootopia*'s anthropomorphising of the cop buddy film complicates and revises to some extent such representational tropes, and shrewdly challenges the studio's wider generic configurations.

Disney animated films have been particularly focused on and criticised for their representation of race, often perceived as reductive, offensive or racist.[4] The studio has striven to distance its more contemporary output from the problematic racial representations that have marked its history. For example, in *Tangled* and *Frozen*, race dissolves into invisible whiteness within exclusively white worlds.[5] Films portraying diverse animated worlds similarly avoid directly engaging with racial issues. In *The Princess and the Frog*, as discussed in Chapter 2, Tiana and Naveen's amphibian 'state' – lasting for two-thirds of the film – is another strategy employed to tone down racial tensions in Disney's idealised version of 1920s New Orleans, discarding issues related to miscegenation (Aza Missouri 2015: 174). Such reimagining, relying on magical transformations and enchanting fairy-tale worlds, is also replicated, to some extent, in the urban action-adventure world of *Big Hero 6*. Set in the imaginary city of San Fransokyo, it seamlessly combines American and Japanese architecture and influences. The way these cultures are mixed, partly in order to create a 'cool and interesting' world – in co-director Don Hall's words (quoted in Lui 2014) – might be considered dubious and opened up to interrogation.[6] *Big Hero 6* never clearly addresses cultural identity, race or race relations as real issues: San Fransokyo appears as a harmoniously hybrid fantasy city with a multicultural superhero team, whose cast include Asian American, Latin American, black and white actors.

Zootopia challenges to some extent such idealised social dynamics: the depiction of the city of Zootopia itself reproduces, then complicates the seemingly harmonious configuration of *The Princess and the Frog* and *Big Hero 6*, appearing at first as another fantasy land, an enchanting theme park. The city's skyline echoes the triangular shape of Disney's theme-park and fairy-tale castles: the buildings are reminiscent of turrets, circled by smaller habitations – the 'kingdom' – and a river (Figure 7.3). Judy's enthusiasm on her train journey to the city is reminiscent of Rapunzel joyfully entering *Tangled*'s kingdom for the first time. Numerous reaction shots foreground Judy's excitement and amazement at the breath-taking urban vistas, self-reflexively mirroring viewers' expected admiration at the eye-catching computer animation. Tracking shots take the audience among skyscrapers, above bridges and under beltways, carried as if on a dizzying and thrilling theme-park ride. The dazzling colour palette – sandy Sahara Square, snowy Tundratown, lush Rainforest District – is matched with impressive state-of-the-art digital effects: variations in temperature and climate are notably showcased through lens flares and photorealistic heat blur, condensation and raindrops.

Such an overwhelming and entertaining theme-park experience was, as for *Tangled*, purposely created: co-director Byron Howard explains that Zootopia was designed 'almost like Disneyland' (quoted in Julius 2016: 44).[7] Zootopia's elaborate environmentally based district division most noticeably echoes Disney World's 'Animal Kingdom', also visited by the filmmakers for inspiration (Julius 2016: 44). The fabricated, performative aspect of all

Figure 7.3 Zootopia as an enchanting Disney theme park. Frame grab from Zootopia *(Howard and Moore, 2016)*.

Disney theme parks, from actors playing Disney characters to staff employees described as 'cast members', has particular implications within the context of the Animal Kingdom: it specifically points to the staged display of animals and their domesticated performance of wilderness. Stephanie Rutherford observes that these look 'docile, organized, and always ready to be "onstage"' (2011: 78). Their more violent behaviour is conspicuously dissimulated, so that the Animal Kingdom appears as a 'natural utopia': like Disney's other theme-park kingdoms, it represents a magical space where visitors 'escape the anxieties of urbanity, crime, difference, and complication' (ibid.: 52). At first, Zootopia appears as an animated version of the Animal Kingdom: a wonderful theme-park city where 'predator and prey live in harmony' – a lion and a giraffe are shown casually standing side by side on an escalator – and 'anyone can be anything'. The city seems to simply anthropomorphise the harmonious and unproblematic social dynamics of Disney's other theme-park and animated fantasy lands – 1920s New Orleans or San Fransokyo.

Yet, the idealistic façade of Disney's contemporary fantasy worlds, reproduced through Zootopia's anthropomorphic utopia, gradually crumbles as Judy and Nick's cop buddy investigation progresses. Inter-species relationships are not as blissfully harmonious as they seem, and underlying prejudices persist. These surface when some predators' behaviour becomes uncontrollably aggressive. As they are shown stalking and mauling other animals, their portrayal shockingly subverts the sanitised version of wilderness staged at the Animal Kingdom and in other Disney animated films. For example, in *The Aristocats* (Wolfgang Reitherman, 1970) and *The Lion King*, predators courteously cease to hunt their prey as soon as they realise that they are the hero's friend. Their seamless switch from wild deadly violence to harmless anthropomorphism re-envisions inter-species relations as a peaceful cohabitation – Disney's tamed 'circle of life' – sharply contrasting with *Zootopia*'s. However, as observed earlier, *Zootopia* relies on a specific kind of anthropomorphism, with entirely 'evolved' animals: predators' 'savage' outbursts are not natural but purposely triggered. Such aggressive behaviour metaphorically prefigures the violence of the species-related slurs and growing tensions following Judy's press conference. To some extent, the film draws a parallel between unconscious, fearful bias and unchecked feral brutality: both are externally triggered, easily manipulated, and have dramatic consequences for inter-species relations. As Arctic shrew Mr. Big (Maurice LaMarche) remarks, 'we may be evolved . . . but deep down we are still animals'. This remark challenges the peaceful and sanitised foundations of Disney's other animal worlds, hinting at their latent violence and wild impulses, and problematises other human-centred, diverse and seemingly harmonious fantasy kingdoms.

While *Zootopia* contrasts with films such as *The Princess and the Frog* and *Big Hero 6* in the way it strikingly exposes racial tensions, it is characterised by a certain degree of ambivalence that perpetuates, to some extent, Disney's problematic approach to race. According to numerous critics and scholars, *Zootopia*'s anthropomorphic lens functions as an 'allegory for the black and white racial dichotomy found within many Western societies' (Beaudine et al. 2017: 231). Gregory Beaudine et al. point out parallels with the experience of predators within the film and that of African Americans within the United States, from their similar demographic numbers (around 10 per cent of the population) to their perception and representation as potentially violent and threatening (ibid.: 228). As noted earlier, the film directly references, explicitly condemns and deconstructs such racial prejudices and discrimination. In this process, authors such as Ahli Chatters and Shearon Roberts argue that *Zootopia* conveys a 'lesson about privilege, stereotypes', and the core tenets of the Black Lives Matter movement (2020: 306). Yet, Dan Hassler-Forest observes that the way *Zootopia* frames this undeniably 'progressive' positioning is at best 'ill-advised', at worst 'offensive' (2018: 367). Although predators' wild outbursts are externally triggered by a toxic serum, the opening scene recalls that 'thousands of years ago', predators did have 'an uncontrollable biological urge to maim and maul'. When Judy clumsily explains the attacks by referring to the animals' 'DNA', her claim can be interpreted as both unknowingly prejudiced – animals have 'evolved' – and based on the prehistoric past of her anthropomorphic world, which helps contextualise the inhabitants' quickly spreading fear. *Zootopia* awkwardly treads a fine line between challenging and perpetuating potentially harmful racial stereotypes, partly playing into 'the very basic racism' that it is set to reject (ibid.: 368). African American activists such as Black Lives Matter protesters have been precisely described as 'acting like "animals"' in numerous news outlets, blogs and social media (Sandlin and Snaza 2018: 1207), and portrayals of young black men as 'ominous criminal predator[s]' have been circulated in the United States since the 1970s with often dramatic consequences (Welch 2007: 277). From this perspective, *Zootopia*'s construction of race seems to echo Disney's past and contemporary portrayals, as illustrated through *The Princess and the Frog*'s amphibious black princess.

Paradoxically, both *Zootopia*'s offensiveness and its more progressive political implications are diluted to some degree through the specific anthropomorphic lens of the film. In other words, as Meghann Meeusen suggests, 'the use of animals allows filmmakers paradoxically both to engage and also avoid engaging a specific critique of power structures' and racism (2019: 348). Unlike animated features such as *The Princess and the Frog* and *Big Hero 6*, there are no recognisably raced bodies onscreen: no ethnic or racial human group is explicitly and unequivocally supported or targeted. Voice casting undermines to some extent the parallels drawn by some authors: black actors such as Octavia Spencer and Idris Elba voice both predators and prey. Both prey and predators encounter micro-aggressions that may be associated with African American experiences, or those of other marginalised groups: fox Nick is mistrusted by the police, and rabbit Judy objects to being called 'cute' as if she were faced with racial slurs – while both are voiced by white actors. As observed by Jennifer Sandlin and Nathan Snaza, *Zootopia*

> has to keep in tension the presentation of enough information for the film to allegorically tap into fears and concerns about race . . . and at the same time displace these concerns into forms different enough that the film cannot be openly and obviously read as direct political commentary. (Sandlin and Snaza 2018: 1199)

Such tension regarding representational identity politics echoes Disney's strategy of 'deniability' (Brown 2021: 136) regarding constructions of queerness, as discussed in Chapter 4. Anthropomorphism combined with generic tropes from the action cop buddy film provide an illuminating framework through which to explore race relations and constructions of race; still, the progressive and subversive potential of such an exploration is at times ambivalently limited. This paradox crystallises the combination of disruption and containment characterising Disney's contemporary output.

Zootopia more effectively subverts Disney's contemporary representations of social dynamics through its challenge of the city's authority figures, supposed to embody Zootopia's idealistic motto of cohesion and harmony. Mayor Lionheart, who launched the 'Mammal Inclusion Initiative' and puts pressure on the city's police force to find the missing mammals, has them secretly imprisoned in a disused hospital. He keeps their inexplicable savage behaviour secret from the public to protect both the city ('It could destroy Zootopia') and his own position ('And how do you think they're gonna feel about their mayor, who is a lion?! I'll be ruined!'). More strikingly, the seemingly harmless Bellwether, who appears sympathetic to Judy from the outset, supports her progress, assists in the investigation and replaces Lionheart when he is arrested, is revealed to be the villainous mastermind behind predators' attacks. Police chief Bogo, Judy's boss, is reluctant to have her investigate a case, ignoring her competence and skills for the job. He is also unaware of Bellwether's schemes, unknowingly following the villain's orders. In typical action cop buddy fashion, the representatives of power cannot be trusted: this challenges the stable, seemingly harmonious configuration of Disney's contemporary narratives.

As the flaws of Zootopia's seemingly utopian system begin to surface, and Judy progresses with her investigation, Disney's generic borders expand into more unexpected territory. Like the typical action cop described by Brown, Judy is ready to 'act outside the law in order to see justice done' (1993: 82), and stops relying on Zootopia's authority figures. Her 'insubordination', in Bogo's term, leads her to abandon her meter maid post and rescue Mr. Big's daughter. As she volunteers to find one of the missing mammals, she is denied access to police resources: as a result, she ends up getting help from Nick, whom she initially describes as a 'hustler' but ultimately partners with. His connections lead them to 'crime boss' Mr. Big who, upon learning that Judy has rescued his daughter, lends his assistance to her investigation. Thanks to his rather unorthodox interrogation methods – threatening to drown animals in icy water – Judy obtains crucial information from a suspect. These encounters, including playful intertextual references to *The Godfather* (Francis Ford Coppola, 1972), notably bring the action cop film into the darker, more dangerous sphere of the crime and gangster film, expanding both the generic scope and tone of the Disney formula.

Throughout these generic changes, Judy's characterisation gradually shifts away from that of the formulaically cheerful and naïve Disney heroine, while *Zootopia* questions and qualifies Disney's perceived sentimentality, blissful optimism and theme-park enchantment. At the start of the film, Judy's innocent idealism is humorously met with incredulity and/or concern. When she announces to her parents that she will become the first 'bunny cop' and 'make the world a better place', they try to discourage her by explaining that 'it's great to have dreams . . . as long as you don't believe in them too much'. Later in the film, Chief Bogo reminds her that 'life isn't some cartoon musical where you sing a little song and all your insipid dreams magically come true. So let it go.' This explicit reference to *Frozen*'s most popular song mocks Judy's naïve optimism; in parallel, it pokes fun at Disney's formulaic reliance on childlike wonder and sentimental idealism, at the core of the studio's fairy tales and musicals – from *Cinderella*'s 'A Dream Is a Wish Your Heart Makes' to Tiana singing 'dreams do come true in New Orleans.' Disney's opening credits song is precisely 'When You Wish Upon a Star', inviting audiences to suspend their disbelief and enjoy a fun and familiar fantasy experience. *Zootopia*'s anthropomorphising of action genres and the associated portrayal of social dynamics and hierarchies disrupt such a predictable 'dream come true' trajectory, forcing Judy to reassess the world and narrative she inhabits: rougher, less harmoniously utopian. Correspondingly, audiences must adjust to this slightly grittier version of the Disney formula.

While *Zootopia* ends on an optimistic note, its conclusion brings some nuance to the unequivocal and typically overly optimistic happy endings mostly associated with Disney animated films, self-reflexively pointing to a more complex version of the studio's representational politics and social dynamics. During Nick's graduation ceremony from Zootopia's Police Academy, Judy gives a commencement address in which she particularly contrasts her initial innocent and simplistic view of Zootopia to its more complicated reality, especially its tense inter-species relationships: 'when I was a kid, I thought Zootopia was this perfect place where everyone got along and anyone could be anything . . . Turns out . . . real life is messy.' Such an observation symbolises the tonal and generic shifts taking place throughout the film. The breath-taking, marvellous, enchanting theme-park world of Zootopia, introduced with Shakira's upbeat pop song 'Try Everything', is gradually revealed to be darker, dangerous and corrupted: as the fantasy cartoon musical turns into an action cop film, the film 'peels away' at Disney's formulaic '"happily ever after" world' (Chatters and Roberts 2020: 296). Judy's final advice, 'try to make the world a better place', hints at Disney's more self-aware understanding and portrayal of social dynamics – and overall generic approach.

Conclusion

Zootopia's anthropomorphising of the action cop buddy genre, transposing its tropes to an exclusively animal world, provides a multilayered reworking and questioning of issues of gendered and racial identity. Such a generic reappropriation re-envisions the gendered dynamics of the action cop buddy film, and challenges the construction of the female cop heroine as depicted in live action. Judy's in-between status as a tough bunny, combining her conventional yet misleading Disney cuteness with a strong, active body, re-envisions post-feminist constructions of the action woman, notably avoiding containment strategies such as the emphasis on a glamorous, sexually attractive appearance. Replacing the live-action cop partners with animated animals from different species, *Zootopia*'s anthropomorphic configuration foregrounds issues and tensions which resonate with wider social dynamics, including certain connotations of racial identity, race relations and racism. The portrayal of species dynamics evokes and foregrounds the dangerous consequences of racial bias and discrimination, and subverts to some extent stereotypes supposedly associated with specific minorities and groups. Through predators' externally altered behaviour and its coverage through news media, the film emphasises the constructed and artificial aspects of racial representations and understandings of race. The characterisation of Nick and Judy challenges such understandings further: species behaviour is also depicted as a calculated performance, pointing to the potentially performative aspects of racial identities. *Zootopia*'s anthropomorphising of the action cop buddy film also functions as a self-reflexive tool which revises Disney's contemporary representational politics and generic tropes more broadly. The film complicates the studio's idealistic representations of social cohesion and racial harmony characterising films such as *The Princess and the Frog* and *Big Hero 6*. *Zootopia*'s action cop configuration qualifies such enchanting theme-park optimism, and reveals the fragility and difficulties of racial cohabitation. However, the anthropomorphic lens of the film also maintains a degree of ambivalence regarding race which dilutes to some extent its more progressive potential. *Zootopia*'s tonal and generic shifts more effectively re-envision Disney's wider formulaic tropes and tone. Like Judy gradually revising her understanding of both Zootopia and the generic narrative she inhabits, Disney gradually revises and expands its formula.

During the 2008–18 decade, Disney strove to challenge viewers' perception of its formula through multiple generic reappropriations and knowing parodies, from heroines discarding the princess label and reflecting on the concept of 'true love' to characters mocking the predictability of their narrative. As the studio's first entry into the action cop buddy film, *Zootopia* represents a new area of generic exploration and expansion for Disney, looking beyond its own cinematic universe. The film also reveals the considerable scope of Disney's contemporary reworking and reimagining of the wider action-adventure genre, and points to the studio's consistent efforts to differentiate its output through the specificity of its animated style, language and generic identity. Relying on an iconic Disney genre, the studio's animated features musically reinterpret the digital action spectacle; relying on the liberating potentials and freedoms of the animated medium, they self-reflexively empower their superheroines; relying on anthropomorphism and Disney's formulaic aesthetic of cuteness, they challenge the dynamics of cop buddy narratives. Considering the distinctly knowing generic reworking and challenging re-envisioning taking place within these films, Disney animated features are pivotal to understanding the contemporary development of and hybridisation between action-adventure genres, from the action musical to the superhero film and cop buddy film.

Notes

1. Although *Zootopia* includes female members of the police force, they are only briefly mentioned (like imposing elephant Francine), and/or Judy has no opportunity to meaningfully interact with them (as with the unnamed Police Academy instructor).
2. The design of Lola Bunny in the 2021 reboot *Space Jam: A New Legacy* (Malcolm D. Lee) was notably altered: contrasting with the 'very sexualised' 1997 original, the character's look was 'reworked . . . making sure she . . . was feminine without being objectified' (Malcolm D. Lee, quoted in Lawrence 2021). The production

discourse and final design of Lola Bunny is interestingly closer to Judy's characterisation, hinting at Disney's influence in terms of contemporary constructions of animated femininity.
3. Such racist connections have wider historical roots, tracing back to antebellum America and the dehumanisation of African American slaves. See Lester 2010: 307.
4. See Chapter 2 for an overview of the debates surrounding Disney's constructions of race throughout its animated canon.
5. For a detailed discussion of the relationship between whiteness and/as invisibility in cinematic constructions of race, see Dyer 1997: 45.
6. This approach becomes notably more problematic when Disney situates its animated world outside of an American and/or Eurocentric world. With *Moana*, for example, Disney located its cultural 'assemblage' within a Polynesian setting, and was accused of 'appropriating' myths and history from across several different cultures while purporting to be 'inclusive' and authentic in its representations (Brown 2021: 127–8). For further discussion of this specific issue, see Anjirbag 2018; Armstrong 2018; Tamaira and Fonoti 2018; Yoshinaga 2019.
7. Byron Howard notably co-directed both *Tangled* and *Zootopia*, which might explain, to some extent, the theme-park correspondences between the former's kingdom and the latter's city.

CHAPTER 8

Reflections of/on Contemporary Disney Animation: Ralph Breaks the Internet

>[I]f we wish to understand contemporary Hollywood animation, we cannot view it as a self-contained entity, but must instead consider how it relates to wider developments in Hollywood. (Brown 2021: 22)

>[T]his place is bonkers! (Vanellope in *Ralph Breaks the Internet: Wreck-It Ralph 2*, Phil Johnston and Rich Moore, 2018)

Contrary to what the trailer for *Ralph Breaks the Internet* suggests, Vanellope is not excited to enter 'Oh My Disney': within the film, she does not ultimately exclaim 'cool!' at the sight of the expansive digital reproduction of Disney's cinematic universe. Instead, puzzled at the great number of Internet visitors rushing through the fairy-tale castle gates, and the myriad of Disney properties scattered around, she describes the place as 'bonkers', 'lame', full of 'princesses and cartoon characters'. Yet, she discovers that, in this iteration of the characters, the animated heroines are highly self-aware and insightful: they playfully teach her about the formulaic performance associated with the Disney Princess, and the empowering potential of the musical. Vanellope experiences her own musical moment outside the gates of 'Oh My Disney', and a resulting epiphany: she decides to leave her predictable, old-school, childlike arcade game 'Sugar Rush' for the dangerous yet highly exciting game 'Slaughter Race'. Vanellope's pivotal journey through 'Oh My Disney' and her overall narrative trajectory throughout the film point to the significant generic shifts that have marked Disney animation since 2008.

This concluding chapter uses *Ralph Breaks the Internet* to map the book's main discoveries regarding Disney's re-envisioning of its contemporary animation. As the studio's first theatrically released animated sequel since *The Rescuers Down Under* (Mike Gabriel, 1990), *Ralph Breaks the Internet* does not solely develop further the characterisations, visuals and generic tropes of *Wreck-It Ralph* (Rich Moore, 2012).[1] Carolyn Jess-Cooke observes that sequels rely on 'important registers of continuation, nostalgia, memory, difference, originality, revision and repetition' (2009: 2) – registers that have also been central to the studio's re-envisioning of its formulaic identity, narratives, aesthetics, constructions of gender and paratexts. As a Disney sequel, *Ralph Breaks the Internet* crystallises the studio's parallel impulses throughout the decade under study in this book: self-reflexive revision and generic expansion, namely engaging with Disney's own past canon, the company's cinematic universe, and wider generic trends within mainstream animation and Hollywood cinema. The film represents an ideal case study in order to look back at this distinct phase of 'regeneration' (Haswell 2019: 97) in the studio's history, marked by the reverberations of Pixar's pioneering computer animation, DreamWorks' irreverent parodic critique of the Disney formula, as well as Disney's unprecedented growth under new creative leadership.

Featuring the leading duo of the first film, *Ralph Breaks the Internet* focuses on Vanellope and Ralph's travels beyond their familiar arcade games and into the Internet. They look for a missing part (a steering wheel) for Vanellope's game, 'Sugar Rush', which broke after the pair tried to alter its set race tracks. As they encounter characters from various websites and correspondingly multifaceted cinematic worlds, comment on their distinctive aesthetics and constructions of gender, and learn from their semantics and syntax, the duo echoes Disney's multiple generic borrowings and reinventions. The chapter will examine their major stopping points ('Oh My Disney', 'Slaughter Race'), illuminating interactions between Disney's contemporary animated output and Hollywood genres, and significant developing trends. As the concluding chapter, it will also highlight generic hybrids specific to Disney, pointing to the ways in which genres of romance and action adventure have come into contact, transformed and sometimes merged throughout the 2008–18 decade.

The first part of this chapter analyses the ways in which *Ralph Breaks the Internet* revisits the portrayal of the Disney Princess, pointing to distinct generic shifts emerging from Disney's contemporary cycle of animated fairy tales and musicals. The film shrewdly mocks and subverts gendered aspects of the Disney formula, amplifying the DreamWorks-style self-referential and parodic approach developed in *Tangled* (Nathan Greno and Byron Howard, 2010). The reintroduction of all of the Disney Princesses, at times reframed as parodic action leads, knowing fairy-tale protagonists, empathetic chick-flick friends and empowered superheroines, crystallises the multifaceted reworking of this character within and beyond the romantic mode, and throughout the post-feminist spectrum.

The second part focuses on the remobilisation of Disney's musical tropes, from the formulaic space of 'Oh My Disney' to the thrilling world of 'Slaughter Race'. Vanellope's performance of 'A Place Called Slaughter Race' not only provides another parodic restaging of a key Disney convention but also sincerely revives its appeal – a dual strategy typical of post-feminism. In parallel, the liberating potential of the Disney song is expanded through the merging of action and musical, a recurring generic combination throughout the studio's contemporary output.

The third part of this chapter explores how *Ralph Breaks the Internet* maps Disney's shifts within and overall move towards the action mode. Vanellope's trajectory from 'Sugar Rush' to 'Slaughter Race', leading to her independence and maturation, as well as Ralph's transformed performance of superhero masculinity illuminate Disney's evolving reappropriation of action-adventure genres since 2008. In parallel, the development of multiple buddy relationships and the reconfiguration of gendered dynamics within the film point to subtle convergences with romantically influenced animated features. Vanellope's attraction to the unpredictable 'Slaughter Race', clashing with Ralph's desire for familiarity and stability, echoes the studio's balance between reinvention and preservation of its own formulaic blueprint.

From a wider perspective, this concluding chapter illuminates the fruitfulness of genre analysis as applied to Disney films. Far from viewing them as a 'self-contained entity' – borrowing Noel Brown's term – this chapter uses *Ralph Breaks the Internet* to foreground the multiple enlightening intersections between Disney animation and Hollywood, live-action cinema and animation. It also considers this film as an entry point for possible avenues of research in relation to Disney's animated output, which evolves within and engages with an ever-expanding cinematic universe.

Self-aware Fairy-tale Leads, Chick-flick Superheroines: The Post-feminist Disney Princess

Vanellope's stop at 'Oh My Disney' and encounter with the fourteen princesses and heroines of the corresponding brand were central throughout *Ralph Breaks the Internet*'s trailers, foregrounding a level of intertextuality and generic self-awareness which borrowed heavily from the DreamWorks formula. Assembling all of these iconic characters from different storylines, time periods and aesthetic styles within the same cinematic space for the first time, the film strikingly reproduces the kind of 'obtrusive intertextuality' (Summers 2020: 191) that has characterised the *Shrek* franchise. The remobilisation of Disney's intertext has been central throughout several television live-action productions since the 2010s, such as the ABC series *Once Upon a Time* (2011–18) and the Disney Channel films *Descendants* (2015, 2017, 2019). What distinguishes *Ralph Breaks the Internet* is the seamless yet explicitly parodic reintroduction of these easily identifiable, iconic animated characters, revealing the significant influence of DreamWorks on Disney's contemporary output.

Shrek the Third (Raman Hui and Chris Miller, 2007) is a particularly important reference point in the context of *Ralph Breaks the Internet*. The former features princesses who are highly reminiscent of Disney's own classic characters through their costumes and hair styles, including Snow White, Cinderella and Sleeping Beauty. The portrayal of these princesses humorously alternates between parodic re-enactment of their traditional and retrograde defining traits, and the calculated subversion of these same traits. For example, when they are kidnapped and imprisoned by vengeful Prince Charming, Sleeping Beauty constantly falls asleep, Cinderella manically cleans the floor of her prison cell, and they and Snow White decide to patiently sit down and wait to be rescued. Encouraged by Princess Fiona, they successfully escape and break into the castle: Snow White's high-pitched vocalising leads forest animals to attack tree guards, Cinderella uses her sharpened glass slipper as a weapon, while other guards trip over Sleeping Beauty's sleeping body. The film also typically relies on contra-diegetic humour to further subvert the internally consistent world of the Disney fairy tale: for example, the princesses all gather to attend Princess Fiona's baby shower, and Sleeping Beauty burns her bra while preparing to escape the prison. This post-feminist joke qualifies the scope of the empowering action-centred sequence: ultimately, all the princesses, including Fiona, have a minor role in the final defeat of Prince Charming, unlike Shrek.

Ralph Breaks the Internet's portrayal of the Disney Princesses strikingly imitates DreamWorks' combination of critical parody, self-reflexive subversion and narrative-cartoonal mode, significantly amplifying both the humorous approach of Disney's contemporary cycle of fairy tales and most particularly *Tangled*'s reappropriation of the DreamWorks formula. When the princesses are first introduced in 'Oh My Disney', their portrayal seems to reproduce the traditionalist construction of femininity perpetuated throughout the Disney Princess franchise: and demure, they wave and smile at their Internet fans. Although most of these characters, from Snow White to Tiana, were initially cel-animated, their transition to computer animation alongside more contemporary Rapunzel, Merida, Anna, Elsa and Moana transforms these different princesses into a particularly homogenised group, crystallising criticisms about the Disneyfication of fairy tales. Later, when Vanellope looks for a place to hide, she glitches into the Princess Room, a behind-the-scenes location revealing that the princesses are cast members 'on break', like Vanellope and Ralph when they are outside of their own games. Still, their behaviour and activities appear to reproduce, once again, Disney's formulaic construction of sentimental fairy-tale femininity: Tiana looks at herself in the mirror, Jasmine smells a flower, and Snow White invites a bird to land on her hand. However, like *Shrek the Third*'s version of Sleeping Beauty, Aurora is shown sleeping in the corner of the frame: this brief gag subtly hints at the parodic tone of the sequence. At the sight of their intruder, the initially passive and demure princesses break out of their formulaic performance and attack Vanellope, their threatening combat poses reframing them as action heroines. While this generic shift is relatively smooth for Elsa, who raises her 'magic hands', Merida, who raises her bow, or even Mulan, who raises her sword, it becomes humorously incongruous for Disney's classical princesses, who repurpose their fairy-tale icons into weapons – most strikingly, Cinderella uses her broken glass slipper (Figure 8.1). This DreamWorks parallel is developed further: humorous role reversals, challenging Vanellope's expectations, are followed by a knowing play with the Disney formula. As the heroines enquire about Vanellope's status as a princess, they gently but comprehensively mock all of its tropes, including princesses' formulaic propensity to talk to animals. In the process, they also expertly list the most recurring criticisms from popular and academic accounts regarding Disney Princesses, from their dependence on patriarchal figures – love interests, fathers – and the absence of mothers to their overall positioning as helpless victims ('Were you poisoned? Cursed? Kidnapped or enslaved?', 'Do people assume all your problems got solved because a big strong man showed up?').[2] Although *Ralph Breaks the Internet*'s critical parody remains light-hearted, the film endows the princesses with a sense of self-awareness which is unprecedented in the Disney fairy-tale canon.

This striking sense of self-reflexiveness highlights the post-feminist doubleness infusing Disney's contemporary animated fairy tales, their oscillation between generic unconsciousness and self-consciousness and – borrowing from Diane Negra and Yvonne Tasker's definition – their combination of empowerment rhetoric with traditionalist identity paradigms (2007: 18). The princesses may only be performing fairy-tale femininity, able to smoothly switch to action mode, but this formulaic role is pivotal for them to bond

Figure 8.1 *The princesses repurpose their fairy-tale icons into weapons. Frame grab from* Ralph Breaks the Internet: Wreck-It Ralph 2 *(Johnston and Moore, 2018)*.

with Vanellope. Once the latter convinces them that she is 'a princess, too', the heroines welcome her and compliment her outfit. What follows is a highly contra-diegetic, DreamWorks-inspired makeover, in which the princesses discard their gowns for hoodies, t-shirts, leggings and shorts, with motifs and messages that include knowing nods to their own narratives: for example, Elsa's top reads 'Let It Go' and Aurora's reads 'Nap Queen'. Such clothing notably imitates the type of items available for purchase on the Disney Store's website, commodifying an updated version of fairy-tale femininity. This sequence also reveals another of Disney's contemporary strategies to renew and revise its fairy-tale formula. As the young women bond over clothes and new outfits, the *mise en scène* echoes the many shopping and makeover scenes of the contemporary chick flick, from *The Princess Diaries* franchise (2001, 2004) and *Sex and the City* (2008, 2010) up to *Crazy Rich Asians* (Jon Chu, 2018) and *Someone Great* (Jennifer Kaytin Robinson, 2019). This genre of romance, which prioritises female relationships, is central to *Frozen*'s (Chris Buck and Jennifer Lee, 2013) syntactic revision of the Disney fairy tale. In this context, it is reappropriated without its heteronormative framework: the princesses' romantic interests are notably absent. Combining tropes of the chick flick with the DreamWorks formula, this sequence crystallises Disney's multiple generic strategies to revisit its fairy-tale formula, while preserving its most essential semantic component, in typically post-feminist fashion: the princess.

Ralph Breaks the Internet's emphasis on such female-centred relationships culminates when all the princesses, spotting Ralph falling from a high tower towards the end of the film, collectively rescue him: from action leads, they are reframed as a team of superheroines. As Catherine Lester points out, Disney animated films have for the most part foregrounded relationships of 'antagonism and competition . . . rather than support between women' (2019: 196). The portrayal of the fourteen princesses actively collaborating to save a male character both functions as a conscious reversal of the Disney formula and showcases a unique, though brief, moment of collective female empowerment. In parallel, it also builds on and consolidates action-adventure and the superhero film as central generic frameworks in Disney's contemporary constructions of gender. With each princess displaying her individual skill, magic or power, the musical theme of their respective films can be heard, reintroducing the fusion of action mode, superhero film and musical developed in *Frozen* and *Moana* (Ron Clements and John Musker, 2016).

Reinterpreting the Disney Song, Performing the Action Musical

Ralph Breaks the Internet's pronounced post-feminist self-awareness impacts another generic facet of the Disney formula, presented as an essential part of princess performance: the musical, and most specifically the 'I Want Song'. In two sequences which magnify the dual strategy of contemporary animated fairy tales, the film ironically parodies and deconstructs, then sincerely celebrates and reclaims this central Disney trope. Dramatically performed by the hero or heroine, the 'I Want Song' expresses yearning for 'a better world beyond the confinements of [their] present situation' (Byrne and McQuillan 1999: 24). In the Princess Room, however, the dramatic potential of the song is quickly undercut. Excited about her makeover, Ariel expresses her happiness at wearing a 'shirt', reprising the melody of 'Part of Your World'. Vanellope's bafflement demystifies her musical performance (Figure 8.2): she points out the non-diegetic soundtrack, the spotlight over Ariel, and the latter's unexpected yet seamless transition from dialogue to song. These conventions may appear natural in a Disney musical, but they become artificial and incongruous in *Ralph Breaks the Internet*, a film which does not explicitly introduce itself as a musical: Vanellope's generic knowledge depends on a different regime of verisimilitude. This generic clash is further emphasised through the description of the formulaic process underlying the 'I Want Song': as Pocahontas explains to Vanellope, the song should 'magically' come to her if she stares at 'a form of water' – a 'wishing well' like Snow White, a 'horse trough' like Mulan, 'the ocean' like Moana – and will convey her dream through a 'metaphor'. Vanellope's reaction echoes that of contemporary Disney male characters, who cynically and pragmatically refuse, at first, to take part in the musical genre: *Enchanted*'s (Kevin Lima, 2007) Robert and *Tangled*'s Flynn. Yet, like these heroes, and in typically post-feminist fashion, initially sceptical Vanellope ends up embracing the core tenets of Disney's musical formula.

Figure 8.2 *Vanellope demystifies the formulaic Disney musical. Frame grab from* Ralph Breaks the Internet: Wreck-It Ralph 2 *(Johnston and Moore, 2018).*

'A Place Called Slaughter Race' amplifies the combination of knowing self-reflexivity and sincere celebration of the Disney formula characterising 'Ma Belle Evangeline' in *The Princess and the Frog* (Ron Clements and John Musker, 2009), and notably developed through the musical pairing of 'I've Got a Dream' and 'I See the Light' in *Tangled*. The song comes to Vanellope at the gates of 'Oh My Disney', after a phone call from Ralph: he has gathered enough money to buy a new steering wheel and save 'Sugar Rush', so that they can all return to their respective games. Vanellope cannot articulate the reason for her malaise on hearing this positive news: staring at a puddle, her reflection is magically transported into 'Slaughter Race'. Her musical performance begins, explicitly signified by a multitude of intertextual references to Disney's animated canon, from the *mise en scène* to the orchestration. The musical transition is conveyed through sparkling fairy dust over the puddle, and an enchanting violin melody. Like Snow White, Aurora and Anna, Vanellope sings while interacting with a bird landing on her hand; when the pace of the song joyfully accelerates, she is greeted by all the characters of 'Slaughter Race', imitating the beginning of *Beauty and the Beast*'s (Gary Trousdale and Kirk Wise, 1991) 'Belle'. Alan Menken's cheerful and upbeat soundtrack, reminiscent of his work on 1990s Disney fairy tales and more recent animated features such as *Tangled*, added to Vanellope's childlike and high-pitched voice, comically contrasts with the threatening and dangerous surroundings of 'Slaughter Race'. Unlike the idyllic pastoral decor of Disney's sentimental fairy tales, peopled by cute anthropomorphic animals, 'Slaughter Race' consists in a violent urban environment, including 'fallen wires, dumpster fires, creepy clowns and burning tires' – Vanellope notably sings to a one-legged pigeon and a white shark. Such an incongruous stylistic clash is accompanied by the initial demystification of Disney's musical generic tropes: Vanellope urges her song to manifest ('Come on, song! I'm reflecting!'), she is blinded by the spotlight above her, and explicitly points out that she is using metaphors and that she is 'rhyming'. Yet, like Disney's contemporary leads, she happily gives in to the musical performance – the spotlight correspondingly disappears after a few verses. She seamlessly joins in and harmonises with the other characters. The 'I Want Song' successfully performs its primary function: Vanellope uses it to convey her longing for the exciting and unpredictable world of 'Slaughter Race', expressing a feeling she was not able to articulate otherwise – in typical musical fashion. The initial playful parody transforms into a more sincere celebration of the 'I Want Song': 'A Place Called Slaughter Race' concludes with the expansive extravagance of Disney's fairy-tale ensemble performances, such as *The Little Mermaid*'s (Ron Clements and John Musker, 1989) 'Under the Sea'.

This sequence not only replicates the doubleness of Disney's contemporary fairy-tale musicals, but it also re-envisions their generic borders through the merging of action-adventure and the musical, as epitomised in *Moana*. By discarding the romantic and heteronormative connotations of Disney's musical formula, the song prioritises instead Vanellope's own narrative of becoming. The liberating performance intrinsic to the musical is enhanced by the dynamic and kinetic tropes of action cinema at work in 'Slaughter Race': choreographed violent fights, thrilling explosions and, most importantly for Vanellope, fast-paced car racing ('flying so fast', 'loving the chase'). In the process, Disney draws on its roots to reimagine and develop further the relationship and parallels between the two spectacular genres. Such merging illuminates the studio's wider strategy throughout its contemporary output in order to renew its formula: reappropriating and re-envisioning action-adventure genres, while expanding its own generic territory. The character of Vanellope acts as a bridge. The action musical princess functions as a converging point between Disney's self-reflexive revision and generic expansion. This post-feminist figure crystallises the enduring appeal of Disney's fairy-tale musical formula ('she is a princess!') mediated through DreamWorks-style parody and contemporary chick-flick tropes, and the empowering potentials of the action mode.

Generic Shifts, Buddy Triangles: The Formula Grows Up

Although Vanellope acts as a generic bridge, her ultimate move to 'Slaughter Race' embodies the self-reflexive approach of contemporary Disney: the studio's wider generic shift towards action adventure, borrowing from genres such as the superhero film and the action cop buddy film, parallels its acknowledgement that the formula requires some revision. From *Bolt*'s (Byron Howard and Chris Williams, 2008) network representative warning that the 'show is too predictable' to *Zootopia*'s (Byron Howard and Rich Moore, 2016) Chief Bogo pointing out that 'life isn't some cartoon musical', contemporary Disney animated films released between 2008 and 2018 have consistently hinted at and reappropriated criticisms surrounding the studio's own formulaic tropes, narratives and gender constructions. The contrasting representation of 'Sugar Rush' and 'Slaughter Race' particularly illuminates such self-awareness and evolution.

With its chirpy theme song and its bright, colourful, miniature world inhabited by young racers and a myriad of anthropomorphic candy characters, 'Sugar Rush' crystallises the childlike, cosy and sanitised world of the Disney formula. Such harmless childishness stands out in Ralph's admirative description to the characters of 'Slaughter Race': 'You should see her racing around in her sweet little track in her cookie wafer car we built together . . . her perfect little game broke.' Vanellope appears embarrassed at the diminutive dimension of the description. The game is starting to feel constraining for her: having mastered all the tracks and consistently won thanks to her glitching powers, she has come to find the game 'kind of predictable'. Her attempts at challenging the game narrative and driving on alternative, bumpier and unruly tracks are met with resistance by the gamers who try to 'steer' her back into her place, which leads to the breaking of the steering wheel within the arcade. By contrast, 'Slaughter Race' represents an opportunity to escape into the unknown, beyond the constraints of the predictable, childlike Disney formula. The construction of this game takes Disney's playful reproduction of the dazzling visuals of the digital action-adventure spectacle further, consolidating and expanding the aesthetic initiated by Pixar, and developed by Disney in *Bolt*, *Wreck-It Ralph* and *Big Hero 6* (Don Hall and Chris Williams, 2014). The characters humorously comment on the imitation of live-action cinematography and effects ('the attention to detail is pretty impressive'): as opposed to the heavily stylised and cartoonish aesthetics of 'Sugar Rush', 'Slaughter Race' showcases photorealistic textures and reflective surfaces, including blurry fog. This more mature action world, with darker sepia tones, is peopled by adults driving racing cars and trucks: their races expand the live-action 'impact aesthetic' playfully imitated in *Bolt* and crystallised within the highly popular action franchise *Fast & Furious*. Vanellope's thrilling race with Shank (Gal Gadot), trying to steal her car to sell it and pay for the steering wheel, makes a strong impression on 'the young girl'.[3] To her, it represents a significant upgrade compared with her own action-centred game: 'it's full of weirdos, the racing is super dangerous . . . and you never know what's gonna happen next'. In other words, she wants to distance herself from the childish, predictable and constraining world of 'Sugar Rush', paralleling Disney's efforts to depart from its formulaic aesthetic, narrative and gender constructions, associated with fairy tales and children's films.

Such desire for change is accompanied by Vanellope's strong sense of her own digital constructedness: like most of Disney's contemporary action-adventure films, *Ralph Breaks the Internet* consistently foregrounds the inner workings of computer animation in order to reveal the *mise en scène* behind the digital action spectacle. In this sequel, glitching and unstable Internet viruses have a significant narrative role, revealing how Disney's generic reworking is rooted in its very animated aesthetic. As *Ralph Breaks the Internet* prioritises 'Slaughter Race' over 'Sugar Rush', it provides an update of *Wreck-It Ralph*'s own primary action-adventure world. In the process, this shift impacts, reframes and renews the superhero narrative trajectory of both of *Wreck-It Ralph*'s leads.

Vanellope's steps towards independence, leaving 'Sugar Rush' and Ralph to move into the Internet and 'Slaughter Race', particularly challenge Ralph's performance of super masculinity: while in the first film he managed to control his overflowing strength to perform heroic acts and notably rescue Vanellope, the sequel questions the very necessity of such a performance. In other words, the film explores whether the typical gendered configuration of genres of romance and action, and of Disney's formula, namely male chivalry and exertion of power in the service of victimised femininity, should be maintained. Like *Moana*'s Maui, Ralph's 'insecurity' is precisely rooted in the fear of rejection by his adoring audience, embodied by Vanellope, who notably made him a medal and called him 'my hero'. Fearing that she will leave for 'Slaughter Race', Ralph frees a virus which threatens the digital integrity of the game: the virus makes significant glitching damage and unexpectedly endangers Vanellope. Upon hearing that she might die in the game, Ralph remobilises his controlled performance of super masculinity, wrecking the entrance of 'Slaughter Race', finding her under some debris and carrying her outside to safety. This spectacular feat is not framed as a heroic act: Ralph is motivated by his own insecurity and selfishness, which leads to a serious argument with Vanellope. The film recurringly points to the gender imbalance behind such performances of super masculinity: Ralph is notably warned not to go to 'Slaughter Race' 'like a white knight'. His refusal to let Vanellope exist beyond his friendship, as an independent being with agency, has disastrous consequences: the Internet virus identifies Ralph as an 'insecurity', duplicating his character until they combine to create a monstrous amalgamation. His attempts at defeating the gigantic, Godzilla-like creature are initially violent and correspondingly unsuccessful: jumping high in the air, punching and wrecking are no longer effective superhero moves. It is only when he reasons with the monster ('you don't own her') and he reconciles with Vanellope that the insecurity digitally disintegrates. This monstrous manifestation notably magnifies *Frozen*'s similar subversion of the archaic figure of chivalrous masculinity. Echoing a syntactic trajectory that is recurring in Disney's contemporary canon, as illustrated in *Moana*, and Disney's wider cinematic universe, as in Pixar's *Incredibles 2* (Brad Bird, 2018) and the rebooted *Star Wars* franchise (2015, 2017, 2019), the male hero must leave space for the independent and empowered heroine, reconfiguring his performance of extraordinary masculinity.

Not only do the rebalanced constructions of gender in *Ralph Breaks the Internet* restore the buddy dynamic between Vanellope and Ralph, but they also allow the multiplication of female-centred relationships, pointing to the influence of the chick flick and the buddy movie throughout Disney's contemporary output. As in *Moana* and *Zootopia*, as well as in *Frozen*, Disney's

Figure 8.3 *Shank, Vanellope and Ralph form a 'buddy' triangle. Frame grab from* Ralph Breaks the Internet: Wreck-It Ralph 2 *(Johnston and Moore, 2018).*

reappropriation of these two genres highlights syntactic parallels with the romantic comedy, while facilitating the gradual disappearance of romance as Disney's primary mode. Ralph's jealousy of Shank creates a 'buddy triangle' of sorts, resolved through Vanellope's reconciliation with Ralph (Figure 8.3). Her sisterly friendship with Shank and her interactions with the princesses are pivotal in her own narrative of becoming.

Familiar Tracks, New Realms: Disney's Contemporary Cinematic Universe

Vanellope's eventful journey throughout *Ralph Breaks the Internet*, from the well-known setting of her game, introduced in *Wreck-It Ralph*, to the highly intertextual world of 'Oh My Disney' and the expansive, unpredictable space of 'Slaughter Race', echoes Disney's strategies to reinvent and regenerate its animated output throughout the 2008–18 decade. Overall, *Ralph Breaks the Internet* crystallises the studio's double impulse: self-reflexive revision and generic expansion. Disney animated films interact with generic tropes and trends within Disney's expanded cinematic universe – Pixar's revisionist approach to the fairy tale and pioneering computer animation, Marvel superhero films – and beyond. They reinterpret the influential DreamWorks formula, and reappropriate genres as varied as the romantic comedy, the chick flick and the cop buddy film. Furthermore, *Ralph Breaks the Internet* points to potential wider shifts for Disney animation beyond 2018, under Jennifer Lee's leadership. These may include the growing convergence of fairy tale and action-adventure, musical and superhero tropes, as suggested by *Frozen II* (Chris Buck and Jennifer Lee, 2019) and *Encanto* (Jared Bush and Byron Howard, 2021). In the former, Elsa's repositioning as an empowered superheroine actively and successfully protecting her kingdom contrasts with her portrayal in all previous *Frozen* properties. In parallel, the gradual disappearance of Disney's sentimental formula, replaced by an emphasis on female-centred relationships, as shown in *Raya and the Last Dragon* (Don Hall and Carlos López Estrada, 2021), suggests that romantic narratives and chivalric princes have become less essential, almost obsolete. The enduring presence of the updated post-feminist Princess reveals its strength as the potentially last icon of the studio's formula.

Ralph Breaks the Internet does not solely represent a self-reflexive panorama of a distinct phase in Disney history, revealing pivotal generic influences and trends in constructions of gender, both within and beyond Disney's cinematic universe: this animated film can also be used as a springboard for future research. As *Ralph Breaks the Internet* explores both familiar tracks and new realms within its diegesis, two themes particularly stand out. The first theme is the relationship between original animated features that re-envision the Disney formula, and films that explicitly revisit and readapt existing animated properties. The emergence of theatrically released sequels with *Ralph Breaks the Internet* and *Frozen II*, and the multiplication of theatrically released live-action remakes since the mid-2010s constitute the most notable examples. At the time of writing, most of Disney's iconic characters reintroduced in *Ralph Breaks the Internet* – from Eeyore and Dumbo to the princesses – have reappeared in such remakes. While some of these, such as the *Maleficent* films (2014, 2019) and *Cruella* (Craig Gillespie, 2021) draw on the revisionist impulse of contemporary animated counterparts such as *Brave* (Mark Andrews and Brenda Chapman, 2012) and *Frozen*, others adopt a post-feminist nostalgic approach and a renewed emphasis on sentimental romance which subsequent animated films have discarded. The ways in which Disney's romantic and musical tropes are remobilised in *Beauty and the Beast* (Bill Condon, 2017) and *Aladdin* (Guy Ritchie, 2019) on the one hand, and *Frozen II* and *Encanto* on the other illustrate such a divergence. By contrast, action-adventure convergences seem to emerge between films like *Mulan* (Niki Caro, 2020) and *Raya and the Last Dragon*. These differing interactions represent further aspects to be explored in relation to Disney's reinvention of its animated canon, its aesthetic, generic and gendered formula.

A second avenue for future research relates to the circulation, reception and afterlives of Disney animated films throughout new media formats and digital platforms. Vanellope's experience in 'Oh My Disney', travelling through new realms while interacting with a multitude of familiar Disney properties, not only echoes the experience of visitors at Disney's theme parks but also prefigures that of viewers of Disney+, Disney's own streaming platform launched the year following *Ralph Breaks the Internet*'s release. This platform represents 'the culmination of the Robert Iger franchise era acquisitions' of Pixar (2006), Marvel (2009), Lucasfilm (2012), BamTech (2017) and Fox (2019) (Scott 2020).[4] Its very home page echoes the design of 'Oh My Disney', with its individual icons corresponding to each Disney property. On this platform, individual animated features are recycled and reinterpreted through original short films, making of series or even 'mood scenes', spectacularly expanding the number of official paratexts for each film: the *Frozen* collection contains close to a dozen such examples. While the creation of such ancillary texts is not new, as illustrated by the numerous animated television series broadcast on Disney Channel, from *Hercules* (1998–9) to *Tangled: The Series* (2017–20), this phenomenon has been amplified with Disney+. Beyond the multifaceted franchising of existing animated films on this new digital platform, their categorisation, repositioning and reception highlight generic meanings and convergences which also deserve further consideration. For example, in February 2021, the digital banner for the 'Valentine's Day' playlist on Disney+ featured the lead couples of *The Princess and the Frog*, Pixar's *Up* (Pete Docter and Bob Peterson, 2009), Disney Channel's *High School Musical* (Kenny Ortega, 2006) and 'Disney+ original' *Lady and the Tramp* (Charlie Bean, 2019). Such repackaging of existing Disney properties, accompanied by suggestions within and beyond its cinematic universe (notably via Star), points to new realms in which to investigate the influence of genres and wider modes – notably romance – examined in this book.[5]

Through a detailed analysis of a distinct decade in the history of the Disney studio, this book has examined the evolving interactions between Disney animation and a continuously growing cinematic universe. The book has not only offered a fresh approach to Disney's contemporary animated films, combining a generic perspective and a focus on gender while examining their positioning on a post-feminist spectrum, but it has also mapped productive intersections between animation scholarship and genre studies. In order to fully understand the generic identity, aesthetics and gender portrayals of Disney animated films, considering the wider Hollywood context is essential; to fully understand contemporary Hollywood cinema, it has now correspondingly become pivotal to consider mainstream animation, and more specifically, Disney animated films.

Notes

1. *The Rescuers Down Under* was one of the least financially successful animated films from the Renaissance era. See Pallant 2013: 92.
2. Examples of such academic accounts include Amy Davis on the princesses' dependence on their fathers (2006: 190–206), Lynda Haas on absent mothers (1995) and Jack Zipes on the overall patriarchal structure of the fairy tales (2011: 86–9). See also the Introduction.

3. The casting of Gal Gadot, who played in three *Fast & Furious* films (2009, 2011, 2013), reinforces this generic intertext.
4. BamTech is a global company specialising in 'direct-to-consumer streaming technology and marketing services, data analytics, and commerce management'. See 'The Walt Disney Company to Acquire Majority Ownership of BAMTech', *The Walt Disney Company*, 8 August 2017, <https://thewaltdisneycompany.com/walt-disney-company-acquire-majority-ownership-bamtech/> (accessed 3 April 2022).
5. In February 2021, the Star brand was added to Disney+, featuring a 'collection of general entertainment movies, television, documentaries' from 'Disney Television Studios (ABC Signature and 20th Television), FX Productions, 20th Century Studios, Searchlight Pictures', along with 'Star-branded exclusive originals'. See 'Disney+ Launches Star in Select Overseas Markets', *The Walt Disney Company*, 23 February 2021, <https://thewaltdisneycompany.com/disney-launches-star-in-select-overseas-markets/> (accessed 3 April 2022).

Filmography

27 Dresses, Anne Fletcher, Fox 2000 Pictures, 2008.
42nd Street, Lloyd Bacon, Warner Bros., 1933.
48 Hrs., Walter Hill, Paramount Pictures, 1982.
(500) Days of Summer, Marc Webb, Fox Searchlight Pictures, 2009.
An Affair to Remember, Leo McCarey, Twentieth Century Fox, 1957.
Akira, Katsuhiro Ôtomo, Akira Studio, 1988.
Aladdin, Ron Clements and John Musker, Walt Disney Pictures, 1992.
Aladdin, Guy Ritchie, Walt Disney Pictures, 2019.
Aladdin and the King of Thieves, Tad Stones, Walt Disney Home Video, 1996.
Alien, Ridley Scott, Brandywine Productions, 1979.
Along Came Polly, John Hamburg, Universal Pictures, 2004.
The Amazing Spider-Man, Marc Webb, Columbia Pictures, 2012.
The American President, Rob Reiner, Columbia Pictures, 1995.
Annie Hall, Woody Allen, Jack Rollins & Charles H. Joffe Productions, 1977.
Antz, Eric Darnell and Tim Johnson, DreamWorks Animation, 1998.
The Aristocats, Wolfgang Reitherman, Walt Disney Productions, 1970.
The Artist, Michel Hazanavicius, Studio 37, 2011.
The Associate, Donald Petrie, Hollywood Pictures, 1996.
The A-Team, Joe Carnham, Twentieth Century Fox, 2010.
Atlantis: The Lost Empire, Gary Trousdale and Kirk Wise, Walt Disney Pictures, 2001.
The Avengers, Joss Whedon, Marvel Studios, 2012.
Avengers: Age of Ultron, Joss Whedon, Marvel Studios, 2015.
Avengers: Endgame, Anthony and Joe Russo, Marvel Studios, 2019.
Avengers: Infinity War, Anthony and Joe Russo, Marvel Studios, 2018.
Bambi, David Hand et al., Walt Disney Productions, 1942.
The Band Wagon, Vincente Minnelli, Metro-Goldwyn-Mayer (MGM), 1953.
Batman Returns, Tim Burton, Warner Bros., 1992.
Batman v Superman: Dawn of Justice, Zack Snyder, Warner Bros., 2016.
Beauty and the Beast, Gary Trousdale and Kirk Wise, Walt Disney Pictures, 1991.
Beauty and the Beast, Bill Condon, Walt Disney Pictures, 2017.
Before Sunset, Richard Linklater, Warner Bros., 2004.
Big Hero 6, Don Hall and Chris Williams, Walt Disney Animation Studios, 2014.
Birds of Prey (and the Fantabulous Emancipation of One Harley Quinn), Cathy Yan, DC Entertainment, 2020.
The Black Cauldron, Ted Berman and Richard Rich, Walt Disney Pictures, 1985.
Black Widow, Cate Shortland, Marvel Studios, 2021.
Blue Steel, Kathryn Bigelow, Lightning Pictures, 1989.

Bolt, Byron Howard and Chris Williams, Walt Disney Animation Studios, 2008.
Brave, Mark Andrews and Brenda Chapman, Pixar, 2012.
Bride Wars, Gary Winnick, Fox 2000 Pictures, 2009.
Bridesmaids, Paul Feig, Universal Pictures, 2011.
Bridget Jones's Baby, Sharon Maguire, Universal Pictures, 2016.
Bringing Up Baby, Howard Hawks, RKO Radio Pictures, 1938.
Brother Bear, Aaron Blaise and Robert Walker, Walt Disney Pictures, 2003.
A Bug's Life, John Lasseter and Andrew Stanton, Pixar, 1998.
Can't Buy Me Love, Steve Rash, Touchstone Pictures, 1987.
Captain America: Civil War, Anthony and Joe Russo, Marvel Studios, 2016.
Captain America: First Avenger, Joe Johnston, Marvel Studios, 2011.
Captain Marvel, Anna Boden and Ryan Fleck, Marvel Studios, 2019.
Casablanca, Michael Curtiz, Warner Bros., 1942.
Catwoman, Pitof, Warner Bros., 2004.
Chicken Little, Mark Dindal, Walt Disney Pictures, 2005.
A Christmas Carol, Robert Zemeckis, Walt Disney Pictures, 2009.
Cinderella, Clyde Geronimi and Wilfred Jackson, Walt Disney Productions, 1950.
Coco, Lee Unkrich, Pixar, 2017.
Crazy Rich Asians, Jon Chu, Warner Bros., 2018.
Crazy Stupid Love, Glenn Ficarra and John Requa, Carousel Productions, 2011.
Cruella, Craig Gillespie, Walt Disney Pictures, 2021.
Dinosaur, Eric Leighton and Ralph Zondag, Walt Disney Pictures, 2000.
Dumbo, Ben Sharpsteen, Walt Disney Productions, 1941.
Easter Parade, Charles Walters, Metro-Goldwyn-Mayer (MGM), 1948.
Edge of Tomorrow, Doug Liman, Warner Bros., 2014.
Elektra, Rob Bowman, Twentieth Century Fox, 2005.
The Emperor's New Groove, Mark Dindal, Walt Disney Pictures, 2000.
Encanto, Jared Bush and Byron Howard, Walt Disney Animation Studios, 2021.
Enchanted, Kevin Lima, Walt Disney Pictures, 2007.
Fantasia, Ben Sharpsteen et al., Walt Disney Productions, 1940.
Fantasia 2000, Hendel Butoy and Eric Goldberg, Walt Disney Pictures, 2000.
Fargo, Ethan and Joel Cohen, Working Title Films, 1996.
Final Fantasy: The Spirits Within, Hironobu Sakaguchi, Chris Lee Productions, 2001.
Finding Nemo, Andrew Stanton, Pixar, 2003.
Forgetting Sarah Marshall, Nicholas Stoller, Universal Pictures, 2008.
The Fox and the Hound, Ted Berman and Richard Rich, Walt Disney Productions, 1981.
Friends with Benefits, Will Gluck, Screen Gems, 2011.
Frozen, Chris Buck and Jennifer Lee, Walt Disney Animation Studios, 2013.
Frozen II, Chris Buck and Jennifer Lee, Walt Disney Animation Studios, 2019.
Frozen Fever, Chris Buck and Jennifer Lee, Walt Disney Animation Studios, 2015.
Get a Horse!, Lauren MacMullan, Walt Disney Animation Studios, 2013.
Ghosts of Girlfriends Past, Mark Waters, New Line Cinema, 2009.
G.I. Jane, Ridley Scott, Hollywood Pictures, 1997.
Gladiator, Ridley Scott, DreamWorks Pictures, 2000.
The Godfather, Francis Ford Coppola, Paramount Pictures, 1972.
Gold Diggers of 1933, Mervyn LeRoy, Warner Bros., 1933.
The Good Dinosaur, Peter Sohn, Pixar Animation Studios, 2015.
The Great Mouse Detective, Ron Clements and John Musker, Walt Disney Pictures, 1986.

Guardians of the Galaxy, James Gunn, Marvel Studios, 2014.
Hancock, Peter Berg, Columbia Pictures, 2008.
Happily N'Ever After, Paul Bolger and Yvette Kaplan, Nitrogen Studios Canada, 2006.
Hawaiian Holiday, Ben Sharpsteen, Walt Disney Productions, 1937.
The Heat, Paul Feig, Twentieth Century Fox, 2013.
Hello, Dolly!, Gene Kelly, Twentieth Century Fox, 1969.
Hercules, Ron Clements and John Musker, Walt Disney Pictures, 1997.
High School Musical, Kenny Ortega, Salty Pictures, 2006.
The Hobbit: The Desolation of Smaug, Peter Jackson, Metro-Goldwyn-Mayer (MGM), 2013.
The Holiday, Nancy Meyers, Universal Pictures, 2006.
Home on the Range, Will Finn and John Sanford, Walt Disney Pictures, 2004.
Hoodwinked, Cory Edwards and Todd Edwards, Kanbar Entertainment, 2005.
How to Be Single, Christian Ditter, New Line Cinema, 2016.
How to Train Your Dragon, Dean DeBlois and Chris Sanders, DreamWorks Animation, 2010.
Hugo, Martin Scorsese, Paramount Pictures, 2011.
Hulk, Ang Lee, Universal Pictures, 2003.
The Hunchback of Notre-Dame, Gary Trousdale and Kirk Wise, Walt Disney Pictures, 1996.
The Incredible Hulk, Louis Leterrier, Marvel Studios, 2008.
The Incredibles, Brad Bird, Pixar, 2004.
Incredibles 2, Brad Bird, Pixar, 2018.
Iron Man, Jon Favreau, Marvel Studios, 2008.
Iron Man 3, Shane Black, Marvel Studios, 2013.
It Happened One Night, Frank Capra, Columbia Pictures Corporation, 1934.
The Jungle Book, Wolfgang Reitherman, Walt Disney Productions, 1967.
Jungle Cruise, Jaume Collet-Serra, Walt Disney Pictures, 2021.
Kate and Leopold, James Mangold, Miramax, 2001.
Knocked Up, Judd Apatow, Universal Pictures, 2007.
L.A. Confidential, Curtis Hanson, Warner Bros., 1997.
La Luna, Enrico Casarosa, Pixar, 2011.
Lady and the Tramp, Clyde Geronimi and Wilfred Jackson, Walt Disney Productions, 1955.
Lady and the Tramp, Charlie Bean, Walt Disney Pictures, 2019.
Laputa: Castle in the Sky, Hayao Miyazaki, Studio Ghibli, 1986.
Lilo & Stitch, Dean DeBlois and Chris Sanders, Walt Disney Pictures, 2002.
The Lion King, Roger Allers and Rob Minkoff, Walt Disney Pictures, 1994.
The Little Mermaid, Ron Clements and John Musker, Walt Disney Pictures, 1989.
Maid in Manhattan, Wayne Wang, Revolution Studios, 2002.
The Matrix, Lana and Lilly Wachowski, Warner Bros., 1999.
Megamind, Tom McGrath, DreamWorks Animation, 2010.
Mission: Impossible: Ghost Protocol, Brad Bird, Paramount Pictures, 2011.
Moana, Ron Clements and John Musker, Walt Disney Animation Studios, 2016.
Monster-in-Law, Robert Luketic, New Line Cinema, 2005.
Monsters, Inc., Pete Docter, Pixar, 2001.
The Moth and the Flame, Burt Gillett, Walt Disney Productions, 1938.
Mrs Doubtfire, Chris Columbus, Fox, 1993.
Mulan, Tony Bancroft and Barry Cook, Walt Disney Pictures, 1998.
Mulan, Niki Caro, Walt Disney Pictures, 2020.
My Neighbour Totoro, Hayao Miyazaki, Studio Ghibli, 1988.
Myth: A Frozen Tale, Jeff Gipson, Walt Disney Animation Studios, 2019.

Olaf's Frozen Adventure, Stevie Wermers-Skelton and Kevin Deters, Walt Disney Animation Studios, 2017.
Oliver and Company, George Scribner, Walt Disney Pictures, 1988.
Once Upon a Snowman, Dan Abraham and Trent Correy, Walt Disney Animation Studios, 2020.
One Hundred and One Dalmatians, Clyde Geronimi and Hamilton Luske, Walt Disney Productions, 1961.
The Other Guys, Adam McKay, Columbia Pictures, 2010.
Paperman, John Kahrs, Walt Disney Animation Studios, 2012.
ParaNorman, Chris Butler and Sam Fell, Laika, 2012.
Persépolis, Vincent Paronnaud and Marjane Satrapi, 2.4.7. Films, 2007.
Peter Pan, Clyde Geronimi and Wilfred Jackson, Walt Disney Productions, 1953.
The Philadelphia Story, George Cukor, Metro-Goldwyn-Mayer (MGM), 1940.
Pinocchio, Hamilton Luske and Ben Sharpsteen, Walt Disney Productions, 1940.
Pirates of the Caribbean: The Curse of the Black Pearl, Gore Verbinski, Walt Disney Pictures, 2003.
Pocahontas, Mike Gabriel and Eric Goldberg, Walt Disney Pictures, 1995.
The Polar Express, Robert Zemeckis, Warner Bros., 2004.
Pretty Woman, Garry Marshall, Touchstone Pictures, 1990.
The Prince of Egypt, Brenda Chapman and Steve Hickner, DreamWorks Animation, 1998.
The Princess and the Frog, Ron Clements and John Musker, Walt Disney Animation Studios, 2009.
The Proposal, Anne Fletcher, Touchstone Pictures, 2009.
Raiders of the Lost Ark, Steven Spielberg, Paramount Pictures, 1981.
Ralph Breaks the Internet: Wreck-It Ralph 2, Phil Johnston and Rich Moore, Walt Disney Animation Studios, 2018.
Ratatouille, Brad Bird, Pixar, 2007.
Raya and the Last Dragon, Don Hall and Carlos López Estrada, Walt Disney Animation Studios, 2021.
Rear Window, Alfred Hitchcock, Paramount, 1954.
Red, Robert Schwentke, Summit Entertainment, 2010.
Red Hot Riding Hood, Tex Avery, MGM Cartoon Studio, 1943.
The Rescuers, John Lounsbery and Wolfgang Reitherman, Walt Disney Pictures, 1977.
The Rescuers Down Under, Mike Gabriel, Walt Disney Pictures, 1990.
The Road to El Dorado, Bibo Bergeron and Don Paul, DreamWorks Animation, 2000.
Robin Hood, Wolfgang Reitherman, Walt Disney Productions, 1973.
Scott Pilgrim vs. the World, Edgar Wright, Universal Pictures, 2010.
Sex and the City, Michael Patrick King, New Line Cinema, 2008.
Shark Tale, Bibo Bergeron and Vicky Jenson, DreamWorks Animation, 2004.
Shrek, Andrew Adamson and Vicky Jenson, DreamWorks Animation, 2001.
Shrek 2, Andrew Adamson, Kelly Asbury and Conrad Vernon, DreamWorks Animation, 2004.
Shrek Forever After, Mike Mitchell, DreamWorks Animation, 2010.
Shrek the Third, Raman Hui and Chris Miller, DreamWorks Animation, 2007.
The Silence of the Lambs, Jonathan Demme, Orion Pictures, 1991.
A Silent Voice, Naoko Yamada, Kyoto Animation, 2016.
Singin' in the Rain, Stanley Donen and Gene Kelly, Metro-Goldwyn-Mayer (MGM), 1952.
Sleeping Beauty, Clyde Geronimi, Walt Disney Pictures, 1959.
Sleepless in Seattle, Nora Ephron, Columbia Pictures, 1993.

Filmography

Snow White and the Seven Dwarfs, David Hand, Walt Disney Productions, 1937.
Someone Great, Jennifer Kaytin Robinson, Feigco Entertainment, 2019.
Something New, Sanaa Hamri, Gramercy Pictures, 2006.
Song of the South, Harve Foster and Wilfred Jackson, Walt Disney Productions, 1946.
Space Jam, Joe Pytka, Warner Bros., 1997.
Space Jam: A New Legacy, Malcolm D. Lee, Warner Bros., 2021.
Spider-Man, Sam Raimi, Columbia Pictures, 2002.
Spider-Man 2, Sam Raimi, Columbia Pictures, 2004.
Spider-Man 3, Sam Raimi, Columbia Pictures, 2007.
Star Wars, George Lucas, Fox, 1977.
Steamboat Willie, Ub Iwerks, Walt Disney Productions, 1928.
The Swan Princess, Richard Rich, Rich Animation Studios, 1994.
Sweet Home Alabama, Andy Tennant, Touchstone Pictures, 2002.
Swingers, Doug Liman, Doug Liman Productions, 1996.
The Sword in the Stone, Wolfgang Reitherman, Walt Disney Productions, 1963.
Tangled, Nathan Greno and Byron Howard, Walt Disney Animation Studios, 2010.
Tangled Ever After, Nathan Greno and Byron Howard, Walt Disney Animation Studios, 2012.
Tarzan, Kevin Lima and Chris Buck, Walt Disney Pictures, 1999.
Terminator 2: Judgment Day, James Cameron, Lightstorm Entertainment, 1991.
Thelma and Louise, Ridley Scott, Metro-Goldwyn-Mayer (MGM), 1991.
Thor, Kenneth Branagh, Marvel Studios, 2011.
Thor: Ragnarok, Taika Waititi, Marvel Studios, 2017.
Thumbelina, Don Bluth and Gary Goldman, Don Bluth, 1994.
Thunder Force, Ben Falcone, Netflix, 2021.
Toy Story, John Lasseter, Pixar, 1995.
Toy Story 2, John Lasseter, Pixar, 1999.
Trainwreck, Judd Apatow, Universal Pictures, 2015.
Treasure Planet, Ron Clements and John Musker, Walt Disney Pictures, 2002.
TRON: Legacy, Joseph Kosinski, Walt Disney Pictures, 2010.
Tropic Thunder, Ben Stiller, DreamWorks Pictures, 2008.
Up, Pete Docter and Bob Peterson, Pixar Animation Studios, 2009.
WALL-E, Andrew Stanton, Pixar, 2008.
Wedding Crashers, David Dobkin, New Line Cinema, 2005.
The Wedding Planner, Adam Shankman, Columbia Pictures, 2001.
When Harry Met Sally, Rob Reiner, Castle Rock Entertainment, 1989.
Winnie the Pooh, Stephen Anderson and Don Hall, Walt Disney Animation Studios, 2011.
Wolf Children, Mamoru Hosoda, Studio Chizu, 2012.
Wonder Woman, Patty Jenkins, Warner Bros., 2017.
Wonder Woman 1984, Patty Jenkins, Warner Bros., 2020.
Wreck-It Ralph, Rich Moore, Walt Disney Animation Studios, 2012.
X-Men, Bryan Singer, Twentieth Century Fox, 2000.
Your Name, Makoto Shinkai, Amuse, 2016.
You've Got Mail, Nora Ephron, Warner Bros., 1998.
Zootopia, Byron Howard and Rich Moore, Walt Disney Animation Studios, 2016.

References

Aaron, Michele (2004), 'Introduction', in Michele Aaron (ed.), *New Queer Cinema: A Critical Reader*, Edinburgh: Edinburgh University Press, pp. 3–14.

Akita, Kimiko and Rick Kenney (2013), 'A "Vexing Implication": Siamese Cats and Orientalist Mischief-making', in Johnson Cheu (ed.), *Diversity in Disney Films: Critical Essays on Race, Ethnicity, Gender, Sexuality and Disability*, Jefferson, NC: McFarland, pp. 50–66.

Alberti, John (2013), *Masculinity in the Contemporary Romantic Comedy: Gender as Genre*, London: Routledge.

Altman, Rick (1984) 'A Semantic/Syntactic Approach to Film Genre', *Cinema Journal*, 23: 3 (Spring), pp. 6–18.

Altman, Rick (1989), *The American Film Musical*, Bloomington: Indiana University Press.

Altman, Rick (1998), 'Reusable Packaging: Generic Products and the Recycling Process', in Nick Brown (ed.), *Refiguring American Film Genres: History and Theory*, Berkeley: University of California Press, pp. 1–41.

Altman, Rick (1999), *Film/Genre*, London: British Film Institute.

Anjirbag, Michelle Anya (2018), '*Mulan* and *Moana*: Embedded Coloniality and the Search for Authenticity in Disney Animated Film', *Social Sciences*, 7: 11, <https://doi.org/10.3390/socsci7110230> (accessed 17 March 2022).

Archer, Neil (2019), *Twenty-first-century Hollywood: Rebooting the System*, New York: Columbia University Press.

Armstrong, Robin (2018), 'Time to Face the Music: Musical Colonization and Appropriation in Disney's *Moana*', *Social Sciences*, 7: 7, <https://doi.org/10.3390/socsci7070113> (accessed 17 March 2022).

Aza Missouri, Montré (2015), *Black Magic Woman and Narrative Film: Race, Sex and Afro-religiosity*, Basingstoke: Palgrave Macmillan.

Barker, Jennifer L. (2010), 'Hollywood, Black Animation, and the Problem of Representation in *Little Ol' Bosko* and *The Princess and the Frog*', *Journal of African American Studies*, 14, pp. 482–98.

Bayless, Martha (2012), 'Disney's Castles and the Work of the Medieval in the Magic Kingdom', in Susan Aronstein and Tison Pugh (eds), *The Disney Middle Ages: A Fairy-tale and Fantasy Past*, Basingstoke: Palgrave Macmillan, pp. 39–56.

Beaudine, Gregory, Aliya Beavers and Oyemolade Osibodu (2017), 'Disney's Metaphorical Exploration of Racism and Stereotypes: A Review of *Zootopia*', *Comparative Education Review*, 61: 1, pp. 227–34.

Beeler, Karin and Stan Beeler (eds) (2015), *Children's Film in the Digital Age: Essays on Audience, Adaptation and Consumer Culture*, Jefferson, NC: McFarland.

Benhamou, Eve (2017), 'When Disney Met Sci-fi: The Marketing of *Lilo & Stitch* (2002)', *Animation Studies 2.0*, 8 May, <https://blog.animationstudies.org/?p=2001> (accessed 28 February 2021).

Billson, Anne (2013), 'How Disney Reinvented the Superhero', *Telegraph*, 10 December, <http://www.telegraph.co.uk/culture/film/10507749/How-Disney-reinvented-thesuperhero.html> (accessed 18 August 2021).
Blu Barnd, Natchee (2013), 'White Man's Best Friend: Race and Privilege in *Oliver and Company*', in Johnson Cheu (ed.), *Diversity in Disney Films: Critical Essays on Race, Ethnicity, Gender, Sexuality and Disability*, Jefferson, NC: McFarland, pp. 67–82.
Boym, Svetlana (2001), *The Future of Nostalgia*, New York: Basic Books.
Brabon, Benjamin A. and Stéphanie Genz (2009), *Postfeminism: Cultural Texts and Theories*, Edinburgh: Edinburgh University Press.
Bradford, Clare (2012), '"Where happily ever after happens every day": The Medievalisms of Disney's Princesses', in Susan Aronstein and Tison Pugh (eds), *The Disney Middle Ages: A Fairy-tale and Fantasy Past*, Basingstoke: Palgrave Macmillan, pp. 171–88.
Bradshaw, Peter (2013), '*Frozen* – Review', *Guardian*, 5 December, <http://www.theguardian.com/film/2013/dec/05/frozen-review> (accessed 18 August 2021).
Brode, Douglas (2005), *Multiculturalism and the Mouse: Race and Sex in Disney Entertainment*, Austin: University of Texas Press.
Brode, Douglas (2010), *From Walt to Woodstock: How Disney Created the Counterculture*, Austin: University of Texas Press.
Brook, Heather (2015), 'Engaging Marriage: Rom Coms and Fairy Tale Endings', in Nadi Fadina and Luke Hockley (eds), *The Happiness Illusion: How the Media Sold Us a Fairytale*, New York: Routledge, pp. 145–61.
Brown, Jeffrey A. (1993), 'Bullets, Buddies, and Bad Guys: The "Action-cop" Genre', *Journal of Popular Film and Television*, 21: 2, pp. 79–87.
Brown, Jeffrey A. (2011), *Dangerous Curves: Action Heroines, Gender Fetishism, and Popular Culture*, Jackson: University Press of Mississippi.
Brown, Jeffrey A. (2015), *Beyond Bombshells: The New Action Heroine in Popular Culture*, Jackson: University Press of Mississippi.
Brown, Jeffrey A. (2017), *The Modern Superhero in Film and Television: Popular Genre and American Culture*, New York: Routledge.
Brown, Noel (2012), *The Hollywood Family Film: A History, from Shirley Temple to Harry Potter*, New York: I. B. Tauris.
Brown, Noel (2021), *Contemporary Hollywood Animation: Style, Storytelling, Culture and Ideology Since the 1990s*, Edinburgh: Edinburgh University Press.
Brown, Noel, Susan Smith and Sam Summers (2017), 'Introduction', in Noel Brown, Susan Smith and Sam Summers (eds), *Toy Story: How Pixar Reinvented the Animated Feature*, London: Bloomsbury Academic, pp. 1–6.
Brugué, Lydia and Auba Llompart (2020), 'The Snow Queer? Female Characterization in Walt Disney's *Frozen*', *Adaptation*, 13: 1, pp. 98–112.
Bruzzi, Stella (1997), *Undressing Cinema: Clothing and Identity in the Movies*, London: Routledge.
Bryman, Alan (2004), *The Disneyization of Society*, London: SAGE.
Buchan, Suzanne (2013), 'Introduction: Pervasive Animation', in Suzanne Buchan (ed.), *Pervasive Animation*, New York: Routledge, pp. 1–21.
Budd, Mike (2005), 'Introduction: Private Disney, Public Disney', in Mike Budd and Max H. Kirsch (eds), *Rethinking Disney: Private Control, Public Dimension*, Middletown, CT: Wesleyan University Press, pp. 1–33.
Bukatman, Scott (2003), *Matters of Gravity: Special Effects and Supermen in the 20th Century*, Durham, NC: Duke University Press.
Bukatman, Scott (2009), 'Secret Identity Politics', in Angela Ndalianis (ed.), *The Contemporary Comic Book Superhero*, New York: Routledge, pp. 109–25.

Bukatman, Scott (2011), 'Why I Hate Superhero Movies', *Cinema Journal*, 50: 3 (Spring), pp. 118–22.

Bukatman, Scott (2012), *The Poetics of Slumberland: Animated Spirits and the Animating Spirit*, Berkeley: University of California Press.

Bunch, Ryan (2017), '"Love is an open door": Revising and Repeating Disney's Musical Tropes in *Frozen*', in K. J. Donnelly and Beth Carroll (eds), *Contemporary Musical Film*, Edinburgh: Edinburgh University Press, pp. 89–103.

Burns, Amy (2013), 'The Chick's "New Hero": (Re)constructing Masculinity in the Postfeminist "Chick Flick"', in Joel Gwynne and Nadine Muller (eds), *Postfeminism and Contemporary Hollywood Cinema*, New York: Palgrave Macmillan, pp. 131–48.

Butler, Jess (2013), 'For White Girls Only?: Post-feminism and the Politics of Inclusion', *Feminist Formations*, 25: 1 (Spring), pp. 35–58.

Byrne, Eleanor and Martin McQuillan (1999), *Deconstructing Disney*, London: Pluto Press.

Carter, Chris (2013), 'An Analysis of the Character Animation in Disney's *Tangled*', *Senses of Cinema*, 67 (July), <https://www.sensesofcinema.com/2013/feature-articles/an-analysis-of-the-character-animation-in-disneys-tangled/> (accessed 31 January 2022).

Cavna, Michael (2011), 'In a Superhero-heavy Summer at the Movies, Stan Lee Talks about Genre's Appeal', *Washington Post*, 10 May, <https://www.washingtonpost.com/lifestyle/style/the-stan-lee-interview-in-this-summer-of-the-superhero-why-does-the-comic-book-genre-mightily-endure/2011/05/08/AF8NAmiG_story.html?utm_term=.7e503465a82f> (accessed 18 August 2021).

Chaney, Jen (2016), '*Zootopia*: A Delightful Menagerie, with a Worthwhile Message', *Washington Post*, 3 March, <https://www.washingtonpost.com/goingoutguide/movies/zootopia-a-delightful-menagerie-with-a-worthwhile-message/2016/03/03/8bed4ac8-defd-11e5-8d98-4b3d9215ade1_story.html?utm_term=.22603713f4b5> (accessed 21 August 2021).

Chang, Justin (2009), '*The Princess and the Frog*', *Variety*, 24 November, <http://variety.com/2009/digital/features/the-princess-and-the-frog-1200477289/> (accessed 1 August 2021).

Chapman, Brenda (2012), 'Foreword', in Jenny Lerew, *The Art of Brave*, San Francisco: Chronicle Books, p. 8.

Charania, Moon and Cory Albertson (2018), 'Single, White, Female: Feminist Trauma and Queer Melancholy in the New Disney', in Susan Talburt (ed.), *Youth Sexualities: Public Feelings and Contemporary Cultural Politics*, Santa Barbara, CA: Praeger, pp. 129–51.

Chatters, Ahli and Shearon Roberts (2020), 'Disney's Social Consciousness: Explaining #BlackLivesMatter through *Zootopia*', in Shearon Roberts (ed.), *Recasting the Disney Princess in an Era of New Media and Social Movements*, Lanham, MD: Lexington Books, pp. 295–310.

Chew, Kevin (2019), 'On War and Cuteness: The Utopian Politics of Disney's *Zootopia*', *Screen*, 60: 4 (Winter), pp. 567–86.

Chion, Michel (2020), 'À propos des fractales glacées de *La Reine des neiges*', *Blink Blank – La revue du film d'animation*, 1 (January), pp. 154–8.

Chmielewski, Dawn C. and Claudia Eller (2010), 'Disney Restyles "Rapunzel" to Appeal to Boys', *Los Angeles Times*, 9 March, <https://www.latimes.com/archives/la-xpm-2010-mar-09-la-fi-ct-disney9-2010mar09-story.html> (accessed 1 August 2021).

Clemetson, Lynette (2007), 'The Racial Politics of Speaking Well', *New York Times*, 4 February, <https://www.nytimes.com/2007/02/04/weekinreview/04clemetson.html> (accessed 22 August 2021).

Cobb, Shelley and Diane Negra (2017), '"I hate to be the feminist here . . . ": Reading the Post-epitaph Chick Flick', *Continuum*, 31: 6, pp. 757–66.
Coggan, Devon (2016), '*Moana*: EW Review', *Entertainment Weekly*, 7 November, <http://ew.com/article/2016/11/07/moana-ew-review/> (accessed 14 August 2021).
Cohen, David S. (2011), 'The Skinny on "Captain America" Vfx', *Variety*, 30 July, <https://variety.com/2011/film/features/the-skinny-on-captain-america-vfx-1118040631/> (accessed 20 August 2021).
Collin, Robbie (2016a), '*Moana* Review: Disney's Beautiful CG Spectacle Will Warm Your Soul', *Telegraph*, 1 December, <http://www.telegraph.co.uk/films/0/disneys-dazzling-moana-cg-animation-has-never-felt-warmer/> (accessed 13 August 2021).
Collin, Robbie (2016b), '*Zootropolis* Is the *Chinatown* of Talking Animal Films – Review', *Telegraph*, 24 March, <https://www.telegraph.co.uk/films/2016/04/14/zootropolis-is-the-chinatown-of-talking-animal-films---review/> (accessed 1 August 2021).
Connor, J. D. (2015), *The Studios After the Studios: Neoclassical Hollywood (1970–2010)*, Stanford, CA: Stanford University Press.
Cook, Pam (2005), *Screening the Past: Memory and Nostalgia in Cinema*, London: Routledge.
Corliss, Richard (2010), '*Tangled*: Disney's Ripping Rapunzel', *Time*, 26 November, <http://content.time.com/time/arts/article/0,8599,2033166,00.html> (accessed 19 February 2018).
Cotta Vaz, Mark (2008), *The Art of Bolt*, San Francisco: Chronicle Books.
Crafton, Donald (2013), *Shadow of a Mouse: Performance, Belief, and World-making in Animation*, Berkeley: University of California Press.
Davis, Adam (2014), 'Never Quite the Right Size: Scaling the Digital in CG Cinema', *animation: an interdisciplinary journal*, 9: 2, pp. 124–37.
Davis, Amy M. (2006), *Good Girls & Wicked Witches: Women in Disney's Feature Animation*, New Barnet: John Libbey.
Davis, Amy M. (2013), *Handsome Heroes & Vile Villains: Men in Disney's Feature Animation*, New Barnet: John Libbey.
Davis, Amy M. (2019), 'Introduction', in Amy Davis (ed.), *Discussing Disney*, New Barnet: John Libbey, pp. 1–14.
De Semlyen, Nick (2016), '*Moana* Review', *Empire*, 2 December, <https://www.empireonline.com/movies/moana/review/> (accessed 14 August 2021).
Debruge, Peter (2014), 'Film Review: *Big Hero 6*', *Variety*, 23 October, <http://variety.com/2014/film/festivals/film-review-big-hero-6-2-1201337195/> (accessed 11 August 2021).
Debruge, Peter (2016a), 'Film Review: *Moana*', *Variety*, 7 November, <http://variety.com/2016/film/reviews/moana-review-walt-disney-animation-studios-1201911413/> (accessed 13 August 2021).
Debruge, Peter (2016b), 'Film Review: *Zootopia*', *Variety*, 12 February, <http://variety.com/2016/film/reviews/zootopia-film-review-1201703504/> (accessed 22 August 2021).
Decker, Todd (2017), 'Racing in the Beat: Music in the *Fast & Furious* Franchise', in K. J. Donnelly and Beth Carroll (eds), *Contemporary Musical Film*, Edinburgh: Edinburgh University Press, pp. 157–73.
Deleyto, Celestino (2009), *The Secret Life of Romantic Comedy*, Manchester: Manchester University Press.
Denis, Sébastien (2020), 'Enfin adulte, le cinéma d'animation?', *Blink Blank – La revue du film d'animation*, 1 (January), pp. 8–13.
Denison, Rayna (2015), *Anime: A Critical Introduction*, London: Bloomsbury Academic.

Do Rozario, Rebecca-Anne (2004), 'The Princess and the Magic Kingdom: Beyond Nostalgia, the Function of the Disney Princess', *Women's Studies in Communication*, 27: 1 (2004), pp. 34–59.
Dole, Carol M. (2001), 'The Gun and the Badge: Hollywood and the Female Lawman', in Neal King and Martha McCaughey (eds), *Reel Knockouts: Violent Women in the Movies*, Austin: University of Texas Press, pp. 78–105.
Doty, Alexander (1995), 'There's Something Queer Here', in Corey K. Creekmur and Alexander Doty (eds), *Out in Culture: Gay, Lesbian, and Queer Essays on Popular Culture*, London: Cassell, pp. 71–90.
Downes, Daniel and June M. Madeley (2011), 'The Mouse is Dead, Long Live the Ogre: *Shrek* and the Boundaries of Transgression', in François Dépelteau, Aurélie Lacassagne and Tim Nieguth (eds), *Investigating Shrek: Power, Identity, and Ideology*, Basingstoke: Palgrave Macmillan, pp. 75–85.
Drotner, Kristen (2004), 'Disney Discourses, or Mundane Globalization', in Ib Bondebjerg and Peter Golding (eds), *European Culture and the Media*, Bristol: Intellect, pp. 91–115.
Duffy, Lisa (2019), 'From the Evil Queen to Elsa: Camp Witches in Disney Films', *Frames Cinema Journal*, 16 (Winter), <https://framescinemajournal.com/article/from-the-evil-queen-to-elsa-camp-witches-in-disney-films/> (accessed 15 March 2022).
Dyer, Richard (1997), *White*, London: Routledge.
Dyer, Richard (2000), 'Action!', in José Arroyo (ed.), *Action/Spectacle Cinema: A Sight and Sound Reader*, London: British Film Institute, pp. 17–21.
Dyer, Richard (2002), 'Entertainment and Utopia', in Steven Cohan (ed.), *Hollywood Musicals: The Film Reader*, London: Routledge, pp. 19–30.
Dyer, Richard (2012), *In the Space of a Song: The Uses of Song in Film*, Abingdon: Routledge.
Edney, Kathryn A. T. and Kit Hughes (2010), '"Hello WALL-E!": Nostalgia, Utopia, and the Science Fiction Musical', in Mathew J. Bartkowiak (ed.), *Sounds of the Future: Essays on Music in Science Fiction Film*, Jefferson, NC: McFarland, pp. 44–66.
Ferguson, Josh-Wade (2016), '"Traded it off for that voodoo thing": Cultural Capital and Vernacular Debt in Disney's Representation of New Orleans', *Journal of Popular Culture*, 49: 6, pp. 1224–40.
Feuer, Jane (1993), *The Hollywood Musical*, Basingstoke: Macmillan.
Flanagan, Martin (2007), 'Teen Trajectories in *Spider-Man* and *Ghost World*', in Ian Gordon, Mark Jancovich and Matthew P. McAllister (eds), *Film and Comic Books*, Jackson: University Press of Mississippi, pp. 137–59.
Flanagan, Martin, Andrew Livingstone and Mike McKenny (2016), *The Marvel Studios Phenomenon: Inside a Transmedia Universe*, New York: Bloomsbury Academic.
Fouladi, Shahriar (2011), '*Smallville*: Super Puberty and the Monstrous Superhero', in Richard J. Gray II and Betty Kaklamanidou (eds), *The 21st Century Superhero: Essays on Gender, Genre and Globalization in Film*, Jefferson, NC: McFarland, pp. 161–78.
Foundas, Scott (2013), 'Film Review: *Frozen*', *Variety*, 3 November, <http://variety.com/2013/film/reviews/frozen-review-1200782020/> (accessed 18 August 2021).
French, Philip (2001), '*Shrek*', *Guardian*, 1 July, <https://www.theguardian.com/film/2001/jul/01/philipfrench> (accessed 25 January 2018).
Furniss, Maureen (2014), *Art in Motion: Animation Aesthetics*, New Barnet: John Libbey.
Furniss, Maureen (2016), *A New History of Animation*, New York: Thames & Hudson.
Furo, Annette, Nichole E. Grant, Pamela Rogers and Kelsey Catherine Schmitz (2016), 'The Corseted Curriculum: Four Feminist Readings of a Strong Disney Princess', in Julie C. Garlen and Jennifer A. Sandlin (eds), *Disney, Culture, and Curriculum*, New York: Routledge, pp. 208–19.

Garlen, Julie C. and Jennifer A. Sandlin (2016), 'Introduction: Feeling Disney, Buying Disney, Being Disney', in Julie C. Garlen and Jennifer A. Sandlin (eds), *Disney, Culture, and Curriculum*, New York: Routledge, pp. 1–26.

Gates, Philippa (2004), 'Always a Partner in Crime: Black Masculinity in the Hollywood Detective Film', *Journal of Popular Film and Television*, 32: 1, pp. 20–9.

Gehlawat, Ajay (2010), 'The Strange Case of *The Princess and the Frog*: Passing and the Elision of Race', *Journal of African American Studies*, 14, pp. 417–31.

Genz, Stéphanie (2009), '"I am not a housewife, but . . .": Postfeminism and the Revival of Domesticity', in Stacy Gillis and Joanne Hollows (eds), *Feminism, Domesticity and Popular Culture*, New York: Routledge, pp. 49–62.

Geraghty, Lincoln and Mark Jancovich (eds) (2008), *The Shifting Definitions of Genre: Essays on Labeling Films, Television Shows and Media*, Jefferson, NC: McFarland.

Gill, Rosalind (2007), *Gender and the Media*, Cambridge: Polity Press.

Gill, Rosalind (2016), 'Post-postfeminism? New Feminist Visibilities in Postfeminist Times', *Feminist Media Studies*, 16: 4, pp. 610–30.

Gill, Rosalind (2017), 'The Affective, Cultural and Psychic Life of Postfeminism: A Postfeminist Sensibility 10 Years On', *European Journal of Cultural Studies*, 20: 6, pp. 606–26.

Gill, Rosalind and David Hansen-Miller (2011), '"Lad Flicks": Discursive Reconstructions of Masculinity in Popular Film', in Hilary Radner and Rebecca Stringer (eds), *Feminism at the Movies: Understanding Gender in Contemporary Popular Cinema*, London: Routledge, pp. 36–50.

Gilligan, Sarah (2011), 'Performing Post-feminist Identities: Gender, Costume, and Transformation in Teen Cinema', in Melanie Waters (ed.), *Women on Screen: Feminism and Femininity in Visual Culture*, Basingstoke: Palgrave Macmillan, pp. 167–81.

Gillis, Stacy and Joanne Hollows (2009), 'Introduction', in Stacy Gillis and Joanne Hollows (eds), *Feminism, Domesticity and Popular Culture*, New York: Routledge, pp. 1–14.

Giroux, Henry A. (1995), 'Memory and Pedagogy in the "Wonderful World of Disney": Beyond the Politics of Innocence', in Elizabeth Bell, Lynda Haas and Laura Sells (eds), *From Mouse to Mermaid: The Politics of Film, Gender, and Culture*, Bloomington: Indiana University Press, pp. 43–61.

Giroux, Henry A. and Grace Pollock (2010), *The Mouse That Roared: Disney and the End of Innocence*, Lanham, MD: Rowman & Littlefield Publishers.

Gledhill, Christine (2012), 'Introduction', in Christine Gledhill (ed.), *Gender Meets Genre in Postwar Cinemas*, Urbana: University of Illinois Press, pp. 1–11.

Gledhill, Christine (2018), 'Preface', in Mary Harrod and Katarzyna Paszkiewicz (eds), *Women Do Genre in Film and Television*, New York: Routledge, 2018, pp. ix–xiv.

Goldmark, Daniel and Charlie Keil (2011), 'What Makes These Pictures So Funny?', in Daniel Goldmark and Charlie Keil (eds), *Funny Pictures: Animation and Comedy in Studio-era Hollywood*, Berkeley: University of California Press, pp. 1–11.

Grant, Barry Keith (ed.) (2012), *Film Genre Reader IV*, Austin: University of Texas Press.

Gray, Jonathan (2010), *Show Sold Separately: Promos, Spoilers, and Other Media Paratexts*, New York: New York University Press.

Gray II, Richard J. and Betty Kaklamanidou (eds) (2011), *The 21st Century Superhero: Essays on Gender, Genre and Globalization in Film*, Jefferson, NC: McFarland.

Greenhill, Pauline and Sidney Eve Matrix (2010), 'Introduction – Envisioning Ambiguity: Fairy Tale Films', in Pauline Greenhill and Sidney Eve Matrix (eds), *Fairy Tale Films: Visions of Ambiguity*, Logan: Utah State University Press, pp. 1–22.

Greno, Nathan and Byron Howard (2010), 'Foreword', in Jeff Kurtti, *The Art of Tangled*, San Francisco: Chronicle Books, p. 7.

Griffin, Sean (1999), *Tinker Belles and Evil Queens: The Walt Disney Company from the Inside Out*, New York: New York University Press.

Haas, Lynda (1995), '"Eighty-six the Mother": Murder, Matricide, and Good Mothers', in Elizabeth Bell, Lynda Haas and Laura Sells (eds), *From Mouse to Mermaid: The Politics of Film, Gender, and Culture*, Bloomington: Indiana University Press, pp. 193–211.

Halfyard, Janet K. (2013), 'Cue the Big Theme? The Sound of the Superhero', in Claudia Gorbman, John Richardson and Carol Vernallis (eds), *The Oxford Handbook of New Audiovisual Aesthetics*, Oxford: Oxford University Press, pp. 171–93.

Hall, Don and Chris Williams (2014), 'Foreword', in Jessica Julius, *The Art of Big Hero 6*, San Francisco: Chronicle Books, p. 7.

Harries, Dan (2002), 'Film Parody and the Resuscitation of Genre', in Steve Neale (ed.), *Genre and Contemporary Hollywood*, London: BFI Publishing, pp. 281–93.

Harrod, Mary and Katarzyna Paszkiewicz (eds) (2018), *Women Do Genre in Film and Television*, New York: Routledge.

Hassler-Forest, Dan (2018), '"Life isn't some cartoon musical": Neoliberal Identity Politics in *Zootopia* and *Orange Is the New Black*', *Journal of Popular Culture*, 51: 2, pp. 356–78.

Haswell, Helen (2014), 'To Infinity and Back Again: Hand-drawn Aesthetic and Affection for the Past in Pixar's Pioneering Animation', *Alphaville: Journal of Film and Screen Media*, 8 (Winter), <http://www.alphavillejournal.com/Issue8/PDFs/ArticleHaswell.pdf> (accessed 15 March 2022).

Haswell, Helen (2017), 'Story Is King: Understanding the *Toy Story* Franchise as an Allegory for the Studio Narrative of Pixar Animation', in Noel Brown, Susan Smith and Sam Summers (eds), *Toy Story: How Pixar Reinvented the Animated Feature*, London: Bloomsbury Academic, pp. 181–96.

Haswell, Helen (2019), 'Fix It Felix! Reviving Walt Disney Animation Using the Pixar Formula', in Amy Davis (ed.), *Discussing Disney*, New Barnet: John Libbey, pp. 91–114.

Herhuth, Eric (2014), 'Life, Love, and Programming: The Culture and Politics of *WALL-E* and Pixar Computer Animation', *Cinema Journal*, 53: 4, pp. 53–75.

Herhuth, Eric (2017), *Pixar and the Aesthetic Imagination: Animation, Storytelling, and Digital Culture*, Oakland: University of California Press.

Hermansson, Casie and Janet Zepernick (2019), 'Children's Film and Television: Contexts and New Directions', in Casie Hermansson and Janet Zepernick (eds), *The Palgrave Handbook of Children's Film and Television*, Cham: Palgrave Macmillan, pp. 1–33.

Hines, Susan and Brenda Ayres (2003), 'Introduction: (He)gemony Cricket! Why in the World Are We Still Watching Disney?', in Brenda Ayres (ed.), *The Emperor's Old Groove: Decolonizing Disney's Magic Kingdom*, New York: Peter Lang, pp. 1–12.

Hoffman, Jordan (2014), '*Big Hero 6* Review: An Adorable Robot Bounces through Mayhem', *Guardian*, 7 November, <https://www.theguardian.com/film/2014/nov/07/big-hero-6-review> (accessed 11 August 2021).

Holliday, Christopher (2016), '"I'm not a real boy, I'm a puppet": Computer-animated Films and Anthropomorphic Subjectivity', *animation: an Interdisciplinary Journal*, 11: 3, pp. 246–62.

Holliday, Christopher (2018a), *The Computer-animated Film: Industry, Style and Genre*, Edinburgh: Edinburgh University Press.

Holliday, Christopher (2018b), 'From Buzz to Business: Hollywood, Fantasy and the Computer-animated Film', in Holliday, Christopher and Alexander Sergeant (eds), *Fantasy/Animation: Connections Between Media, Mediums and Genres*, London: Routledge, pp. 210–26.

Holliday, Christopher (2019), 'Let It Go? Towards a "Plasmatic" Perspective on Digital Disney', in Amy Davis (ed.), *Discussing Disney*, New Barnet: John Libbey, pp. 115–36.

Holliday, Christopher and Alexander Sergeant (2018), 'Introduction: Approaching Fantasy/Animation', in Christopher Holliday and Alexander Sergeant (eds), *Fantasy/Animation: Connections Between Media, Mediums and Genres*, London: Routledge, pp. 1–19.

Holmes, Su (2014), 'Cold and Hungry: Discourses of Anorexic Femininity in *Frozen* (2013)', *Auteuse Theory: A Blog on Women's Cinema*, 21 November, <http://auteusetheory.blogspot.co.uk/2014/11/cold-and-hungry-discourses-of-anorexic_21.html> (accessed 21 August 2021).

Honeycutt, Kirk (2009), '*The Princess and the Frog* – Film Review', *Hollywood Reporter*, 24 November, <http://www.hollywoodreporter.com/review/princess-frog-film-review-93780> (accessed 21 August 2021).

Hornaday, Ann (2009), 'Movie Review: Disney's "The Princess and the Frog," Starring Anika Noni Rose', *Washington Post*, 11 December, <http://www.washingtonpost.com/wp-dyn/content/article/2009/12/10/AR2009121001278.html> (accessed 9 February 2018).

Hornaday, Ann (2010), '*Tangled*: Disney's Take on Rapunzel Is as Gorgeous as It Is Engaging', *Washington Post*, 24 November, <http://www.washingtonpost.com/wp-dyn/content/article/2010/11/23/AR2010112306966.html> (accessed 1 August 2021).

Howe, Alexander N. and Wynn Yarbrough (eds) (2014), *Kidding Around: The Child in Film and Media*, New York: Bloomsbury.

Huddleston, Tom (2010), '*The Princess and the Frog*', *Time Out*, 26 January, <http://www.timeout.com/london/film/the-princess-and-the-frog> (accessed 1 August 2021).

Hui, Christine (2019), 'Sun Flowers and Moon Powers: Princesses and Magical Agency in *Tangled* and *The Tale of the Princess Kaguya*', *Frames Cinema Journal*, 16 (Winter), <https://framescinemajournal.com/article/sun-flowers-and-moon-powers-princesses-and-magical-agency-in-tangled-and-the-tale-of-the-princess-kaguya/> (accessed 15 March 2022).

Husbands, Lilly and Caroline Ruddell (2019), 'Approaching Animation and Animation Studies', in Nichola Dobson, Annabelle Honess Roe, Amy Ratelle and Caroline Ruddell (eds), *The Animation Studies Reader*, New York: Bloomsbury Academic, pp. 5–15.

Ingraham, Chrys (2008), *White Weddings: Romancing Heterosexuality in Popular Culture*, New York: Routledge.

Jancovich, Mark (2001), 'Genre and the Audience: Genre Classifications and Cultural Distinctions in the Mediation of *The Silence of the Lambs*', in Melvyn Stokes and Richard Maltby (eds), *Hollywood Spectatorship: Changing Perceptions of Cinema Audiences*, London: BFI, pp. 33–45.

Jeffers McDonald, Tamar (2007), *Romantic Comedy: Boy Meets Girl Meets Genre*, London: Wallflower Press.

Jeffers McDonald, Tamar (2009), '*Homme*-com: Engendering Change in Contemporary Romantic Comedy', in Stacey Abbott and Deborah Jermyn (eds), *Falling in Love Again: Romantic Comedy in Contemporary Cinema*, London: I. B. Tauris, pp. 146–59.

Jenkins, Claire (2014), 'Splitting the Nuclear Family? The Superhero Family in *The Incredibles* and *Sky High*', in Julian C. Chambliss, Thomas Donaldson and William Svitavsky (eds), *Ages of Heroes, Eras of Men: Superheroes and the American Experience*, Newcastle upon Tyne: Cambridge Scholars Publishing, pp. 214–28.

Jenkins, Claire (2015), *Home Movies: The American Family in Contemporary Hollywood Cinema*, London: I. B. Tauris.

Jess-Cooke, Carolyn (2009), *Film Sequels: Theory and Practice from Hollywood to Bollywood*, Edinburgh: Edinburgh University Press.

Julius, Jessica (2014), *The Art of Big Hero 6*, San Francisco: Chronicle Books.

Julius, Jessica (2016), *The Art of Zootropolis*, San Francisco: Chronicle Books.

Julius, Jessica and Maggie Malone (2016), *The Art of Moana*, San Francisco: Chronicle Books.
Jolin, Dan (2014), '*Big Hero 6* Review' *Empire*, 19 July, <https://www.empireonline.com/movies/big-hero-6/review/> (accessed 11 August 2021).
Kaklamanidou, Betty (2014), *Genre, Gender and the Effects of Neoliberalism: The New Millennium Hollywood Rom Com*, London: Routledge.
Kamen, Matt (2015), '*Big Hero 6* and the Future of Animation', *Wired*, 20 March, <http://www.wired.co.uk/news/archive/2015-03/20/big-hero-6-animator-interview> (accessed 19 August 2021).
Karlyn, Kathleen (1995), *The Unruly Woman: Gender and the Genres of Laughter*, Austin: University of Texas Press.
Karlyn, Kathleen (2011), *Unruly Girls, Unrepentant Mothers: Redefining Feminism on Screen*, Austin: University of Texas Press.
Keegan, Rebecca (2016), 'Did a Disney Animated Film Really Say That? If It's *Zootopia*, Prepare to Be Shocked', *Los Angeles Times*, 4 March, <http://www.latimes.com/entertainment/movies/la-et-mn-zootopia-production-20160304-story.html> (accessed 21 August 2021).
Kennedy Haydel, Sheryl (2020), '#NolaBorn: Tiana and the Road Home for New Orleans Residents', in Shearon Roberts (ed.), *Recasting the Disney Princess in an Era of New Media and Social Movements*, Lanham, MD: Lexington Books, pp. 137–49.
Kent, Miriam (2021), *Women in Marvel Films*, Edinburgh: Edinburgh University Press.
King, Geoff (2000), *Spectacular Narratives: Hollywood in the Age of the Blockbuster*, London: I. B. Tauris.
Kois, Dan (2010), '*Tangled* Looks and Feels Great, So Why Is Disney Selling It Short?', *Village Voice*, 24 November, <http://www.villagevoice.com/film/tangled-looks-and-feels-great-so-why-is-disney-selling-it-short-6429266> (accessed 1 August 2021).
Krutnik, Frank (2002), 'Conforming Passions? Contemporary Romantic Comedy', in Steve Neale (ed.), *Genre and Contemporary Hollywood*, London: British Film Institute, pp. 130–47.
Kuhn, Annette and Guy Westwell (2012), *A Dictionary of Film Studies*, Oxford: Oxford University Press, <http://www.oxfordreference.com/view/10.1093/acref/9780199587261.001.0001/acref-9780199587261-e-0080> (accessed 10 April 2018).
Kurtti, Jeff (2009), *The Art of The Princess and the Frog*, San Francisco: Chronicle Books.
Kurtti, Jeff (2010), *The Art of Tangled*, San Francisco: Chronicle Books.
Lacroix, Celeste (2004), 'Images of Animated Others: The Orientalization of Disney's Cartoon Heroines from *The Little Mermaid* to *The Hunchback of Notre Dame*', *Popular Communication: The International Journal of Media and Culture*, 2: 4, pp. 213–29.
Lane, Anthony (2001), 'Fantasy Land', *New Yorker*, 21 May, <http://www.newyorker.com/magazine/2001/05/21/fantasy-land> (accessed 1 August 2021).
Langford, Barry (2005), *Film Genre: Hollywood and Beyond*, Edinburgh: Edinburgh University Press.
Langsdale, Samantha (2014), 'Disney Classics and "Poisonous Pedagogy": The Fairy-tale Roots of *Frozen* (2013)', *Animation Practice, Process & Production*, 4, pp. 27–43.
Langsdale, Samantha and Sarah Myers (2018), 'The Evolution of Reproductive Fantasies: An Interdisciplinary Feminist Analysis of Disney's *Tangled* (2010)', in Christopher Holliday and Alexander Sergeant (eds), *Fantasy/Animation: Connections Between Media, Mediums and Genres*, London: Routledge, pp. 243–60.
Law, Michelle (2014), 'Sisters Doin' It for Themselves: *Frozen* and the Evolution of the Disney Heroine', *Screen Education*, 74, pp. 16–25.

Lawrence, Derek (2021), 'New Legacy, New Lola: Why *Space Jam* Wanted to Do Better by One Tune', *Entertainment Weekly*, 5 March, <https://ew.com/movies/space-jam-new-legacy-lola-bunny/> (accessed 27 August 2021).
Lee, Jennifer (2013), '*Frozen*, Written by Jennifer Lee', *IMSDb*, 23 September, <https://imsdb.com/scripts/Frozen-(Disney).html> (accessed 18 August 2021).
Lee, Jennifer and Maggie Malone (2012), *The Art of Wreck-It Ralph*, San Francisco: Chronicle Books.
Leonard, Suzanne (2007), '"I hate my job, I hate everybody here": Adultery, Boredom, and the "Working Girl" in 21st Century American Cinema', in Diane Negra and Yvonne Tasker (eds), *Interrogating Postfeminism: Gender and the Politics of Popular Culture*, Durham, NC: Duke University Press, pp. 100–31.
Lerew, Jenny (2012), *The Art of Brave*, San Francisco: Chronicle Books.
Lester, Catherine (2019), 'Frozen Heart and Fixer Uppers: Villainy, Gender, and Female Companionship in Disney's *Frozen*', in Amy Davis (ed.), *Discussing Disney*, New Barnet: John Libbey, pp. 193–216.
Lester, Neal A. (2010), 'Disney's *The Princess and the Frog*: The Pride, the Pressure, and the Politics of Being a First', *The Journal of American Culture*, 33: 4 (December), pp. 294–308.
Letts, Will (2016), 'Camp Disney: Consuming Queer Subjectivities, Commodifying the Normative', in Julie C. Garlen and Jennifer A. Sandlin (eds), *Disney, Culture, and Curriculum*, New York: Routledge, pp. 148–60.
Lichtenfeld, Eric (2007), *Action Speaks Louder: Violence, Spectacle, and the American Action Movie*, Middletown, CT: Wesleyan University Press.
Lowther, Tricia (2012), 'Brave Just Enough', *The F Word*, 21 August, <http://www.thefword.org.uk/reviews/2012/08/Brave> (accessed 11 August 2021).
Lui, John (2014), '*Big Hero 6* a Nod to "sentimentality found in great anime films"', *Straits Times*, 12 November, <https://www.straitstimes.com/lifestyle/entertainment/big-hero-6-a-nod-to-sentimentality-found-in-great-anime-films> (accessed 18 January 2022).
Ma, Sheng-Mei (2003), 'Mulan Disney, It's Like, Re-orients: Consuming China and Animating Teen Dreams', in Brenda Ayres (ed.), *The Emperor's Old Groove: Decolonizing Disney's Magic Kingdom*, New York: Peter Lang, pp. 149–64.
Macaluso, Michael (2016), 'The Postfeminist Princess: Public Discourse and Disney's Curricular Guide to Feminism', in Julie C. Garlen and Jennifer A. Sandlin (eds), *Disney, Culture, and Curriculum*, New York: Routledge, pp. 73–86.
McMillan, Graeme (2014), 'Disney's *Big Hero 6*: A Primer on the Obscure Marvel Comic', *Hollywood Reporter*, 21 May, <http://www.hollywoodreporter.com/heat-vision/disneys-big-hero-6-a-706328> (accessed 19 August 2021).
McRobbie, Angela (2009), *The Aftermath of Feminism: Gender, Culture and Social Change*, Los Angeles: SAGE.
McSweeney, Terence (2020), *The Contemporary Superhero Film: Projections of Power and Identity*, New York: Columbia University Press.
Maddaus, Gene (2017), 'Pixar's John Lasseter Was the Subject of a "Whisper Network" for More than Two Decades', *Variety*, 21 November, <https://variety.com/2017/film/news/john-lasseter-pixar-disney-whisper-network-1202620960/> (accessed 29 August 2021).
Maier, Kodi (2019), 'Princess Brides and Dream Weddings: Investigating the Gendered Narrative of Disney's Fairy Tale Weddings', in Amy Davis (ed.), *Discussing Disney*, New Barnet: John Libbey, pp. 173–92.

Malcolm, Paul (2001), 'Trouble in Fairyland', *LA Weekly*, 16 May, <http://www.laweekly.com/film/trouble-in-fairyland-2133359> (accessed 25 January 2018).

Manovich, Lev (2001), *The Language of New Media*, Cambridge, MA: MIT Press.

Marotta, Jenna (2018), 'Jennifer Lee and Pete Docter to Replace John Lasseter as Disney/Pixar Chief Creative Officers', *IndieWire*, 19 June, <https://www.indiewire.com/2018/06/jennifer-lee-pete-docter-john-lasseter-disney-pixar-1201976513/> (accessed 29 August 2021).

Meades, Alan (2015), 'Beyond the Animated Landscape: Videogame Glitches and the Sublime', in Chris Pallant (ed.), *Animated Landscapes: History, Form and Function*, New York: Bloomsbury, pp. 269–85.

Meeusen, Meghann (2019), 'Power, Prejudice, Predators, and Pets: Representation in Animated Animal Films', in Casie Hermansson and Janet Zepernick (eds), *The Palgrave Handbook of Children's Film and Television*, Cham: Palgrave Macmillan, pp. 345–61.

Merry, Stephanie (2013), '"Frozen" Movie Review: Kristen Bell and Idina Menzel Dazzle in Disney's Latest', *Washington Post*, 26 November, <http://www.washingtonpost.com/goingoutguide/movies/frozen-movie-review-kristen-bell-and-idina-menzel-dazzle-in-disneys-latest/2013/11/26/3b030292-5390-11e3-9fe0-fd2ca728e67c_story.html> (accessed 19 February 2018).

Mihailova, Mihaela (2019), 'Animation and Realism', in Nichola Dobson, Annabelle Honess Roe, Amy Ratelle and Caroline Ruddell (eds), *The Animation Studies Reader*, New York: Bloomsbury Academic, pp. 47–57.

Miller, Susan and Greg Rode (1995), 'The Movie You See, the Movie You Don't: How Disney Do's That Old Time Derision', in Elizabeth Bell, Lynda Haas and Laura Sells (eds), *From Mouse to Mermaid: The Politics of Film, Gender, and Culture*, Bloomington: Indiana University Press, pp. 86–103.

Mitchell, Elvis (2001), '"FILM REVIEW; So Happily Ever After, Beauty and the Beasts', *New York Times*, 16 May, <https://www.nytimes.com/2001/05/16/movies/film-review-so-happily-ever-after-beauty-and-the-beasts.html> (accessed 28 February 2021).

Mittermeier, Sabrina (2021), 'Disney's Queer Queen – *Frozen*'s Elsa and Queer Representation', *Fantasy/Animation*, 5 February, <https://www.fantasy-animation.org/current-posts/disneys-queer-queen-frozens-elsa-and-queer-representation?rq=frozen> (accessed 18 August 2021).

Moen, Kristian (2013), *Film and Fairy Tales: The Birth of Modern Fantasy*, London: I. B. Tauris.

Moine, Raphaëlle (2008), 'Semantic-syntactic Definitions of Genre', in Alistair Fox and Hilary Radner (eds), *Cinema Genre*, Oxford: Blackwell, pp. 55–62.

Mollet, Tracey L. (2020), *A Cultural History of the Disney Fairy Tale: Once Upon an American Dream*, Cham: Palgrave Macmillan.

Naidu Parekh, Pushpa (2003), '*Pocahontas*: The Disney Imaginary', in Brenda Ayres (ed.), *The Emperor's Old Groove: Decolonizing Disney's Magic Kingdom*, New York: Peter Lang, pp. 167–78.

Napier, Susan J. (2005), *Anime from Akira to Howl's Moving Castle: Experiencing Contemporary Japanese Animation*, Basingstoke: Palgrave Macmillan.

Nathan, Ian (2001), '*Shrek* Review', *Empire*, 29 June, <https://www.empireonline.com/movies/shrek/review/> (accessed 25 January 2018).

Neale, Steve (2000), *Genre and Hollywood*, London: Routledge.

Negra, Diane (2009), *What a Girl Wants? Fantasizing the Reclamation of Self in Postfeminism*, London: Routledge.

Negra, Diane (2015), 'Postfeminist Perfectionism and Failure in *Frozen*', Keynote Address 2, Symfrozium: A Study Day on Disney's *Frozen* (2013), 12 May, University of East Anglia, Norwich.

Negra, Diane and Yvonne Tasker (2007), 'Introduction: Feminist Politics and Postfeminist Culture', in Diana Negra and Yvonne Tasker (eds), *Interrogating Postfeminism: Gender and the Politics of Popular Culture*, Durham, NC: Duke University Press, pp. 1–25.

Nilsen, Sarah (2019), 'Living in *Zootopia*: Tracking the Neoliberal Subject in a Colorblind World', in Sarah Nilsen and Sarah E. Turner (eds), *The Myth of Colorblindness: Race and Ethnicity in American Cinema*, Cham: Palgrave Macmillan, pp. 61–88.

Nugent, John (2016), '*Zootropolis* Review', *Empire*, 25 March, <https://www.empireonline.com/movies/zootropolis/review/> (accessed 21 August 2021).

O'Hara, Helen (2015), '*The Princess and the Frog* Review', *Empire*, 9 December, <https://www.empireonline.com/movies/princess-frog/review/> (accessed 26 January 2018).

Ohmer, Susan (2011), 'Laughter by Numbers: The Science of Comedy at the Walt Disney Studio', in Daniel Goldmark and Charlie Keil (eds), *Funny Pictures: Animation and Comedy in Studio-era Hollywood*, Berkeley: University of California Press, pp. 109–28.

Orange, Michelle (2016), 'Disney's *Zootopia* Paws at Segregated City Life', *Village Voice*, 1 March, <https://www.villagevoice.com/2016/03/01/disneys-zootopia-paws-at-segregated-city-life/> (accessed 22 August 2021).

Orenstein, Peggy (2006), 'What's Wrong with Cinderella?', *New York Times Magazine*, 24 December, <http://www.nytimes.com/2006/12/24/magazine/24princess.t.html>, (accessed 22 January 2018).

Osmond, Andrew (2002), '*Lilo & Stitch* Revisited: Part I', *Animation World Network*, 31 December, <https://www.awn.com/animationworld/lilo-stitch-revisited-part-i>, (accessed 24 April 2021).

Pallant, Chris (2010), 'Neo-Disney: Recent Developments in Disney Feature Animation', *New Cinemas*, 8: 2, pp. 103–17.

Pallant, Chris (2013), *Demystifying Disney: A History of Disney Feature Animation*, New York: Bloomsbury.

Pallant, Chris (2015), 'Introduction', in Chris Pallant (ed.), *Animated Landscapes: History, Form and Function*, New York: Bloomsbury, pp. 1–12.

Parasher, Prajna (2013), 'Mapping the Imaginary: The *Neverland* of Disney Indians', in Johnson Cheu (ed.), *Diversity in Disney Films: Critical Essays on Race, Ethnicity, Gender, Sexuality and Disability*, Jefferson, NC: McFarland, pp. 38–49.

Price, David A. (2009), *The Pixar Touch: The Making of a Company*, New York: Vintage Books.

Projansky, Sarah (2007), 'Mass Magazine Cover Girls: Some Reflections on Postfeminist Girls and Postfeminism's Daughters', in Diane Negra and Yvonne Tasker (eds), *Interrogating Postfeminism: Gender and the Politics of Popular Culture*, Durham, NC: Duke University Press, pp. 40–72.

Purse, Lisa (2011a), *Contemporary Action Cinema*, Edinburgh: Edinburgh University Press.

Purse, Lisa (2011b), 'Return of the "Angry Woman": Authenticating Female Physical Action in Contemporary Cinema', in Melanie Waters (ed.), *Women on Screen: Feminism and Femininity in Visual Culture*, Basingstoke: Palgrave Macmillan, pp. 185–98.

Purse, Lisa (2013), *Digital Imaging in Popular Cinema*, Edinburgh: Edinburgh University Press.

Radner, Hilary (2011), *Neo-feminist Cinema: Girly Films, Chick Flicks and Consumer Culture*, New York: Routledge.

Rechtshaffen, Michael (2014), '*Big Hero 6*: Film Review', *Hollywood Reporter*, 23 October, <https://www.hollywoodreporter.com/review/big-hero-6-film-review-742707> (accessed 11 August 2021).

Robey, Tim (2013), '*Tangled*, Review', *Telegraph*, 25 December, <http://www.telegraph.co.uk/culture/film/filmreviews/8286988/Tangled-review.html> (accessed 19 February 2018).

Romney, Jonathan (2000), 'Arnold through the Looking Glass', in José Arroyo (ed.), *Action/Spectacle Cinema: A Sight and Sound Reader*, London: British Film Institute, pp. 34–9.

Rutherford, Stephanie (2011), *Governing the Wild: Ecotours of Power*, Minneapolis: University of Minnesota Press.

San Filippo, Maria (2021), 'Introduction – Love Actually: Romantic Comedy Since the Aughts', in Maria San Filippo (ed.), *After 'Happily Ever After': Romantic Comedy in the Post-romantic Age*, Detroit, MI: Wayne State University Press, pp. 1–24.

Sandlin, Jennifer and Nathan Snaza (2018), '"It's called a hustle, sweetheart": Black Lives Matter, the Police State, and the Politics of Colonizing Anger in *Zootopia*', *Journal of Popular Culture*, 51: 5, pp. 1190–213.

Schumaker, Justin S. (2011), 'Super-intertextuality and 21st Century Individualized Social Advocacy in *Spider-Man* and *Kick-Ass*', in Richard J. Gray II and Betty Kaklamanidou (eds), *The 21st Century Superhero: Essays on Gender, Genre and Globalization in Film*, Jefferson, NC: McFarland, pp. 129–43.

Schwarzbaum, Lisa (2009), '*The Princess and the Frog*', *Entertainment Weekly*, 18 December, <http://ew.com/article/2009/12/18/princess-and-frog-2/> (accessed 26 January 2018).

Scott, A. O. (2010), 'Back to the Castle, Where It's All about the Hair', *New York Times*, 23 November, <http://www.nytimes.com/2010/11/24/movies/24tangled.html?_r=0> (accessed 13 August 2021).

Scott, A. O. (2016), 'Review: *Moana*, Brave Princess on a Voyage with a Chicken', *New York Times*, 22 November, <https://www.nytimes.com/2016/11/22/movies/moana-review.html> (accessed 13 August 2021).

Scott, Jason (2020), 'Disney+: It All Adds Up', *Media Commons*, 4 May, <http://mediacommons.org/imr/content/disney-it-all-adds> (accessed 23 January 2022).

Sells, Laura (1995), '"Where do the mermaids stand?" Voice and Body in *The Little Mermaid*', in Elizabeth Bell, Lynda Haas and Laura Sells (eds), *From Mouse to Mermaid: The Politics of Film, Gender, and Culture*, Bloomington: Indiana University Press, pp. 175–92.

Shareef, Hannah (2020), 'In Memoriam of the Woman Behind Tiana', in Shearon Roberts (ed.), *Recasting the Disney Princess in an Era of New Media and Social Movements*, Lanham, MD: Lexington Books, p. 17.

Shoard, Catherine (2010), 'How *The Princess and the Frog* Really Breaks the Mould', *Guardian*, 5 February, <https://www.theguardian.com/film/filmblog/2010/feb/05/princess-and-the-frog> (accessed 10 February 2018).

Smith, Susan (2011), 'The Animated Film Musical', in Raymond Knapp, Mitchell Morris and Stacy Wolf (eds), *The Oxford Handbook of the American Musical*, New York: Oxford University Press, pp. 167–78.

Smith, Susan (2017), 'Toy Stories through Song: Pixar, Randy Newman and the Sublimated Film Musical', in Noel Brown, Susan Smith and Sam Summers (eds), *Toy Story: How Pixar Reinvented the Animated Feature*, London: Bloomsbury Academic, pp. 105–26.

Solomon, Charles (2013), *The Art of Frozen*, San Francisco: Chronicle Books.

Sperb, Jason (2012), *Disney's Most Notorious Film: Race, Convergence, and the Hidden Histories of Song of the South*, Austin: University of Texas Press.

Sperb, Jason (2016), *Flickers of Film: Nostalgia in the Time of Digital Cinema*, New Brunswick, NJ: Rutgers University Press.

Staiger, Janet (2008), 'Film Noir as Male Melodrama: The Politics of Film Genre Labeling', in Lincoln Geraghty and Mark Jancovich (eds), *The Shifting Definitions of Genre: Essays on Labeling Films, Television Shows and Media*, Jefferson, NC: McFarland, pp. 71–91.

Staninger, Christiane (2003), 'Disney's Magic Carpet Ride: *Aladdin* and Women in Islam', in Brenda Ayres (ed.), *The Emperor's Old Groove: Decolonizing Disney's Magic Kingdom*, New York: Peter Lang, pp. 65–77.

Streiff, Madeline and Lauren Dundes (2017), 'Frozen in Time: How Disney Gender-Stereotypes Its Most Powerful Princess', *Social Sciences*, 6: 2, <https://doi.org/10.3390/socsci6020038> (accessed 17 March 2022).

Summers, Sam (2017), 'From Shelf to Screen: Toys as a Site of Intertextuality', in Noel Brown, Susan Smith and Sam Summers (eds), *Toy Story: How Pixar Reinvented the Animated Feature*, London: Bloomsbury Academic, pp. 127–40.

Summers, Sam (2019), 'Adapting a Retro Comic Aesthetic with *Spider-Man: Into the Spider-Verse*', *Adaptation*, 12: 2, pp. 190–4.

Summers, Sam (2020), *DreamWorks Animation: Intertextuality and Aesthetics in Shrek and Beyond*, Cham: Palgrave Macmillan.

Sweeney, Gael (2013), '"What do you want me to do? Dress in drag and do the hula?": Timon and Pumbaa's Alternative Lifestyle Dilemma in *The Lion King*', in Johnson Cheu (ed.), *Diversity in Disney Films: Critical Essays on Race, Ethnicity, Gender, Sexuality and Disability*, Jefferson, NC: McFarland, pp. 129–46.

Tamaira, A. Mārata Ketekiri and Dionne Fonoti (2018), 'Beyond Paradise? Retelling Pacific Stories in Disney's *Moana*', *The Contemporary Pacific*, 30: 2, pp. 297–327.

Tasker, Yvonne (1993), *Spectacular Bodies: Gender, Genre, and the Action Cinema*, London: Routledge.

Tasker, Yvonne (1998), *Working Girls: Gender and Sexuality in Popular Cinema*, London: Routledge.

Tasker, Yvonne (2011), '*Enchanted* (2007) by Postfeminism: Gender, Irony, and the New Romantic Comedy', in Hilary Radner and Rebecca Stringer (eds), *Feminism at the Movies: Understanding Gender in Contemporary Popular Cinema*, London: Routledge, pp. 67–79.

Tasker, Yvonne (2015), *The Hollywood Action and Adventure Film*, Chichester: John Wiley & Sons.

Tasker, Yvonne (2020), 'Vernacular Feminism: Gendered Media Cultures and Historical Perspectives on Postdiscourse', *Television & New Media*, 21: 6, pp. 671–5.

Taves, Brian (1993), *The Romance of Adventure: The Genre of Historical Adventure Movies*, Jackson: University Press of Mississippi.

Taylor, Richard (ed.) (2006), *The Eisenstein Collection*, London: Seagull Books.

Te Vaka (n.d.), 'Lyrics: LOGO TE PATE (Listen to the Pate)', *Te Vaka*, <https://tevaka.com/track/2048641/logo-te-pate> (accessed 14 August 2021).

Telotte, J. P. (2008), *The Mouse Machine: Disney and Technology*, Urbana: University of Illinois Press.

Telotte, J. P. (2010), *Animating Space: From Mickey to WALL-E*, Lexington: University Press of Kentucky.

Thomas, Deborah (2000), *Beyond Genre: Melodrama, Comedy and Romance in Hollywood Films*, Moffat: Cameron & Hollis.

Travers, Peter (2016), '*Zootopia*', *Rolling Stone*, 3 March, <https://www.rollingstone.com/movies/reviews/zootopia-20160303> (accessed 20 May 2018).

Turan, Kenneth (2010), 'Movie Review: "Tangled"', *Los Angeles Times*, 24 November, <http://articles.latimes.com/2010/nov/24/entertainment/la-et-et-tangled-20101124> (accessed 19 February 2018).

Turner, Sarah E. (2013), 'Blackness, Bayous and Gumbos: Encoding and Decoding Race in a Colorblind World', in Johnson Cheu (ed.), *Diversity in Disney Films: Critical Essays on Race, Ethnicity, Gender, Sexuality and Disability*, Jefferson, NC: McFarland, pp. 83–98.

Wagner, Keith B. and In-gyoo Jang (2016), 'The 3-D Animated Codescape: Imperfection and Digital Labor Zones in *Wall-E* (2008) and *Wreck-It Ralph* (2012)', *animation: an interdisciplinary journal*, 11: 2, pp. 130–45.

Waldrep, Shelton (1995), 'Story Time', in The Project on Disney (eds), *Inside the Mouse: Work and Play at Disney World*, Durham, NC: Duke University Press, pp. 79–97.

Walker, Prinsey (2020), 'Tiana at Ten', in Shearon Roberts (ed.), *Recasting the Disney Princess in an Era of New Media and Social Movements*, Lanham, MD: Lexington Books, pp. 15–17.

Walker, Tim (2014), '*Big Hero 6*: Disney's Japanese Superheroes', *Independent*, 18 November, <https://www.independent.co.uk/arts-entertainment/films/features/big-hero-6-disney-s-japanese-superheroes-9866371.html> (accessed 18 January 2022).

Ward, Annalee (2003), *Mouse Morality: The Rhetoric of Disney Animated Film*, Austin: University of Texas Press.

Warner, Helen (2013), '"A new feminist revolution in Hollywood comedy"? Postfeminist Discourses and the Critical Reception of *Bridesmaids*', in Joel Gwynne and Nadine Muller (eds), *Postfeminism and Contemporary Hollywood Cinema*, Basingstoke: Palgrave Macmillan, pp. 222–37.

Warner, Marina (1995), *From the Beast to the Blonde*, London: Vintage.

Wasko, Janet (2020), *Understanding Disney: The Manufacture of Fantasy*, 2nd edn, Cambridge: Polity Press.

Watts, Steven (1997), *The Magic Kingdom: Walt Disney and the American Way of Life*, Boston, MA: Houghton Mifflin.

Weetch, Owen (2016), *Expressive Spaces in Digital 3D Cinema*, London: Palgrave Macmillan.

Welch, Kelly (2007), 'Black Criminal Stereotypes and Racial Profiling', *Journal of Contemporary Criminal Justice*, 23: 3 (August), pp. 276–88.

Wells, Paul (1998), *Understanding Animation*, London: Routledge.

Wells, Paul (2002a), *Animation: Genre and Authorship*, London: Wallflower Press.

Wells, Paul (2002b), *Animation and America*, Edinburgh: Edinburgh University Press.

Wells, Paul (2009), *The Animated Bestiary*, New Brunswick, NJ: Rutgers University Press.

Weltzien, Friedrich (2005), 'Masque-ulinities: Changing Dress as a Display of Masculinity in the Superhero Genre', *Fashion Theory*, 9: 2, pp. 229–50.

Whelan, Bridget (2014), 'Power to the Princess: Disney and the Creation of the Twentieth-century Princess Narrative', in Alexander N. Howe and Wynn Yarbrough (eds), *Kidding Around: The Child in Film and Media*, New York: Bloomsbury, pp. 167–91.

Whelehan, Imelda (2010), 'Remaking Feminism: Or Why Is Postfeminism So Boring?', *Nordic Journal of English Studies*, 9: 3, pp. 155–72.

Whitfield, Sarah (2017), '"For the first time in forever": Locating *Frozen* as a Feminist Disney Musical', in George Rodosthenous (ed.), *The Disney Musical on Stage and Screen: Critical Approaches from Snow White to Frozen*, London: Bloomsbury, pp. 221–38.

Whitley, David (2012), *The Idea of Nature in Disney Animation: From Snow White to WALL-E*, Burlington, VT: Ashgate Publishing.

Wilkins, Heidi (2016), *Talkies, Road Movies and Chick Flicks: Gender, Genre and Film Sound in American Cinema*, Edinburgh: Edinburgh University Press.

Williams, Linda (2001), *Playing the Race Card: Melodramas of Black and White from Uncle Tom to O.J. Simpson*, Princeton, NJ: Princeton University Press.

Willis, Susan (1995), 'The Problem with Pleasure', in The Project on Disney (eds), *Inside the Mouse: Work and Play at Disney World*, Durham, NC: Duke University Press, pp. 1–11.

Wood, Aylish (2015), *Software, Animation and the Moving Image: What's in the Box?*, Basingstoke: Palgrave Macmillan.

Yockey, Matt (ed.) (2017), *Make Ours Marvel: Media Convergence and a Comics Universe*, Austin: University of Texas Press.

Yoshinaga, Ida (2019); 'Disney's *Moana*, the Colonial Screenplay, and Indigenous Labor Extraction in Hollywood Fantasy Films', *Narrative Culture*, 6: 2 (Fall), pp. 188–215.

Zipes, Jack (1995), 'Breaking the Disney Spell', in Elizabeth Bell, Lynda Haas and Laura Sells (eds), *From Mouse to Mermaid: The Politics of Film, Gender, and Culture*, Bloomington: Indiana University Press, pp. 21–42.

Zipes, Jack (2011), *The Enchanted Screen: The Unknown History of Fairy-tale Films*, New York: Routledge.

Zipes, Jack (2016), 'The Great Cultural Tsunami of Fairy-tale Films', in Pauline Greenhill, Kendra Magnus-Johnston and Jack Zipes (eds), *Fairy-tale Films beyond Disney: International Perspectives*, New York: Routledge, pp. 1–17.

Index

27 Dresses, 62–3, 90, 109, 122n
42nd Street, 137
48 Hrs., 8, 181, 189, 191
(500) Days of Summer, 108

action adventure, 10–13, 17, 19–20, 22, 39, 46, 79–80, 88, 90–1, 100, 117, 121, 125–205, 207–11, 214–18
action genre *see* action adventure
action mode, 10, 19–20, 121, 126–8, 148, 150, 153–4, 185, 208, 210–11, 214
action musical *see* musical
action spectacle, 125–49
An Affair to Remember, 59
Aladdin (1992), 12, 26–8, 32, 36, 39–41, 52, 54–5, 83–4, 93, 103
  'A Whole New World' (song), 32, 93
  Aladdin (character), 28, 81
  Jasmine (character), 28–9, 40, 71, 81, 209
Aladdin (2019), 218
Aladdin and the King of Thieves, 61
Alien, 149n
Along Came Polly, 114
Altman, Rick, 4–5, 10
The Amazing Spider-Man, 170
The American President, 73
animation
  computer animation, 1, 5, 7, 19, 22, 31–4, 37, 41, 55–7, 95–8, 127–9, 131, 133, 143, 162, 171, 198, 207, 209, 215, 217
  cut-out animation, 5, 7, 141

  hand-drawn animation, 31, 34, 41–3, 45–6, 51, 54–7, 64, 75, 94–7, 99n, 126–8, 132, 135–6, 140, 143, 148n, 149n
  silhouette animation, 7, 169, 172
  stop motion, 140
  see also plasticine
anime, 20n, 148n, 156
Annie Hall, 59
anthropomorphism, 5, 9, 20, 24–5, 32, 40, 42, 51–3, 62, 71–4, 79, 87, 115, 127, 132, 159, 178, 180–205, 213–14
Antz, 34
The Aristocats, 199
The Artist, 95
The Associate, 194
The A-Team, 129
Atlantis: The Lost Empire, 39, 126
The Avengers (2012), 127, 134, 166–7
Avengers: Age of Ultron, 160, 178n
Avengers: Endgame, 178n
Avengers: Infinity War, 178n

Bambi, 25, 27, 41, 183
  Bambi (character), 193
The Band Wagon, 137
Batman (character), 162; *see also* Christopher Nolan
Batman Returns, 173
Batman v Superman: Dawn of Justice, 159
Beauty and the Beast (1991), 12, 18, 26, 28, 31, 36–7, 40–1, 45, 54, 60, 65, 89, 126, 145, 213
  'Beauty and the Beast' (song), 28, 32, 40, 44, 61

Belle (character), 27, 29, 69, 104, 144
'Belle' (song), 213
Beauty and the Beast (2017), 27, 218
Big Hero 6, 2, 19, 125–7, 129–30, 132, 135–6, 138, 141–4, 147, 150–1, 153–62, 177–8, 185, 197–8, 200, 204, 215
    Baymax (character), 125, 127, 132, 138, 151, 154, 156, 159–61, 166, 175, 178
    Hiro (character), 125, 127, 132, 138, 144, 151, 154, 156–61, 175, 178
Birds of Prey (and the Fantabulous Emancipation of One Harley Quinn), 178n3
The Black Cauldron, 12
Blue Sky Studio, 22–3, 31, 45n, 126
Blue Steel, 186
Bolt, 2–3, 19, 22, 125–30, 132–8, 141–2, 147, 214–15
Brave, 18, 101–5, 107–8, 113–14, 119–21, 218
Bride Wars, 62–3, 109, 111
Bridesmaids, 109, 111
Bridget Jones (franchise), 91, 122n
Bridget Jones's Baby, 91
Bringing Up Baby, 70, 122n
Brode, Douglas, 12, 30
Brother Bear, 39, 51
Brown, Jeffrey A., 12, 150, 153, 157, 162, 176–8, 190–1, 202
Brown, Noel, 3, 5, 20n, 21n, 46n, 66, 74, 82, 88, 98, 101, 107, 118, 184, 201, 205n, 206, 208
buddy film, 181–3, 185–6, 192; *see also* cop buddy film
A Bug's Life, 31
Bukatman, Scott, 65, 131, 171, 178n

camp, 119–20, 148, 174
Can't Buy Me Love, 47n
Captain America: Civil War, 159
Captain America: First Avenger, 154, 157
Captain America/Steve Rogers (MCU character), 157–8, 162, 174, 178n
Captain Marvel, 178n
Casablanca, 59

Catmull, Ed, 3, 31, 42, 79, 99n
Catwoman, 173, 178n
Chapman, Brenda, 101–3
Charlie's Angels (franchise), 135, 173
chick flick, 10, 18, 62, 101, 109, 111–12, 120, 122n, 122n, 207–8, 211, 214, 216–17
Chicken Little, 17, 24, 41–3, 58, 96
children's film 5, 153, 215; *see also* family film
A Christmas Carol (2009), 56
Cinderella (1950), 4, 12, 17, 27, 33–4, 58, 61–2, 65, 75n, 80, 85, 89, 93, 105, 112, 114, 173, 202
    Cinderella (character), 28–9, 43, 64, 69, 87, 104–5, 113, 119, 210, 212
    'A Dream Is a Wish Your Heart Makes' (song), 105, 202
    'So This Is Love' (song), 61, 93, 105, 113
'Cinderella' (fairy tale), 45
Coco, 47n6
cop buddy film, 8, 20, 178, 180–1, 183–5, 189–91, 196–7, 201, 203–4, 214, 217; *see also* buddy film
Crazy Rich Asians, 45, 109, 211
Crazy Stupid Love, 90, 99n6
crime film, 8, 183, 202
Cruella, 99n7, 218
cuteness, 24–5, 40, 43, 87, 106, 135–6, 177, 181, 185, 187, 189, 191, 193–4, 201, 203–4, 213

Davis, Amy M., 3, 6, 12–13, 76n, 80, 118, 149n, 175, 219n
Descendants, 208
Despicable Me (franchise), 126
Dinosaur, 47n
Disney, Walt, 13, 27
Disney+, 21n9, 218–19, 220n
Disney fairy tale, 2, 8, 10, 12–18, 20, 23, 27–30, 33–46, 51–4, 57–61, 64–5, 67–75, 77–8, 80–7, 89–90, 92–109, 111–13, 117–21, 125, 152, 155, 181–4, 197, 202, 207, 209–14, 219; *see also* fairy tale
Disney Fairy Tale Weddings, 64, 76n

Disney formula, 6–7, 10–11, 17–18, 22–47, 51–4, 57, 59–61, 63–4, 69–71, 74–5, 77–94, 98, 100–21, 125, 127–8, 130, 136, 143, 147–8, 150, 152, 156, 168, 177–8, 181–5, 187, 189, 193, 197, 202–4, 206–18

Disney Prince (character), 18, 27, 29–30, 35, 43, 45, 51, 62, 69, 72, 80–1, 90, 92, 98, 105–6, 112–14, 125, 177, 218; see also Prince Charming

Disney Princess (character), 1, 3, 18, 11–13, 15, 29, 35, 43, 46, 64–5, 69, 71–2, 74–5, 81–2, 86–9, 98, 103–5, 107, 112, 118–19, 122, 125, 128, 150, 177, 182–3, 204, 206–14, 217–18, 219n; see also princess (trope)

Disney Princess franchise, 29–30, 57, 63, 86, 104, 209

Disneyland (Resort), 36, 64, 66, 84, 198; see also Walt Disney World (Resort)

DreamWorks, 1, 5, 7–8, 17–18, 22–4, 31, 33–4, 36–9, 41–2, 46, 77–81, 83–7, 90–2, 94, 97–8, 100–1, 105, 107, 114, 126, 155, 192, 207–11, 214, 217

Dumbo (1941), 4, 24, 32, 183
  Dumbo (character), 1, 47n, 218
Dyer, Richard, 137, 144–6, 148, 205n

Easter Parade, 137
Edge of Tomorrow, 188
Eisner, Michael, 23, 26, 42, 46n
Elektra, 178n
The Emperor's New Groove, 39
Enchanted, 8, 17, 24, 43–6, 47n13, 51, 57, 59, 69, 73, 75n, 81–2, 99n, 106, 113, 117, 212
The Expendables (franchise), 129
fairy tale (genre), 2, 4, 27–9, 34–8, 43–6, 51, 57–65, 67–70, 75, 77–84, 86–9, 94, 97–102, 104–7, 112–16, 118–21, 126, 128, 148, 150, 152, 168, 173, 178, 182, 184, 197–8, 206–7, 209–11, 215, 217; see also Disney fairy tale
family film, 5–6, 11, 21n, 127, 184
Fantasia, 24, 26

Fantasia 2000, 38
Fantastic 4 (franchise), 159, 165
Fargo, 186
Fast & Furious (franchise), 144, 215, 220n3
femininity (constructions of) see gender
Final Fantasy: The Spirits Within, 32
Finding Nemo, 31, 33
formula see Disney formula
Forgetting Sarah Marshall, 115
The Fox and the Hound, 33
Friends with Benefits, 108
The Frog Prince, 57–8
Frozen, 2, 5, 8, 13, 15, 17–19, 20n, 21n, 51, 96, 100–3, 105–22, 127–8, 136, 145, 150–4, 168–77, 179n, 181, 183–4, 197, 202, 211, 216, 218–19
  Anna (character), 8, 100, 102–3, 105–10, 112–17, 120, 145, 151–2, 169, 174–6, 209, 213
  Elsa (character), 13, 15, 18–19, 100–3, 107–13, 115, 117–21, 148, 151–3, 155, 168–77, 179, 209–11, 218
  'Fixer Upper' (song), 110, 115
  'For the First Time in Forever' (song), 105, 109, 112, 145
  Hans (character), 18, 100, 102–3, 106–7, 109–10, 112–17, 148, 152, 175
  Kristoff (character), 100, 107–10, 112–17, 152, 175
  'Let It Go' (song), 117–20, 170–6, 202, 211
  'Love Is an Open Door', 113
Frozen Fever, 21n, 176
Frozen II, 21, 120, 179n, 217–18

G.I. Jane, 188
gender (constructions of), 2, 4, 6, 9, 11–20, 28–9, 36–7, 43–6, 51–4, 69–70, 73–4, 78–80, 87–92, 94, 98, 99n, 101–2, 104, 107, 112–16, 118–21, 125, 148, 150–87, 189–90, 196, 203, 207–8, 211, 214–16, 218–19
  femininity (constructions of), 12–16, 19, 30, 62, 69, 74, 88, 102, 104, 118–20, 151–2, 154, 168, 173–8, 180, 188, 204n, 209–11, 216

masculinity (constructions of), 14, 16, 80, 90–1, 112–17, 151–2, 154–5, 158, 161–8, 177–9, 208, 216
Get a Horse!, 95–6
Ghosts of Girlfriends Past, 90
Gill, Rosalind, 14–15, 75, 78, 90
Giroux, Henry A., 29, 65
Gladiator, 162
Gledhill, Christine, 12, 21n
The Godfather, 183, 202
Gold Diggers of 1933, 137
The Good Dinosaur, 56, 131–2, 182
The Great Mouse Detective, 33
Guardians of the Galaxy, 171

Hancock, 162
Happily N'Ever After, 38
Haswell, Helen, 2–3, 31–2, 42, 47n, 78–9, 95–6, 207
Hawaiian Holiday, 171
The Heat, 185
Hello, Dolly!, 47n
Hercules, 39–40, 57, 126, 143, 162–3
  TV series, 219
heteronormativity, 12, 15, 19, 59–60, 69, 74–5, 89, 92, 100, 103, 109, 114, 117–19, 211, 214
The Hobbit: The Desolation of Smaug, 7
The Holiday, 91
Holliday, Christopher, 3, 6–9, 26, 28, 30, 33–4, 41, 43, 46n, 47n, 78, 83, 87, 97, 105, 112, 139, 183, 194
Home on the Range, 41
homme-com, 18, 114–16, 120
Hoodwinked, 38
How to Be Single, 111
How to Train Your Dragon, 7, 97
  franchise, 126
Hugo, 95
Hulk, 131, 178n; see also *The Incredible Hulk*
Hulk/Bruce Banner (MCU character), 155, 160, 162, 165–7, 170, 178n
The Hunchback of Notre-Dame, 52, 145

Ice Age (franchise), 126
Iger, Robert, 23, 42, 219

Illumination, 22–3, 31, 46n, 126
The Incredible Hulk, 151, 167, 178n; see also *Hulk*
The Incredibles, 31, 150, 152–3, 155, 159
Incredibles 2, 216
intertextuality, 2, 8, 10, 14, 18–19, 32, 36, 41–3, 47n9, 57, 59–60, 62, 65, 77–9, 82–6, 94, 105, 108, 110, 112, 114, 121, 127, 156, 161, 182–3, 202, 208, 213, 217, 220n
  contra-diegetic intertextuality, 36, 42–3, 77–9, 84, 90, 98, 99n, 209, 211
Iron Man, 3, 151, 156
Iron Man/Tony Stark (MCU character), 1, 156, 159–60, 162
Iron Man 3, 142, 159, 165
It Happened One Night, 70

Jeffers McDonald, Tamar, 18, 53, 59, 69–71, 114, 116–17, 152
The Jungle Book, 30, 33, 51, 75n
Jungle Cruise, 99n

Karlyn, Kathleen, 74, 87
Kate and Leopold, 59, 73
Katzenberg, Jeffrey, 23, 34
kiss (true love's), 34, 37, 44, 60, 62, 70, 77, 106, 110, 112–13
Knocked Up, 115
Kung-Fu Panda (franchise), 126

L.A. Confidential, 8
La Luna, 95, 97
Lady and The Tramp (1955), 51
Lady and The Tramp (2019), 219
Lara Croft: Tomb Raider (franchise), 173
Lasseter, John, 3, 20n, 31, 33, 42, 131, 158, 182
Lee, Jennifer, 2–3, 21n9, 51, 96, 100, 102, 112, 120, 127–8, 136, 148n, 150, 152, 176, 179n, 181, 211, 217
Lee, Stan, 152
Lethal Weapon (franchise), 135, 181, 191
Lilo & Stitch, 17, 23, 39–42, 46, 126–7

The Lion King, (1994), 26, 32, 40–1, 54, 57, 183, 199
    'Can You Feel the Love Tonight' (song), 32
The Little Mermaid, 12–13, 26–8, 32–3, 37, 40–1, 45, 54–5, 60–1, 65, 72, 80, 88, 92, 106, 118–19, 128, 145, 213
    Ariel (character), 13, 29, 32, 40, 71, 80, 88, 106, 119, 145, 212
    Eric (character), 80, 106
    'Kiss the Girl' (song), 61, 92
    'Part of Your World' (song), 28, 40, 145, 212
    'Under the Sea' (song/ride), 32, 65, 213
    Ursula (character), 118–19
Lucasfilm, 3, 31, 219

Maid in Manhattan, 45
makeover, 30, 45, 84, 104, 173–4, 211–12
Maleficent (franchise), 218
Marvel, 1–3, 7, 11, 19, 121, 127, 150–79, 184, 217, 219
Marvel Cinematic Universe (MCU), 3, 151, 154–5
masculinity (constructions of) *see* gender
The Matrix, 36, 135
Megamind, 155
memory film, 18, 52, 54, 64, 66, 68, 75
Men In Black (franchise), 191
Mission: Impossible – Ghost Protocol, 142
Moana, 2, 13, 19, 125–30, 135–6, 140–7, 150–5, 161, 163–4, 168, 177, 181, 187, 193, 205n, 211, 214, 216
    'How Far I'll Go' (song), 144–7
    'Logo Te Pate' (song), 144, 147, 149n, 168
    Maui (character), 125, 135, 140–4, 146–7, 149n, 151, 155, 161, 163–8, 170, 172, 175, 177, 178n, 181, 216
    Moana (character), 125, 128, 135–6, 141–7, 151, 167–8, 178n, 181, 209, 212
    'We Know the Way' (song), 143, 147
    'Where You Are' (song), 145
    'You're Welcome' (song), 140, 149n8, 164, 172
Monster-in-Law, 109
Monsters, Inc., 31, 33

monstrosity, 154, 165–8, 177; *see also* superhero film
The Moth and the Flame, 171
Mrs Doubtfire, 21n
Mulan (1998), 29, 36, 57, 126, 143
    Mulan (character), 30, 210, 212
    Shang (character), 143
Mulan (2020), 218
musical, 2, 4–5, 10, 13, 19–20, 23–4, 27–30, 32–4, 36, 38–44, 46, 47n, 51–2, 66, 78–9, 82–3, 86–7, 92, 94, 97, 100, 110, 114, 118, 120, 126, 128–30, 137, 139, 141–7, 164, 168, 170, 172–3, 175–6, 194, 202–4, 206–8, 211–14, 217–18
    action musical, 19, 143–7, 204, 211–14
    backstage musical, 137, 141

Negra, Diane, 14, 16, 62, 111, 174–5, 210
New Orleans, 51, 60, 64–9, 74, 197, 199, 202
New Orleans Square (Disneyland), 64, 66
Nolan, Christopher, 150
nostalgia, 18, 44, 46, 51, 53–7, 59–60, 62–5, 69, 74–5, 78, 85, 91, 94–5, 149n, 206
    post-feminist nostalgia, 53–4, 63, 75, 91

Obama, Barack, 76n, 190–1
Oh My Disney, 1, 20, 206–9, 213, 217–19
Olaf's Frozen Adventure, 21n, 115, 176
Oliver and Company, 40
Once Upon a Time, 208
One Hundred and One Dalmatians, 39, 75n
opening credits (Disney), 94–5, 99n, 202
The Other Guys, 129

Pallant, Chris, 3, 7, 26, 38–9, 41, 131, 151, 219n
Paperman, 96
ParaNorman, 118, 122n
paratext, 8, 10–11, 14, 18, 23, 32, 36, 41, 45, 52–5, 57, 59, 63, 65, 78–9, 83, 85–7, 91, 94, 96, 98, 101, 104, 152, 184, 207, 219; *see also* trailer

parody, 18, 23, 34, 36–7, 40, 58, 77–8, 80–1, 83–8, 70, 101, 107, 114, 121, 134, 166, 209–10, 213–14
Persépolis, 75n
Peter Pan, 4, 40, 56, 126
Pinocchio, 27, 40, 56–7, 75n, 83–4
  'When You Wish Upon a Star' (song), 57, 94, 202
photorealism, 32, 47n, 55–6, 95, 97, 129–33, 135, 139, 141–2, 169, 198, 215; *see also* stylised realism
Pirates of the Caribbean (franchise), 99n
Pirates of the Caribbean: The Curse of the Black Pearl, 135
Pixar, 1, 3, 5, 7–8, 11, 17–19, 22–4, 31–3, 36, 38–9, 41–3, 46, 47n, 55–6, 75n, 78–9, 94–5, 97, 99n, 101, 104–5, 120–1, 126, 129–32, 139, 150–1, 153, 155, 182, 207, 215–17, 219
plasmaticness, 171–2, 176–7
plasticine, 7, 140, 143
Pocahontas, 29, 66, 76n
  Pocahontas (character), 30, 212
The Polar Express, 32
post-feminism, 2, 4, 11, 14–17, 19–20, 45–6, 53–4, 59–64, 69, 73–5, 78, 87–94, 97–8, 101, 108, 111–13, 116, 121, 122n, 155, 168, 173, 177–8, 180, 185, 188, 203, 207, 209–12, 214, 218–19; *see also* nostalgia
Pretty Woman, 45, 108
Prince Charming (trope), 35, 47n, 52, 57, 60, 69, 74, 101, 107; *see also* Disney Prince
The Prince of Egypt, 34
princess (trope), 34, 57, 62, 64, 69, 70, 74, 79, 83–4, 101–4, 209; *see also* Disney Princess
The Princess and the Frog, 2, 8, 15, 17–18, 42, 51–79, 81, 86–90, 92, 94–5, 98, 99n, 100, 102, 104, 106, 114–16, 119, 121, 148n, 181, 185, 197–8, 200, 204, 213, 219
  Charlotte (character), 53, 57, 60, 63–7, 69, 74, 88, 100, 104, 106, 114, 119

'Down in New Orleans' (song), 65, 67, 202
'Ma Belle Evangeline' (song), 60–1, 71, 92, 213
Naveen (character), 53, 58, 60–4, 69–74, 79, 90, 106, 114, 117, 197
Tiana (character), 52–3, 57–8, 60–74, 76n, 79, 86, 90, 100, 106, 117, 197, 200, 202, 209
The Princess Diaries (franchise), 211
The Proposal, 73, 91
Purse, Lisa, 129–31, 133–5, 144, 153–4, 162, 165, 173–4, 195

queerness, 15, 118–21, 122n, 201

race (constructions of), 15, 18, 20, 51–2, 54, 66–9, 74, 75n, 76n, 122n, 148, 180–4, 188, 190–2, 194, 196–8, 200–1, 203–5
Raiders of the Lost Ark, 42
Ralph Breaks the Internet: Wreck-It Ralph, 2, 1–3, 19–20, 206–20
  'A Place Called Slaughter Race' (song), 207, 213
  Shank (character), 215, 217
Ratatouille, 139
Red (2010), 129
Red Hot Riding Hood, 136
The Rescuers, 12, 46n
The Rescuers Down Under, 46n, 206, 219n
The Road to El Dorado, 34
Robin Hood (1973), 75n, 126
romantic comedy, 2, 11–13, 18, 21n, 44–6 52–4, 59–62, 69–70, 73–5, 78, 87, 89–92, 98, 100, 108–9, 111–17, 120–2, 152–3, 173, 181, 184, 186, 217
  neo-traditional romantic comedy, 53, 59–61, 75, 98, 100, 108, 114, 117, 122n
  see also chick flick, homme-com, screwball comedy
romantic mode, 10, 18, 100, 120, 207, 217
Rush Hour (franchise), 181, 191

Satrapi, Marjane, 56, 75n, 95
science fiction, 22, 39, 46, 126, 128, 149n, 191
screwball comedy, 4, 10, 18, 53, 61, 70–1, 73, 75, 101, 117, 120–1, 122n
self-reflexivity, 1, 3, 9, 18, 20, 35, 43, 57, 59–60, 63, 69, 77, 82–3, 92, 94, 101, 105, 107–18, 112, 121, 125, 129, 136–7, 139, 143, 163, 171, 177, 181, 184, 198, 202–3, 207, 209–10, 213–14, 217–18
Sex and the City, 62, 109, 111
franchise, 211
Shark Tale, 192
Shrek, 34–41, 43–4, 47n, 51, 58, 60, 75, 77–86, 94, 99n, 105, 107, 113–14, 135, 155, 192
Fiona (character), 35–7, 77, 114, 135, 209
franchise, 5, 18, 98, 99n, 114, 121, 208
Robin Hood (character), 35, 135
Shrek (character), 34–5, 37, 59, 77, 209
Shrek Forever After, 77
Shrek 2, 136
Prince Charming (character), 114, 209
Shrek the Third, 99n, 208–9
Cinderella (character), 209
Sleeping Beauty (character), 209
Snow White (character), 209
The Silence of the Lambs, 186
Singin' in the Rain, 143
Sleeping Beauty, 4, 12, 27, 34, 60, 65, 75n, 80, 85, 91, 103, 106, 110, 112–14, 118
Aurora (character), 27–9, 35, 43, 81, 87, 106–7, 110, 209, 211, 213
Maleficent (character), 118
Prince Phillip (character), 27, 35, 81, 91, 110
Sleepless in Seattle, 59, 122n
Smith, Susan, 4, 30, 32, 47n, 52, 172
Snow White and the Seven Dwarfs, 12, 17, 24, 27, 31, 33–5, 40–1, 58, 60–2, 65, 72, 75n, 106, 112–13, 118, 126
Snow White (character), 1, 13, 26, 28–9, 43, 62, 60, 69, 87, 106, 209, 212–13

'Some Day My Prince Will Come' (song), 60
'Whistle While You Work', 43
'Snow White' (fairy tale), 99
Something New, 74
Song of the South, 66
Space Jam, 188, 204n
Space Jam: A New Legacy, 204n
Sperb, Jason, 55–6, 66, 95, 149n
Spider-Man, 131, 154, 156, 170
Spider-Man franchise: 150, 165
see also *The Amazing Spider-Man*
Spider-Man/Peter Parker (MCU character) 156–8, 170, 174
Spider-Man 2, 165
Spider-Man 3, 171
Star Wars (1977), 21n
Star Wars (property), 1
Star Wars (rebooted franchise), 216
Steamboat Willie, 95–6
stylised realism, 32, 41, 47n, 55, 131; see also photorealism
Summers, Sam, 22, 25, 27, 32–9, 41–2, 46n, 47n, 78–9, 192, 208
superhero film, 2–3, 10, 12, 19, 125, 127, 131, 148, 150–79, 182, 184, 198, 204, 207–8, 211, 214–18
The Swan Princess, 27
Sweet Home Alabama, 47n
Swingers, 114
The Sword in the Stone, 75n, 126

Tangled, 2, 8, 17–18, 42, 47n, 51, 65, 77–100, 102, 113, 115–16, 121, 128, 135, 145, 181, 197–8, 205n, 207, 209, 212–13
Flynn/Eugene (character), 18, 77–85, 87–94, 96–8, 99n, 100–1, 104, 113, 135, 212
'I See the Light' (song), 92–4, 97–8, 128, 213
'I've Got a Dream' (song), 82, 92–4, 213
Rapunzel (character), 1, 18, 65, 71, 77–85, 87–93, 96–7, 104, 145, 198, 209
'When Will My Life Begin' (song), 87, 145

Tangled Ever After, 78, 89
Tangled: The Series, 219
Tarzan, 36, 41, 163
Tasker, Yvonne, 10, 12, 14, 16, 45, 74, 93, 128–9, 134, 138, 143, 145, 153–4, 173, 181, 185–6, 210
Telotte, J. P., 25, 57, 131
Terminator 2: Judgment Day, 153
Thelma and Louise, 153
Thor, 162, 164
Thor (MCU character), 155, 162, 164–5, 167
Thor: Ragnarok, 178n
Thumbelina, 27
Thunder Force, 178n
Toy Story, 31–3, 131, 182
  franchise, 5, 33, 126, 139
  'You've Got a Friend in Me' (song), 32–3
Toy Story 2, 31
  'When She Loved Me' (song), 33
trailer, 1, 3, 20n, 54, 79–80, 85, 100, 126, 156, 206, 208
  retrospective trailer, 27–8, 40–1, 54, 57
Trainwreck, 108
Treasure Planet, 39, 126
Tropic Thunder, 129
Trump, Donald, 191

Up, 55, 97, 104, 219

verisimilitude
  aesthetic verisimilitude, 25
  generic verisimilitude, 18, 107–8, 111, 142, 212

WALL-E, 47n, 104
Walt Disney World (Resort), 64; *see also* Disneyland (Resort)
Warner Bros., 25, 27, 36, 188

wedding
  culture, 63–4, 90
  film, 62
  scene, 37, 61–3, 73–5, 89–90, 105, 107, 109–11, 121
  see also Disney Fairy Tale Wedding
Wedding Crashers, 62
The Wedding Planner, 62
Wells, Paul, 6–7, 9, 21n, 24–5, 72–3, 182–3
When Harry Met Sally, 45
Winnie the Pooh, 1, 148n
Wonder Woman, 174, 178n
Wonder Woman 1984, 178n
Wreck-It Ralph, 1–2, 13, 19, 96, 123, 125–30, 134–6, 138–44, 147, 148n, 149n, 150–5, 161, 163, 165–70, 172, 175–7, 181, 187, 193, 206, 215, 217
  'Shut Up and Drive' (song), 144
  Vanellope (character), 1, 125, 139, 144, 150–1, 155, 166–9, 176–7, 181, 206–18
  Wreck-It Ralph (character), 1, 125, 134, 139–40, 150–1, 155, 161, 165–70, 174–7, 181, 207–9, 211, 213–14, 216–17

X-Men, 154
  franchise, 150, 152, 165, 174

You've Got Mail, 45, 122n

Zipes, Jack, 6, 12–13, 28, 37, 81, 197, 219n
Zootopia, 2, 8, 19–20, 127, 178, 180–205, 214, 216
  Judy (character), 180–1, 184–93, 195–205
  Nick (character), 180–1, 184–7, 189–95, 197, 199, 201–3

EU representative:
Easy Access System Europe
Mustamäe tee 50, 10621 Tallinn, Estonia
Gpsr.requests@easproject.com